Foreign
Ownership
of
Canadian
Industry

Foreign Ownership of Canadian Industry

Third Edition

A. E. Safarian

University of Toronto Press

© University of Toronto Press 2011
Toronto Buffalo London
www.utppublishing.com
Printed in the U.S.A.

Originally published by McGraw-Hill Company of Canada Ltd. 1966
Reprinted by University of Toronto Press 1973

ISBN 978-1-4426-1222-8

Printed on acid-free paper

Library and Archives Canada Cataloguing in Publication

Safarian, A. E., 1924–
Foreign ownership of Canadian industry / A. E. Safarian. – 3rd ed.

ISBN 978-1-4426-1222-8

1. Corporations, American – Canada.   2. Corporations, Foreign – Canada.
I. Title.

HG5152.S3 2011   332.67'373071   C2011-904015-8

University of Toronto Press acknowledges the financial assistance to its publishing
program of the Canada Council for the Arts and the Ontario Arts Council.

    Canada Council Conseil des Arts    ONTARIO ARTS COUNCIL
for the Arts   du Canada   CONSEIL DES ARTS DE L'ONTARIO

University of Toronto Press acknowledges the financial support for its publishing
activities of the Government of Canada through the Canada Book Fund.

Acknowledgments

I have been fortunate in securing financial aid from a number of institutions at various points of this study. The study was conceived at the Institute for Economic Research at Queen's University. The initial costs were underwritten by a grant from the Social Science Research Council of Canada; I am particularly grateful for the encouragement given at this early stage by persons associated with the Council, particularly John Meisel. The Canada Council and the University of Saskatchewan each made several grants in support of research costs. Through a sabbatical leave from the University of Saskatchewan and the award of a Faculty Research Fellowship by the Ford Foundation, I was able to spend the academic year 1963-64 in full-time research at the University of Toronto. I am grateful to all of these institutions for making this year of intensive research possible.

Various persons have been helpful over the years as my work progressed. It was a most useful experience to assist Irving Brecher and S. S. Reisman with their earlier study in this field. Some of the interviews were conducted in co-operation with D. E. Armstrong and John Lindeman who prepared a study for the Canadian-American Committee. Walter L. Gordon was especially helpful in arranging interviews. C. D. Blyth and E. B. Carty have helped sharpen my understanding of the official data and supplied information. For various specific kinds of information and other help or useful discussions I am indebted to Denis Amyot, W. Mackenzie Hall, Samuel Pizer, J. N. Behrman, G. S. Watts, B. A. Griffith, Arthur J. R. Smith, H. E. English, H. C. Eastman, J. H. Dales, and Harry G. Johnson. Criticisms by C. P. Kindleberger of a paper I wrote on exports of subsidiary companies have helped clarify the presentation of some topics. I have been fortunate in the research assistance supplied at different times by Mary Winch, T. J. Courchene, Shirley Spafford, and J. D. Rowlatt.

Thank you as well to Jennifer DiDomenico and University of Toronto Press for working to bring this book back into print in 2011.

My greatest debt is to the many businessmen who spent much of their time in supplying information through interviews, questionnaires, and correspondence. Without their co-operation this study would literally have been impossible.

The entire responsibility for what appears in this study must rest with the author. The views expressed here are not necessarily those of any of the persons or institutions mentioned above. Some of them, indeed, have disagreed or will disagree with parts of what is said here. My acknowledgement of their help is all the warmer for this.

A. E. Safarian

Contents

List of Tables

A Note on the Tables

All tables in this book refer to the companies replying to the question-naires shown in Appendix B and to the year 1959, except where otherwise noted. The number of non-resident owned companies involved in Chapters 2 to 8 is 280. The voting stock of 227 of these is controlled in the United States, of the remaining fifty-three in overseas countries. Where a distribution by size of assets is given, the total for all companies will not add to 280 because sixteen companies could not be classified by size of assets. The shortfall is fourteen where only the American-owned companies are shown. Distributions by size are usually given in intervals of under $1 million, $1 to $4.9 million, $5 to $24.9 million and $25 million and over. The major exception is the analysis relating to the cross-classifications of selected characteristics in tables 17, 20, 25, 31, 44, 52, and 53, where the distributions by size are in intervals of under $1 million, $1 to $4.9 million, and $5 million and over.

In Chapter 9 the tables refer to 160 non-resident owned companies and ninety-six resident-owned companies with assets of $1 million or more which answered the questionnaires, and to the year 1959, except where otherwise noted.

Some of the tables in this book show what appear to be unusually high non-responses to particular questions by companies returning the question-naires. In most cases these reflect the fact that 50 of the 280 non-resident owned firms and 35 of the 96 larger resident-owned firms which returned the questionnaires did not answer any of the general questions on the last page of the questionnaires. Further details on this appear on page 35 and Appendix B.

Preface to the Third Edition

All four of my major books were devoted to exploring how a relatively small country situated in close proximity to a large one could thrive in an open economy. The first was *The Canadian Economy in the Great Depression* (1959). In the course of researching that book I found there was very little data or analysis, especially at the firm level, to help explain how the high degree of foreign ownership of Canadian industry would affect the relatively steep decline and slow recovery of the Canadian economy in the 1930s. The two notable exceptions for my purposes at the level of the firm were Marshall et al. (1936) for Canada and Dunning (1958) for the United Kingdom. Indeed, the international academic literature more generally on foreign direct investment (FDI) and multinational enterprises (MNEs) was limited when I started on *Foreign Ownership of Canadian Industry* (1966) in the late 1950s, and had grown rather slowly when I finished it almost a decade later. I had attempted a dry run on the performance of MNEs, based largely on a limited set of interviews with company managers, recorded in several chapters published in Brecher and Reisman (1957).

While the availability of economic analysis was still limited in the 1960s, there was a surge in public interest and media coverage of the effects of FDI on Canada. This was sparked initially by efforts to persuade wholly owned subsidiaries to issue a minority of their shares. More dramatic were the different international policy positions taken by Canada and the United States as they affected MNEs. The United States had banned exports to communist countries, including exports of U.S.-made products through subsidiaries of U.S. firms abroad. Canada and most other countries continued to trade with such countries, although generally cooperated with the United States in preventing the export of defence-related goods and technologies. A series of incidents involving trade with China and Cuba in particular strained relations between the United States and other countries.

Questions had arisen also about the economic performance of FDI in Canada, which was alleged to be inferior to that of domestic direct investment (DDI) in exports, research and development, and other respects. The federal government launched several investigations in the late 1960s and early 1970s, then expanded significantly the sectors closed to FDI and began review of inward FDI.

Foreign Ownership of Canadian Industry concentrated on the organization of the subsidiaries and the division of powers with parent company managers; transfers of knowledge within the MNEs; the extent of subsidiary research, exports, and imports; comparative costs of production in the MNEs; patterns of ownership and finance; and how nationality of ownership affected these matters. While every available source was used, the analysis focused especially on a unique set of data for large FDI and DDI, data collected initially by interviews with subsidiary, parent, and DDI firms, then by detailed questionnaires sent to the managers of the first and third sets of firms. The research methodology and the pitfalls involved are discussed fully in Chapter 2. While there were significant differences by ownership for many of the topics noted above, the economic performance of FDI was surprisingly close to that of DDI for exports, R&D, and some other aspects, although FDI was more import-intensive.

Results beginning to appear in some other countries showed FDI led to better performance than did DDI. Comparisons with other countries also suggested that performance of both FDI and DDI in Canada was equally bad in terms of Canadian welfare. These results quickly entered the controversy in Canada over the effects of FDI and, for a time, I found myself involved in the public debate in Canada and elsewhere on the benefits and costs of FDI and MNEs. My results also attracted attention in the literature that began to flourish in the 1970s. The large growth in research on economic performance undertaken at Statistics Canada alone is summarized in Baldwin et al. (2010). Some of the later results confirmed my own; some did not – unsurprisingly, given the different databases, methodologies, and time periods. The longer-term impact of the 1966 book can be assessed in Eden and Dobson (2005).

It should be added that economic and political issues other than the performance of the firm attracted much attention to MNEs and the related spread of trade and investment. Some findings on these other issues were discussed in the Preface to the 1973 edition of this book, reprinted here without change. More recent data and analysis can be found in annual reports on MNEs published by the United Nations and in Dunning and Lundan (2007).

Recent reviews consider at least two other issues of significance. First is the spread in the number of important home countries for MNEs and also of alliances between firms engaging in international investment. Second is the growing predominance of international mergers and acquisitions in FDI. The issues raised by outward FDI by Canadian-owned firms are discussed in Globerman (1994), while the causes and consequences of the spread in international mergers and acquisitions more generally are examined in Safarian (2011).

In writing the first and second books noted in the opening paragraph of this Preface, I was puzzled by the fact that macro and micro policies respectively were far from what seemed optimal for welfare, not only in terms of what economics and political economy suggested but also by experience elsewhere. For example, Australian policies on FDI seemed to be both more clearly focused on a few key priorities and more stable over time than those in Canada. My third book focused on the regulatory problems raised more generally by the type of federalism involved, especially the constitutional division of economic powers and subsequent court and parliamentary interpretation and modification. My fourth major book returned to FDI, but in this case examined the development of policy on it in the industrial countries after 1945. The focus was on departures from optimum economic policies and on which explanations of policy determinants, both economic and political, best explained policy developments. That volume noted that policy had developed over time from closed sectors and regulation of FDI to fewer of the former and less restrictiveness of the latter, in the sense that governments were more likely to subsidize and work with FDI to restructure industry and develop key sectors, especially by the 1980s. The book closed by noting that the effects of large firms, both FDI and DDI, were such that continued liberalization, as distinct from policy swings, was unlikely. Indeed, security issues raised by new sources of FDI, particularly state-owned firms, led to new policy interventions in the 1990s and later. In addition, the rapid ownership and restructuring changes resulting from major international mergers and acquisitions in the first decade of the twenty-first century have led to enhanced FDI review and closing of more sectors in many countries (Safarian 2011). Finally, the effects on the environment, working conditions, and a variety of other socio-economic issues have received increasing attention, especially because of the efforts of non-governmental organizations. These newer concerns are examined in issues of the *World Investment Report* (UN, various years) and elsewhere.

A. E. Safarian
October 2010

References

Baldwin, J. R., G. Gellatly, G. Wulagong, and Y. Beiling. 2010. *The Contribution of Multinationals in Canada to Economic Performance*, Ottawa: Statistics Canada, Economic Analysis Division, April. Mimeo.

Brecher, J., and S. Reisman. 1957. *Canada-United States Economic Relations*. Ottawa: Queens Printer: Royal Commission on Canada's Economic Prospects.

Dunning, J. H., and S. Lundan. 2007. *Multinational Enterprises and the Global Economy*. 2nd edition. Cheltenham, U.K: Edward Elgar.

Dunning, J. H. 1958. *American Investment in British Manufacturing Industry*. London: Allen and Unwin.

Eden, L., and W. Dobson (eds.) 2005. *Governance, Multinationals and Growth*. Papers at a Conference in Honour of the Work of A. E. Safarian. Cheltenham, U.K.: Edward Elgar.

Globerman, Steven, ed. 1994. Canadian-Based Multinationals. Ottawa: Industry Canada Research Series, volume 4.

Marshall, H., F. A. Southard, Jr., and K. W. Taylor. 1936. *Canadian-American Industry: A Study in International Investment*. New Haven: Yale University Press.

Safarian, A. E. 1959. *The Canadian Economy in the Great Depression*. Toronto: University of Toronto Press.

Safarian, A. E. 1966. *Foreign Ownership of Canadian Industry*. Toronto: McGraw-Hill. Reissue with a new preface, Toronto: University of Toronto Press, 1973.

Safarian, A. E. 1974. *Canadian Federalism and Economic Integration*. Ottawa: Privy Council Office, Government of Canada

Safarian, A. E. 1993. *Multinational Enterprise and Public Policy: A Study of the Industrial Countries*. Aldershott, U.K.: Edward Elgar.

Safarian, A. E. 2011. "International Mergers and Acquisitions." In M.N. Jovanovic, ed., *International Handbook on the Economics of Integration*, volume 3, pp. 110–41. Cheltenham, U.K.: Edward Elgar.

United Nations. Annual. *World Investment Report*. Geneva: UNCTAD.

Preface to the Second Edition

For about two decades now there has been persistent criticism of the role of foreign investment in Canadian industry. This has raised questions at both the overall level of the national economy and at the level of the firm, in both the economic and political context. It has led to legislation designed to ensure Canadian ownership of certain industries and the maximum use and development of Canadian personnel and facilities in the foreign-owned sector.

The first edition of this study appeared in 1966 and was confined to one aspect of these issues—the performance of the foreign-owned firm in the commodity-producing sectors of Canadian industry. The emphasis was on the relation with the parent firm abroad and the consequences for the subsidiary's policies and performance in the hiring of senior personnel, exports, imports, research, and financing. The approach was highly quantitative, because there was a serious lack of data on the operations of foreign-owned firms and because such a lack was inhibiting and distorting discussion of these issues. It will be appreciated that there are considerable limitations to the private statistical studies of this kind (as detailed in Chapter 2), but if careful attention is paid to the qualifications throughout, the data remain, I think, useful in understanding the operations of the firms and some of the consequences for Canadian economic welfare.

It took a long time simply to prepare and describe the data, and there are still gaps in the information. One result is that the study is less analytical than one would want. I stayed fairly close to the data, though trying to draw out some key relationships throughout the text—and producing at times what *Punch* used to call "a shattering glimpse of the obvious." That was perhaps a useful first step in examining these complex controversial questions, but I dealt with the overall economic issues only as extensions of some questions raised at the level of the firm, and the broader political questions were barely touched upon.

It seemed therefore desirable, given the opportunity of a second edition,

to include in the preface* some discussion of these broader issues as they
have been shaped in more recent years, particularly in terms of the effects of
the growth of American-owned corporations in Canada. Conclusions about
what has happened in Canada may not be always relevant to other higher-
income countries and would probably be quite different from conclusions
about the effects on some lower-income countries. Nevertheless, the issues
are important, both economically and politically, and the Canadian case is
especially significant.[1]

Three related questions are considered here. There is a concern that the
economic benefits traditionally associated with foreign direct investment
are accompanied by high economic costs, both as conventionally defined and
otherwise. There is an even greater concern that, whether or not economic
progress narrowly defined is involved, foreign direct investment poses a
threat to political sovereignty or to the exercise of political power, and to
cultural distinctiveness. This is particularly the concern about the large
American firms so prevalent in Canada, a concern sometimes indistinguishable from the fuller range of questions in the relations between Canada and
the United States. Lastly, there is growing frustration at the inability to
mount effective policies to modify perceived problems, given the differing
view on their importance and the highly regional nature of Canada and of
its government.

Economic Benefits and Costs

The expansion of domestic production in a country at full employment is
determined broadly by increases in the supplies of the agents of production,

---

*What follows here is, with minor editorial changes, a paper presented at a joint
session of the American Economic Association and the American Finance Association
at Toronto, 28 December 1972, and published in the *Journal of Finance* (May 1973).
[1]The scope of direct investment in Canada can be put briefly. Canada accounts for
29 per cent of all United States direct investment abroad. Almost 80 per cent of all
foreign direct investment in Canada is from the United States. In 1969 between 24
and 29 per cent of all business assets in Canada were in firms whose voting stock was
controlled abroad, depending on whether 50 per cent or 25 per cent of foreign ownership is taken as constituting control. Foreign direct investment is highly concentrated
in manufacturing, petroleum and gas, and other mining and smelting industries, where
foreign control of capital amounted in 1967 to 57, 74, and 65 per cent respectively
(or 45, 60, and 56 per cent respectively for the United States alone). Such firms are
much better represented among the larger firms; of the 556 corporations in Canadian
non-financial industries in 1969 with assets of $25 million or more, fully 298 were
foreign-controlled. See Statistics Canada, *Canada's Internal Investment Position 1926
to 1967*, and Corporation and Labour Unions Returns Act, *Report for 1969*, Information Canada, Ottawa,

and by increases in productivity arising both from the improved quality and more efficient use of these agents and also from economies of scale. Foreign direct investment contributes to these sources of expansion to the extent that it supplies capital, and also where it makes available a range of technology, access to markets, and entrepreneurship which are otherwise not available or only at greater overall net costs. These potential gains from increased capital stock and improved technology may appear as one or more of higher real wages rates, fuller employment, lower prices, or better quality of output. An important benefit is the tax payments to various governments from the higher level of output, since double-taxation agreements between countries allow the host country to tax such firms without losing the investments.

It will be clear that whether these gains are realized for the recipient country and how they are realized depends on a number of assumptions with respect to public policy. In particular, how far can competition in the system be relied on to ensure that the impact of new entry to an industry via new products and processes does spill over from the firm, increasing general productivity or lowering prices rather than being captured solely by the firm? If competition cannot ensure that these potential benefits are realized, can tax and other policies so ensure? A critical point in assessing the effects of foreign direct investment is involved in these questions, and they will be considered further below. I am assuming now that the host country taxes these investments at an optimal rate consistent with other objectives of tax policy, and does not largely or fully forgo taxes or use subsidies to attract foreign capital. This is clearly a set of decisions within the power of its governments, but it is not costless. The difficulty resides in part in taxing international firms effectively, given the problem of determining transfer prices for unique services within the firm where there is no market price or equivalent, and given the opportunities in such firms for shifting taxable income so as to minimize taxes internationally over time.

One major question then is the nature and extent of the benefits which occur through spillovers from the firm, and whether they can be achieved at less cost in other ways. It has been suggested that two of these—benefits from manpower training and uncaptured productivity spillovers—may be important potential benefits. The gains can come from the movement to domestic firms by executives and others trained in the foreign firm at the latter's cost, education of suppliers in production and quality control and of customers in better use of products, and in numerous other ways. The significance of this to the question of the benefits from foreign direct investment has been recognized for some time. Unfortunately, the empirical tests, admittedly difficult, are still very limited in nature and number.[2]

The costs to offset against these benefits are quite direct in some cases, such as payments abroad for interest, dividends and business services. Unlike the return on portfolio investment, these costs are variable and tend to grow without further capital inflow to the extent that the firms are successful and the capital base is expanded by re-investment of earnings. The commitment from the viewpoint of the recipient country, in brief, is open-ended and unknown—terminable by the liquidation of the firm or its sale to domestic owners.

Despite considerable shortcomings of both theory and measurement in this area, some useful measures have been attempted of the overall net economic impact of portfolio and/or direct investment in Canada. One approach indicated that, under the full employment conditions prevailing in 1950–56, net foreign investment (*both* portfolio and direct) contributed up to 20 per cent of the growth in per capita real income in that period.[3] A second study, which also uses an aggregate production function, deduces what Canadian domestic output and income might be if the withholding taxes on payments abroad were raised so that foreign investment in Canada became less attractive. This approach assumes that a Cobb-Douglas function is a plausible approximation to the production process, particularly in terms of the assumed ease with which labour can be substituted for capital in production. Perhaps more fundamentally, it is explicitly assumed that full employment can be maintained as the adjustment to increased reliance on domestic capital (and labour, at lower wage rates) occurs. Assume that the tax is raised all the way to the point where only domestic capital is used in production. Under these assumptions, it is estimated that the gross domestic product (produced in Canada) would be 16.5 per cent lower. Gross national income (received by

---

[2]See Richard E. Caves, "International Corporations: The Industrial Economics of Foreign Investment," *Economica* (February 1971), pp. 1–27. On the general point, see the classic statement of the effects of foreign direct investment in high-income host countries, G. D. A. MacDougall, "The Benefits and Costs of Private Investment from Abroad: A Theoretical Approach," *Economic Record* (March 1960). Some suggestive empirical work is in J. Dunning, *American Investment in British Manufacturing Industry*, Allen and Unwin, London, 1957, and Donald T. Brash, *American Investment in Australian Industry*, Australian National University Press, Canberra, 1966.

[3]Rudolph G. Penner, "The Benefits of Foreign Investment in Canada, 1950–1956," *Canadian Journal of Economics and Political Science* (May 1966), pp. 172-83. The range of the contribution was from 8 to 20 per cent with the higher figure more relevant to the extent that a significant part of technical progress is implemented by additions to capital stock. The estimate deducts Canadian investment abroad; the contribution of gross inflows alone would be greater.

Canadians) would be only 3 per cent lower, since income payments to foreigners would fall. It is noted that there may be further costs in terms of slower future growth if access to foreign techniques by other means is less satisfactory, but this possibility is discounted. The study concludes that two years normal growth would be lost at most, provided the assumptions are realistic.[4]

It is possible to cite other evidence which might be taken as reassuring in terms of the existence of gains to a higher-income host country, such as evidence that the cost of foreign equity capital as conventionally measured is comparatively low.[5] But this would be to miss some of the more fundamental questions. A whole range of externalities, both positive and negative, have been claimed for direct investment. The list of negative effects is long. What they have in common is a view that important decisions about Canadian-based facilities, made in the context of the international firm and heavily influenced or determined abroad, lead to less than the maximum efficient development of the subsidiary. This outcome is attributed to various forces, such as poor information or lack of interest by the parent's officers, private or public pressures on them to favour facilities at home at the expense of the subsidiary, or limiting of the subsidiary's initiatives by the habit of dependence on decisions abroad. Thus the recipient country's development is geared away from manufactured exports and research and towards reliance on imports and technology from abroad. More generally, the comparatively large size of the parent companies in the investing country and the subsidiaries in the recipient, in both cases relative to their domestic counterparts, has raised questions about welfare effects which are familiar from the theories of oligopolistic market structures.

This approach raises a prior question about the motives for direct investment, particularly about what one might infer from them with regard to

---

[4]Philip A. Neher, "Capital Movement, Foreign Ownership and Dependence on Foreign Investment in Canada and British Columbia," and John Helliwell and Jillian Broadbent, "How Much Does Foreign Capital Matter?" both in *B.C. Studies*, Department of Economics, University of British Columbia, Vancouver, no. 13 (spring 1972), pp. 31-42.

[5]Rates of return for United States direct investment in Canada, measured as net earnings as a percentage of book value, were 8 per cent in the late sixties, having declined from 10.7 per cent in the early fifties. These are well below rates of return for United States direct investment elsewhere. Some serious qualifications must be attached to such figures, including the difficulty of determining both the types of returns and the capital base in internationally integrated enterprises. See Donald T. Brash, "United States Investment in Australia, Canada and New Zealand," in Peter Drysdale, ed., *Direct Foreign Investment in Asia and the Pacific*, University of Toronto Press, 1972, pp. 95-136.

welfare effects for the recipient country. The theory of foreign direct investment is still in an indeterminate state. Two approaches have been particularly fruitful in recent years, that emanating from work on industrial organization and emphasizing the long-term strategy of large oligopolistic firms, and that from international trade theory placing emphasis on national comparative advantages in the production of new products. The industrial organization approach has emphasized such motives as international competition for market shares by oligopolists, assurance of raw material supplies, and protection as an inducement to foreign direct investment.[6]

Richard Caves has recently examined this approach in a·systematic way, stressing the parallelism between domestic and international mergers where markets are geographically separate. To operate abroad successfully, the firm must possess some special advantage in production or marketing which it can draw on in the new location at a cost which more than offsets the costs of location abroad. Moreover, the return from this advantage is tied to the process of production and distribution, thus favouring transfer abroad by direct investment rather than sale of the advantage. Oligopoly with differentiated products leads the firm to produce abroad the same goods as at home, while attempts to reduce competition or uncertainty by oligopolists (differentiated or not) lead to investment in extractive industry. Differentiated oligopoly has the important effect that it tends to equalize rates of return on equity capital in the same industry across nations but (given barriers to entry of new firms) not necessarily to equalize rates of return between industries in a nation.[7]

The trade theory approach has recently been explored by Harry Johnson in particular. Some recent research on the economics of new product development by Raymond Vernon and his colleagues has strongly suggested that direct investments is frequently identified with comparative advantage in the production of new commercial knowledge in some national markets and in its subsequent application in others. Johnson notes that the return on superior technology can be absorbed entirely by the foreign company. Provided there is no change in prices or quality of commodities to consumers, or prices of factors of production in the economy, and assuming no additions occur to tax revenue, then the firm captures all the benefits of investment. If the foreign firm simply replaces domestic output under these conditions, no

---

[6]S. H. Hymer in particular put early and major emphasis on industrial organization as an approach to direct investment. See his "The International Operations of National Firms: A Study of Direct Investment," M.I.T. doctoral dissertation, 1960.
[7]Caves, "International Corporations."

gain accrues to the host country. He regards this as unlikely, however, partly because the existing double taxation agreements permit the country to collect a share of earnings on foreign capital and rents on foreign knowledge. More fundamentally for present purposes, his conclusion that there are gains to the recipient country rests on the view that knowledge cannot be permanently monopolized but ultimately becomes a free good. It is easy enough to criticize oligopolistic direct investment firms by reference to more competitive situations, up to and including pure competition. It is not as easy to fault them if the situation in a given market before and after their entry is compared, as has been done in several European countries, for there the evidence most often points to an increase in competition and general productivity.[8]

The view that foreign direct investment *per se* yields a pattern of industrial development in high-income host countries which is inimical to certain kinds of growth is particularly strongly held in Canada. Paradoxically, this view appears to co-exist with a number of careful empirical studies which largely refute it. In the typical case, other things constant, the performance of foreign-owned firms in these respects in Canada appears to be as good (or bad) as that of their resident-owned counterparts. This is the case for exports, where performance of foreign-owned firms has been found to be similar to that of resident-owned firms whether one considers all such firms, larger ones only, or only those in manufacturing. The Canadian research performance of foreign-owned firms is at least as good as that of resident-owned firms whether considered as a percentage of sales or degree of sophistication. Again, while both positive and negative effects appear when examining the relation of foreign ownership to industrial concentration and merger activity, the most general conclusion which appears possible is that the extent of foreign ownership has not clearly increased or decreased the degree of competition looked at in these ways. This conclusion is stronger for firms owned in the United States, incidentally, than for firms owned overseas. General empirical tests do suggest, however, that such firms have a higher share of imports in purchases, despite evidence of substantial import substitution over time.[9]

---

[8]See the following by Harry G. Johnson: "The Efficiency and Welfare Implications of the International Corporation," in Charles P. Kindleberger, ed., *The International Corporation*, M.I.T. Press, Cambridge, Mass., 1970; and "Survey of the Issues," in Drysdale, ed., *Direct Foreign Investment in Asia and the Pacific*. The Vernon thesis is discussed in his book, *Sovereignty at Bay: The Multinational Spread of U.S. Enterprises*, Basic Books, New York, 1971, Ch. 3. For evidence on competition and productivity effects, see the sources listed on pp. 158-59 of Vernon.

[9]For export, imports, and research, see below, Ch. 9; for exports and imports, see B. W. Wilkinson, *Canada's International Trade*, Canadian Trade Committee, Montreal, 1968; for research see N. H. Lithwick, *Canada's Science Policy and the Economy*, Chs. 4 and 5, Methuen, Toronto, 1969; for concentration, see G. Rosenbluth, "The

If one considers experience in other high-income countries, the proposition that nationality of ownership is causally and systematically related to poor economic performance of the firm looks even more dubious. On the contrary, studies for the United Kingdom, Australia, the Federated Republic of Germany, and France, among others, both on an individual industry basis and more broadly, generally have a much more positive set of conclusions than those just cited. United States firms in those countries are criticized for exactly the opposite reason to that advanced in Canada—they are believed, usually correctly as these studies suggest, to have a performance record in exports, research, productivity, and other respects which is generally superior to that of domestic firms.

The Canadian studies lead to some further questions. The performance of foreign-owned firms in Canada, while it may not be as bad as some fear, is nevertheless not as good as many might have expected from the assumed advantages in access to foreign research, financing, and marketing. Why is performance typically not better than in the Canadian-owned counterparts where they exist, and why is the performance of both sets of firms so often worse than the best-practice techniques in the United States and elsewhere over long periods? The large and long-standing gap in productivity between Canadian and United States manufacturing generally, and the direct comparisons of subsidiaries with parents, raise questions of this kind. It has been established by aggregative and industry studies that the large foreign-owned manufacturing sector and its domestic counterpart both suffer from too many firms, too many products, and too short runs. It is fairly convincingly established that the most important ultimate determinants of this inefficient industrial structure have been Canadian and foreign protection against trade, a lack of effective competition (partly because of tariffs and a weak anti-combines policy), and badly devised government industrial policies on research and other matters.[10] Industrial policy may well have dissipated part of the potential gain from both foreign and domestic investment in an inefficient and fragmented structure of industry. Indeed, until recent years,

---

Relation between Foreign Control and Concentration in Canadian Industry," *Canadian Journal of Economics* (February 1970), 3. For the experience in other countries, see the sources noted in Vernon in the preceding footnote.

[10]For studies in this area see H. C. Eastman and S. Stykolt, The *Tariff and Competition in Canada*, Macmillan, Toronto, 1967; H. E. English, *Industrial Structure in Canada's International Competitive Position*, Canadian Trade Committee, Montreal, 1964; Economic Council of Canada, *Scale and Specialization of Canada's Manufacturing Industry*, Queen's Printer, 1968; and Ch. 7 below.

much of what passed for industrial strategy in Canada consisted simply of inducing firms to invest in Canada (rather than importing goods) via a high effective rate of protection. In recent years this has been combined with substantial tax concessions as well, by both federal and provincial governments, partly to induce them to locate in certain regions or to undertake more research activity. To the extent such policies do not succeed, not only is the specific policy goal unrealized but much of the potential benefit from direct investment is lost both by way of tax loss and inefficient industry.

It would be easy to ascribe this general state of affairs to the "branch-plant economy" with which it is associated, without asking where the fundamental causes lie. I suggest that the main responsibility should be borne by the complex of policies historically used to speed industrial development in this country. Even if one shares that view (and especially if one does not), certain opportunities nevertheless exist for potentially profitable intervention in the initial investment or subsequent operations by such firms. A firm with many international affiliations by investment, trade, or otherwise—regardless of nationality of ownership—has more opportunities for such matters as tax shifting and sourcing of supplies, whether it uses these opportunities or not. Foreign subsidiaries may certainly have advantages, but it does not follow in any particular case or industry that they necessarily benefit the recipient country or benefit it as much as is feasible with a more intelligent use of policies to capture more spillovers and/or taxes. While my presumption would be that there is generally more competition with foreign firms than without, in principle they can either increase or decrease the degree of monopoly or competition. More generally, as Johnson has noted, there is an important dilemma in the creation of new knowledge, for incentives to its production are usually necessary; but the knowledge should be made available to all users without charge in order to maximize the social benefit from it.

All of this raises questions perhaps more fundamental than whether foreign direct investment is likely to create net economic gains. The first question is whether these net gains can be maximized, or better, optimized. One set of answers exists in improving the set of policies which determine the social gains of corporate policies generally, without regard to nationality of ownership. My earlier comments suggest much remains to be done in Canada in this regard. Second, even if the gains exist, they might be derived with less cost by alternative forms of access to foreign technology. There is a range of ways in which a project can be undertaken: licensing, joint ventures, purchase of management services, protection for domestic firms whether private or public, direct investment of various types, or state purchase of technology and distribution without charge to all. These have quite different economic costs and benefits, as well as different political and social consequences. The presumption in some of the literature is that the direct investment "package" of capital, of production and distribution techniques, and of management skills is most often indivisible. Unfortunately it is not yet possible to say, from a social rather than private viewpoint, how far this is so and in what industrial situations a split of the package is least costly with given objectives.[11] The idea that knowledge created elsewhere is costless, however, may prove expensive to a nation in some of the manufacturing industries undergoing rapid technical changes. There is sometimes an assumption in the literature that, without direct investment, such techniques can be bought or created at least as cheaply or effectively by alternative means with no loss in other respects, or perhaps even with gains in them.[12]

If a country goes the route of discrimination against direct investment, it should be noted that the best alternative is not necessarily protection of domestic inputs. There is a range of alternatives in terms of access to foreign technology, as just noted, any one of which may be preferable in given circumstances. One can make an infant industry type of argument for domestic ownership, of course, extending protection to inputs by the nationality of the supplier. The constraints of that approach should be noted. They include (1) an argument that there are social benefits from investment in creating new knowledge which cannot be captured by the firm which invests in knowledge; (2) that these are greater for domestically owned firms than foreign-owned firms; (3) that there is no lower-cost way to acquire that knowledge.[18]

Thirdly, there is the question of technique, that is the extent to which one relies on general tax and other policies or on specific policies directed at particular industries or even firms, whether the object is to improve the economic setting for all firms or to try to distinguish between them on the basis of ownership. In both cases the mood in government and to some extent other circles seems to be to attempt direct case-by-case intervention through a screening agency or similar institution, rather than general or market-oriented policies. Either the latter is mistrusted or the former is regarded as yielding more predictable outcomes, apparently assuming that present knowledge and skills give one some confidence in the welfare effects. The direct

[11]For a discussion with respect to licensing especially, see Jack Baranson "Technology Transfer through the International Firm," *Papers and Proceedings of the American Economic Association* (May 1970), p. 60.
[12]Penner and Neher appear to favour this assumption, for example, in the studies cited above.
[18]For this range of issues, see the two articles by Johnson cited above.

case-by-case approach also increases bureaucratic costs and powers.[14]

Perhaps even more fundamentally, it has been suggested that a high degree of dependence on imported techniques has created an environment in which entrepreneurial effort is dampened permanently. A considerable literature has developed around this theme in low-income countries, but the argument has also been extended to high-income countries. One example is the "truncation" argument which provides the framework for a recent government study of foreign investment in Canada. Direct investment, it is argued there, leads to many important activities being performed in the parent firm or country, with the result that significant gaps have occurred in Canada's domestic capacities in these respects. How far have managerial, technical, distributive, and financial capabilities been "stunted" because of easy access to supplies of these abroad, mainly through subsidiaries? If one accepts that a certain mass of such activity on an integrated basis is necessary either to give autonomous capacity to exploit innovation privately or to implement policy in this area publicly, the case is made to create more capacity in this area.[15]

Such arguments can be regarded simply as a plea for more protection for skilled domestic groups. As such, their justification would have to be put in terms of infant industry arguments extended to nationality of ownership, with the constraints just noted.

Some doubts must be expressed, however, about how relevant this argument is in high-income host countries. First, it is not obvious that it is supported by the evidence directly bearing on it. It has been noted, for example, that the American challenge through foreign direct investment has been met by a quite formidable response from firms in Western Europe and Japan in particular.[16] It is certainly true that foreign direct investment predominates in oligopolistic industries with high entry barriers, but the one test in Canada

---

[14]For a defence of the direct approach and a discussion of policy approaches generally, see Government of Canada, *Foreign Direct Investment in Canada*, Ottawa, 1972.

[15]*Ibid.* See also Kari Levitt, *Silent Surrender: The Multinational Corporation in Canada*, Macmillan, Toronto, 1970, where the argument is extended to the possible effects of economic dependence on the capacity for political decisions as well. The theme noted in this paragraph is an important but inadequately explored assumption in the literature on divesting foreign direct investment. See Albert O. Hirschman, *How to Divest in Latin America and Why*, Princeton Essays in International Finance, 1969.

[16]Stephen Hymer and Robert Rowthorn, "Multinational Corporations and International Oligopoly: The Non-American Challenge," in Kindleberger, ed., *The International Corporation*, pp. 57-91. The authors, it should be added, are critical of the consequent spread of multinational corporations, partly because of the limits which they see this placing on the scope for national planning.

as to whether this association is because of foreign direct investment yields results which are inconclusive.[17] The frequent assertion that foreign firms monopolize markets or stifle domestic entrepreneurs is not yet rigorously tested by the counter-hypothesis that there are external benefits from such direct investment—training of managers who then move outside the subsidiary, the education and financing of suppliers, the stimulus from competition, and so on. It may be noted that an aggregative test of whether foreign direct investment merely substituted for domestic capital without adding to capital stock in Canada turned out negatively.[18]

My second reason for doubting this proposition is that it fails to take into account the ways in which extended protection itself inhibits the development of entrepreneurial skills by removing competition, restricting market horizons, and leading to an inefficient structure of industry. The "truncation" argument fails to test the counter-hypothesis that the continuing reliance on imported inputs associated with foreign direct investment is due not to the presence of such investment but to the policies (including protection) which foster inefficient industrial development and which also entice to Canada excessive direct investment in some industries. A more promising approach would be to achieve more efficient organization of industry through more liberal foreign trade policy, a far more efficient use of competition policy, and more effective government tax and subsidy and regulatory policies. An associated approach is to tackle directly the many market and societal imperfections which continue to make it difficult to mobilize entrepreneurial capital for many purposes. The hindrance to effective national financial markets because of differences in provincial securities regulations is a case in point. The historic official restrictions on merchant banking roles, or even on noncontrolling equity participation, for many major financial institutions must have formed a formidable barrier to entrepreneurship through much of the history of this country. Finally, under-investment in those educational skills which are more closely related to economic growth is still capable of correction; the graduation of four doctorates in business administration in 1970–71 in all of Canada is hardly a warrant that we are taking seriously the need for research on distinctive business problems here. The linguistic and social barriers to managerial roles for significant portions of the population are

---

[17]Rosenbluth, "Foreign Control and Concentration."

[18]For the period 1951-62 as a whole every $1.00 of new direct investment from abroad was associated with $2.00 of additional domestic investment—a figure falling to $1.50 in recession and risng to $3.00 in boom. See Richard S. Caves and Grant L. Reuber, *Capital Transfers and Economic Policy, 1951-1962*, Harvard University Press, Cambridge, 1971, Ch. 4.

being corrected, but the pace is still slow. Some of the changes involve minor tax or expenditure changes, others need fundamental attitudinal changes. They are worth taking on their own merit, and they lead to an approach which yields more self-reliant expansion while maximizing rather than sacrificing the gains possible from foreign investment. They also have the major effect that they do not sacrifice the interests of those parts of the country or population whose real incomes are still deplorably low.

As Vernon has pointed out, the argument about the effects of direct investment is concerned to an important degree with the form of the question being asked.[19] The measures cited, with some improvement, can perhaps tell what was the effect in quantifiable, largely economic, terms. They cannot tell you what *would* have been the effect without direct investment, because we do not know what would have been the quality of the response by domestic entrepreneurs (both public and private) which would have ensued on the one hand, or the terms of access to technology abroad by alternative means, on the other. "What might have been" is an interesting and often important question. At any time in the past an alternative tax or spending or regulatory policy can, with the benefit of hindsight, compound interest, and some sacrifice by preceding generations, give an alternative preferred by the present generation and hence indicate to the present generation the sacrifices it can make for succeeding ones. More seriously, I am sure that careful historical studies can provide much light on the effects of direct investment, provided they allow for the role of other variables in growth and test counter-hypotheses. A related question which should be tackled systematically on an analytic, historic, and comparative basis, as noted earlier, is the extent to which the "package of indivisible inputs" accompanying direct investment is in fact indivisible, and on what terms.

In concluding this section, it should be noted that there is a roundabout nature to the argument on gains from foreign investment. If a country is willing to make the sacrifices required to support domestic saving and entrepreneurial groups for long, substantial growth will certainly occur without foreign direct investment or with non-controlling forms of access to foreign technology. In that sense, foreign direct investment is neither necessary nor sufficient for adequate growth. The question is what sacrifices are involved in that approach and why one should impose such sacrifices on a community. The answer does not lie, I suggest, in any evidence of substantial economic damage, however much one may argue for a correction of particular abuses

---

[19]Vernon, *Sovereignty at Bay*, p. 157.

or for improving the terms of access directly or by a better domestic policy framework.

Balance of Payments Effects

Fears about the balance of payments effects of direct investment come largely from two sources. The fact that direct investment, unlike portfolio, has no term for repatriation, and that retained earnings cause the liability to grow with no continuing capital inflow, is one source of concern. The other is the evident relation between direct investment and substantial imports from the parent firm to the subsidiary. Such imports at first reflect the fact that direct investment in manufactures is to some considerable degree a substitute for trade, which in turn is (only partly) blocked by restrictions of various kinds. Despite considerable import substitution in older products, the import relation continues over time as the parent develops new products.

The only way to ·resolve this range of issues is to do a stage-by-stage analysis of the long-term effects of direct investment on the balance of payments, both directly and indirectly. The comprehensive analyses of this type which are available lend little support generally to such fears from the viewpoint of high-income host countries.[20] The empirical results for manufacturing, while related to a large number of variables, depend particularly on the assumption with regard to import substitution. Where the subsidiary's production is assumed to displace exports which would otherwise have occurred from the parent, direct investment makes a net overall contribution to the host country's balance of payments. If it is assumed the products would have been produced in the host country in any case, the net effect of direct investment on the host country's payments position is small. In Canada's case, the former assumption yields balance of payments results which are strongly positive, the latter yields results which are slightly negative. Since there is a great deal of historical and other evidence that Canadian governments have persistently attempted to induce manufacturing direct investment in Canada by means of a high degree of protection and otherwise, the former outcome seems the likely one.[21]

---

[20]See G. C. Hufbauer and F. M. Adler, *Overseas Manufacturing Investment and the Balance of Payments*, Government Printing Office, Washington, D.C., 1968; and W. B. Reddaway and Asscociates, *Effects of U.K. Direct Investment Overseas, Final Report*, Cambridge University Press, 1968.

[21]See Herbert Marshall *et al.*, *Canadian-American Industry: A Study in International Investment*, Yale University Press, New Haven, 1936, p. 209. For a recent empirical study indicating that Canadian tariff policy has had an impact on the choice between exporting to Canada from the United States and producing in Canadian subsidiaries,

Two other interpretations of the balance of payments effects appear to have gained widespread currency. One is the view that the benefit from direct investment disappears at the point where the annual inflow of foreign capital is less than interest, dividends, and business services paid out in the same year. This is a view particularly prevalent in some writing on low-income countries. Perhaps it had some justification in such situations as a first approximation to short-run balance of payments effects, given the critical role of foreign exchange in development planning and the frequent absence of better estimates. One must emphasize, nevertheless, that the comparison is meaningless either as a measure of the net gain from direct investment or of the overall balance of payments effects. The former measure, as noted earlier, is derived by approximating increases in output directly attributable to the capital minus owners' returns, plus adjustments for social benefits and costs. The latter measure depends not only on capital inflow and earnings paid out currently, but on exports generated and imports displaced by foreign firms, on assumptions about the effects of foreign investment on the capital stock and income (and hence the balance of payments) in the host country and abroad, and other variables as noted in the studies mentioned earlier. There is no relation, to put it briefly, between income paid out on the total stock of foreign-owned capital in Canada and the annual *inflow* of capital.

A related type of misunderstanding arises from the observation that the host country's domestic savings are typically used to finance the expansion of such firms, after some initial financing by inflows of direct investment capital. In Canada this misunderstanding arises from the observable fact that about 90 per cent of the capital used by subsidiaries of United States firms is from sources within Canada. The inference drawn is that Canadians are financing the "takeover" of Canadian industry. Let me leave aside certain issues this begs—why sourcing in Canada for supplies and technology is desirable, but not for capital, and indeed the whole issue of whether capital is the critical input from direct investment. On closer examination it turns out that fully 70 per cent of the funds used by such subsidiaries in Canada in

see Thomas Horst, "The Industrial Composition of U.S. Exports and Subsidiary Sales to the Canadian Market," *American Economic Review*, March 1972, Vol. 62, pp. 37-45. It may be noted that other relatively simple measures, which are heavily affected by the problem of identifying the return on direct investment, suggest that the Canadian capacity to produce, to export, and to service debt has at least kept pace with the considerable expansion of direct investment. As a percentage of gross national product, for example, payments abroad of interest and dividends by all firms and governments (not just direct investment firms) have declined from 2.9 per cent in the late twenties to 1.9 per cent in the late fifties and the sixties. As a percentage of sales of goods and services abroad they have fallen from 16 per cent to 9 per cent over the same period.

the year 1967, for example, were cash flows generated within the subsidiaries from retained earnings and depreciation and depletion allowances. These funds are no more owned (or their disposition privately controlled) by Canadians than are the assets which give rise to them, except for some minority shareholdings in subsidiaries. If we define the assets as foreign-owned or controlled, the income which accrues to them must be so defined. That earnings retained in Canada are equivalent to new inflows of capital from abroad would be evident if the earnings were shown as paid out to the parent then reinvested in Canada, as many balance of payments statisticians recommend.

Primary Resources

In principle it is not clear why primary resources should be treated differently from manufacturing in so far as direct investment is concerned. A general theory of direct investment, for example, should be capable of explaining both phenomena. In practice there are sufficient differences of degree to warrant the separate treatment of resources as a sub-category of a more general phenomenon. One difference is that the benefits external to the firm are often smaller by way of manpower training and productivity effects, because, for example, the subsidiary is capital-intensive or buys little in domestic markets. A second point is that the profits of foreign subsidiaries in primary resources often include substantial rents which the government should collect for maximum benefit, and can collect without adverse supply effects.[22]

It is very uncertain what the rents are, however, until the resources have been discovered, the technical problem of production solved, the transport and other infrastructure built, and financing and markets provided. Any bargain struck before all of this has been successfully undertaken quickly obsolesces afterwards, and generates pressures to capture more of the rents, to secure more processing, and so on.[23] A second difficulty is that the bargaining power of governments in such circumstances varies widely by resource, depending on the ease of access to the resource in other countries, the degree of collusion among firms, and the co-operation (if any) among governments controlling the major resources. In Canada the situation is complicated still

---

[22]See Caves, "International Corporations." The discussion here focuses on the case where a primary resource firm is integrated with a parent abroad, rather than with a manufacturing subsidiary in Canada.
[23]Vernon, *Sovereignty at Bay*, Ch. 2. This chapter also reviews the extensive literature on attempts to control foreign investment in primary resources.

further by the competition between provinces to attract resource development through various concessions, compounded by the fact that some provinces have relatively few development alternatives. The outcome is to reduce even further the net gain from such investment to the recipient country.

One possible alternative is for governments to set leases and other aspects of contract as short and as flexible as possible, thus permitting renegotiation more easily, but with variations by type of resources reflecting problems of exploration, the degree of bargaining power in each case with regard to concessions, and the effects on the economy more generally. It is even more important to recognize that the comparative advantage in some types of resource development which Canada possesses cannot be realized more fully without greater and continued freedom of access for processed products to foreign markets.

The substantial presence of many large foreign-controlled corporations in Canada should not obscure that what is involved in these issues, and in issues such as environmental control or tax subsidization, is more a matter of government policy and control of the large corporation in resource development than of domestic to foreign ownership. It is not at all clear why resident-owned firms in primary resource development should be exempted from such questions. There is a presumption for more regulation in the primary resource field than elsewhere for reasons noted above. Whether domestic ownership as such is necessary depends on one's assessment of how far foreign ownership limits the possibilities for effective regulation, as well as the kinds of questions on economic benefits and costs raised earlier. It is time to turn to these broader issues.

Some Political and Social Issues

The economic consequences of foreign direct investment in relatively high-income countries would not, by themselves, explain the reaction to such investment. When an economist moves to such issues as national independence he is on slippery ground, not only because the issues do not lend themselves readily to his customary approaches but also because other social scientists have failed to give them the systematic attention they deserve. Nevertheless, venture we must or we evade the issue most often and most fervently raised about foreign direct investment.

A major relevant question is the ways and the extent to which foreign direct investment affects the ease with which a state can implement its policies, and how far any losses here can be said to cancel out any net economic gains. The question is not strictly amenable to a cost-benefit approach, for people differ widely on both the meaning and the value they will put on independence in the sense just noted. In particular, they differ on which aspects of it should be regarded as an absolute which cannot be traded off whatever the gain in other respects.

One useful distinction, although sometimes blurred, is between those aspects of direct investment which are largely or wholly related to the actions of firms in pursuit of their own objectives, and those which are largely or wholly related to the state in the pursuit of its objectives through direct pressures on the firm.

Does the nation state have something to fear, in terms of its capacity to mount programs, from foreign direct investment as such? The answer must surely be that it does in some directions, but there are important offsets. A multinational firm by definition involves some assets, including important head-office assets, which are located outside the borders of the host country. The multinational firm allocates these and other resources over time among its affiliates, within the important constraints of law, economic circumstances, and the organizational settings of such firms. If one poses this situation against a firm whose entire assets are located in one country, or the great bulk of whose assets and head office facilities are so located, then clearly there is more *potential* control for a government in the operations of such domestic firms. This is particularly so for the range of administrative policies where corporations are subject to that blend of persuasion and coercion which often appears necessary, at least to government bureaucrats, to implement duly passed law. The point involved goes beyond this type of situation. Whatever the actuality, for example, the opportunities for tax minimization through transfer pricing among differing tax jurisdictions are greater for multinational firms. If multinational firms continue to spread, and if governments cannot singly or together implement their policies except at great cost, then there is clearly a loss of sovereignty. And that is true even if one agrees that there is some gain to the national and international community in other respects.

Stating the issue in this way raises important qualifications and questions. It is clear that there are different kinds of international business with different degrees of integration with the recipient and investing countries. It is also true that foreign investment is to some extent a substitute for foreign trade,[24] and the latter also offers considerable scope for "dependence." It is not clear

---

[24]See Horst, "Industrial Composition."

whether foreign firms are less responsive in practice to government policies, or more likely to escape laws. The studies of *economic* performance of subsidiaries in high-income countries, as noted earlier, do not lend support to such views on any generalized basis, whatever specific cases one may take to the contrary. Nor is there much point in discussing actual or potential political costs without looking at actual or potential benefits. Too often the assumption is made that economic integration merely limits or complicates the exercise of some forms of policy. There are both opportunities and constraints in practice, with the opportunities arising in part from the larger and enriched economic base which is available to support initiatives in both domestic and foreign policy. If only constraints were involved in foreign direct investment, or it was fairly easily matched by alternative forms, then governments would long since have acted to severely restrict it.

The fact is that we know rather too little to comment in a general way on the effects of the spread of multinationals on a country's capacity to implement policies. There is no general study of the probable degree of harmonization of national policies which the spread of multinational firms will require, comparable to the studies which approach this same question from the viewpoint of integration by foreign trade. Nor is there any major empirical study on such important specific topics as the effects of transfer pricing practices on tax revenues. In the area of short-run stabilization policy, however, a recent study is fairly encouraging on the question of policy implementation. It covered the period 1951 to 1962, when Canada was on a flexible exchange rate, with some work on later years, and suggested two conclusions. The first is that autonomous changes in capital flows were accommodated fairly easily by corresponding changes in the current account, and did not require major policy adjustments or major changes in the rate of capital formation out of, domestic savings. Direct investment required much less adjustment in the balance of payments than did portfolio investment, and under average conditions was fully accommodated through automatic income adjustments. The study also suggests that foreign capital flows do not alter the ability of a country like Canada to pursue independent stabilization goals so much as they give more leverage to some types of policy and less to others, thus affecting the manner in which policy instruments can be used to achieve these goals.[25]

---

[25]Caves and Reuber, *Capital Transfers.* See also Reuber, "Foreign Investment in Canada: A Review," in Douglas Auld, ed., *Economics: Contemporary Issues in Canada*, Holt, Rinehart and Winston, Toronto, 1973.

Earlier it was noted that one can distinguish in principle the effects on independence of the spread of direct investment firms as such from the attempt by the government of the home country to exercise sovereignty over subsidiaries in the host country. There have been a series of situations in the past fifteen years where United States law has been interpreted as extending to American-owned subsidiaries in Canada and elsewhere. These include regulations under the United States Trading with the Enemy Act which, by threatening to levy penalties on the parent, prohibited all trade by such subsidiaries abroad with North Korea, North Vietnam, Cuba, and China. Canadian law included no such general prohibition, although strategic goods were not exported to them. Exemptions could be secured from this prohibition on a case-by-case basis, but little is known on how this worked in practice. These regulations have now been substantially relaxed in the case of China, but not the other three countries, provided the transactions do not involve strategic goods. There has also been some relaxation on trade by subsidiaries with Eastern Europe and the Soviet Union. There have been similar problems in the area of United States anti-trust law, which has on occasion been interpreted to apply to subsidiaries abroad because of the effects of the latter on United States trade. Some of the balance-of-payments guidelines of the United States government have been interpreted by some writers as bordering on extra-territorial extension of law.

In each of these cases there is a United States, as well as Canadian, interest. On occasion, also, the effect of the United States policy may even be beneficial to Canada economically, as with some anti-trust decisions. Nevertheless, there is a serious problem of erosion of sovereignty for a host country if it fails to assert the principle that its laws, regulations, and policies take precedence over foreign in so far as its residents are concerned.

It will be noted that the problem arises not because of foreign direct investment as such, but because of the unilateral extension of law abroad through the international firm, which then finds itself caught between two sovereigns with different laws or policies. It is a problem of intergovernmental relations, and the optimal solution involves intergovernmental negotiation and agreement. The Canadian government in particular is well placed to launch such proposals, and there are some precedents in international or bilateral law which might be helpful. The field of competition policy might be a good place to start. Meanwhile, few issues are as likely to jeopardize the future of direct investment, at least in Canada, for these types of issues dramatically confirm the view that the presence of such firms directly limits sovereignty and serves as a vehicle for imposing the values and policies of foreign governments on other countries.[26]

A phenomenon as widespread as multinational corporations inevitably becomes bound up both with the question of the social and political consequences of large corporations and the larger range of issues in the field of Canada–United States relations. When one state is much more powerful than the other and is a major world power as well, terms such as interdependence are often likely to take on a one-sided meaning; one state has more of it than the other, and more than it wants on occasion. Here we are at the heart of the Canadian dilemma—the ties through investment, trade, communications, military alliances, population transfer, and in many other ways to the powerful and restless giant to the south. I do not have a handy panacea on how to deal with the complications of this relationship, which will always challenge our ingenuity. I would suggest that when larger issues are linked closely to foreign direct investment there is likely to be considerable mis-specification. One example noted earlier is the attempt to link foreign firms to the production of what some regard as socially undesirable commodities, or to private wants at the expense of public sector spending. No one would deny that such corporations transmit or create certain kinds of wants, but so do many other processes which involve no direct investment. Another example is the view that such firms may be incompatible with a high degree of planning and, of course, with state ownership, both of which would tend to integrate a firm more fully within a country rather than integrate an industry internationally. Direct investment firms appear to co-exist with varying degrees of planning, but let us grant the point that direct investment as now generally conceived is certainly more compatible with a capitalist than a socialist orientation to enterprise. This leaves a prior question, however, for the difficulty of controlling such firms in a more highly planned society cannot be treated as both necessary and sufficient evidence of the undesirability of such firms or the desirability of more direct planning. We are not even in a position yet to know how far it is possible to deal with the problems created by such firms simply by more active and effective use of present instruments of policy, applied either nationally or internationally.

What is more likely to determine the fate of direct investment is the kind

---

[26]Cases involving home governments other than the United States are not unknown. These situations have drawn more protest in Canada than in other countries, presumably because more national firms exist elsewhere which can undertake the business prohibited to the subsidiaries. For an analysis of this issue, see the Report of the Task Force on the Structure of Canadian Industry, *Foreign Ownership and the Structure of Canadian Industry*, Privy Council Office, Ottawa, 1968.

of monetary and trading system one envisages for the future. Short-term instability in the inflow of long-term capital can probably be handled to some considerable degree by new approaches to conventional policy instruments, as noted earlier. Whether recipient countries would be willing to live with the economic and political costs to them of major sporadic attempts by the United States government to regulate the capital outflow, the operations of subsidiaries abroad, or the trade balance in particular, is quite another matter. That kind of approach to direct investment, coupled with independent attempts by host countries to improve the social return from it or otherwise regulate it, is likely to be more restrictive of foreign direct investment than the kinds of concerns just noted.

An important point about the political and social aspects is the uneven effect of foreign direct investment on private groups within the host country. This may help explain some types of policy responses to direct investment, particularly those which prevent its competitive effects and perhaps those which attempt to secure some of the economic rents for domestic investors.

The most convincing general long-term result of more direct investment is that the real wage rate will rise given the addition of capital and the improvement and spread of technology. Given some degree of competition with domestic owners or other subsidiaries, the benefit will come in part through lower prices and improved products. These gains, of course, might be taken in terms of population increase or employment opportunities, depending on such matters as immigration policy and the extent to which technology is labour-saving. Domestic owners of capital and suppliers of technology (i.e. high-skill labour) may gain to the extent they are complementary to foreign-owned firms and to the extent that capital formation and national income have risen. But domestic owners of capital and suppliers of technology may lose if they are competitive with foreign-owned firms, since the presence of the latter can require them to face higher wages rates, lower market prices, or a reduced share of the market. Where these competitive effects are not the likely ones but entry to an industry is barred for a time, potential domestic entrants lose in other ways. Moreover, foreign subsidiaries are likely to cause further resentment among local capital owners because of their evident dislike of minority share issues, i.e. their unwillingness to share the quasi-rents which are a return on their knowledge or on their market power.[27]

---

[27] While there may be various reasons for this, one of the most general seems to be that the value of the subsidiary to prospective domestic owners is less than to the parent. For a discussion of this in the context of a theory of direct investment which emphasizes the minimization of transaction costs, see John McManus, "The Theory of the Inter-

The effects on the demand for senior personnel are less clear. Foreign investment increases the scope for employing such persons directly and in some cases in the affiliates abroad, and supplies managerial and technical training which may subsequently spill over into the economy. What is also evident in the host country is that some significant percentage of the most senior positions in the subsidiary are filled by nationals of the parent company—more so in Canada, incidentally, than in Australia and the United Kingdom.[28]

All of this produces significant group differences in views on the effects of direct investment, and on policy proposals which might curb such investment. Significant regional differences also occur, and for similar reasons. The low-income regions, such as most of the Maritimes, eastern Quebec, and northern Ontario, are unable to compete with the more developed parts of the country for capital and technology. Since they have fewer alternative sources of jobs and tax revenue than other parts of Canada, they tend to view with suspicion any measures which might further reduce their access to these. There are also a considerable number of persons in eastern and western Canada, and not only in Quebec, who appear to be almost neutral in their attitudes between direct investment from Ontario and direct investment from abroad.[29]

A policy which reduces the inflow of foreign capital and technology—and does nothing to substitute for it—may well shift income away from labour and to domestic owners of capital and professionals. One of the studies noted earlier suggests that, if withholding taxes on income paid abroad are raised so that Canada relies entirely on domestic capital, and assuming full employment can be maintained, the rate of return for domestic savers will rise 40 per cent while the real wage drops 17 per cent.[30] Restrictive policies might also tend to widen the already wide and persistent regional income differentials in Canada. These effects on personal and regional income distribution can be offset in principle by tax and transfer policies. Whether they could be fully offset in practice is a complicated question, as recent Canadian experience with both tax and transfer policies suggests. The other critical assumption is that nothing is done to substitute for the capital or technology to which access is restricted, or to compensate for any other

national Firm," in Gilles Paquet, ed., *The Multinational Firm and the Nation State*, Collier-Macmillan, Toronto, 1972.

[28]See my *Performance of Foreign-Owned Firms in Canada*, Canadian-American Committee, Montreal, 1969, Ch. 2.

[29]See, for example, the introduction by A. D. Scott to the issue of *B.C. Studies*, no. 13.

[30]Helliwell and Broadbent, "How Much Does Foreign Capital Matter?" p. 40.

losses such as marketing connections. Of course, some substitutes would be found abroad or created at home, with benefits and costs which are unclear as noted earlier.

While it is desirable to find or develop substitutes for some types of direct investment which appear less costly in economic and political terms, some questions about the political process by which decisions of this kind are made raise some doubts that this will be the most probable path for policy. There are other and perhaps easier ways to reconcile group differences to yield agreed policies, especially in a setting where some become convinced that national survival itself is at stake. Breton and others have suggested a theory of the economics of nationalism which helps explain how group differences are reconciled to yield agreed policies in circumstances such as those described here.[31] In essence, nationalism is regarded as a collective consumption good which yields both general and particular benefits. The general benefits accrue to all of those who derive psychic income from investment in nationalism. The particular benefits accrue to those who benefit directly by way of higher real income or better jobs (as well as deriving psychic income) from policies of economic nationalism. The particular beneficiaries, as already noted, tend to be in the higher income groups. The political process involves persuading those who lose economic income or jobs to accept the policies because their psychic income is increased. Most major policies will have some differential impact by groups, of course. Policies in an area as divisive as this one should give close attention to the effects on the policy objective of levelling up economic incomes and opportunities for Canadians. That issue, in my view, has had far more to do with the survival of the country historically than any issues raised by foreign direct investment.[32]

In noting this approach as an explanatory aid to certain types of policies I

[31]Albert Breton, "The Economics of Nationalism," *Journal of Political Economy*, Vol. 72 (August 1964), pp. 376-86. See also Harry C. Johnson, "A Theoretical Model of Economic Nationalism in New and Developing States," *Political Science Quarterly*, Vol. 80 (June 1965), pp. 169-85.

[32]Other elites are involved, as Vernon has argued (*Sovereignty at Bay*, Ch. 6). Government officials may believe administrative control of business activity more difficult to maintain. As noted earlier, those who promote a competing ideology understandably oppose the extension of the largest and often most successful examples of capitalism to their country. The issue becomes even more complicated if important elements of the media, whether for reasons of the psychic income of nationalism or because of competition or both, determine that they have a direct stake in the outcome. The debate on this subject in Canada is not uninfluenced by the fact that the national broadcasting system, the daily newspaper with the largest circulation and the public affairs magazine with the largest circulation, all generally warmly support economic as well as cultural nationalism.

hope you will not infer that I favour it. On the contrary, national feeling and national self-interest ought to serve better ends than this particular form of protection for special groups, and national investment and regulation can yield higher real income and satisfaction where social and private costs or returns diverge. And that is true of both domestic and foreign corporations in Canada. One of the heavier costs of economic nationalism is the way in which it diverts public attention from such issues, focusing it on multinational corporations and encouraging policies which will have little or even negative effects on the more important issues.

Conclusions

From the viewpoint of the higher-income host country, a large multi-national presence in the corporate area brings both benefits and costs, either actual or potential. There are likely to be net economic benefits, with the size depending on how well domestic policy options are exercised in tax policy, competition, or regulation. Some other forms of access to international technology may be less expensive economically, and will certainly create less political tension. It is difficult to know the types of industries and situations where this is likely to be the case given present knowledge of the consequences of splitting the package of inputs which come over time with direct investment, and the various possible mechanisms for international transfer of such inputs. The quality of the domestic policy and private entrepreneurial response is the other critical determinant of an outcome where less or little direct investment is specified. Indeed, it is suggested that many of the problems allegedly associated with multinational corporations are not, in fact, due to them. The term has become a catch-all for the problems of control of the large corporation, the failures of domestic policies in correcting abuses of the market system, and a protest against a particular life-style. Canadian policy is an object lesson in this respect, both for the inefficiency and excessive foreign direct investment which Canada's industrial policies have encouraged and for the failure to encourage a stronger capacity to undertake efficient ventures or to transmit knowledge from abroad in other ways.

It is inevitable, and in some cases desirable, that host countries will attempt to improve the net gain from direct investment, in part by developing techniques to offset the bargaining power which such firms have because of location in several nation states. Some countries will have a high degree of public planning for other reasons, extended also to any direct investment firms. In other countries, I am doubtful that detailed administrative controls are either justified by the evidence of damage or likely to give clear improvements in national welfare given the problems of operating such controls and the state of knowledge of the subject. If I am correct in my view that the economic literature suggests such firms are highly responsive over time to economic stimuli, and that the influence of ownership as such is far less important than relative prices as determined by comparative advantage and by economic policy, then there are ways to influence such firms' policies far short of direct controls.

This takes us to my final point. If one assumes that the recipient and investing country can both gain from direct investment in the case of high-income countries, then independent policy approaches to the distribution of these gains are not likely to maximize the combined outcome. The same is likely to be true of independent policy approaches to limit some of the disadvantages which accompany direct investment. Indeed, it is not difficult to see situations today across boundaries where unrestricted competition for direct investment or unco-ordinated regulation of it are diminishing the combined social return which might be expected from it. I have restricted myself here largely to a national framework. Ultimately, domestic policy in this and other respects depends on the extent to which one considers that an international setting for trade and investment and the resulting improvement of international resource allocation is also most likely to be conducive to the national interest. One does not have to accept the view of the unconditional supporters of direct investment, who regard it as nothing less than the basis for a new political world order, to suggest that binational or multinational policy approaches to some of the opportunities and constraints posed by such investment would be in the national interest—particularly if one believes that only a few of the criticisms of such firms may amount to mountains of evidence, some of the evidence consists of foothills capable of being ascended by governments, and all too many of the alleged shortcomings amount to nothing more than molehills.

1
Introduction

The flow of private international capital played a significant role in the development of a number of countries in the hundred years up to 1914. First the United States, then Argentina, Australia, and Canada, were major recipients of such investment, particularly from the United Kingdom. Most of this capital was in the form of bonds, guaranteed by governments. It underwrote the rail and other investments required to develop regions which were rich in natural resources but thinly populated. The borrowing of capital was accompanied not only by real imports of equipment and supplies, but also by a mass migration of population to the borrowing lands particularly from Europe.

This pattern of capital flow was partially restored in the 1920s, only to be largely disrupted by the great depression of the thirties. Capital flows since World War II stand in contrast to the major flows of earlier periods. Government grants and loans and direct foreign investments dominate. The development problems of most of the major recipients are markedly different from those of the earlier recipients, and the migration of population is on a much more modest scale.[1]

Many authorities have noted the differences between direct investment and portfolio investment when discussing long-term international capital investment. The essential distinction is that legal control of the asset is in-

---

[1]For a more extended treatment of the contrasts noted here, see Penelope Hartland, "Private Enterprise and International Capital," *The Canadian Journal of Economics and Political Science*, vol. XIX (1953), p. 70.

volved in direct investment.[2] Foreign direct investment, therefore, represents capital investment in a branch plant or subsidiary corporation abroad where the investor has voting control of the concern. Foreign portfolio investment is involved where the form of the investment (in bonds or loans) or the amount (in voting stock) does not involve legal control of the asset, at least short of bankruptcy. The distinction is clearly not the same as that between foreign equity and debt investments. There is a relation, however, in that foreign direct investment is largely represented by equity capital in the form of shares of incorporated subsidiaries and net assets of unincorporated branches. Foreign portfolio investment may take either form also, though in the Canadian experience it has been mainly in government and corporate bonds and debentures.

Most direct investment carries a variable rate of return dependent on profits and on a decision to withdraw them, in contrast with a payment fixed by contract in the case of a bond. It usually carries ownership rights of no fixed duration in contrast with the requirement of repayment or refinancing at a given time in the case of bond financing. The former is directly associated with the extension of the products, technology, and management techniques of the investing enterprise, as well as the financing associated with the latter. These and other differences, while useful for broad analytical purposes, become less clear in some circumstances. The fixed returns may become variable with default and moratoria, for example, and the import of capital through bond issues may be accompanied by the import of technology.[3]

---

[2]The Dominion Bureau of Statistics draws the following distinction on p. 21 of *Canada's International Investment Position 1926-1954.* (The Dominion Bureau of Statistics is henceforth referred to as D.B.S.). "Portfolio investments are typically scattered minority holdings of securities which do not carry with them control of the enterprises in which the investments occur. Usually securities are public issues such as bonds and debentures of governments, municipalities, and corporations and the stock of companies listed on stock exchanges, although less marketable issues may also constitute some parts of this type of investment. Direct investments on the other hand are those investments in business enterprises which are sufficiently concentrated to constitute control of the concerns. The nature of the classification is such that potential control is implied rather than an actual exercise of control over business policy, although the latter may be present as is usually the case. The investors supply the capital assuming the largest burden of risk, technical knowledge, and skills. The division of investments into the two groups is a useful form of analysis, but there may be exceptional border line instances of holdings contained in each which are not representative of the characteristics shown by the more typical cases included."

[3]For a discussion of the differences between direct and portfolio investment, see August Maffry, "Direct Versus Portfolio Investment in the Balance of Payments" and the Discussion by Vincent W. Bladen and H. J. Dernburg, *Papers and Proceedings of the American Economic Association,* vol. XLIV, No. 2 (May 1954), pp. 615-633.

Economists have long been concerned with certain questions regarding international long-term capital flows. The question of the mechanism of adjustment in the balance of payments in response to, among other things, foreign long-term borrowing has received much attention. Studies of international adjustment also illuminated some aspects of the processes of economic growth, particularly in the case of those dealing with changes in the stock of capital and in industrial structure.[4] In a general way a number of empirical studies of the experience with foreign investment in the nineteenth century and early decades of the twentieth century also came to conclusions about the benefits of foreign investment to the receiving and lending countries. Particular aspects of theories of foreign trade have also illumined the nature and effects of capital transfers. Two questions regarding foreign investment have received rather scant attention from economists until recently. The effects of international direct investment have not been given much separate attention, perhaps because its role was relatively small until recent decades. The benefits and costs of foreign investment generally have not been systematically analysed from the national point of view of either the capital exporting or importing country. Recently there have been several attempts to systematically analyse economic benefits and costs from the point of view of both countries. The most notable example from the viewpoint of the borrowing country is an article growing out of Australia's experience with private foreign investment in recent years.[5] The major

---

[4] There is a voluminous literature on the long-term mechanism of adjustment in the balance of payments in response to capital imports. The Canadian experience of 1900-1913 has been examined with particular thoroughness. Some key publications are Jacob Viner, *Canada's Balance of International Indebtedness, 1900-1913*, Harvard University Press, Cambridge, 1924; C. G. Meier, "Economic Development and the Transfer Mechanism: Canada 1895-1913," *Canadian Journal of Economics and Political Science*, vol. XIX (February 1963), pp. 1-19; J. C. Ingram, "Growth in Capacity and Canada's Balance of Payments," *American Economic Review*, vol. 47 (March 1957), pp. 93-104; and A. K. Cairncross, *Home and Foreign Investment 1870-1913*, Cambridge University Press, 1953, Chapter 3.

[5] G. D. A. McDougall, "The Benefits and Costs of Private Investment from Abroad: A Theoretical Approach," *Bulletin of the Oxford University Institute of Statistics*, vol. 22, (August 1960), pp. 189-210 (reprinted from *The Economic Record*, March, 1960). See also Paul B. Simpson, "Foreign Investment and the National Advantage: A Theoretical Analysis, *"U.S. Private and Government Investment Abroad*, ed. Raymond F. Mikesell, University of Oregon Books, Eugene, 1962. For the view that private investment abroad under competitive conditions may be excessive, from the point of view of the national economic welfare of the lending country, see J. Carter Murphy, "International Investment and the National Interest," *The Southern Economic Journal*, vol. XXVIII, No. 1 (July 1960), pp. 11-17; Murray C. Kemp, "Foreign Investment and the National Advantage," *The Economic Record*, vol. XXXVIII (March 1962), pp. 56-62; and Marvin Frankel, "Home Versus Foreign In-

conclusion of that article, under a number of assumptions, is that "The most important direct gains to Australia from more rather than less private investment from abroad seem likely to come through higher tax revenue from foreign profits (at least if the higher investment is not induced by lower tax rates), through economies of scale and through external economies generally, especially where Australian-owned firms acquire 'know-how' or are forced by competition to adopt more efficient methods."[6] The author also indicates a number of indirect gains which (depending on government policy) may result from more foreign investment, such as more domestically-financed investment.

The topic of foreign direct investment has received limited attention by economists. Much attention has been given to international capital flows on the one hand and the theory of the firm on the other. The former has usually been at the aggregative level, however, while the latter has been largely outside the context of international transactions and often of location theory. Research on this topic from the point of view of business administration has usually been directed to methods of operation within the international firm, with less systematic emphasis on economic issues. Research on direct investment, particularly where related to corporate policies and practices, necessarily cuts across these areas. It may also involve broader political and social considerations, depending on the specific topic and the approach to it. Direct investment has received increasing attention in recent years. There has been a revival of interest in the question of the sharing of benefits when direct investments are made in economically poor countries by firms in relatively wealthy lands.[7] Direct investment between countries at similar stages of development has also received more attention, in terms of both the effects on investing and receiving countries and the nature and desirability of policies designed to impede or increase such investments. Literature on the management of international business operations has also grown rapidly. One should not overestimate what is available for economic analysis in this area since there are large gaps in information and analysis and much of what is available is concerned with consequences for the firm

vestment: A Case Against Capital Export," *Kyklos*, vol. XVIII, Fasc. 3 (1965), pp. 411-433. A. E. Jasay has criticized this general position in his article "The Social Choice Between Home and Overseas Investment," *The Economic Journal*, vol. LXX, No. 277 (March 1960), pp. 105-113.

[6]McDougall, *ibid.*, p. 209-210. The term "external economies" refers to services rendered by one producer to another without compensation.

[7]For a discussion of this literature, see Benjamin Higgins, *Economic Development*, Norton, New York, 1959, Ch. 15.

rather than for the economy, but the quickening of interest and information is unmistakable.

Canada offers unusual scope for research in this area, and her experience with direct investment is a long one. While international investment in Canada before World War I was largely in the form of debt, direct investment was a significant portion of the total. The first official estimates, those for 1926, show direct investment of $1.8 billion out of total foreign long-term capital in Canada of $6 billion.[8] At that time non-residents owned 37 per cent and controlled 17 per cent of the combined capital in manufacturing, mining, railways and other utilities, and merchandising. Moreover, there has been a substantial increase of direct investment in the last two decades, absolutely and as a percentage of all foreign capital invested in Canada. At the end of 1963 the book value of direct investment in Canada was $15.4 billion out of a total of $26.2 billion for all foreign long-term investment. Foreign ownership and control of capital in the industries noted above was 35 per cent and 34 per cent respectively in 1962. High and rising ratios of ownership and control in the manufacturing and mining sectors in particular have led to increasing concern in the past decade with the possible economic and political consequences, and resulted in some legislation as noted below.

In view of this it is surprising that there is so little serious research on the Canadian experience with direct investment. In particular, rather little is known in any systematic and generalized way about the characteristics and consequences of the international firm in Canada. The only major empirical and analytical study on this subject was published thirty years ago.[9] More recent analyses are restricted to specific issues or lack a strong empirical base.

The present volume attempts to fill one of the gaps by examining certain policies and results of the international business firm in Canada. The objective of this study is to attempt to establish data on the characteristics of those Canadian firms which are owned by non-residents, and to analyse some of the consequences with respect to the structure and development of the Canadian economy. Particular attention will be given to some basic economic characteristics of the firms; to the organizational framework of

[8]Unless otherwise indicated, all data on the total amount of foreign capital invested in Canada are from publications of the Dominion Bureau of Statistics as listed in the bibliography.
[9]Herbert Marshall, Frank A. Southard, Jr., Kenneth W. Taylor, *Canadian-American Industry: A Study in International Investment,* Yale University Press, New Haven, 1936.

the companies involved, including the nature of senior personnel and the relationship with affiliates abroad; to export and import policies and results; to research and development; and to some aspects of financial operations.

These issues deserve analysis in their own right, as aspects of a complex phenomenon which has spread rapidly in Canada and elsewhere during recent years. An understanding of many aspects of Canada's economy and of economic policy would be advanced by further studying the characteristics of its foreign-owned sectors. The issues involved here cut across questions of efficiency, employment and growth in which the economist has a special interest. In addition, the issues are particularly relevant to the controversy in Canada of the past decade concerning problems of equity and of nationalism in which the political economist has an interest. Anyone familiar with this controversy will appreciate that it has affected the choice of issues analysed here. This will be emphasized in what follows, yet it should be emphasized also that certain tasks have not been undertaken in this study, either because there is not enough information for relatively convincing conclusions or because they would take us far afield from our main focus of research. No attempt has been made to weigh the net overall economic benefits and costs of direct investment, nor to analyse overall balance of payments aspects. Several specific topics are not dealt with directly, particularly in the area of investment in primary resources.[10] Nor has an attempt been made to examine the larger topic of Canadian-American relations, political, social, and economic, of which this issue forms a part. This study will inevitably overlap and perhaps contribute to an understanding of some of these areas, but it does so from the point of view of an examination of the organization and operation of the international firm.

Direct Investment in the Canadian Economy

It is well known that Canada borrowed substantial amounts from abroad in the nineteenth century and the first three decades of the present century for government projects and railroad construction. These fixed-interest loans were very largely on government account or guaranteed by

---

[10]For an attempt at an overall assessment of net benefits see Rudolph G. Penner, "The Benefits of Foreign Investment in Canada, 1950 to 1956," Paper delivered to the Statistics Conference of the Canadian Political Science Association, Vancouver, June 1965. Some of the overall balance of payments aspects are examined in Irving Brecher, *Capital Flows Between Canada and the United States*, Montreal, Canadian-American Committee, 1965; and David W. Slater, *Canada's Balance of International Payments — When is a Deficit a Problem?*, Canadian Trade Committee, Montreal 1964.

governments. What is less well appreciated is the substantial direct investment in Canada from Confederation onwards. It has been estimated that the total inflow of capital was about $850 million from 1870 to 1900, of which $710 million was in government or railroad securities.[11] Most of the remainder was American direct investment in Canada. The number of foreign-owned manufacturing branches and subsidiaries in Canada rose rapidly after 1900, as did American investments in primary resources. By 1913 direct investment accounted for over one-fifth of all foreign capital invested in Canada. It is not known what proportion of the capital invested in industry was foreign-owned in the early years of this century, but the evidence suggests it was not small.[12]

Official estimates of foreign capital invested in Canada were first prepared in the late twenties. The first such estimate, for 1926, indicated the United States had already supplanted the United Kingdom as the major source of external capital. Direct investment in 1926 amounted to 30 per cent of total foreign long-term capital in Canada of $6 billion.[13] Depression and war slowed the increase in foreign capital even absolutely. The 1948 total of $7.5 billion for foreign long-term investment was just about the same as that for 1930, although the proportion represented by direct investment was considerably higher. Rapid general development in the next decade, and particularly large foreign investment in petroleum and natural gas, very substantially raised the absolute value of foreign capital invested. The total continued to rise in subsequent years when economic growth had moderated. At the end of 1963 the book value of foreign long-term investments in Canada was $26.2 billion, with 78 per cent of it owned by residents of the United States. Direct investment constituted 59 per cent of the total compared with 38 per cent two decades earlier.[14] As to the immediate

[11]See Hartland, "Private Enterprise and International Capital," pp. 77-78.
[12]See Marshall et al., *Canadian-American Industry*, pp. 1-21.
[13]It is important to note that common and preferred stocks are included at book values as shown in the balance sheets of the issuing companies. In periods of rising prices such values will be less than market values. Bonds and debentures are valued at par, liabilities in foreign currencies being converted into Canadian dollars at the original rate of exchange. See D.B.S., *Canada's International Investment Position, 1926-1954*, for a discussion of valuation, classification and other statistical problems.
[14]It may be noted in passing that Canadian long-term investments abroad have risen from $2 billion in 1945 to $6.7 billion in 1963. This rate of increase is almost as rapid as that for foreign investment in Canada. The composition of the totals differs with government loans and subscriptions a third of Canadian long-term foreign assets, and non-residents have a significant equity in Canadian direct investments abroad through their ownership of Canadian corporations. Details on Canadian assets abroad and on net international indebtedness are available in the annual and quarterly publications by D.B.S. on the balance of international payments.

factors underlying the increase in the value of total foreign direct investment in Canada, it may be noted that the retention of profits on such investment (as against net international capital inflows) accounted for 39 per cent of the increase in the value of direct investment in the period 1946-1961. Moreover, 61 per cent of the gross inflow for direct investment from the United States in 1946-1961 went to the petroleum, natural gas, and mining industries.[15]

These absolute values need to be put into some perspective. One question is whether the production base and international receipts (created in part with the help of foreign capital) are growing sufficiently to help finance it. This is difficult to measure directly and the answer lies partly in the future. It may be noted here that the national product in current dollars rose somewhat more slowly than did foreign capital during the fifties, but this tendency was reversed in the early years of the sixties. National product in current dollars has risen about twice as fast as the total of foreign capital since the twenties. Such comparisons should be qualified by the observation that quite different valuation techniques are involved in the two series.[16] Perhaps more relevant are historical comparisons with the payments abroad which have arisen to date from recent foreign investment. Interest and dividends paid abroad as a percentage of gross national product have fallen from 2.9 per cent in the late twenties and 6.4 per cent in the depressed thirties to 1.9 per cent in the period 1957-1964 inclusive. As a percentage of earnings from the sale abroad of goods and services such payments have declined from 16 per cent in the late twenties and 25 per cent in the thirties to 9 per cent in the period 1957 to 1964 inclusive. Such historical comparisons require further analysis, however, since direct investment is a much larger portion of the total now and the return on it is variable. In later chapters the nature of the return on direct investment and the relationship of direct investment to exports and imports will be considered in detail.

Direct investment tends to be concentrated in certain sectors of the economy. Before presenting data on these sectors it is well to note more precisely the meaning of the terms "direct investment" and "control" and the coverage of the series. These points are clear in reports on Canada's investment position but are sometimes overlooked in discussions of the

---

[15]D.B.S., *The Canadian Balance of International Payments, 1961 and 1962*, pp. 48-9.
[16]If one takes foreign capital invested as a percentage of national product in constant (1949) dollars, a procedure even more questionable than that in current dollars, the percentage are 87, 48 and 89 for 1930, 1948 and 1963 respectively.

subject.[17] First, a direct investment company is either an unincorporated branch owned by non-residents, or a concern incorporated in Canada in which the effective control of voting stock is held, or believed to be held, by non-residents. There is a difference between the legal position of effective control of voting stock and the question of the extent to which that control is in fact exercised. Official data on foreign ownership and control of Canadian industry relate only to the former point. The word "control" is a convenient short way to refer to this legal position, but it should always be remembered that the data alone tell us nothing about the extent to which the officers of the major or sole shareholder abroad do in fact exercise their influence. In fact, very little is known about this matter except that there is a wide range of situations from a high degree of centralization of responsibility and decision-making to virtually complete decentralization.[18] Similarly, the convenient terms "parent" and "subsidiary" are used in the

---

[17]See footnote 2 above and note the following from p. 24 of D.B.S. *Canada's International Investment Position, 1926-54*: "The concept of control also needs to be carefully examined particularly before conclusions are drawn from the data. The category of direct investments shown here generally includes all concerns in Canada which are known to have 50 per cent or more of their voting stock held in one country outside Canada. In addition a few instances of concerns are included where it is known that effective control is held by a parent firm with less than 50 per cent of the stock. In effect this category includes all known cases of unincorporated branches of foreign companies in Canada and all wholly-owned subsidiaries, together with a number of concerns with a parent company outside of Canada which holds less than all of the capital stock. In addition there are a relatively small number of Canadian companies included in cases where more than one-half of their capital stock is owned in a single country outside of Canada where there is not a parent concern. These exceptional cases are confined to instances where control is believed to rest with non-residents." See also the *Canadian Balance of International Payments, 1961 and 1962*, pp. 95-97.

Since some comparisons will be made with data collected by the U.S. Department of Commerce, it is well to note here that their definition differs somewhat from this. Direct foreign investment is defined by them to include "all those foreign business enterprises in which a U.S. resident person, organization, or affiliated group, owned a 25 per cent interest, either in the voting stock of a foreign corporation, or an equivalent ownership in a non-incorporated foreign enterprise. . . . In a few important instances foreign companies were included as direct investments although the U.S. stock ownership was slightly less than 25 per cent but where strong management relationships were known to exist. Publicly-owned foreign corporations, 50 per cent or more of the stock of which was owned in the United States, were included even when there was no single controlling U.S. interest." U.S. Department of Commerce, *U.S. Business Investments in Foreign Countries*, A Supplement to the *Survey of Current Business*, Washington, 1960, p. 76.

[18]See Irving Brecher and S. S. Reisman, *Canada-United States Economic Relations*, Royal Commission on Canada's Economic Prospects, 1957, pp. 132-137, and Marshall et. al., *op cit.*, pp. 229-230.

legal sense throughout this book to describe company affiliations which vary considerably in the degree of decentralization of decision-making which is involved.

TABLE 1

FOREIGN LONG-TERM CAPITAL INVESTED IN CANADA *

Selected Year-Ends 1900-63

Year	Total ($ billions)	Direct investment as % of total	U.S. as % of total	Total as % of gross national product in current dollars
1900	1.2	—	14	—
1913	3.5	23	22	—
1926	6.0	30	53	117
1930	7.6	32	61	133
1939	6.9	33	60	123
1945	7.1	38	70	60
1948	7.5	44	74	50
1957	17.5	58	76	55
1961	23.6	58	76	63
1963	26.2	59	78	61

NOTE: The estimates prior to 1926 are from Jacob Viner, **Canada's Balance of International Indebtedness, 1900-13**, ch. 6, and Frank A. Knox, "Canadian Capital Movements and the Canadian Balance of International Payments, 1900-1934," **Excursus** in Marshall et al., **op. cit.**, p. 296. The remaining figures were calculated from various D.B.S. sources.

* The adjective foreign is used in many places in this book as a convenient way to refer to assets owned by non-residents, not all of whom are necessarily nationals of other countries. Similarly the term Canadian is sometimes used to refer to assets owned by residents, not all of whom are nationals of Canada.

The second point to note is the considerable variety of situations involved even in the statistical concept of foreign direct investment because of variation in the extent and manner of ownership of these firms. The relative importance of the four more or less distinct major categories can be designated for firms with assets of $25 million or more at the end of 1960. These large firms accounted for $8.0 billion of the total of $12.9 billion of direct investment at that time. First, there were twelve branch plants with an investment of $0.8 billion representing assets in Canada owned by non-residents but not incorporated separately under the Canadian provincial or federal Companies Acts. There are three types of incorporated concerns in the data. The forty-four Canadian enterprises whose voting stock was wholly owned by foreign concerns made up $2.9 billion of the total. Forty Canadian enterprises in which the foreign concern does not hold all of the voting stock accounted for $3.2 billion of the total; generally, but not necessarily always, the foreign concern holds at least 50 per cent of the voting stock. The remaining group of fifteen firms would consist largely or wholly of firms where there is no foreign concern which has effective control of the voting stock of the Canadian enterprise, but at least 50 per cent of the latter's stock is held by residents of a foreign country and it is believed that non-residents have control. This last category, while involving few Canadian companies, accounted for $1 billion of the total of $8.0 billion.[19] As will be pointed out at the beginning of Chapter 8, the last of the four types noted here appears to be so different from the others in terms of the key concept of control that it has been excluded entirely from the material prepared for the present study.

Accordingly, the statistical concept of control must not be confused with the question of the extent and manner in which the shareholder exercises it, and the statistical concept itself covers a wide variety of situations. It need hardly be added, though it is sometimes overlooked in discussing the implications of the data on direct investment, that the extent to which the owners and officers of both the foreign concern and of its Canadian branch or subsidiary are free to decide corporate policies and operations is still another matter. They are obviously free to decide on the use and disposition of their property, as circumscribed by private circumstance and public law. Those circumscriptions are variable but are clearly important, ranging all the way from law and governmental influence generally to the degree of competition in the markets in which the agents of production are hired and those in which the products are sold.

It should be emphasized that the major portion of private and public wealth in Canada is *not* covered by the official data on foreign ownership and control of selected Canadian industries. There are, in fact, no comprehensive data on Canadian wealth and its ownership. There are large gaps in information as well as conceptual problems once one moves beyond fixed capital in industry and social capital. The estimates for these items

---

[19]D.B.S., *The Canadian Balance of International Payments, 1961 and 1962*, p. 88, and data supplied by the National Accounts and Balance of Payments Division of D.B.S.

alone are interesting in this connection. An estimate of the net stock of fixed capital in industry in 1955, valued in 1949 prices, placed the total at $25 billion. The net stock of social capital in government, housing, and institutions (i.e. schools, universities, churches, and hospitals) in 1955, again valued in 1949 prices, was placed at $22 billion.[20] The D.B.S. ratios⋅ for foreign ownership and control of selected industries, which are noted below, refer to about $20 billion of the former figure; the major part of the remaining $5 billion is the net stock of capital in agriculture, an industry which is very largely owned by residents. Canadians own most of the debt underlying the social capital of $22 billion (in 1949 prices) noted above. In 1960 only 4 per cent of Government of Canada debt was held abroad, as was 27 per cent of provincial and municipal debt. The former ratio had fallen sharply from 24 per cent in 1936, while the latter had risen by two points.[21]

Data available under the Corporations and Labour Unions Returns Act, first reported for 1962, throw further light on this question. These data cover only firms with gross revenues exceeding $500,000 in 1962 or assets exceeding $250,000. The assets of reporting corporations which are more than 50 per cent non-resident owned (corresponding closely with direct investment) have been related to the estimated total assets of businesses in Canada.[22] The reporting corporations which were more than 50 per cent owned by non-residents accounted for 1.3 per cent of the estimated total assets in agriculture, 57.7 per cent of those in mining and manufacturing together, 9.2 per cent of those in construction, 4.0 per cent of the assets in utilities, 16.4 per cent of assets in trade, 10.1 per cent of assets in ser-

---

[20]William C. Hood and Anthony Scott, *Output, Labour and Capital in the Canadian Economy,* Royal Commission on Canada's Economic Prospects, Ottawa, 1957, pp. 435-450.

[21]It should be noted that the data for net capital stock used in this paragraph are quite different in concept, valuation, and timing from the book value series for foreign investment which are used elsewhere in this chapter.

[22]See the *Corporations and Labour Unions Returns Act, Report for 1962,* Queen's Printer, Ottawa, 1965, pp. 16-17. The measures given here are approximations since the smallest non-resident owned firms are not included. It is believed that greater coverage would not raise non-resident ownership much except for the category of finance, where chartered banks and most insurance firms have been exempted from the Act. The finance industry as a whole appears to be mainly owned by residents, but there are substantial holdings by non-residents in some sectors. In 1954 the capital of banks was owned and controlled by residents to the extent of 75 per cent and 98 per cent, while the corresponding ratios for insurance of all kinds were 38 per cent for ownership and 57 per cent for control. See D.B.S., *The Canadian Balance of International Payments for 1960,* pp. 53 and 63 and for *1961 and 1962,* p. 74; and Brecher-Reisman, *op. cit.,* pp. 287-290.

vices, and 8.9 per cent of those in finance. The last of these excludes chartered banks and most insurance companies.

Let us look now at the group of selected industries where official estimates of the percentage of foreign ownership and control have been made over the years. Only certain years will be shown here, including the earliest year for which data are available, the first post-war year for which the estimates are available, and the year 1957 when economic growth became slower. In comparing the percentages by different industries it is useful to keep in mind the relative sizes of the industries. The book value of total capital employed (wherever owned) in these industries at the end of 1962, in billions of dollars, was 13.1 in manufacturing, 6.8 in petroleum and natural gas, 3.6 in mining and smelting, 5.4 in railways, 10.6 in other utilities, and 9.5 in merchandising and construction.[28] It is also useful to keep in mind the statistical difference between ownership and control ratios. The foreign *ownership* ratios measure equity and debt capital owned by non-residents as a percentage of total capital employed in the industries. The foreign *control* ratios measure equity and debt capital invested by residents as well as non-residents in those companies whose voting stock is controlled by non-residents, all of which is taken as a percentage of the total capital employed in the industries. The ownership ratio for a particular industry will exceed the control ratio by the extent to which non-residents invest in companies they do not control, but will fall short of it by the extent to which residents invest in companies which non-residents control.

Considering first of all the data on all non-resident ownership in table 2, several points stand out. First, the long-term increase in ownership and control is confined to three of the six industrial groups for which measures exist, namely manufacturing, petroleum and gas, and mining and smelting.[24]

---

[28]*Quarterly Estimates of the Canadian Balance of International Payments*, Fourth Quarter 1964, p. 19.
[24]Comparable data over time are not available for petroleum and natural gas together. It is known that from 1945 to 1955 the resident ownership of the petroleum sector alone fell from 59 per cent to 36 per cent, and control from 43 per cent to 20 per cent. It should also be added that the book value of investment in the industry rose ninefold over this period. *The Canadian Balance of International Payments, 1956*, pp. 33-34. The sharply different movements of the overall ownership and control ratios for the six industrial groups between 1926 and 1962, with the former almost constant while the latter doubled, reflects differential movement in the major sectors. In the three commodity-producing sectors as a whole both ownership and control have risen, the latter rising more quickly. In the three service sectors together the ownership percentage has fallen while the control ratio has remained low and stable. While control in the commodity-producing sectors has risen considerably, one should also note the effect of the apparent treatment of railways, which

TABLE 2

NON-RESIDENT OWNERSHIP AND CONTROL AS A PERCENTAGE OF CAPITAL INVESTED IN SELECTED CANADIAN INDUSTRIES

Selected Year-Ends 1926-62

Industry	Non-resident ownership					Non-resident control				
	1926	1948	1957	1959	1962	1926	1948	1957	1959	1962
Percentage of total capital owned or controlled by all non-residents:										
Manufacturing	38	42	50	51	54	35	43	56	57	60
Petroleum and natural gas	—	—	63	62	63	—	—	76	73	74
Mining and smelting	37	39	56	58	62	38	40	61	61	57
Railways	55	45	30	27	23	3	3	2	2	2
Other utilities	32	20	14	14	13	20	24	5	5	4
Merchandising and construction	—	—	—	9	9	—	9	—	9	12
Total of above industries	37	32	34	34	35	17	25	32	32	34
Percentage of total capital owned or controlled by United States residents:										
Manufacturing	30	35	39	41	43	30	39	43	44	45
Petroleum and natural gas	—	—	57	55	52	—	—	70	67	62
Mining and smelting	28	32	46	49	54	32	37	52	53	51
Railways	15	21	11	9	9	3	3	2	2	2
Other utilities	23	16	11	12	11	20	24	4	4	4
Merchandising and construction	—	—	—	6	7	—	6	—	6	6
Total of above industries	19	23	26	26	28	15	22	27	26	27

SOURCES: D.B.S., **The Canadian Balance of International Payments 1960**, pp. 59, 80, 81 and **Quarterly Estimates of the Canadian Balance of International Payments**, Fourth Quarter 1964, pp. 18-19.

NOTE: A number of changes in coverage, concepts, and construction have occurred over the years. Components of the petroleum and natural gas industry were included in other industrial groups until 1954: non-resident ownership and control of the industry in that year was 60 per cent and 69 per cent respectively. Corporations in construction were not included until the post-war period. The estimates for merchandising are founded on less satisfactory data than the other series. Because of statistical problems, changes over short periods may have limited significance.

In the case of the other industry groups shown, foreign ownership has fallen sharply over time for railways and other utilities and has always been small in merchandising. Taking all of these industries together, ownership by non-residents has been just about unchanged at one-third of the total over the period of 35 years. The long-term rise in the control ratio is entirely due to increases in the three industrial sectors noted above, and now stands at one-third also. It is interesting to note that in the period 1957 to 1962, during which economic growth slowed considerably, the overall ownership and control ratios were virtually unchanged at about one-third each. Even in industries where foreign ownership and control is high and has grown over time there is by no means an even pattern of growth in recent years. Much depends, of course, on the years one chooses for comparison, and the smaller changes upward or downward in complex series such as these should not be overemphasized.

Trends similar to those in the overall ratios are evident if one considers the major country component, namely the ownership and control ratios for residents of the United States. These trends include the long-term rise in the United States ownership and control ratios, the different direction of change and different levels for the two sets of industries noted above, and the relative stability in the overall ownership and control ratios in the most recent period.

Foreign ownership and control ratios are high, therefore, in three industry groups which account for half of the capital employed in the selected industries for which data are available, but low in the remaining three industry groups. In industry groups where ownership and control are high, this is not uniformly the case, of course. In manufacturing, for example, the extreme cases are automobiles and parts, and rubber, where foreign ownership was close to 90 per cent and control close to 100 per cent in 1959. The ratios are much lower in industries such as pulp and paper and agricultural machinery, which are roughly evenly divided between resident and non-resident ownership and control, and lower still in primary iron and steel and in beverages, which are largely resident-owned and controlled. The official data are produced in table 3 for the year 1959,

---

made up fully one third of total capital employed in the six sectors combined in 1926 as against only 11 per cent in 1962. It appears that both of the major railways were treated as resident-controlled in 1926, although it was not until the mid sixties that over half of the stock of one of them was held in Canada. For absolute figures on capital employed and its ownership in 1926 and 1962 see D.B.S., *The Canadian Balance of International Payments, 1958* p. 6, and *Quarterly Estimates of the Canadian Balance of International Payments, Fourth Quarter 1964*, p. 19.

TABLE 3
NON-RESIDENT OWNERSHIP AND CONTROL OF TOTAL CAPITAL EMPLOYED IN SELECTED INDUSTRIES, END OF 1959

	% ownership by		% control by		Total capital
	All non-residents	U.S. residents	All non-residents	U.S. residents	employed* ($ millions)
Petroleum and natural gas	62	57	73	69	5,609
Mining					
Smelting and refining of non-ferrous native ores	56	42	66	66	922
Other mining	59	53	59	47	2,145
Total Mining	58	50	61	53	3,067
Manufacturing					
Beverages	26	23	13	12	456
Rubber	86	79	98	90	203
Textiles	22	13	23	14	622
Pulp and paper	52	43	49	38	1,889
Agricultural machinery†	43	43	55	55	170
Automobiles and parts	89	89	97	96	407
Transportation equipment, n.o.p.	58	27	73	27	267
Primary iron and steel	25	15	23	9	707
Iron and steel mills‡	30	—	25	—	—
Electrical apparatus	74	65	81	67	526
Chemicals	61	44	77	52	1,073
Other manufacturing§	52	41	61	48	5,351
Total manufacturing	51	41	57	44	11,671
Total for above industries	55	46	62	52	20,347

SOURCES: **The Canadian Balance of International Payments 1960**, pp. 60-61 and 82-84, and 1961 and 1962, pp. 83 and 135.
* Owned by residents and non-residents.
† Agricultural machinery includes enterprises also engaged in the manufacture of other heavy equipment, a fact which tends to overstate foreign ownership and control ratios for capital employed in the agricultural implements industry proper. In this industry minor amounts of capital attributable to overseas countries have been included with the United States and offsetting adjustments made in **Other manufacturing**.
‡ The figures for this industry refer to the end of 1960. The capital employed is included with **Other manufacturing**.
§ Of the foreign investment of $2,796 million in this category, $369 million was in other vegetable products, $128 million in other animal products, $244 million in other wood products, $686 million in other iron products, $766 million in other non-ferrous products, $227 million in non-metallic minerals and products, $92 million in miscellaneous products, and $284 million in "other enterprises."

the year for which the data prepared for the present study apply. The ownership and control ratios are subject to considerable statistical problems which become magnified as the industry groups become more specific.[25] For this reason, presumably, such ratios are not available for almost half of the investment in the manufacturing sector.[26]

The Controversy about the International Firm

The major series noted in the preceding section were available for some time prior to the mid fifties. Their consolidation and extension at the time, along with the hearings and reports of the Royal Commission on Canada's Economic Prospects, concentrated public attention on them and on the operations of the international firm in Canada. Since the mid fifties there has been considerable controversy over the role of the international firm in Canada and some new legislation regarding it. This controversy has focused particularly on the role of United States direct investment in Canada. As such, it has at times become inter-twined with and enhanced

---

[25]Briefly, the foreign capital invested and the total capital invested are estimated from different sources, raising considerable problems of classification, valuation and timing. It is also worth noting that the book value data on foreign investment are generally derived from consolidated balance sheets of the *enterprises* in Canada (i.e. of firms or aggregations of firms under common ownership and financial control). As a result the entire investment in Canada of a corporation together with its subsidiaries is normally attributed to their principal activity. Moreover, a company established to provide facilities for a particular enterprise is normally classified with it. It is obvious that all of this will considerably affect the meaning of particular industrial sub-divisions. In addition, it is not possible to compare directly the industrial statistics compiled on the *establishment* basis with financial statistics for firms or enterprises classified industrially. The establishment is the smallest independent operating unit for which the required input and output data can be obtained, and which is therefore classifiable to an industry. The term *concern* is used to refer to combinations of various forms of organization, such as unincorporated branches and incorporated subsidiaries. For further comment on the nature and significance of these points, see D.B.S. *Canada's International Investment Position, 1926-54*, pp. 64-70, and *The Canadian Balance of International Payments, 1960*, pp. 55 and 62.

[26]Somewhat more detail on manufacturing and mining, showing assets, equity, sales and profits, have become available in the *Corporations and Labour Unions Returns Act, Report for 1962*, p. 25 and pp. 49 ff. The data cover only corporations whose gross revenues for the year exceeded $500,000 or whose assets exceeded $250,000. The most detailed industrial data are those for United States-controlled manufacturing enterprises with assets of one million dollars or more for the year 1953. The statistics show the proportion of total employment, earnings, and production in Canadian manufacturing which was represented by these particular direct investment companies, compiled for about 40 industry groups. See D.B.S., *Canada's International Investment Position, 1926-54*, pp. 42-44 and 92-93.

by disputes with the United States in one or other of the many economic and non-economic links between the two countries.[27]

This controversy has taken several directions. It has been part of the controversy over the process of adjustment (or lack of it) in the balance of payments, involving not only long-term capital flows but also the handling of monetary, exchange rate and fiscal policies over much of the period. It has been embodied, largely in an unspecific way, as part of the fear in some quarters about American cultural and political influences in Canada. And it has taken the form of persistent and specific criticisms of the assumed operating characteristics of the foreign-owned firm. It is this last point which forms the heart of this study.

Usually the criticisms of the international firm begin with recognition of the advantages involved in direct investment. These have been summarized as "an indivisible package of money, technology, skills and markets. It is this kind of package which non-residents have provided, thereby performing vital tasks which Canadians alone could do either less efficiently, more slowly or in some cases perhaps not for a very long time to come."[28] The critics go on to state, however, that there are, or can be, adverse consequences from direct investment due to conflicts of interest, actual or potential, between the interests of the subsidiary and those of the foreign owners of the firm. Since the maximum feasible development of the subsidiary companies can be taken to be in the Canadian interest, at least so long as the resources involved are used efficiently, there is a conflict then between the interests of Canada and of the foreign owners of the subsidiaries. This situation arises because, it is stated, the international firm seeks to maximize its global profit over time, an objective which is not

---

[27]It has been necessary to summarize briefly the tone and conclusions of several reports below which deal in general terms with complex issues. Footnote references should help the reader who wishes to check his recollections against mine. There are good general summaries of many of the issues in Aitken, *American Capital and Canadian Resources*, Cambridge, Harvard University Press, 1961; in Aitken (ed.) *The American Economic Impact on Canada*, Duke University Press, Durham, N.C., 1959, especially the chapters by Aitken and Brecher; and in Frank A. Knox, "United States Capital Investments in Canada," *The American Economic Review*, vol. XLVII, No. 2 (May, 1957), pp. 596-609. For a criticism of recent Canadian policies regarding foreign investment, see Harry G. Johnson, *The Canadian Quandary: Economic Problems and Policies*, especially the foreword, Chapters 1-3 and 8-10, McGraw-Hill, Toronto, 1963. See also the publications noted in the remainder of this section. For a comparison of current and earlier attitudes, see A. W. Currie, "Canadian Attitudes Towards Outside Investors," *The Canadian Banker*, vol. 68, No. 1 (Spring, 1961), pp. 22-35.

[28]Irving Brecher and S. S. Reisman, *op. cit.*, p. 121.

necessarily in the best interest of the subsidiary. Decisions which may appear reasonable from the point of view of the overall profit position of the international firm may not be in the best feasible interest of the subsidiary and of Canada. Such conflicts of interest might arise in a large number of instances — indeed, wherever a choice arises in the international firm over the present use or the future development of Canadian facilities and resources as against the use or development of facilities and resources located abroad. The possibilities involved are very large. A few of the claims are listed below.

1. Many direct investment firms in Canada, it is claimed, are run simply as extensions of the United States market, in contrast with overseas affiliates of the parent. Therefore the opportunities for Canadians to secure positions among senior management and on boards of directors are limited. The consequences of these two points are to limit the development of Canadian managerial resources, to ensure that resident managers from parent companies make decisions in the interests of the international firm, and, regardless of the nationality of the managers, to limit greatly the range of decision-making permitted to them.

2. Except for firms established to supply raw materials and partly finished goods to the parent, direct investment companies are often not allowed to export, or can export only to markets where imperial preferences are available. The limited export franchise is designed to prevent competition in the markets of the parent and its other affiliates. The result is to prevent exports which are either economically feasible or which could be if the subsidiaries were given the right to seek and develop foreign markets.

3. The development of Canadian production and of service industries in Canada is limited (whether within or outside the subsidiary) because of limitations on the sources from which the subsidiary may buy, and particularly because of requirements to buy parts, equipment, and services from the parent and its affiliates abroad or from their foreign suppliers.

4. The centralization of research and development facilities in the parent abroad, and the control over the size and purpose of such facilities in Canada, inhibit the development of this important expenditure in Canada, further restrict the sales potential of the subsidiary, and limit the development of technical and scientific personnel.

5. The financial policies of such firms, particularly where they are wholly owned by non-residents, may reflect the requirements of parent companies more than those of the subsidiary, may lead to an under-

developed state for some sectors of the domestic capital market, and may cause serious balance of payments problems.

These brief comments are designed simply to state the general nature of the criticisms. The list could be extended considerably. What they share in common is the view that decisions about Canadian-based facilities, made in the context of the international firm, may lead to something less than the maximum feasible development of Canadian resources, as well as to distortion of the direction of development away from certain areas such as secondary manufactures and research facilities. This result, be it noted, is assumed to be caused by the fact that the firm is foreign-owned. There is little point in blaming the foreign-owned firm for the limitations of the Canadian environment if these limitations, independently, are the reason for lack of adequate performance on the part of the subsidiary. Similarly, it is often stated or implied that a Canadian-owned firm in similar circumstances would act in a way yielding better results from the national point of view, since it does not have to consider the effect on the facilities of affiliates abroad when making decisions of the same kind.

There is another general way in which the international firm has been criticized, a way not always consistent with that just noted. This particular approach does not concentrate, at least directly, on the global profit maximization of the international firm but on its alleged defects. Thus the head-office personnel are assumed to be uninformed about or insufficiently interested in the potential for the subsidiary, while still retaining some power of decision-making; hence the full potential for the subsidiary (and for the Canadian economy) is not realized. It is sometimes suggested that the administrative problems of large international firms directly inhibit the development of the subsidiaries; for example, international market-sharing within the global firm may be used to minimize inter-subsidiary conflicts. Again, the international firm may enjoy monopoly advantages, or have monopoly agreements with other firms which have the effect of limiting domestic development. There may also be personal preferences on the part of head-office personnel favouring the parent country in decisions on purchasing, location, and the like, at least where there is no significant advantage one way or the other. The suggestion here is not that the foreign-owned firm avoids profit maximization, but that lack of knowledge or uncertainty or inertia plus a preference for the home location in such cases gives results which are different from those of Canadian-owned firms in similar circumstances.

These are disadvantages which are claimed to be inherent in the nature of the international firm itself, acting as a private organization. Consideration of the economic operations of the firm will form the heart of this study. It is well to note also the suggestions that from time to time the government of the investing country may be tempted to exert pressure on the subsidiary, via the parent, in order to serve its own interests. These interests may or may not coincide with those of Canada. There are a few known examples in recent Canadian history which include political as well as economic overtones. Several will be noted in subsequent chapters as part of the evidence on the possible consequences accompanying foreign direct investment.

These and related views pose a conflict of interest between the interests of the nation and those of the international firm with its locus of operations in several nations. If these views are correct, they indicate what may be significant disadvantages to direct investment as offsets to the advantages traditionally associated with it for the recipient country. In the past decade there have been many examples of such criticisms in the reports of Royal Commissions and in statements in and outside Parliament by Ministers of successive governments. The mass media of communication have from time to time emphasized heavily particular criticisms and legislation. Books and articles on aspects of the subject have been written, albeit rather few in number and generally guarded in approach. A few examples must suffice here to give some idea of the controversy.

The place to start is with the report of the Royal Commission on Canada's Economic Prospects.[29] The hearings of the Commission, many of the submissions to it, and its *Final Report* created a strong impression that there were or might develop significant adverse effects and conflicts of interest, as well as advantages, from direct investment.[30] The comments in

---

[29]Royal Commission on Canada's Economic Prospects, *Final Report*, Queen's Printer, Ottawa, 1958. For comments on the Report, including its views on foreign investment, see Simon Kuznets, "Canada's Economic Prospects," *The American Economic Review*, Vol. XLIX, No. 3 (June, 1959), pp. 358-385, and Willard L. Thorp, "Canada-United States Economic Relations," *The Canadian Journal of Economics and Political Science*, Vol. 26, No. 2 (May, 1960), pp. 326-334. See also Royal Commission on Canada's Economic Prospects, *Preliminary Report*, Queen's Printer, Ottawa, 1956, and comments on it by Jacob Viner, "The Gordon Commission Report," *Queen's Quarterly*, Vol. LXIV (Autumn, 1957), pp. 305-325, and Harry G. Johnson, "Canada's Economic Prospects," *The Canadian Journal of Economics and Political Science*, Vol. 24, No. 1 (February, 1958), pp. 104-110.

[30]It is interesting to note that the subject of foreign ownership and control is not specifically mentioned in the order in council (P.C.: 1955-909), which set out the terms of reference of the Commission. See pp. 471-472 of the *Final Report*. The Commission attempted to justify its interest by a brief and not entirely clear reference in

the *Final Report* itself on the actual or potential adverse effects are very brief and are qualified by suggesting they are not frequent and that economic benefits far outweigh economic disadvantages.[31] Indeed, a careful reading of Chapter 18 of the *Final Report* suggests the ultimate justification for the legislation proposed in it rests on a brief paragraph which raises the question whether the economic integration associated with United States direct investment might not lead to loss of political independence (p. 390) and a warning that "to do nothing would be to acquiesce in seeing an increasing measure of control of the Canadian economy pass into the hands of non-residents and to run the risk that at some time in the future a disregard for Canadian aspirations may create demands for action of an extreme nature" (p. 399). In any case, the Commissioners went on to make certain recommendations. They urged foreign-owned companies to use Canadian personnel and facilities wherever possible. To ensure that such companies were susceptible to Canadian influences and opinions when making decisions, they urged that the companies include independent Canadians on their boards, issue a sizable minority of their equity stock to Canadians, and publish the financial and other results of Canadian operations. The Commissioners suggested that companies which issue shares and appoint Canadian directors be given a lower rate of withholding tax on dividends paid abroad than that paid by companies which do not meet these requirements, as well as other special tax concessions. The Report also suggests that stronger action be taken to preserve Canadian control of principal financial institutions.

The circumstances of the late fifties and early sixties were conducive to questions about the impact of foreign-owned companies. On the one hand the decline in the rate of economic growth and the persistence of substantial deficits in foreign trade in goods and services became linked with the capital inflow and the overvalued exchange rate. Foreign ownership

---

(p. 390) to the political consequences of foreign ownership. There can be no doubt, however, about the interest which the hearings and Report of the Commission aroused in the issue. See, for example, the briefs submitted to the Commission by the Trades and Labour Congress of Canada and the Canadian Congress of Labour (Joint Submission), the Security Analysts' Association of Toronto, the Investment Dealers' Association of Canada, the Labour-Progressive Party (especially the Appendices to its Brief). Many of the submissions by individual companies, industry associations, trade unions, and other sources, and the added comments in hearings before the Commissioners also carry criticisms and defences of particular corporate practices and policies.

[31]The specific adverse effects, in fact, are limited largely to two pages (390-391) in a Report of about 500 pages.

and control, and the capital inflows, bore some of the brunt of criticisms of this state of affairs, even though much of it could more logically be ascribed to inappropriate federal fiscal and monetary policies. A series of political and economic problems in Canada's relations with the United States on such matters as trade with Communist countries, military alliances, the export of energy, labour relations on the Great Lakes, integration of automobile production, and attempts by each country to improve its balance of payments and employment became involved with the issue of foreign ownership or affected the atmosphere in which it was considered. Exhortations to subsidiary and parent companies to reform their practices and policies became almost a set piece in literally dozens of speeches by Ministers of both the Conservative and Liberal governments of the late fifties and early sixties, including the Prime Ministers, Ministers of Finance, and Ministers of Trade and Commerce in particular.[32] Other public and private figures have added their comments with regard to general effects or specific incidents. The hearings of the Royal Commission on Energy raised a number of questions about the relations between foreign companies and their Canadian affiliates in the petroleum industry. This was particularly true of the marketing of Western Canadian crude in the United States and in Eastern Canada, where it was alleged there were or might be conflicts of interest with the marketing of supplies controlled by foreign affiliates. Nor has the debate been one-sided, for some authoritative voices have been raised to question the existence or extent of adverse effects, both economic and political.

It must be admitted that the analytical framework within which the criticism of the international firm has proceeded has been rather loosely articulated. It is also true that the empirical evidence has been limited, either in terms of its preciseness or its generality of application. There have been only two studies which have attempted to overcome these difficulties in the area of corporate practices and policies by adding detailed new information on a number of such companies and by analysing the implications thereof.[33] One is the staff study prepared for the Royal Commission

---

[32]To refer to only two of many examples, see the *Notes* for the speeches by the Honourable Walter L. Gordon, Minister of Finance of the Government of Canada, to the Sixth Annual Industrial and Municipal Relations Conference, Peterborough, Ontario, October 28, 1964, and to the Albion College Regional Meeting of the American Assembly, Albion, Michigan, May 14, 1965, Department of Finance Press Releases. See also footnotes 37 and 38 of this chapter.

[33]There are also a few studies of the operations of particular companies in depth. See Benjamin Barg, *A Study of United States Control in Canadian Secondary Industry*, unpublished Ph.d. thesis, Columbia University, 1960.

on Canada's Economic Prospects. This study drew on Commission hearings and submissions, studies by the staff of the Commission, and interviews with the executives of twenty-two major industrial corporations whose voting stock is mainly owned by corporations in the United States. The report considered the characteristics and responsibilities of senior personnel, research, marketing, purchasing, some aspects of pricing and production, and capital investment. The study found scattered evidence, some concrete and some speculative, of corporate practices which had or could have adverse effects on Canada's economic welfare. It went on to note that, on analysis, many of the adverse situations turned out to be due not to external control of the firms but to the economic and institutional setting (such as lack of competition, the economics of location and production, and United States tariff policy) and as such would apply to Canadian-owned firms also. Its conclusions were, first, that adverse economic effects arising from foreign control as such were small compared with the gains which direct investment brought; and second, the net gains to Canada could be even greater if any adverse effects were removed.[84]

The second report was published in 1960 for the Canadian-American Committee, the material having been compiled through interviews with the senior officers of more than 50 corporations. The great bulk of the report is an examination of six aspects of the behaviour of United States subsidiaries in Canada, namely, the sale of equity shares, Canadianization of senior personnel, publication of data, commercial policies (i.e. sales, purchases, and degree of manufacturing), research, and contributions to charity and education. The conclusion of the report in this regard is as follows:

> As the detailed chapters in Part II will show, the staff found that none of the six points of criticism of U.S. subsidiary operations in Canada could stand up as a generalized indictment. In some cases the evidence collected in the course of this study clearly does not support the implications of the criticism. In other cases, where the record of performance is mixed, there are sound reasons why some companies do not adopt the practice which Canadians expect of them. In still other cases, it would appear that the responsibility for remedial action would rest with the Canadian authorities, and not with business management.

The report goes on to add, in effect, that some criticisms of some subsidiaries are justified, and urges them to adjust to Canadian views on these

---

[84]Brecher and Reisman, *op. cit.*, Part II.

practices wherever possible in order to avoid unnecessary worsening of Canadian-American relations and, possibly, restrictive or discriminatory legislation.[35]

Informative as these reports have been it seems fair to say that the evidence on each of the practices under consideration is less than satisfactory. Indeed, consideration of the issues has been greatly hampered by the lack of firm information which has undergone careful statistical analysis as well as by lack of attention, in some cases, to that which is available.

The lack of information has not prevented legislation on the issue of the international firm, in an attempt to prevent further foreign ownership of industry and influence corporate practices.[36] Amendments to the federal government's insurance legislation in 1957 and later allowed the directors of such companies considerable discretion in the transfer of stock, gave the Canadian companies the right to buy out shareholders and thus become owned by policyholders, and permitted them to hold equities as a larger share of their investment portfolios. The motive for these changes was in large part to reduce transfers of ownership and control to non-residents. New regulations in 1960 and 1961 restricted the granting of leases for oil, gas and mineral development in territories under federal jurisdiction to corporations in which 50 per cent of the issued shares are owned by Canadians or in which shares of the corporation are listed on a recognized Canadian stock exchange and thus are available to the public. The force of these regulations was blunted by the fact that most of the major firms involved were already in the latter category. The Income Tax Act was amended to remove the differential in withholding tax on income paid abroad, which favoured wholly-owned subsidiaries, and to encourage capital inflows in the form of debt securities rather than equity investment. In 1958 and 1960 revised legislation provided that for new radio, television,

[35]John Lindeman and Donald Armstrong, *Policies and Practices of United States Subsidiaries in Canada*, Canadian-American Committee, Montreal, 1961, p. 11 and Ch. 9.

[36]It should be noted that the Corporations and Labour Unions Returns Act, effective January 1, 1963, yields information on the officers, directors, share ownership, and financial statements of foreign-owned firms and resident-owned firms with annual gross revenues exceeding $500,000 or assets exceeding $250,000. (It also covers trade unions with 100 or more members resident in Canada). The first returns, for 1962, became available late in 1965. The original version of this Act, which was withdrawn, was discriminatory, requiring information from wholly-owned subsidiaries of foreign corporations which was not required of other Canadian private companies. Unfortunately, information is not asked on most of the economic issues which have been under discussion in Canada and which have remained unclarified with regard to both resident-owned and non-resident owned companies.

and cable companies Canadians must own well over half of the voting stock and comprise well over half of the directors. Consideration of Canadian participation is a factor, albeit in less specific terms, in other legislation such as that creating the National Energy Board. Measures have been placed before Parliament to ensure Canadian control of chartered banks; to prevent foreign control of Canadian newspapers; and to establish a Canada Development Corporation, which will finance large new enterprises and also provide a pool of equity capital designed to thwart foreign takeover bids for large Canadian firms.[37]

The most extensive experiment in dealing with foreign ownership and control to date was in the budget of June, 1963. The stage had been set for this in the budget of December, 1960. At that time certain exemptions from withholding tax on interest paid abroad were repealed, and the tax on dividends paid abroad, which was formerly 5 per cent if the company was wholly-owned abroad, was raised to a uniform 15 per cent. The budget of June, 1963 proposed a 30 per cent takeover tax where resident companies listed on the Canadian stock exchanges were purchased by non-residents, subject to certain restrictions on the size of transactions. This proposal was dropped because of its unworkability and after strong protests from the financial community. Withholding taxes on income paid abroad were changed to attract relatively more foreign financing in fixed-interest securities. The major change in such taxes was an attempt to secure more Canadian participation in ownership and directorships of foreign-owned companies, the objective being to reduce the degree of foreign ownership of industry and influence corporate practices to conform more with Canadian interests. Withholding taxes on dividends were reduced from 15 per cent to 10 per cent immediately for companies beneficially owned by Canadian interests to the extent of at least 25 per cent of their voting stock, and also in cases where the parent company and its associates held no more than 75 per cent of the voting shares and the stock of the subsidiary was listed on a Canadian exchange. In addition, 25 per cent of the directors of such companies had to be residents of Canada. The tax was to be raised from 15 per cent to 20 per cent by January 1, 1965, for companies not in

---

[37]On the proposed Canada Development Corporation see Canada, *House of Commons, Debates*, April 26, 1965, pp. 10-11 and 21, and Notes for a speech by the Honourable Walter L. Gordon, Minister of Finance of the Government of Canada, to the Annual Meeting of the Canadian Textiles Institute, Ste. Adele, Quebec, June 3, 1965, Department of Finance Press Release. See also E. P. Neufeld, *The Canada Development Corporation — An Assessment of the Proposal*, Canadian Trade Committee, Montreal, 1966.

these categories, though provision was made for refunds if companies moved into these categories by 1967. Provisions for accelerated depreciation on new machinery and equipment, which, in effect, amount to giving business firms an interest-free loan, have been restricted to firms having this required degree of Canadian ownership, except for certain designated areas of high unemployment.

These changes were the subject of widespread discussion in the year which followed. In the budget of March, 1964 the increase in withholding tax on dividends was withdrawn and certain technical matters were clarified. The decrease in withholding tax for companies with a given degree of Canadian participation, and other incentives to this end, remained in effect.[38]

These are not the only items of legislation on the issue of corporate policy in the past decade. The export incentive schemes for automobile parts in recent years, for example, appear to include as one of their assumptions the view that the fact of foreign ownership of almost the entire automobile industry in itself is a significant cause of the large net imports and small exports of automobile parts from Canada. It is also not unlikely that the very frequent urging of "good corporate practices" in the speeches of cabinet ministers, almost always directed at foreign-owned firms or their parent companies, has been accompanied by administrative encouragement to such companies in the day-to-day business of government.

Finally, early in 1966, in response to "guidelines" issued by the American government urging parent companies to take steps to improve their balance of payments with their foreign subsidiaries, the Canadian government issued 12 principles of operation to subsidiary companies in Canada. These urged the firms to pursue sound growth and full realization of productive potential, realize maximum competitiveness especially through specialization, develop markets abroad and sources of supply in Canada, process natural resources in Canada as far as possible, assure a fair return on exports by the subsidiary, develop research and design capability in Canada, Canadianize their senior personnel, retain sufficient earnings for growth after paying a

---

[38]The detailed changes and the reasoning underlying them can be found in Canada, *House of Commons, Debates*, 26th Parliament, Ottawa, 1st session (1963), June 13 (especially p. 1001), July 8, and October 16 (especially pp. 3638-39); and 2nd session (1964) March 16 (pp. 977-79). For an analysis of these moves, see the publication of the Canadian-American Committee entitled *Recent Canadian and U.S. Government Actions Affecting U.S. Investment in Canada*, Montreal, 1964. See also my article, "Foreign Ownership and Control of Canadian Industry" in Abraham Rotstein (ed.), *The Prospect of Change*, McGraw-Hill, 1965, Toronto, pp. 220-244.

fair return to the owners, issue shares in Canada and report publicly on operations, and support national objectives and community activities.[39]

It bears emphasis, in conclusion, that the controversy over the international firm has several facets. It has strong cultural and political overtones, and at various points merges into the whole fabric of Canadian-American relations. One can hardly cover that vast, complex, and often subjective area in the present volume, nor has an attempt been made to do so. The choice of corporate policies and the questions asked about them inevitably border on this area, however. There are some larger economic questions deserving fuller analysis which enter this study only in specific contexts; the overall adjustment problem in the balance of payments and the total net economic gain from foreign investment are examples. This study concentrates on the decision-making process in the international firm, and the results for the firm and the national economy. It deals with selected aspects only of the policies and practices of such firms, specifically those five aspects noted at the beginning of this section, which appear to permit systematic quantification. It also attempts to distinguish the characteristics of foreign-owned and Canadian-owned companies where they can be compared, partly as a reference point but particularly to delineate if possible any characteristics peculiar to the former because they are foreign-owned.

The emphasis of this study, then, is measurement and understanding of corporate characteristics and their effects. The complex nature of the exercise requires a warning that some of the measurements are rather qualitative ones. The next chapter is devoted to an analysis of the sources and quality of the statistical material underlying the study. It is crucial to an understanding of the uses and limitations of this volume.

---

[39]See the *Financial Post*, April 9, 1966, p. 5.

2
The Statistical Background to the Study

The statistical material in this volume, drawn largely from a questionnaire, has been supplemented by interviews, and by the limited public sources of information for part of the analysis. Apart from the general advantages and disadvantages of these research techniques there are specific limitations imposed by their use in the present context. In this chapter the major techniques used are described, some comparisons are drawn between the respondent companies and all direct investment firms, and some qualifications introduced about the data.

The Nature of the Interviews and Questionnaire

The first step was to select a number of companies for interviews. The purpose of the interviews was twofold. First, a qualitative exploration of the issues with company officers seemed desirable before preparing the questionnaire to determine the best way to phrase the questions. Even apparently simple questions can pose unforeseen problems without such exploration. The difficulties in phrasing the questions and understanding the responses become much greater where, as in the present case, a number of questions required the respondents to interpret complex company and inter-company policies and practices. Second, the interviews permitted a more flexible study of corporate policies than is possible in a written questionnaire survey. In the latter, one is dependent on the written replies of the respondents to a uniform set of questions. The interviews also involved a common list of topics, sent to the interviewee beforehand, and a given set of more specific questions on each topic were asked as the interview proceeded. The technique itself and the fact that, with a few exceptions, the interview was not relied on for the statistical data made it possible to be fairly flexible in the approach to particular topics from company to company. Indeed, one function of the interviews was to explore intensively specific issues which prior research indicated was particularly relevant to each company, and to get behind the results of operations to the circumstances and policies underlying them.

About sixty firms, covering the entire range of commodity-producing industries, were involved in the interviews, which took place in 1959.[1] In seven cases the affiliate was located overseas. In the majority of cases the Canadian assets of the firms involved in interviews were over $25 million and in all but a few cases they were over $10 million; the few exceptions were among the six largest firms in the industry concerned. The firms involved had Canadian or American head offices in or easily accessible from Montreal, Toronto, Detroit, Chicago and New York. Most frequently the interview was with the chief executive officer of the Canadian company along with one or more other senior officers, but one-third of the interviews were with senior officers of the parent company in the United States. In most cases the interviews lasted about three hours.

The next step was to prepare a detailed questionnaire to be sent to the firms interviewed and to as many other direct investment firms owned in the United States and overseas as could be identified. This questionnaire, which covered the general characteristics of the company and the five major topics noted earlier, is reproduced, along with the covering letter, in Appendix B. The questionnaire was checked by several persons who have studied direct investment companies, but was not pre-tested before being sent out since the interviews were designed in part for this purpose. It was mailed in September, 1960 to about 1,500 firms and it was followed up in December of that year by a second request to 130 of the firms believed to

---

[1]For many of these interviews we joined forces with Donald Armstrong and John Lindeman who were undertaking a related but independent study for the Canadian-American Committee. Their assistance, and that of members of the Canadian-American Committee in arranging for interviews, is gratefully acknowledged. Valuable insights into corporate policy were gained also a few years earlier in connection with interviews conducted with Irving Brecher and S. S. Reisman for the Royal Commission on Canada's Economic Prospects. Information on these firms, preparatory to the interviews, was gleaned from the *Financial Post Corporation Service* and its various *Surveys,* the *Financial Post* itself, the *Canadian Mines Handbook, Moody's Industrial Manual,* reports to the Department of the Secretary of State, Company reports, the *Stock Exchange Official Yearbook,* Company *Submissions* to the Royal Commission on Canada's Economic Prospects, *Reports* under the Combines Investigation Act, *Hearings and Reports* of the Royal Commission on Energy, and a variety of other private and government publications.

be medium-sized or larger ones.[2] The available questionnaires were 310 in all, of which thirty were removed from the study because closer examination indicated their voting stock was actually Canadian controlled, or that they were essentially sales agencies, or in a few cases, the questionnaires were useless because so few questions had been answered.[3] Thus the response rate was almost 20 per cent. This is probably not atypical for private questionnaires generally, though it should be added that the present questionnaire was unusually detailed and complex and a number of the questions asked for material normally treated as confidential by most firms. The 280 usable questionnaires which form the heart of this study account for something between 9 per cent and 12 per cent of all firms owned by non-residents in the manufacturing, mining and petroleum industries, and for about 40 per cent of the total assets of all such firms in these industries. The latter ratio is greater than the former because proportionately more of the larger and medium-sized firms received the questionnaire compared with smaller firms and also because, among the recipients, there was a better response rate for the larger and medium-sized firms. The firms involved accounted for about 40 per cent of the aggregate book value of investment in all non-resident owned manufacturing companies, over 40 per cent for non-resident owned petroleum and natural gas companies and over 25 per cent in the case of mining. It should be added that the last percentage and the coverage of all direct investment would both be raised considerably if those companies with no parent abroad were to be excluded

---

[2]The basic list of firms was derived from the list of *Foreign Direct Investment in Canadian Manufacturing* compiled by the Industrial Development Branch of the Department of Trade and Commerce in Ottawa. This was supplemented by information assembled at the Royal Commission on Canada's Economic Prospects, extending into older firms and those in primary resource industries (see Appendix B of Brecher-Reisman, *op. cit.*) and a variety of other sources some of which were noted in the previous footnote. There are several other lists of Canadian direct investment firms, but they give the parent rather than the subsidiary or are based on the Trade and Commerce list or, in some cases, are greatly out of date. Information on the ownership of all but the smallest firms became available in 1965 under the Corporations and Labour Unions Returns Act. See the Introduction of the Report for 1962 under the Act.

[3]Most of the companies interviewed also completed the questionnaire in detail. In some of the remainder the material from interviews plus that from public sources was such as to permit completion of substantial portions of the questionnaire (especially the more objective questions) with reasonable precision. While few such companies are involved, it is important to note that this procedure does yield relatively high non-response rates for larger companies for some of the more qualitative questions in particular.

from the figures for direct investment, as they are from the present study.[4]

It is important to note that the data are for the Canadian firm or enterprise, and that an effort was made to secure data for the most central administrative unit in Canada. The data contained in this study cannot be compared with statistical data for the establishment in such matters as industry groups.[5] Many of the 280 Canadian subsidiaries themselves have branches or subsidiaries in Canada, whose operations are administered from the Canadian head office and whose results are included in the questionnaires from the Canadian head office. In some cases, however, the foreign parent company has two or more quite distinct operations in Canada, which are fully responsible to quite separate divisions of the parent abroad: in these cases separate questionnaires were filed. In any case, it should be noted that the questionnaire has been prepared for the overall decision-making level of the corporation in Canada, which may not be the production level. Admittedly, this distinction tends to break down for single-plant firms in Canada and where the parent exercises directly many financial and other functions for the subsidiary.

It should also be noted that the material from interviews and questionnaires was requested and supplied on a strictly confidential basis. It was agreed that the companies participating in the study would not be identified, and that none of the material supplied in confidence would be released in a form which might reveal the identity of individual companies. Anonymous

---

[4]See Chapter 8 below for a discussion of this point. The coverage of capital invested refers to the ratio of the total Canadian and external investment in the companies involved in the study to the total Canadian and external investment in all companies controlled outside Canada in the industries concerned. As to coverage by numbers of firms, the 280 studied here amount to almost 9 per cent of the 3,269 Canadian concerns in the industries noted which were controlled abroad at the end of 1959. The latter figure includes, however, 971 wholly-owned subsidiaries of Canadian companies which are in turn controlled abroad. In many cases the present 280 firms are at a higher level of aggregation since an effort was made through the instructions with the questionnaire and otherwise to secure consolidated returns from the most central administrative unit in Canada. If all 971 wholly-owned subsidiaries of direct investment companies are excluded, the present study covers 12 per cent of the total population by numbers. Data were compiled from D.B.S., *The Canadian Balance of International Payments, 1960*, p. 80, and estimates supplied by Mr. E. B. Carty of the Dominion Bureau of Statistics.

[5]See footnote 25 of Chapter 1 for a comment on the enterprise and the establishment. Some companies which had subsidiaries of their own outside Canada had great difficulty in deconsolidating their accounts for some of the questions noted here in order to distinguish domestic operations and foreign operations. Where this deconsolidation was not possible and results greatly affect the data, the specific questions have been omitted. The same problem arose with a few of the firms which received the questionnaire to resident-owned companies, as outlined in Chapter 9.

replies were accepted; fifty-eight companies chose not to identify themselves on the questionnaire.

The replies were received to a large extent from the major industrial cities: about 190 replies were from Ontario, with almost 100 from Metropolitan Toronto; fifty replies from Quebec included about forty from the Montreal area; another twenty were from other parts of Canada. While the questionnaires and covering letters were mailed to the president of the Canadian firm in almost all cases, about twenty replies were received from points in the United States. It should be recalled that these responses would be at the level of the enterprise, but it is not known how the production units of the respondent firms were actually distributed across Canada. It is also of interest to note the position of the respondent officers insofar as they identified themselves. One must note that in many cases it is clear that a number of persons or departments were involved in preparing information which was used to complete the questionnaire: all that can be identified precisely, however, is the position of the officer who signed the questionnaire or accompanying communications, hence was given or assumed the responsibility for completing it. About two-thirds of the respondents identified their positions. In 45 per cent of these it was the president, the managing director, or general manager of the subsidiary who signed the questionnaire. In 10 per cent of the cases it was a vice-president, with no further identification by function. In 35 per cent the controller, treasurer, secretary-treasurer or (in a few cases) the assistant to these officers signed the questionnaire. In half of the remainder the secretary of the firm was the officer who signed. The rest were a miscellaneous group ranging from chairman of the board to plant manager.

The quality of the replies to the questionnaire must be considered at various levels. It will be immediately evident that the extensive questionnaire survey used here, briefly covering a wide range of questions over a wide number of companies, is more suited to certain kinds of analyses. It necessarily sacrifices the individual characteristics of the particular respondents in a search for generality. In other words, it helps one to note the extent to which given characteristics are repeated from firm to firm and how they vary with other characteristics of the firms. It has its uses in establishing statistics on company characteristics which are known in about the same way from company to company, such as data on dollar sales and ownership. It can be used to probe further, with some qualifications, into such structural characteristics as the type of business of the company. It can also be used to enquire to a limited extent into the policies of the firm. Here its use must be considerably qualified by problems of interpretation by the respondent or the enquirer or both. Any of the techniques used to frame questions and checks on questions leave room for bias arising from the nature of the question and the interpretation placed on it. A very intensive survey of a few companies is much more suited to answering such questions as that on the degree of decentralization between parent and subsidiary, though even such intensive surveys leave some room for interpretation.

Parts of the present study have pushed the use of the questionnaire rather far in analysing corporate policy and other more or less subjective topics. There may be some justification for this on a subject where previous studies are few, and where the prior experience of the interviews may have helped to avoid some errors and also to supplement the questionnaire. Nevertheless, the reader is warned that the material is at varying levels of quality. The highest quality should appear in the statistical data covering such matters as age and size of firm, proportion of output exported, and percentage of earnings paid as dividends. Even such apparently simple matters as these involve some judgement, as will be noted later. A second level of quality appears where an opinion is involved but the question or comparison is more or less quantitative, for example, where firms are asked to specify the range of products in the Canadian subsidiary compared with the parent. This can be a difficult comparison in multiplant firms given a variety of products, the problem of the weight to be attached, if any, to the importance of the products in overall output, and so on. A third level of quality appears where the question or comparison is of a qualitative nature, for example, the degree of decentralization of operations and policies between parent and subsidiary. There are shades of quality within each group, of course. In some cases the detail of the replies has indicated problems of interpretation which have led to discarding the question, or to indicating explicitly the limitations thereof. A good deal of information on the limitations of various questions has been given in the body of the study, in order to permit the reader to judge for himself whether the degree of quantification and the evaluation placed thereon is justified.

In this connection it should be noted that the response rate varies within the questionnaires received.[6] Not all respondents answered all of the questions, so the response rate within the firms which answered the questionnaire is given separately for most questions. Sometimes the officers of the Canadian firm did not know what the situation was in the parent firm on

---

[6]See footnote 3 of this chapter for the low response rate by larger companies to certain questions.

a given point; in other cases the respondent answered some questions but was unable or unwilling to answer particular questions of a highly confidential or complex kind. In particular, certain broad questions on which more extensive replies were desirable (but which many companies might not be prepared to spend the time required to answer) were placed at the end of the questionnaire on a separate page, and the respondents asked to reply to these on a separate sheet. A number gave very detailed statements on these and most replied briefly to them, *but fifty of the respondents did not answer any part of the page at all. Where response rates within the firms returning the questionnaire are compared by questions it is important to keep this point in mind.*[7] One should be careful also to note that, where firms did not answer some particular questions but did return the questionnaire, it cannot be assumed that their replies to the unanswered questions would have followed the pattern of those who answered them. This assumption has in fact been made in many places of necessity; that is, by ignoring the non-replies to particular questions, the inference is that they are randomly distributed among respondent groups. At the same time it is important to determine if there is any consistent pattern to the lower responses to some questions, particularly those at the end of the questionnaire. In several places in this study the firms which did not answer certain key questions listed at the end of the questionnaire are compared with those which did, by examining their responses to related questions which both groups answered within the body of the questionnaire. No marked general bias appeared by these tests.[8] It may be noted also that in many cases where a specific question was answered with a dash or left blank it was very likely because it was not applicable to the firm or the answer was nil. One can make this claim, even though the instructions to the questionnaire asked that dashes not be used, because internal evidence on related questions supports it. Except for a very few cases where this evidence was completely unambiguous, however, it was decided to treat these replies as "no response" while drawing the attention of the reader to their probable interpretation.

Every item on every questionnaire has been checked carefully to ensure that there is internal consistency of the material. This involved not only

---

[7]As noted in Chapter 9, a questionnaire with a somewhat similar last page designed for more extensive replies was sent to a number of resident-owned firms. Of the ninety-six firms with assets of $1 million or more which answered that questionnaire fully thirty-five did not answer the last page of it.

[8]The possible exception is the question on the degree of decentralization. As examples of these tests, see footnotes 27, 40, and 9, in Chapters 3, 4 and 5 respectively.

checking the arithmetic but also ensuring that the replies to closely related questions were not inconsistent for individual firms. Where necessary, further correspondence with the firms involved cleared up the matter, but in a few cases the specific reply had to be omitted. It should be made clear that no general attempt was made to secure the replies for those questions which the respondent firms chose to leave unanswered. It was believed that follow-ups in these cases would be fruitless. The possible effects of such omissions have already been noted, and the omissions will be drawn to the attention of the reader throughout.

The experience with the interviews suggested that the variety of situations was often too great or complex to permit simple presentation of alternative choices, with a residual category, for the responses to a number of questions. While this technique simplifies tabulation it also runs the risks of oversimplification, combined with suggesting responses where the answers are not really known in full detail in advance. In these cases the companies were asked to reply in their own words and an attempt was made to classify the responses afterwards. This involves imposing one's own judgement on the categories in which the responses will be placed.

It should be emphasized that this entire study has been made in the context of a given environment for the firm, as determined by private circumstance and public law in the late fifties. The questions were answered within that context and apply fully only to that environment. No doubt the characteristics and relationships shown here can be used to help project the effects of changes in environment, but this is a derived use which can only be speculative. The statistical material is for the year 1959, with some important exceptions where data typical of a period of time or the change over a period were requested. The results, therefore, are conditioned by the year for which the data were collected.

The question of time raises a related issue. In a number of cases, as explained further later, some variables have been classified in terms of one or two other variables. The age of the firm is used as one such classification. It should be clear that what is involved here is the assumption that a variety of firms existing in a given environment at a given time can be usefully distinguished by the length of time they have been in existence. This is one way to look at the effects of time on performance, that is, with the environment given. Another approach is to secure observations on the performance of given firms at different points of time. This method is quite different in concept, since time is introduced directly while the environment in which the firms operate is a variable one. Whatever the relative merits of the two approaches, the latter did not appear feasible because of the difficulty of securing reliable statistics for many of the characteristics for earlier years.

One final point remains, that of the possibility of bias in the responses to the questions. Some of the issues involved were the subject of public controversy in 1960 when the questionnaires were mailed, as well as before and since. The responses could be coloured by this in two ways. First, those firms which had what was considered to be an unsatisfactory performance might be less likely to answer the questionnaire. Second, some of those who answered might phrase replies on the more controversial issues so as to present the best case for the firm. An approach to the first point will be made in the next section, where the extent to which the 280 firms deviated from the 1,500 firms to which questionnaires were sent is examined, as is the extent to which both deviated from the overall population. In the chapters dealing with individual characteristics, further data on all firms is presented. It must be admitted that relatively little is known about the overall population's characteristics as regards several of the key questions asked in this study, and therefore little is known about the extent to which the 280 firms reflect "desirable" performance compared with the overall population. At the same time, it should be added that few firms would have what has been labelled "undesirable" performance in all parts of all six areas covered by the questionnaire. The great majority are more likely to have undesirable performance in some areas only.

The possibility that the replies are deliberately slanted would seem improbable as a general observation. Quite apart from the implied question of probity, it seems very unlikely that senior management would spend a good deal of time preparing the answers to a very detailed questionnaire, only to slant these answers in a particular direction, especially since it is not always clear just what the direction should be. The simple alternative was to consign the entire questionnaire to the wastepaper basket. The companies were under no obligation whatsoever to reply to the questionnaire, and, since it was made clear that the individual companies would not be identified, they had nothing to gain for their company by such a procedure. There remains the possibility of unconscious bias, however, a possibility which suggested certain checks should be made. As noted earlier every question on every questionnaire was carefully checked to discern not merely any errors of a simple kind but also any internal inconsistency between related questions or related information. Several of the questions on each major topic were necessarily closely related in order to give an overall picture of the topic. Other questions were inserted precisely in order to permit one to consider the same point from somewhat different focuses: several important cross-checks are referred to in footnote 8 of this chapter. There were extensive interviews with a significant minority of the firms in this study, in addition to questionnaires. In preparation for the interviews and in the course of the study more generally, moreover, a very large number of public sources of information on the companies involved were investigated. During the year 1961 and in some cases into 1962 there was a considerable amount of correspondence with some of the firms, not only to discuss the problems involved in having them fill out particular questions in the way required, but also to clarify any internal inconsistencies. One should not leave the impression that there was a substantial amount of contradictory evidence in the questionnaires, interviews and public sources, for this was definitely not the case. The vast majority of the questionnaires gave every evidence of having been filled out carefully and consistently. The most serious problems in the questionnaires, in fact, arose because of the original phrasing of some questions, phrasing which failed to take into account the variety and complexity of company situations. A few questionnaires were rejected where inconsistencies could not be cleared up or, more commonly, replies were not sufficiently detailed. Some questions have been omitted or qualified because of unforeseen problems arising from the wording or/and a poor response rate.

Finally, one should note that the questions are of quite different kinds. There is no good reason why purely statistical questions, such as the size of the company or the percentage of output exported, should be slanted in the circumstances. On the other hand, it is possible that questions on policy may pose a problem of interpretation since they are qualitative rather than quantitative. In short, the answers to such questions report the views of the persons involved, a matter of considerable interest in itself, and it is in that sense that they are presented here.

Comparisons of Respondent Firms with All Direct Investment Companies

To what extent are the respondent firms representative of the overall population of such firms? One should be quite clear in noting that a private study of this kind cannot claim to be representative of anything but the firms directly involved, for the simple reason that there is no way in which one can control the pattern of responses. The firms involved are in no sense a scientific sample of the overall population, on the basis of which one can make probability analyses of the characteristics of the latter. It is necessary, nevertheless, to compare the firms in this study (and the group to which questionnaires were sent) with the overall population of such firms, insofar as the data permit. Such comparisons may suggest any bias between respondents and non-respondents, in the sense that particular kinds of firms may have been more likely to answer the questionnaire. In any case, intelligent use of the data is conditional on understanding the characteristics of the firms involved. The great limitation throughout, unfortunately, is that there is quite limited information on the characteristics of the overall population of firms, as well as the group to which the questionnaires were sent, against which to test the known characteristics of the 280 firms.

The group of 1,500 firms which received the questionnaire differed from the overall population in various ways, a fact which in itself would affect the nature of the 280 respondent firms. In terms of numbers, the larger and medium-sized firms are over-represented compared with smaller firms, as witnessed by the fact that somewhere between 9 per cent and 12 per cent of the overall number of firms or enterprises are included while about 40 per cent of the assets of all such firms are covered. This over-representation is partly due to a better rate of response from larger firms. It was partly achieved deliberately, as noted earlier, since there is an interest in the larger firm as a result of the dominant role in production played by larger firms in most of the industries involved. The 1,500 firms to which questionnaires were sent included most of the larger or medium-sized firms, which are more easily identified. Size of firm is used as a basic classification throughout this study. In order to assess this effect, and also because size of firm is one of the determinants of other characteristics of firms, the size distribution of the firms in this study is given in table 4. It is known that at the end of 1960, one year later than the present series, the distribution by asset size of all direct investment enterprises in petroleum, mining, and manufacturing was as follows: ninety-two had assets in excess of $25 million, ninety-five had assets from $10 million to $25 million, 625 had assets from $1 million up to $10 million, and 1,483 had assets under $1 million.[9] For the 280 firms in this study the distribution of firms by the same intervals was thirty-five, twenty-four, 101 and 104 respectively. Of the sixteen firms which did not specify assets in the intervals requested, at least half probably had assets in excess of $1 million — in most cases,

[9]D.B.S., *The Canadian Balance of International Payments, 1961 and 1962*, p. 92. More detailed size classifications for all direct investment companies appear in *Corporations and Labour Unions Returns Act, Report for 1962*, pp. 32, and 81-86. Unfortunately the data are classified in ways which are both broader and narrower than the coverage of the 280 firms, so that detailed comparisons are not possible.

probably well in excess. The 280 firms in this study, in brief, are much more representative of the larger firms.[10]

For brevity of presentation and to avoid small numbers in some groups, in most cases the data will be given for only four size groups. In 37 per cent of the firms the assets involved were under $1 million, in 29 per cent from $1-4.9 million, in 15 per cent from $5-24.9 million, in 13 per cent they were $25 million or more and in 6 per cent, unknown. Since a number of comparisons will be made between firms owned by United States residents and those owned by overseas residents, and since size of firm itself is often a determining factor, it is well to note here the size distribution of firms by these geographic areas. In the under $1 million category lay 35 per cent of U.S. owned firms and 45 per cent of firms owned overseas; in the $1-4.9 million category the percentages were 32 per cent and 19 per cent respectively; in the $5-24.9 million category they were 14 per cent and 23 per cent; in the $25 million and over category there were 13 per cent and 9 per cent and among non-responses 6 per cent and 4 per cent. The differences in size distribution in small, medium-sized and large firms should not seriously affect the comparisons in most cases for other purposes.

It is also possible to compare the age distribution of the firms in this study with that of all such firms. About 24 per cent of the firms in this study were established or purchased by the present major or sole owner in 1955 or later, a further 30 per cent in 1946 to 1954, 15 per cent from 1930 to 1945, 13 per cent from 1919 to 1929, 16 per cent prior to 1919, and 2 percent unknown. The only data for the overall population which give an age distribution at a point of time are those for United States direct investment firms in manufacturing, mining and petroleum. These show that 48 per cent of all United States direct investment companies in these fields in Canada in 1957 were established prior to 1946, 16 per cent from 1946 to 1950, and 36 per cent from 1951 to 1957.[11] The present data show that 58 per cent of the companies classified as United States direct investments in

[10]Data available from the *Corporations and Labour Unions Returns Act, Report for 1962*, p. 35 indicate there were 138 firms in mining and manufacturing (including petroleum) at the end of 1962 with assets of $25 million or more in which half or more of the voting stock was held by non-residents. Sixty-five of these had assets up to $49.9 million, forty-seven from $50 million to $99.9 million, twenty-six with $100 million or more. For a more detailed analysis of the role of larger firms by industry see Brecher-Reisman, *op. cit.*, Appendix B, and the source listed in the previous footnote.

[11]U.S. Department of Commerce, *U.S. Business Investments in Foreign Countries*, p. 100. The terms direct investment and company may not be comparable. See footnote 17 of Chapter 1.

TABLE 4

SIZE AND AGE DISTRIBUTIONS OF RESPONDENT COMPANIES

(Number of companies)

	Size in 1959				Age of Company		
$ millions	Sales	Assets		Year		Under present ownership	
						All	U.S. only
Under .5	43	72		1955-60		66	52
.5 — .9	43	32		1950-54		61	40
1 — 4.9	85	82		1946-49		23	14
5 — 9.9	22	19		1939-45		11	9
10 — 24.9	26	24		1930-38		33	31
25 — 49.9	18	13		1919-29		35	32
50 — 99.9	12	10		1900-18		39	38
100 or more	12	12		Before 1900		5	5
Not given	19	16		Not given		7	6
Total	280	280				280	227

NOTE: For definitions of size and age, see the questionnaire in Appendix A. At least half of the sixteen companies which did not specify asset size probably had assets in excess of $1 million.

1957 and earlier were established prior to 1946, 9 per cent from 1946 to 1950 and 33 per cent from 1951 to 1957. These differences in age may have a substantial effect on the operating characteristics of firms. It is well to note, therefore, that age in table 4 refers to the date when the present owner acquired ownership. Many of the firms had a history long before this, which will be taken into account for certain purposes. In 62 per cent of the firms in this study the present major or sole owner established the firm, in 23 per cent the present owner purchased it from residents and in 13 per cent of the cases from non-residents. The remaining 2 per cent represents combinations of methods and a few non-replies. It will also be apparent from the table that the firms owned by residents of the United States are older on average than those owned overseas. This should be kept in mind in comparing the performance of these two sets of firms. Similarly, in considering the relative performance of firms with assets under $1 million, it should be noted that about 70 per cent of them were established or acquired in the fifties by the present owner, as against 37 per cent of those with assets of $1-4.9 million and about 30 per cent each for the two largest size groups.

One way in which the firms receiving the questionnaire differed from the overall population was that unincorporated branches are somewhat less easily identified and hence less well represented in these firms. In addition, however, the questionnaire is better suited to incorporated firms. Only ten of the 280 firms in this study are not incorporated in Canada. The ratio of the number of unincorporated branches to the number of branches and incorporated subsidiaries for the overall population in 1959 was about one in fourteen, compared to one in twenty-eight here for the same group of industries. On the other hand the ratio of concerns owned in the United States to the total, 227 out of 280 or about 80 per cent, is almost identical with that for the overall population of direct investment concerns in the industries noted.[12]

The 1,500 firms to which questionnaires were sent were definitely more representative of manufacturing firms than was the case for primary resource industries. There were a large number of relatively small direct investment companies in petroleum and mining, often with complex interlocking ownership patterns, which could not be identified and separated even to a significant extent. It was decided to concentrate, therefore, on the larger and medium-sized firms in these categories, a fact which is reflected

[12]The characteristics of the overall population of firms in these respects are available from *The Canadian Balance of International Payments, 1960*, p. 80.

in the group of 280 firms. In other words there is strong over-representation by *numbers* of firms for manufacturing compared with petroleum and other mining. Industrial classifications are extremely difficult to make when dealing at the level of the firm or enterprise, given the many products (and often quite different industries) involved in many firms. The attached classification, based on the major types of products produced in the firm, will serve to indicate the point. It is well to note that small numbers have made it necessary to combine some industries, even at the major industry levels used here, in order to avoid identifying firms. The classification is based on the Standard Industrial Classification at the highest level of aggregation, that is, twenty major industry groups in manufacturing plus mining. This was modified to eliminate a few industries where one or two firms were involved (shown with miscellaneous industries) and to show components of the paper and allied industries, particularly to show lumber, pulp and newsprint separately from paper products. It should be noted that firms producing crude petroleum and natural gas are included with the integrated producers: a split between them at the level of the firm or enterprise was not feasible. Finer industry breakdowns and a breakdown by primary and secondary manufacturers in particular does not seem feasible with the data on the firm available to us, although a crude approximation to primary and secondary manufactures will be attempted for some purposes.

Because of the Corporations and Labour Unions Returns Act somewhat more detailed data became available in 1965 on the overall number and value of direct investment by major industry groups of the Standard Industrial Classification. This material has not been reproduced here alongside the 280 firms because of differences in the years covered, in the exclusions by size of firm, and because of what might be different bases for classification by industry. Even a casual glance at the industrial groupings for all firms will confirm that petroleum and mining firms are under-represented by numbers, and manufacturing greatly over-represented. Given the fact that mainly the larger firms are included for the first two, however, there is much more even representation of the three industry groups by value. The reader will find it useful to compare the classification in table 5 by numbers of firms to the related classification in table 3 showing total capital employed and the portions owned by non-residents.

Finally, it is possible to compare some aspects of the ownership pattern of the firms in this study with that for the overall population. One estimate is for all firms owned in the United States at the end of 1953. As shown in table 6, the range of resident participation in the equity of all such firms in the commodity-producing sector is very similar to the range in the respondent companies for 1959. A second comparison is possible using data for 1962 reported under the Corporations and Labour Unions Returns Act, though it will be recalled that small companies are excluded from the provisions of that Act. The respondent firms appear to be somewhat more heavily concentrated among wholly-owned firms, although the differences are not great. A third comparison, not shown in the table, can be made using census data of the United States Department of Commerce for the year 1957. The data for the overall population of United States direct investment firms in all Canadian industries (commodity-producing and service) in that year show the percentage of United States ownership was 95 per cent or more in 83 per cent of the firms, 50 to 95 per cent in 12 per cent and less than 50 per cent in 5 per cent of the firms.[18] In the present study, covering only the commodity-producing industries, 74 per cent of the respondent firms are in the first category, 20 per cent in the second, 4 per cent in the third, and 3 per cent did not give this information. As will be noted in Chapter 8, there are wide differences in ownership patterns within these aggregates.

The major conclusion must be that too little is known about the overall population of firms and those to which questionnaires were sent to permit most of the significant comparisons required to determine the degree of representativeness of the firms in this study. The firms in the study correspond broadly with the overall population in terms of several of the rough comparisons (ownership pattern, age distribution) which can be made. In terms of numbers, however, there is over-representation of larger and medium-sized firms compared with small ones, of incorporated concerns compared with branches, and of manufacturing compared with mining and petroleum. In terms of value of overall assets, the three broad industry groups are not as widely different in coverage. Other comparisons between the firms in this study and the population as a whole will be made as each specific aspect of corporate practice is examined, insofar as the limited data on the latter permit.

Cross-classifications of the Variables

Many of the questions raised in this study can best be approached by

---

[18]U.S. Department of Commerce, *U.S. Business Investments in Foreign Countries*, p. 101. Apart from the fact that the Commerce data cover all industries and not just commodity-producing industries, it should be noted that their data refer to all equity ownership in the United States while ours refer specifically to the parent firm's ownership. There are significant investments in a number of firms by non-residents other than the parent.

TABLE 5

INDUSTRIAL CLASSIFICATION OF RESPONDENT COMPANIES

(Number of companies)

Industry group	Total	Assets of $10 million or more*	Industry group	Total	Assets of $10 million or more*
Petroleum and products	11	9	Metal fabricating	28	2
Primary mining and smelting	6	5	Machinery (except electrical)	39	6
Foods and beverages	15	5	Transportation equipment	22	8
Rubber products	6	5	Electrical products	42	4
Textile and clothing	8	0	Non-metallic mineral products	9	3
Wood and furniture	7	0	Chemicals and products	35	6
Lumber, pulp, newsprint	5	5	Miscellaneous and unclassified	26	0
Paper products	7	1	No reply to question	7	0
Primary metals	7	0	Total	280	59

* Sixteen firms did not give size of assets, including four in metal fabricating industries, three in chemicals and products, two each in transportation equipment and miscellaneous and unclassified, and one each in food and beverages, textile and clothing, non-metallic mineral products, machinery (except electrical), and electrical products.

TABLE 6

RESIDENT PARTICIPATION IN COMMON STOCK EQUITY OF DIRECT INVESTMENT COMPANIES IN MANUFACTURING, MINING AND PETROLEUM

(Percentage distributions)

Resident ownership	U.S. owned companies		Resident ownership	Firms owned in U.S. and overseas	
	All (1953)	Respondents (1959)		All (1962)	Respondents (1959)
0 — 1%	76	74	5% or less	72	77
2 — 24%	12	13	6 — 25%	13	11
25 — 49%	8	8	26 to 50%	15	9
50% and more	4	3	No reply	—	3
No reply	—	3			
Total	100	100	Total	100	100

SOURCES: The U.S. data for 1953 are from D.B.S., **Canada's International Investment Position 1926-54**, p. 86. They include 539 unincorporated branches but exclude 564 wholly-owned subsidiaries in Canada of Canadian corporations controlled in the United States. The data for all firms are from **Corporations and Labour Unions Returns Act, Report for 1962**, Table IV. They exclude smaller firms whose gross revenues did not exceed $500,000 or assets did not exceed $250,000.

considering the relationship between different variables. In considering the percentage of output exported by the various companies, for example, one might wish to see if, and how, this varied with unit cost of production relative to the affiliate. The percentage of output exported may also vary with other factors, such as the industrial mix of the products of the firm and the size of the firm. It may also be desired to ascertain if, and how, the percentage exported varied with such differences among firms as the country in which the affiliate was located or the degree of ownership by the affiliate. One needs a measure of the net relationship between the "dependent variable" of exports and the "independent variable" of unit costs after any effect of industry or of size or of other independent variables has been taken into account. The same problem occurs in examining any other relationship in the information collected.[14]

---

[14]It need hardly be added that, while such terms as explanatory variables and relationships are used, it is not intended to imply that these statistical cross-classifications *in themselves* are proof of causation. Quite apart from the limitation of technique

The standard methods of multiple regression can be used to advantage in determining and measuring such net relationships, under certain conditions. Unfortunately, the present information appears not to meet these conditions for a good number of key relationships which should be drawn. In the first place, several of the variables are not directly expressed quantitatively on a meaningful scale. The information is simply grouped in classes serving to distinguish the companies by some characteristic, such as nature of industry. This is not an insurmountable problem, at least where the dependent variable is suitably quantified. Unfortunately, it is complicated by the fact that the numerical values of several important variables are not well distributed throughout the relevant ranges. Data for the percentage of output exported are concentrated at zero per cent, for example, and for degree of ownership by the affiliate at 100 per cent. The effect of this is to reduce the observations in other parts of the range, a matter of considerable importance where there are more than two or three independent variables.[15] Incomplete data for some companies also reduce the number of individual observations.

Multiple regressions using a number of variables could be quite misleading in such circumstances, however desirable in principle. It has been necessary to be content generally with much simpler procedures involving two or three variables. It is doubly important in the present context, accordingly, to interpret them with care, and to present, even if crudely, the other significant relationships which may be involved.

Most of the data in this volume have been shown by size groups, and a breakdown by United States ownership and overseas ownership was also given in most instances, or can be derived by simple deduction. In addition, some key variables have been classified by some or all of the following explanatory variables: age of firm, type of business, type of product, nature and range of products made in Canada compared with those made in the affiliate, size of Canadian firm relative to the affiliate, degree of supervision by officers of the parent, and degree of ownership

---

noted below and the fact that weights are not assigned to the explanatory variables, it is recognized that the ultimate justification for assumptions about explanatory values must be in the rationale underlying the relationship rather than in the statistical techniques used.

[15]The same limitation apparently arises when the values of the different variables are used to establish classes of company, with one set of classes for each variable. A frequency distribution representing this data could be treated, theoretically, by the method available for complex contingency tables. This method is not recommended generally for frequency arrays with more than two or three dimensions.

of voting stock of the subsidiary by the parent. Since there was frequently a relationship between absolute size of the Canadian firm and the key variables under examination, the classification of the key variables and the explanatory variables in each case was made within different size groups for the firms involved. This was done for three size groups only, and not the four size groups used elsewhere in this volume. The three size groups were firms with assets under $1 million, from $1-4.9 million, and $5 million or more. The restriction to three size groups, which limits the conclusiveness of analysis by size, was necessary because of the relatively small numbers of medium sized and larger firms involved. It will be appreciated that the firms must be distributed over a number of analytical groups, such as age of firm and type of business, as well as by three size groups. Even with three size groups there were cases where few firms or none appeared in a given cross-classification, thereby prohibiting analysis. The tables throughout this book show only the overall cross-classifications between the key variables and the explanatory variables. The detailed tables showing these classifications within three size groups have not been reproduced, although the results are summarized where relevant.

The problem of small numbers in some groups of the cross-classifications used here is complicated by the non-response to some questions by firms which answered the questionnaire. As noted earlier, no explicit assumptions were made about the distribution of these non-responses, although several were checked against related questions. Similarly, the non-responses are not given any specific treatment in the cross-classifications. The reader can secure the non-responses by particular sub-groups for most questions by checking other data presented in this volume, since the number of respondent firms not answering any given question is identified in the main tables.

The classification which involves the greatest dispersion of the data by classes is that for type of product. The observations are spread far too thinly among the sixteen groups involved, plus whatever number of groups are used for the other variable involved. Partly to get around this problem, and partly as a matter of interest in its own right, the industries have been combined in some cases to show primary products and primary manufacturing on the one hand as distinct from secondary manufacturing on the other. With considerable oversimplification the former group has been taken to be most clearly represented by petroleum products, primary mining and smelting, wood and furniture, lumber, pulp and newsprint, primary metals, and non-metallic minerals.[16]

It will be clear that these cross-classifications of two variables within given size groups are an inadequate substitute for the regressions which could be drawn if the numbers and distribution of the firms, and perhaps our technical capacity, permitted. The cross-classifications clarify many aspects of the data, provided they are used carefully with an eye on the small numbers and other limitations of the data.

---

[16]There are firms in primary manufacturing elsewhere in the other groups, such as in parts of the chemical industry, and there are firms in secondary manufacturing within these groups, including a few producing furniture. It does not appear that the conclusions would be changed by more refined analysis, as a glance at the numbers of firms in the secondary manufacturing industries will suggest. Lack of data on establishments, and some rather broad descriptions of industry, prevent a more acceptable classification. For a classification of primary and secondary manufacturing sub-groups, see D. H. Fullerton and H. A. Hampson, *Canadian Secondary Manufacturing Industry*, Appendix A, Ottawa, Royal Commission on Canada's Economic Prospects, 1957.

3
The Managers and Their Powers

Two objectives dominate this chapter. First, an attempt will be made to identify the organization of responsibility, in its formal sense, between the subsidiary and its parent. Certain characteristics of the management and of the board of the subsidiary will be examined, especially the extent to which they are residents and nationals and the extent to which they have been associated with the parent. The forms of contact with officers of the parent will also be considered. Formal titles and organization in themselves tell only a limited amount about the relationship between the companies. The second and much more difficult objective is to examine the division of responsibility between the officers of the subsidiary and those of the parent. These questions are of interest in themselves; they are also relevant to the economic results of direct investment operations, which form the remaining chapters of this study.

The Senior Executives

One of the key problems facing the officers of the parent company in their relationship to the subsidiary is the selection of the senior officers. As will be noted later in this chapter, constant supervision of the subsidiary by the parent's officers is impractical in most cases. There must be considerable reliance on the decisions made or recommended by the management of the subsidiary. Who these persons are, where they are located, what powers they can exercise, all become important decisions.

For the parent company's officers, acting as directors of the subsidiary, or as the persons to whom the subsidiary reports, there are contrasting factors to take into account when making such decisions.[1] There is obviously a desire to ensure that the persons involved are thoroughly acquainted with the international firm's products and policies. Where a substantial new venture is involved the experience of the parent's personnel may be invaluable to its success. These and other reasons often result in selecting senior management and technical personnel from the parent, particularly in the early stages of the subsidiary's existence. There may also be some inclination to keep a person from the international firm as head of the subsidiary and perhaps in one or two other key posts, well after the early years of the establishment of the subsidiary, to ensure that the interests of the international firm are kept to the forefront as the subsidiary settles more fully into its national environment. There are also such considerations as the use of appointments to subsidiary firms abroad as training for persons who may subsequently occupy positions with the parent. Against these is the interest of the international firm in having the subsidiary develop nationals for key positions, partly because success will depend over time on familiarity with the laws and customs and economic conditions of the country in which the subsidiary is located; partly because competent managerial and technical personnel are scarce and worth developing or acquiring in their own right; partly because there are frequently salary, tax and other barriers to the mobility of senior personnel; partly also for reasons of public relations. There are also important questions of internal morale and recruitment to consider. Firms which are believed to reserve senior positions for nationals of the country of the affiliate usually find they cannot recruit the most promising nations of the country in which the subsidiary is located. A compromise between these contrasting considerations is the appointment of nationals of the country of the subsidiary who have or are given some experience or training in the parent or its affiliates abroad.

It should be evident that the balance between these considerations is going to differ a good deal by country. Transfer of executives between Canada, the United States and the United Kingdom is much easier than where language and law and social conditions are quite different. At the same time it is easier to recruit nationals of Canada who can serve satisfactorily in senior positions. Finally, it should be noted that the interests of Canada are twofold in this regard. She has an interest in ensuring that those of her nationals who have the requisite skills, or can acquire them, are not barred from the senior positions of substantial sectors of her

---

[1]See the discussion of this and related points in John Fayerweather, *Management of International Operations*, McGraw-Hill, New York, 1960, pp. 372 to 387.

industry. If the benefits of direct investment are to be realized and her industry to be as efficient as possible, she should not deny the import of skilled management and technical personnel to supplement her own scarce resources.[2] Here as elsewhere no absolute test can be laid down in balancing the demands of national independence with those of national efficiency.[3]

The data available heretofore, while limited, do not suggest that international firms in Canada have discriminated generally and markedly against nationals of Canada in their appointments to senior positions. The only reasonably comprehensive study of all skilled groups noted that in 1957 only 1,000 of the 35,000 supervisory, professional and technical personnel in United States direct investment companies in Canada had been sent from the United States.[4] These data include far more than senior management.

[2]In this connection it is of interest to note the following comment by the Economic Council: "Senior management has a very important role in making a company and its employees and capital facilities productive, efficient and profitable. There is evidence from the 1961 Census of Canada and the 1960 Census of the United States to suggest that the educational attainment of the owner and management group is very significantly lower in Canada than in the United States. The average differences between the two countries in this regard appear to be wider than in almost all other major categories by the labour force. Furthermore, interviews undertaken by members of our staff indicate that there is increasing recognition and concern about the need for higher educational levels for future management in Canadian business firms, as a basis for more aggressive and imaginative approaches to risk-taking, innovation, new product development, and marketing." Economic Council of Canada, *Second Annual Review*, Queen's Printer, Ottawa, December, 1965, p. 62.

[3]It is of interest to note the views of Albert Breton in his article "The Economics of Nationalism," *The Journal of Political Economy*, Vol. LXXII, No. 4 (August, 1964), pp. 376-386. Breton argues that nationality or ethnicity can be considered a collective capital good. Societies in which political nationalism exists invest resources in nationality, with profit for specific groups. Essentially this involves redistribution of income rather than its creation. To some extent in his theory, but more especially in his examples, Breton tends to identify this redistribution mainly in terms of the creation of high-income jobs for nationals of a given territory. Legislation passed with regard to foreign ownership in Canada, as listed in Chapter 1 above, suggests that the diversion of investor income to middle-class and upper-class persons has been at least of equal importance as an objective. It may be that the situation in Quebec was primarily what he had in mind, in which case the relatively greater emphasis on high-income jobs in describing policy may be justified. Our study did not include any detail on the backgrounds of the nationals of Canada who were in executive positions in foreign-owned firms. Of the nineteen senior executives of foreign-owned firms who were interviewed in Montreal in 1959, however, the majority of whom were Canadians, only one was a French-Canadian.

[4]U.S. Department of Commerce, *U.S. Business Investments in Foreign Countries*, p. 122. There were 241,000 other employees in these firms for whom similar data were available, of whom 1,000 were sent from the United States. A further 149,000 employees of these firms were not allocated precisely in this way, but it was known that only about 1 per cent of them could have been sent from the United States.

TABLE 7

CHARACTERISTICS OF CHAIRMEN OF THE CANADIAN BOARDS

(Number of companies)

	Country of control			Asset size in $ millions			
	U.S.	Overseas	All Countries	Under 1	1-4.9	5-24.9	25 and over
Resident in Canada	35	15	50	12	11	11	13
Non-resident	60	16	76	30	24	10	8
No board or no chairman*	30	4	34	11	4	6	11
Board inactive	54	9	63	27	23	8	2
No response to question	48	9	57	24	20	8	1
Total	227	53	280	104	82	43	35
Number of **residents** formerly employed with parent or its affiliates outside Canada	8	3	11	6	3	1	0
Number of **chairmen** (wherever resident) who are nationals of country of affiliate	59	15	74	29	22	12	6

* Ten firms were not incorporated in Canada. Six of these were not incorporated anywhere and definitely had no boards.

The most comprehensive survey of senior management of the United States direct investment firms in Canada until the mid sixties was limited to about 110 U.S. corporations which had large Canadian subsidiaries. That survey showed that in 1955 the presidents of 47 per cent of the subsidiaries were Canadians, as were 57 per cent of the four senior executives taken as a group. By 1958 these percentages had risen to 50 per cent and 61 per cent respectively. Moreover, the older firms and the larger firms tended to have the highest proportions of Canadians among their senior officers.[5] In 1965 data for the year 1962 became available from the Corporations and Labour

[5]See the *Empire Trust Letter*, published by the Empire Trust Company, October, 1958, No. 60.

Unions Returns Act for 138 corporations in manufacturing, mining, and petroleum whose stock was owned abroad to the extent of at least 50 per cent, and which had assets of $25 million or more. In 103 of these corporations the president was resident in Canada, and in sixty-two of these he was a Canadian citizen. These larger corporations had 865 other officers resident in Canada, of whom 706 were Canadian citizens.[6]

It seemed useful to design the questionnaire for the present study as if each subsidiary had a chairman, president and senior officers all formally designated, realizing that this was a rather rigid test for some multi-firm concerns. For many such firms the most senior resident officer may be a general manager, with the officers of the parent bearing the more senior titles for the subsidiary, or such titles not being used at all with regard to the subsidiary. In addition, one should note that the degree of decentralization is not necessarily a function of the apparent seniority of the titles of resident officers. A resident vice-president or manager may be the active head of the subsidiary, and the more senior titles may be nominal except at the highest level of approval of some key decisions. The actual degree of decentralization of authority will be dealt with after commenting on the formal organization of responsibility.

The first thing to note is that the proportion of the 280 firms which did not answer the questions on the chairman and the president is unusually high compared with most questions in the body of the questionnaire. Most of these probably did not have a chairman or a president; that is, they are probably similar to those which replied explicitly that there were no such officers for the subsidiary.[7] A significant number of boards are inactive, as noted in the next section; in the tables any consideration of the chairmen of such boards has been eliminated. One must be careful, therefore, in describing the characteristics of senior officers, for many firms do not conform to the prototype assumed in the questionnaire: this is particularly true of the chairmen. There are some large firms with very active boards in this study which have no formal chairman, or where the president shares that title. In over half of the firms the board is inactive, or there is no chairman or no board, or the question was not answered. The chairman was resident in Canada in fifty of the remainder, and non-resident in seventy-six cases. The latter, of course, are usually officers of the parent

---

[6]*Corporations and Labour Unions Returns Act, Report for 1962*, p. 36.
[7]It will be noted that the smaller firms in particular did not answer the question on chairman and president, but almost all replied to that on the next three senior officers, suggesting that many of them do not have a chairman or president.

firm. It is particularly in the smaller firms that one is likely to find non-resident chairmen (or inactive boards, or non-responses) although there are some quite large firms with non-residents as chairmen. It will be noted that there is a somewhat larger proportion of resident chairmen for overseas companies than for firms owned in the United States, a result which does not hold, however, for presidents. It is also interesting to note that a relatively small proportion of the resident chairmen were formerly employed with the parent or its affiliates abroad when compared with the presidents of the subsidiaries. A large number of the chairmen are nationals of the country of the affiliate, in fact almost exactly that group which is resident abroad.[8]

By contrast, the presidents are mainly residents of Canada. There were 158 residents and eighty-five non-residents, excluding cases where there was no president and non-responses to this question. The non-residents were very largely concentrated in the smaller firms; only three of the thirty-five firms with assets of $25 million or more had a non-resident president. Over a third of the residents had been employed in the parent or its affiliates outside Canada. This proportion includes, of course, both Canadians and foreigners who began their careers with the company abroad or acquired experience with the parent before returning to Canada. As indicated in table 8, 119 of the 243 presidents for whom data are available were nationals of the country of the affiliate.[9]

It is of interest to record how data on the nationality of the president appeared when classified by some other variables. As just noted, 49 per cent of the firms had presidents who were nationals of the country of the affiliate, disregarding those with no president or which did not answer this question. Table 8 indicates that in subsidiaries with asset size under $1

[8]With regard to the residency of the senior officers reported on here it cannot be assumed that all of the non-residents are foreigners. It is not rare, for example, for Canadians to move into the senior ranks of the parent firms. Similarly, the question on nationality was whether the senior officers were nationals of the country of the affiliate: it cannot be assumed that all of those replying in the negative were nationals of Canada. It does not appear likely that either of these would greatly affect the overall picture given here. It should also be recognized that not all of the executives who are nationals of the country of the affiliate were formerly employed by the affiliate. For a discussion of the conflicting issues involved for such persons with regard to the question of citizenship, specifically, the possibility of transfer abroad as against the desire for full membership in the community, see the article in the *Toronto Daily Star*, May 2, 1959, p. 9.

[9]Data collected under the *Corporations and Labour Returns Act* for all of the larger firms, presented a few paragraphs above, suggest our data on the largest firms greatly overstate residency of presidents while being very similar on nationality.

TABLE 8

CHARACTERISTICS OF PRESIDENTS OF THE CANADIAN CONCERNS
(Number of companies)

	Country of control			Asset size in $ millions			
	U.S.	Overseas	All Countries	Under 1	1-4.9	5-24.9	25 and over
Resident in Canada	129	29	158	37	42	34	32
Non-resident	70	15	85	48	25	7	3
No president	8	2	10	7	3	0	0
No response to question	20	7	27	12	12	2	0
Total	227	53	280	104	82	43	35
Number of residents formerly employed with parent or its affiliates outside Canada	50	10	60	11	12	19	14
Number of presidents (wherever resident) who are nationals of country of affiliate	99	20	119	56	29	20	10

million about 65 per cent of the presidents were nationals of the country of the affiliate. This proportion was about 40 per cent for firms with assets of $1-4.9 million, 50 per cent for those with assets of $5-24.9 million, but fell sharply for firms with assets of $25 million or more where only about 30 per cent had presidents who were nationals of the country of the affiliate. It may be noted that if one measures the size of the subsidiary as a percentage of that of the affiliate, as against absolute size, there is no such change among the various size groups. If this same question is considered in relation to the age of the Canadian firm, measured by the date it was acquired or established by the parent, it turns out that 61 per cent of the firms established or acquired in the fifties had a president who was a national of the country of the affiliate, 73 per cent of those established or acquired in 1940-49, 48 per cent of those in the period 1919 to 1939 and only 19 per cent of those established or acquired before then. If these data are examined within three asset size groups the fourth of these still stands out sharply, i.e. the firms which are oldest have a much lower per cent of presidents who are nationals of the country of affiliate, but the differences among the other three age groups become relatively small.[10] It may be noted also that the great majority of the sixteen broad industry groups used in this study are fairly close to the average of 49 per cent in terms of nationality of the president. In twelve of the sixteen industries between 40 per cent and 60 per cent of the firms involved reported that the president was a national of the country of the affiliate. Two of the remaining four were above and two below these limits; since they refer to industries where quite small numbers of firms reported, it is probably more meaningful to emphasize the more uniform pattern of the other industries. There was no difference between primary industries and primary manufacturing, on the one hand, and secondary manufacturing on the other, in the proportion of firms whose presidents were nationals of the country of the affiliate.

No attempt was made to secure the next three senior officers by their titles, since the interviews suggested there was a great deal of variation in actual practice in this respect. In some cases, particularly among the smaller firms as shown in table 9, there were less than three other senior officers. These particular persons, whatever their titles, are very largely resident in Canada. In 143 firms all three were residents, and in another twenty-nine where the other senior officers were fewer than three they were all resident in Canada. All but four of the firms with assets of $25 million or more fall into these categories. At the other extreme there were twenty-four firms in which none of the next three senior officers resided in Canada; all but four of these firms had assets under $1 million. The great majority of the next three senior officers are not nationals of the country of the affiliate. In 108 firms none of the three (or one or two) was in this category, and in fifty-six more firms only one of the three was a national of the country of affiliation. Once again, most of the largest firms are in these two groups. At the other extreme, all of the next three senior officers were nationals of the country of affiliation in fully fifty-seven firms, including a number of large and medium-sized firms. In relative terms, firms owned overseas have a somewhat larger proportion of residents among the next three senior officers than do firms owned in the United States, but they also have a moderately larger number of nationals of the country of their affiliate among these officers.

---

[10]The three size groups used in such cross-classifications, as noted in Chapter 2, are under $1 million, from $1-4.9 million, and $5 million or more.

One should add a word of warning about the use of the data on nationality of senior personnel. Whatever the interpretation placed on their significance, one should note that they reflect persons with quite different lengths of residence. The interviews indicated some persons who had resided in Canada for a number of years on being transferred from the parent or from its other foreign affiliates, and some of whom might well be transferred elsewhere within the international firm. There were also a

TABLE 9

RESIDENCY AND NATIONALITY OF NEXT THREE SENIOR OFFICERS OF THE CANADIAN CONCERNS

(Number of companies)

	Country of control			Asset size in $ millions			
	U.S.	Overseas	All Countries	Under 1	1-4.9	5-24.9	25 and over
Resident in Canada							
0 of 3	23	1	24	20	3	1	0
1 of 3	28	3	31	17	9	4	0
2 of 3	33	8	41	13	18	4	4
3 of 3	108	35	143	34	38	32	31
1 of 1 or 2 of 2*	25	4	29	17	8	2	0
No response to question	10	2	12	3	6	0	0
Total	227	53	280	104	82	43	35
Nationals of country of affiliate (wherever resident)							
0 of 1 or 0 of 2*	17	4	21	14	6	1	0
0 of 3	73	14	87	27	21	19	16
1 of 3	43	13	56	12	23	7	11
2 of 3	25	9	34	14	12	4	3
3 of 3	48	9	57	28	13	8	3
No response to question	21	4	25	9	7	4	2
Total	227	53	280	104	82	43	35

* In order to simplify the presentation, other categories involving either more or less than three senior officers have been classified as follows: for **residency,** 0 of 3 includes 2 firms with 0 of 2, 2 of 3 includes one with 2 of 4, and 3 of 3 includes seven with 4 of 4; for **nationality,** 1 of 3 includes four firms with 1 of 4, 2 of 3 includes four with 2 of 4, 3 of 4, or 3 of 6, and 3 of 3 includes eight with 1 of 1, 2 of 2, or 4 of 4.

significant number of United States nationals in particular who had been resident in Canada for long periods of time, extending up to several decades in a few cases. It is a moot point whether some of these persons will ever be transferred abroad, or agree to it, although the possibility remains. Nor was it rare to come across former nationals of the United States or other countries who were now nationals of Canada and had obviously settled down permanently. In such circumstances nationality of officers can only be a rough guide, over time, to the policies of parent firms regarding appointment of senior personnel, since the data are necessarily tempered by the personal inclinations and future intentions of the officers involved as regards nationality.

By way of summary of the data it is of interest to look at the combined figures for all senior officers expressed as total numbers of persons. Fully 798 of the 1,131 officers were resident in Canada in 1959. Of the resident group, 193 had been formerly employed in the parent or its affiliates abroad, including Canadians who began their careers or spent some years with the international firm. Of the 1,131 officers, 476 were nationals of the affiliate. As an approximate measure of the nationality of the 798 residents, one can say that approximately 143 (i.e. 476 − 333 non-residents) were foreigners. Residents of Canada predominate except for the position of board chairman. There are only twenty firms in which none of the five senior officers reside in Canada. All but three of these had assets under $0.5 million (the others were under $5 million) and half of them were less than five years old as companies. While nationals of Canada are also in the majority, again excepting the chairman, there are a significant number of firms in which most of the senior persons are nationals of the country of affiliation. While data are not available on this point, it was clear from the interviews that the length of residency of such persons varied from what had turned out to be a lifetime appointment all the way to a short Canadian term of duty that took on the aspects of an intercompany training program.

It may be of interest to summarize what these firms had to say about their policies regarding transfers of senior personnel between the Canadian firm and its foreign affiliates.[11] The great majority of firms, 130 in all,

---

[11]Excluded here are transfers for training purposes, usually for short periods and involving junior or middle management and technical experts. Many of the executives who were interviewed indicated that such personnel of the Canadian firm had access to the parent's management development program. Several of them also noted that there was a significant movement to the Canadian firm for management training, particularly in the case of overseas affiliates of the parent, for whom the size and nature of the Canadian operation involved some advantages for training purposes.

TABLE 10

SUMMARY OF CHARACTERISTICS OF SENIOR OFFICERS
(Number of persons)

	Chairman of Board	President	Next three	Total persons
Resident in Canada	50	158	591	798
Non-resident	76	85	174	333
Number of **residents** formerly employed with parent or its affiliates abroad	11	60	122	193
Number of persons (wherever resident) who are nationals of country of affiliate	74	119	286	476

NOTE: Totals may not add because of adjustments for officers with dual titles.

have no defined policy or objective on the movement of senior personnel from the parent or its other affiliates to the Canadian company, or on the reverse movement. This does not rule out the possibility of such movement between these firms, of course, but simply indicates there is no position clear enough to be reported as such. Sixty-five firms did not answer the question, which was included among the general ones at the end of the questionnaire. The remaining eighty-five firms made a specific statement on the matter. About one-quarter of these were really references to existing situations rather than policies or even strong preferences. These references to existing situations were equally divided among those which pointed to the fact of senior personnel who were largely or entirely Canadian and those who were largely or entirely from the parent; all but three of the latter were new companies formed since 1950, whose personnel came to Canada to start the company and have remained. Among the remaining three-quarters, the ratio of those with policies favoring the use of Canadians as senior personnel in the Canadian firm was about eight to one. This was stated in a variety of ways. In most cases it was an explicit statement of company policy to use Canadians in key positions, or against movement of parent personnel to senior positions in Canada, which had been largely or completely put into practice. In a substantial minority of cases, however, it was given as an objective, or even a strong preference, often with an accompanying statement that it would be put into effect as qualified Canadians were trained or found. The remaining companies defined their policies as a free interchange of senior personnel among the various affiliates. Only three companies appeared to favour the use of parent personnel in key positions in their subsidiaries as a distinct policy, apart from the early years of the subsidiary and similar qualifications.

Typical of these positions are the following replies from companies owned in the United States:

> The policy of the Company is to use Canadian citizens in all key positions. There has been no transference of executive personnel to the Company from our parent company. (A large firm acquired just after the second world war.)
> Declared policy is for Canadian personnel to take over the company as soon as practical. (A medium-sized firm established just after the second world war.)
> The policy of the board of directors (of the Canadian company) is to exchange men freely back and forth between Canadian and American companies whenever necessary. In addition to strengthening the management for the two companies, the policy serves as a management development program by broadening individual horizons. (A large firm acquired in the early fifties.)

Most of the companies which made a specific statement on movement to the Canadian company also indicated the situation regarding movement to the parent company and its affiliates abroad. There is a significant transfer of personnel, often both ways, for short periods of training, particularly at the level of junior management. In terms of longer-term movements of senior personnel, however, a rather unexpected situation has developed. It was noted earlier that most firms have no defined policy. A relatively small portion of the firms have policies favouring a free inter-change in both directions, as already noted. The great bulk of the remaining responses fell about equally into two other categories. In one group there is a policy, or at least a strong preference, against movement in either direction. The other group has a policy or preference against movement from the parent to the Canadian firm (that is, the firms attempt to appoint Canadians only), but in one way or another either assists or cannot prevent the movement of senior personnel to the parent.

Along with a question on policy, the respondents were also asked to identify significant historical changes in the characteristics of officers and board of the Canadian company. About one-third of the respondents did not answer the question, a high proportion even for the general questions at the end of the questionnaire, which suggests the question may have been too broadly phrased. In the majority of cases, 135 in all, the respondents did not identify any significant changes. This appears consistent with data presented in this chapter indicating age of firm is only moderately related to Canadianization of senior personnel. All but a few of the remainder indicated that residents of Canada, and particularly Canadians, have formed over a period of time a significantly increasing portion of the executive or of the board or, in most cases, of both. Many referred to specific significant changes such as the election of the first Canadian president or other senior officer after a succession of persons from the parent or its other affiliates in that position, the appointment of resident management or of "outside" directors for the first time to the board of the Canadian firm, the activation of "paper boards," the establishment of a quorum of resident members for the board, and so on. A few companies indicated only that plans were under consideration for similar moves. Half a dozen companies, by contrast, indicated a distinct and apparently deliberate movement in the reverse direction.

One must be careful of interpretations on the points considered in this section, given the very large number of companies with no defined policy or which did not identify significant historical changes. One can only suggest that the evidence given here on senior personnel and boards suggests that these firms generally have appointed substantial numbers of residents and Canadians to the key positions. There are, of course, a number of firms where many, and in a few cases all, of the senior personnel or directors are from the parent, and a few where there has been a sharp increase in the proportion of executives and directors from the parent. Sometimes this refers to relatively new firms, though by no means to all of them. In other cases it involves a temporary injection of parent management to reinvigorate a lagging subsidiary. It may also be a technique for assuring standardization of procedures in an international firm generally exercising, or about to exercise, close management control of subsidiary policies. However, these generally refer to a minority of cases. One might, in fact, suggest some concern in the other direction, as judged by some of the replies from firms with defined policies or preferences. Both in the interviews and in the responses to the questionnaire it is significant that a rather small group of firms had policies favouring mobility both ways. In some firms the sensitivity of the Canadian public to having Americans in particular in the senior Canadian positions has tended to block off the top positions abroad for Canadians. In others, it has lead to the export of talent without a compensating import, and sometimes, one suspects, to preventing or delaying the import of additional skilled managers when the Canadian firm has been having difficulties. Not all of these situations benefit Canadian welfare, whatever they may do to the opportunities for individual persons. Moreover, an active interest of qualified directors from the parent company, so long as it does not stifle the initiative of local management, can do much to improve the quality of performance of the Canadian subsidiary, in the interest of both the Canadian economy and the international firm.

The Board of Directors

At the outset it is well to recognize that the board of a subsidiary may be purely a legal institution, established because of the requirement of the Act under which the subsidiary is incorporated. It is non-existent, of course, for an unincorporated branch. Many boards are precisely in this position, meeting only infrequently to ratify decisions already made, and the composition and other characteristics of such boards need not detain us. Other boards may play a role in the affairs of subsidiary companies which varies all the way from one form of regular direct communication between officers of the Canadian company and of the affiliate to active and sometimes even minute direction of the company's affairs.

Eight concerns had no board and one did not answer a question on whether the board was active. Fully sixty-three companies (including two with assets over $25 million each) indicated their boards were not active. The comments which follow apply only to the remaining 208 concerns, with adjustments as noted in the tables for some cases where some related characteristic was not available.[12]

Directors who are associated with the parent, or with the parent's affiliates outside Canada, form the single largest group on the boards. There were 634 such persons among the 1,505 directors involved, while only eleven of the companies with active boards had no such director. The most common representation was from two to four such directors, which was the case in 126 companies. It may be noted from table 11 that the most fre-

---

[12]The interpretation placed on the world "active" would vary, of course. For many purposes one might wish to deduct from this group the thirty companies whose boards met only once yearly, for example, yet which classified their boards as active. It should be noted, however, that frequency of meeting is not the only criterion of how actively the board is involved in the affairs of the company. A board may meet infrequently, for example, while exerting a substantial influence when it does meet, or its committees may be active.

quent size of board was from five to nine members, with 138 companies in this range.

The senior management of the Canadian company was almost as well represented on the boards, with 565 of the 1,505 directors in this group. Only seven companies with active boards had no such directors, while most had from one to three such persons.[13] It is interesting to note also that "outside" directors, numbering 221 in all, exist in 40 per cent of the companies with active boards.[14] These persons were defined as "resident 'outside' directors not otherwise associated with parent, with its other affiliates or with Canadian company as employees, legal counsel, or significant owners." The representatives of other significant owners accounted for only thirty-five persons, and all other persons, such as legal counsel, for fifty persons.

The total of 1,505 directors includes some double counting, particularly as some firms could not distinguish the first two groups noted above and consequently listed the person in both categories when reporting on the composition of the board. The net total membership on these boards was 1,466, and, of this number, 759 were reported as residents of Canada. The non-residents include basically the directors associated with the parent and its affiliates abroad, with a further small group from the other categories in amounts which were not determined. Only ten boards were without a single resident of Canada, and only four were composed entirely of residents of Canada. Resident directors formed from 1 per cent to 24 per cent of the membership in twenty-three companies, 25 per cent to 49 per cent of the membership in fifty-five companies, 50 per cent to 74 per cent in eighty companies, and 75 per cent to 99 per cent in thirty-one companies. It will be noted that only thirty-three of these companies fail to meet the directorship requirement of recent legislation which raised withholding taxes on dividends paid abroad for many foreign-owned companies, and that only two of the largest firms are in this group.[15] It is a striking fact that in all but six of the thirty-five companies with assets of $25 million or more at least half of the directors were residents of Canada.[16]

---

[13]As noted in the next paragraph there is some duplication between the numbers for this and the preceding group of directors. As a result, the figure of seven companies with no director from senior management and eleven with no director associated with the parent or its affiliates abroad must be considered minimal.

[14]The survey by the Empire Trust Company in their *Letter* of October, 1958, found that 40 per cent of the 110 larger firms they examined had one or more 'outside' Canadians on their boards and that the proportion was higher for the very large firms.

[15]This legislation was outlined at the end of Chapter 1.

[16]In 1962 the 138 firms in manufacturing, mining and petroleum, with at least 50 per

TABLE 11

COMPOSITION OF BOARDS OF DIRECTORS AND FREQUENCY OF MEETINGS
(Number of companies)

Categories—All companies*	0	1	2	3	4	5	6	7	8	9	10	11	12	13	14	15	16	17	Other	No reply to question	Not applicable	Total companies	Total number of persons
Management of company	7	41	51	44	22	22	9	4			1									8	71	280	565
Associated with affiliates abroad	11	20	34	60	32	23	12	5	2											10	71	280	634
Resident "outside" directors	118	23	20	14	10	5	2	1	4											12	71	280	221
Other significant owners	181	4	5	4	1	1														13	71	280	35
Other	156	30	7	2																14	71	280	50
Total number on board†				15	12	45	23	25	23	22	12	8	7	2	4	3		2		6	71	280	1,466
Residents of Canada only	10	28	45	27	25	15	27	11	4	2	5	2	2							6	71	280	759
Frequency of meetings																							
Companies owned in U.S.	25	21	21	38	17	13	0	0	3	0	2	0	10						5	11	61	227	
Companies owned overseas	5	6	2	7	4	6	0	1	1	0	1	1	6						2	1	10	53	
All companies	30	27	23	45	21	19	0	1	4	0	3	1	16						7	12	71	280	
All companies with assets of $25 million or more	0	0	0	3	7	6	0	1	1	1	2	0	7						3	2	3	35	

NOTE: For further details, see Appendix A

* In response to an introductory question "Is the Canadian Board an active one?" 208 replied yes, sixty-three no, eight there was no board, and one did not reply. The composition for the first group only was reported, with allowances for non-responses as indicated.

† The total for number of persons shown in the last column will not add vertically because of double counting of persons among the categories shown for some companies. This double counting does not exist in the figure for the total number of persons on the board.

The senior management of the Canadian company forms about 37 per cent of the directors both for companies which are owned by residents of the United States and for companies owned by overseas residents. There is a difference in the other two major groups of directors, in that persons associated with foreign affiliates play a relatively larger role in the former companies while outside directors play a correspondingly smaller role. In the case of companies owned by residents of the United States, 44 per cent of the directors are associated with foreign affiliates while 13 per cent are outside directors. For companies owned by overseas residents, mainly residents of the United Kingdom, the corresponding figures are 34 per cent and 21 per cent. In line with this, 60 per cent of the directors of companies owned overseas are resident in Canada compared with 50 per cent for companies owned in the United States. The distance from the parent company seems to be the most convincing factor which might account for this. As will be noted later, the two sets of companies do not differ markedly in other characteristics which might account for this difference, such as degree of supervision by the affiliate or the number of firms in which minority shareholders exist. The role of distance can be seen in the very different frequency of attendance at board meetings by directors associated with the parent.

All of the boards of companies with assets of $25 million or more had representatives of senior management, and all but one had directors associated with the non-resident affiliate. In each case the range of two or three to six or seven such directors covered almost all such companies. The proportion of outside directors rose markedly with the size of company, although many larger companies do not have such outside directors. Only one-quarter of the companies with assets under $1 million had one or more such directors, as compared with 40 per cent of those with assets up to $4.9 million and 55 per cent for each of the two largest size groups.

The frequency of board meetings is one clue to the role of the approximately 200 active boards for which data were available. Fully thirty met only once a year, a figure which, as noted earlier, raises some question about the interpretation placed on the word "active." A further twenty-seven boards usually met twice yearly, twenty-three usually met three times a year, forty-five met quarterly, twenty-one met five times a year, nineteen usually met every two months, and only the remaining thirty-two

---

cent of their stock held outside Canada and assets of $25 million or more, had 1,332 directors. Of these, 706 were residents of Canada and 592 were citizens of Canada. See *Corporations and Labour Unions Returns Act, Report for 1962*, p. 35.

met more frequently, most often on a monthly basis.[17] The boards of companies owned by overseas residents met more frequently on the average than did those of companies owned in the United States. This may reflect the presence of relatively more outside directors on such boards, though in some cases the boards met frequently and prepared detailed minutes as one device for keeping officials overseas informed of Canadian developments. In all companies with assets of $25 million or more the boards met at least quarterly, in two-thirds of them at least six meetings a year were held, and in about half of them at least eight meetings were held each year. Directors associated with the parent or its affiliates abroad attended all of the meetings of the Canadian board, regardless of the frequency of meeting, in two-thirds of all companies reporting active boards. Full attendance by such directors for companies owned overseas was much less common; in only about half of these firms did the representatives of the affiliate attend one fourth or more of the meetings of the boards.

No effort will be made to disentangle the authority in practice of the board of directors from that of senior management. The questions which were phrased on the autonomy of the subsidiary, to be noted below, include this point but also go well beyond it; nevertheless, a comment on the role of boards in subsidiary companies is in order. Much of the literature on boards of directors suggests that, in practice, their role is usually limited and that the executives, who are often on the boards, exercise the active leadership functions in business corporations. It is true that particular directors may be influential as advisors, that those representing large stockholder interests will usually have a decisive veto, and that the board has legal authority. Nevertheless, both the making and execution of decisions in practice often lies with full-time officials, and board approval may be highly formal in most circumstances.[18] If this is the case for large American corporations, what should one expect of typically smaller Canadian firms which, in most cases, are largely or wholly owned by a single firm abroad? There is a temptation in such circumstances to sweep the board aside as simply a formal legal requirement arising from a particular form of business

---

[17]For comparative purposes it may be of interest to note the number of regular board meetings per year of 644 manufacturing firms in the United States, as reported in the National Industrial Conference Board, *Corporate Directorship Practices*, Studies in Business Policy, No. 90, New York, 1959. The most frequent number was ten to twelve meetings per year, which was the case for 52 per cent of the firms. Fully 33 per cent of the firms met only four or five times a year, however. It should be kept in mind that these firms are probably typically larger than the firms in the present study.
[18]See Robert Aaron Gordon, *Business Leadership in the Large Corporation*, University of California Press, 1961, Ch. 6.

TABLE 12

RESIDENCY OF DIRECTORS AND FREQUENCY OF ATTENDANCE
AT MEETINGS OF THE BOARD
(Number of companies)

Interval in percentages	Resident directors as % of all directors		% of meetings attended by representatives of affiliate	
	All companies	Assets of $25 million or more	All companies	Assets of $25 million or more
0	10	1	15	3
1-24	23	1	14	3
25-49	55	4	18	2
50-74	80	20	8	1
75-99	31	5	4	3
100	4	1	127	16
Not applicable*	71	3	71	3
No reply to question	6	0	23	4
TOTAL	280	35	280	35

*No board, or board inactive.

organization. What is said in the next section on decentralization of powers, and particularly on the extensive direct executive consultation on major policy with the officers of the parent, confirms this view of the board. Yet it is easy to overemphasize this approach to the role of the board. The point of some of the analysis regarding the limited actual role of boards in general is the divorce of ownership and management in large corporations where stockholdings are widely dispersed, and the consequent rise to effective power of salaried executives. The point of most of the firms under discussion, however, is precisely that the ownership of stock is concentrated, that the owners, or their managers, are well represented on virtually all of the boards, and that a significant portion of the senior officers served in the parent firm or its other affiliates and may return to them. These are executive-dominated boards, more so than in public companies, but many of the executives have present, past, or possibly future, direct association with the owner firms. In these circumstances the relevant question becomes, in significant part, whether the parent's approach to foreign subsidiary operations includes an active board. Many of the boards are clearly quite inactive, meeting only to satisfy legal requirements and playing no role in the overall policies of the firm. That many have chosen to regard the boards otherwise is suggested by several things: only sixty-three replied that the boards were not active; in 70 per cent of the remainder the boards met at least three times a year, and in 60 per cent at least four times a year; and in two-thirds of the active boards persons associated with the parent attended all meetings.

Why should the owners of a wholly-owned company bother with more frequent meetings than required by law? It may be suggested tentatively that this is used in some companies as one convenient form of more or less regular and direct communication between executives of the subsidiary, of its parent and perhaps of other affiliates, especially where decentralization of operations is emphasized by management attitudes. In some cases the management of the Canadian company is the prime mover in having active boards with outside directors, in an attempt to consolidate their own position *vis-à-vis* officers of the parent or to secure advice and contacts outside the company. The active boards will also reflect at times the carry-over or creation of minority stock holdings.[19]

It should be made clear that these comments are not intended to challenge the view that many boards of directors play a limited role in the affairs of the firm, or that the owners have the ultimate right to exert their legal powers through the board if they so wish. What has been questioned is the view that the boards are irrelevant in the parent-subsidiary context. It may be of interest, nevertheless, to note here a point which will be made in Chapter 9, where the performance of the 160 non-resident owned firms in this study with assets of $1 million or more is compared with that of ninety-six resident-owned firms in the same industries with assets of $1 million or more. Neither set generally met frequently, but the boards of the resident-owned met more frequently than those of the non-resident owned firms. Thus only forty-eight and forty-one of each respectively met at least bi-monthly, and only seventeen of either group met at least once a month.

It was noted earlier that firms with assets of $25 million or more have a

---

[19]It may be noted in passing that the role of many outside directors is also different. In public companies in which ownership is dispersed the outside director may have a fighting chance in disagreements with manager-directors who are not significant owners. In companies which are largely or wholly-owned abroad, some of the directors are executives representing owners and still other directors are executives whose careers will be determined in part by the owners. No doubt many outside directors supply useful advice and business and financial contacts (as their role on management or executive committees indicates, as noted below) but their position between two groups of inside directors must be awkward at times, should they choose to exercise it.

higher proportion of resident directors than do smaller firms. The proportion of resident directors to total directors does not appear to vary significantly in other respects measured here. Thus half or more of the directors were residents in 53 per cent of the firms acquired or established by the present owner in the decade of the fifties; the corresponding percentages were 55 per cent, 59 per cent, and 66 per cent for firms acquired or established in 1940 to 1949, 1919 to 1939, and before 1919 respectively. The increase in the ratio by age of firm is moderate, and it virtually disappears if one examines the relation between these two variables within three groups of firms segregated by size of assets. It is probably more meaningful, therefore, to note that, in a small majority of firms in each age group, resident directors form half or more of the total number of directors. Nor is there any tendency for the proportion of resident to total directors to vary with the size of the Canadian firm when the latter is measured as a percentage of the size of the parent firm. Detailed analysis of the residency of directors by type of business is limited by the fact that the great majority of the firms are concentrated in the fully processed or manufactured goods category, so that there are relatively few firms in other categories. In the major category 56 per cent of the firms reported at least half of their directors resided in Canada, including 15 per cent where at least three quarters were residents. In a related group, those engaged in assembly operations, 47 per cent of the firms reported half or more directors resident in Canada. The corresponding percentages for the small number of firms involved in extractive industry, semi-fabricated products, and fully integrated production were 66 per cent, 43 per cent and 69 per cent. The last of these, which includes many of the largest firms, was the only group to report that there were no firms at all in which less than one-quarter of the directors were residents of Canada. That the practice of appointing resident directors is widespread is suggested also by considering the data classified by the sixteen major industry groups used in this study. In only four such industry groups was there a majority of firms in which less than half of the board were resident in Canada.

As one might expect, the extent to which the parent holds the voting stock of the subsidiary appears to be a significant factor in the ratio of resident to non-resident directors. Where the subsidiary's stock was held entirely by the parent 49 per cent of the firms involved reported that at least half of their directors were residents. This percentage rose to 61 per cent for firms in which the parent held 75 per cent or more of the stock but not all, and to 79 per cent for firms in which the parent held under three-quarters of the stock. The same pattern persists when the evidence is considered within three groups of firms classified by size. More will be said of this point in Chapter 9.

The Management or Executive Committee

The making of decisions by groups rather than by individuals is commonplace in corporations, especially as they become larger or more complex. Formal and informal committees of senior executives and/or directors often play a major role in the initiation of general policy and the co-ordination of its implementation, as well as assuming more specific and limited functions. An attempt was made to determine the existence and composition of the former type of committee, which has broader supervisory duties than the latter. These general supervisory committees can be committees of either management or of the board (there is often an overlap in personnel, of course) and can go under various names. The problem of distinguishing one from the other is particularly difficult in firms whose boards are largely composed of executives of related companies. In the case of companies with inactive boards the two types of committees might well amount to the same thing in practice as far as general supervisory powers are concerned. The best brief approach appeared to be to ask simply, "Is there an active management or executive committee with major responsibilities?"[20] Ninety-eight companies have no such committee. Most of these, seventy-four in all, were companies with assets under $5 million, but ten with assets over $25 million also had no such committee. A further twenty-nine companies did not reply to this question, in most cases probably because it was not relevant. Of the 153 companies with such committees, about 70 per cent supplied detailed figures on composition according to the same categories as those given for the board. The most typical size of these committees is from three to five persons, with about half of those reporting on size located in this range. They are overwhelmingly composed of residents of Canada, with fully 80 per cent of the total membership in that category. The senior management of the Canadian company formed 72 per cent of the total numbers, persons associated with the parent and its affiliates 12 per cent, outside directors 14 per cent and other groups only 2 per cent. Membership by persons associated with the parent and also that by outside directors was restricted to relatively few of the companies reporting on this, about a quarter and a fifth of the total respectively.

---

[20]The data below as well as internal evidence in the questionnaires clearly suggest these are very largely committees of management rather than committees of the board.

Other Methods of Maintaining Contact with the Affiliate

Apart from representation on the Canadian board, the executives of the parent companies or major owners are informed of the operations and policies of the Canadian subsidiaries in a variety of ways, some of which are related to management or executive committees but most of which go well beyond these. Chief among these are informal contacts, such as visits, letters, and telephone calls, and written reports or copies of documents. These personal contacts and reports have a variety of purposes: in part they are the standardized accounting or reporting items which are required by the officers of the parent in order to permit them to check the progress of the subsidiary; in part they are the means of securing advice or guidance from the officers of the parent on major plans or problems and ensuring that the overall objectives of the international firm are maintained as the plans progress and the problems are resolved; in part they are a method of keeping officers of subsidiary companies informed of developments in the parent and its affiliates. Two hundred firms supplied details on these other methods. The following comments apply to contacts at senior levels of management, while the purely technical liaison will be dealt with in a later chapter.

Informal contacts dominate, with 159 firms referring to them and forty-eight of these using only such methods, apart from contacts through the board. It is fairly common practice for the Canadian firm's manager or president to make a regular annual or semi-annual visit to the parent, or for a senior officer or officers of the parent to visit the Canadian company. In a few firms regular quarterly and even monthly visits to the parent company are the rule, especially if the Canadian officer reports to, or is a member of, the parent's management committee or board. In addition, *ad hoc* visits may become necessary on particular problems. Contact is maintained by telephone or letter in the meantime, but with considerable variation by company. A very few executives reported they were in almost daily contact with senior executives of the parent, while others were not in contact except for extraordinary developments.

Regular written reports on an intra-annual basis are made by 122 of the 200 companies which gave details. About one-third of these 122 companies appear to be making financial reports, such as selected balance sheet or income items, profit estimates, cash balances, quarterly budgets, or capital spending, whether actual or forecast. About one-seventh of these companies appear to be making non-financial reports, loosely construed since the categories overlap, such as general progress reports, current and prospective business, bookings, production, sales, or inventories, whether actual or forecast. The remainder are making both types of reports. Reporting on a monthly basis predominates with sixty-eight firms reporting some item on such a basis, while quarterly reports are also frequent. A few firms report certain items weekly and even daily, usually through copies of documents on production and sales figures. A large proportion, as indicated above, do not submit written intra-annual reports at all. [21]

A considerable variety of other methods serve to keep parent company officers informed of the absolute and relative performance of the subsidiary and of special situations.[22] Some of these work directly, as in those few companies where the senior resident officer of the Canadian firm is a member of the parent board or of its management committee or is expected to report personally to one of these at monthly intervals. In others the contact may arise as a result of procedures designed for other purposes, for example, situations where specific capital purchases beyond a certain value must be referred to the parent company. These will be discussed further below. What needs emphasis here is the variety of contacts beyond those at the board, and it should also be emphasized that there is very great variation among companies in these respects. In some cases, as long as all goes reasonably well the parent or major owner is content with an annual budget and related statements usually presented directly to the board of the Canadian company, and informal advisement of major changes which will affect its investment. In others, there are frequent oral or written presentations to meetings of executives of the two firms and a huge volume of regular reports or documents at frequencies of anything from a day onwards, not to mention detailed procedure manuals, frequent informal contacts, and so forth. These procedures reflect in part the wide differences in actual parent-subsidiary relationships subsumed under the term direct investment, including very different ownership situations, very different market and technological situations, different concepts among parent company managements about the degree and kind of reporting and of decentralization which is desirable, and the particular personal and historical characteristics which affect any organization.

---

[21]Companies owned overseas do not appear to differ very much from those owned in the United States in the nature and frequency of informal contacts and written reports, except that personal visits are somewhat less frequent.

[22]Some of these methods were indicated in replies to various questions, but not with sufficient detail and consistency among different companies to permit quantification.

The Delegation of Powers

The management relationships between parent and subsidiary Canadian firms cover many forms of organization and degrees of delegation of responsibilities. At any given time these will reflect a variety of factors, including, for example, the economic circumstances with regard to the nature, production and distribution of the product, government policies, the past history of the firms, and the characteristics and attitudes of their senior personnel. The management relationships between parent and subsidiary firms inevitably change over time as these and other factors change. It is perhaps hazardous to attempt to disentangle this complex of factors, even if specialized knowledge of management relationships could be claimed. Yet it is important in its own right, and in relation to some questions raised later in this study, to attempt at least a tentative examination of this aspect of the subject.

It is not our purpose to examine the extensive literature on the delegation of powers in multi-company enterprises.[23] The rationale of centralized decision-making, or at least of review of major local decisions, is easy to grasp. Some group must decide whether, from the point of view of the overall enterprise, the channelling of funds and development of products is bringing maximum returns, and whether the operation of particular firms measures up to given criteria of efficiency. Those who have substantial investments in a variety of companies will want at the minimum to be informed of the degree of success of the firms involved, and to be in a position to approve at least the major financial decisions which affect their investments. Indeed, major financial decisions, product change, and the appointment of the chief executive officer of the firms within an enterprise are decisions particularly likely to be performed by or reviewed at the centre. But much more than this may be involved, since direct investment is typically an extension of management techniques and products to a new setting. Extensive overlapping of functions can be costly, and resultant conflicts of interest must be resolved; it is often economic to centralize certain specialized management functions common to all of the companies. Depending on the nature of the firms, a good many other specific factors

---

[23]A general discussion of the principles involved, with several case studies, will be found in Geo. Albert Smith, *Managing Geographically Decentralized Companies*, Harvard University Graduate School of Business Administration, Cambridge, Mass., 1958, and John Fayerweather, *Management of International Operations*, McGraw-Hill, New York, 1960, Ch. 6. For three different approaches, as seen by the executives of the parent companies, see Dan H. Fenn (ed.), *Management Guide to Overseas Operations*, McGraw-Hill, New York, 1957, pp. 156-180.

may point to centralization of given functions. All of this necessarily carries with it the implication of reporting from the various firms to the centre if certain decisions are to be made at the centre or if major local decisions are to be reviewed. Standardized accounting becomes desirable, consequently, to facilitate at least some comparisons among firms in the enterprise as well as to consolidate accounts. Improved communications and improved centralized data analysis favour review by those at the centre. At the same time it is well to note that all of this need not imply actual centralized decision-making on any detailed basis in order to secure broad conformance with important parent policies. Particularly after the early years of the subsidiary, clear overall policy and procedure guides to the subsidiary's officers and effective conformance by them, to the extent that both are feasible, can secure some degree of centralization without the need for detailed supervision from the centre.

The case for delegation of powers is also strong. The circumstances facing companies in the same enterprise will vary because they are producing a different product mix, are located in different regions or countries, are facing different kinds of competition, are of widely differing size, and so on. The initiative of officers of the various firms may be stifled by over-centralization; moreover, in such circumstances the firm may find it difficult to attract competent personnel. Speed of decision, flexibility of operations, close knowledge of local circumstances, and incentives to the maximum development of local management may all favour considerable delegation of authority. There will be variation, accordingly, in the degree of delegation or centralization of responsibilities which is appropriate to any given set of circumstances, and the organizational forms within the international firm which are appropriate thereto. The purpose of the present section is the limited one of attempting to indicate the degree of delegation of responsibilities which existed in fact in the particular setting of foreign-owned industry at a given time, to suggest how this compares with that in other geographically decentralized firms, and to indicate how it is related to various variables.[24] It is well to keep in mind that the situations summarized here are essentially as seen by the resident managers of the subsidiaries, since the questionnaire was mailed to them.

[24]For an analysis of the form of organization and degree of supervision of a number of Mexican subsidiaries of American firms, see E. R. Barlow, *Management of Foreign Manufacturing Subsidiaries,* Harvard University Graduate School of Business Administration, Cambridge, Mass., 1953, Ch. 3 and Ch. 4. The same topics are covered for American firms in the United Kingdom in John H. Dunning, *American Investment in British Manufacturing Industry*, Allen and Unwin, London, 1958, Ch. 3.

At the outset a note of caution may be necessary about oversimplified views on the process of control in a multi-company enterprise. This warning is all the more appropriate because, for purposes of generalization, it has been necessary in this study to submerge important aspects of the operations of some individual firms which may be at the heart of the issue of control in their cases. The warning is also necessary because of the exaggerated simplicity with which many persons view the process of decision-making in modern firms, not excluding many of the smaller firms. In the first place, the freedom of action of the executives, directors and major shareholders is necessarily curtailed by the actions and views of those most directly involved in its environment — namely governments, competitors, labour, purchasers, and suppliers, to name the more significant. These are the external checks to action by management and major owners. The internal checks may be as important, given the various levels of management with different responsibilities and viewpoints which is characteristic of the multi-unit, multi-product firm.[25] The diversity of views among management, and the resultant conflict, is likely to be greatest among firms which are organized primarily geographically, as against those organized primarily by products or by functions. A close student of geographically decentralized companies has observed that "All the problems of multi-unit companies seem, in the author's experience, to appear in their most virulent form in companies organized by geographical units. Tensions are undoubtedly heightened because lines of authority in such firms are almost always not very clear, levels of authority are numerous, and people who are supposed to work closely together are not close together physically." He notes also that "there is a tendency for all branch officers to be suspicious of people at headquarters — of both their motives and their ideas."[26] If one extends this to enterprises where the component plants or firms are located in different countries and are most frequently organized on a national basis for purposes of delegation of responsibilities and reporting, the possibilities of divergent approaches and looser organizations are magnified, as are the differences in external or environmental checks.

---

[25]As one observer put it: "The word 'control' brings to mind a picture of a sort of omnipotent being sitting at a central switchboard from which he manipulates every policy and every transaction of a concern. Yet any large business concern is a loose aggregation of departments which run to a very large extent on their own, facing problems many of which are puzzling even to the head of the concern, and if this is true of a single company, it is all the more true of a varied collection of companies and of the men who sit in a banking office and supposedly 'control' them." F. L. Allen, *The Great Pierpont Morgan*, (Harper and Brothers, 1949).
[26]Geo. Albert Smith, *op. cit.*, pp. 107 and 89.

Before considering the actual degree of decentralization it is of interest to note the officer or division in the foreign affiliates to which the Canadian companies are responsible. The firms in this study are responsible in most cases to the most senior officers of the foreign affiliate. Fully 137 firms indicated they were responsible to the president, the chairman or the board of the latter company. A further fifty-six indicated responsibility to general senior officers just below the president, while thirty-five reported they were responsible to officers who had specific functions, such as the international division, manufacturing or sales. Twelve firms reported they were responsible only to the Canadian board or, in one case, its executive committee. Ten of these twelve had assets of $25 million or more each and almost all have been established in Canada for decades. Eleven further firms

TABLE 13

OFFICER OR DIVISION IN FOREIGN AFFILIATE TO WHICH CANADIAN FIRM IS RESPONSIBLE
(Number of companies)

Officer or division	All companies	U.S. only	Under 1	1-4.9	5-24.9	25 and over
Chairman and/or board*	34	16	16	9	6	3
President	103	96	45	36	11	9
Executive vice-president, vice-president, or general manager	56	44	19	21	10	5
Functional vice-presidents or managers						
International division	19	16	5	5	4	2
Other divisions or functions	16	10	10	4	2	0
Not specific or varies	5	5	1	1	1	2
Canadian company's board	12	11	0	0	2	10
None†	11	10	4	3	1	2
No reply to question	24	19	4	3	6	2
Total companies	280	227	104	82	43	35

By asset size in $ millions

* Includes four responsible to executive committee.
† These replied they were not responsible to any officer or division in the foreign affiliate, but did not explicitly place the locus of responsibility in the Canadian board. Special ownership or management situations are involved in some cases.

indicated simply that they were not responsible to any officer or division of the affiliate; several of these could probably be classified with the above twelve, but others represent special ownership or management situations. The firms in this study which are owned by overseas companies tend to be more frequently responsible to the chairman or board of the affiliate, rather than to the president, compared with companies owned in the United States.

For many companies it is not possible to compare the locus of responsibility for the Canadian company with that for other foreign subsidiaries of the parent. In eighty-three cases, all but seven of which were American-owned companies, the parent had no other foreign affiliate. In sixty-nine further cases the question was not answered, many of the respondents indicating they did not know to whom other foreign subsidiaries were responsible. A further eighteen are not strictly comparable since one or both of the Canadian or overseas affiliates are not responsible to an officer or division of the parent. This left eighty-three companies where the Canadian firm and other foreign affiliates of the parent were responsible to the same officer or division of the parent, and only twenty-seven companies where a different one was involved. American-owned companies accounted for sixty and twenty-four of these respectively. The Canadian companies reporting to a different officer or division mainly tended to report to a higher level in the parent, but this probably reflected the fact that two-thirds of them were in the two largest size groups of firms.

While the subsidiary is responsible to the officers or divisions indicated, it is well to note that in practice the initial approach to such persons may at times be at a lower level of the parent firm's organization, since senior executives of large companies are usually busy with many responsibilities. This is not to deny that the ultimate responsibility is that shown on a company's organizational charts. It is simply to note that in many circumstances the approach to such persons will be through other executives whose role in the final resolution of the question may be a significant one.

The Degree of Decentralization of Responsibility

One of the most complex questions involved in this study was the actual degree to which decisions were decentralized between officers of the parent and those of the subsidiary. An effort was made to secure information on this at the end of the questionnaire in the form of the following question.

With respect to the operations and policies of the Canadian company, please describe the degree of decentralization of responsibility and decision making as between persons associated with the Canadian company and those (primarily) associated with your affiliate; for example, with respect to such matters as production planning, financial policies, introducing new products or techniques or markets, capital expansion, marketing, labour relations.

Sixty-nine of the respondents did not answer this question, a figure not greatly out of line with that for other general questions listed at the end of the questionnaire.[27] The 211 companies which did reply to it did so in varying degrees of detail, and this, combined with the wide variation in degrees of actual decentralization, makes a meaningful classification difficult. The available detail is an improvement, however, over a separate question noted below asking simply for the degree of supervision, which is related to this question though not identical, and it permits the establishment of a degree of uniformity within any grouping. The replies can be classified very broadly within the following groups which reflect the stated degree of decentralization on the one hand and the stated nature of qualifications thereto on the other. The complexity of the term "decentralization" and the variation in the detail of replies to the question combine to lower the quality of any summary. One should emphasize that there is variation within the groups, that they overlap, and that there is likely to be some arbitrariness at the margin of each group, and quite possibly a few errors.[28]

To avoid misunderstanding it is necessary to emphasize that the question attempts to establish some general propositions on the *effective* degree of decentralization which exists between two more or less distinct groups of persons within a given set of circumstances.[29] The ultimate legal powers of

---

[27]As noted below, the questionnaire also asked in another section if the Canadian firm was "supervised extensively, partly, or negligibly" by the affiliate. All but twenty-three of the respondents answered this question, including almost all of those which did not answer the question on the degree of decentralization. The latter firms had about the same percentage of replies giving "extensively" as the answer as did those which also answered the question on degree of decentralization, but they had a somewhat higher percentage answering "partly" and a correspondingly lower percentage answering "negligibly." See also the third paragraph of the next section.

[28]In classifying replies to this question the temptation to infer additional details on the degree of decentralization from other parts of the questionnaire has been generally resisted, since this would involve imposing one's explicit judgement of the role of (say) boards and market ties as reported elsewhere, rather than reporting what the executives believe to be the end result of all such ties. The exception is the three firms noted in the footnote to table 14.

[29]This distinction between the groups of persons is not always clear. A certain amount of corporate schizophrenia may develop for a time, for example, in the case of a former long-time resident president of the Canadian firm who becomes a full-time officer of the parent, resident in the United States, but serves also as chairman of

shareholders, their representation on boards, the financial and other reports they receive on the operations of the firms, and the ties exercised by technology and other economic factors, are considered explicitly elsewhere.

The first major group of thirty-seven firms to be considered claimed full decentralization on both operations and policies, without any significant explicit qualifications. One group of twenty-five firms included statements such as "operations and policies are entirely the responsibility of Canadian executives", from a well-established large firm; and, "there is complete decentralization of responsibility and decision making in the Canadian subsidiary relative to the parent company. As mentioned previously there is a free exchange of ideas between the two companies which can be used or rejected by either company according to the decision of management," from a small firm established in Canada early in the fifties. Almost all of these had representatives of the parents on their boards, of course. In the remaining twelve firms this was made explicit in that the responsibility for the matters shown was specifically stated to be with the board of the Canadian company and, in most cases, its senior officers. Typical of the situations in this group are the following replies, both from large firms which were established many decades ago:

Responsibility for and decision making with respect to operations and policies of Canadian company are completely decentralized from parent. As indicated previously, senior officers and Board of Directors are completely responsible for the operations of the Canadian company. The only authoritative influence of the parent is through its representation on the Board.

The only influence of the parent company on basic policies is through representation on the Canadian board of directors. Budgeting and capital expenditures are handled entirely by the local board without reference to the parent. All final decisions rest with the Canadian board.

Some of the answers in this group were rather brief; more detailed answers in these cases might conceivably have placed them in the next category. Nevertheless, these firms appear to enjoy a substantial degree of autonomy while remaining legally accountable to their owners. The direct

---

the Canadian board and as the officer in the parent to which the Canadian company reports. This type of situation is not rare, given the frequent movement of Canadians, or of returning Americans, to senior positions in the parent firm. Such situations may lead both to informed spokesmen for the Canadian company and a close interest in its operations.

influence of the parent is limited to its contact through the board. There is reporting, of course, and there are many indirect influences via similar technology or products or other contacts. The policy in most cases is to select competent managers and to let them run the Canadian firm so long as the results are favourable, subject to the overall regular review by the board.

A second major group of 111 firms claimed a substantial degree of decentralization in both operations and policies, but explicitly qualified as to major policy changes and major financial changes. Typically, operations were quite decentralized but major policies were referred. By types of functions the greatest degree of decentralization was in production planning, marketing, and labour relations; there was a limited degree of decentralization on new products and techniques, while decisions on capital expansion and financial policies tended to be centralized in part at least. This group covers a rather wide range of companies, all of which appear to have a high degree of decentralization but most of which state some significant qualification thereto. Usually the qualification consists of some form of consultation with officers of the parent, mainly on major policy and on major financial items, as a reference either from Canadian management or from the Canadian board.

Sixteen of these companies gave general statements indicating a large degree of autonomy but not stating precisely the qualifications. Most of these noted at least that the initiative on policy changes came from those primarily associated with the subsidiary. Thirty-three companies indicated that the responsibility for the matters noted in the question rested with the officers or board of the Canadian company, but decision-making on broad policy matters involved some form of participation by executives of both the parent and the subsidiary.[30] The sense in which the executives of the parent company were involved varied all the way from a largely advisory one to explicit determination based on the advice of Canadian officers, with various degrees of joint determination in between. It is probably hazardous to classify the shades of decentralization which might be involved, at least from the present material. The relevant points are that the initiative on policy usually rests with the Canadian officers and/or board, that the parent's officers are consulted directly on major policy changes, and that the recommendations of the subsidiary carry much — perhaps usually decisive — weight. The

---

[30]It might be noted that thirteen of the firms gave major financial changes as a specific matter on which the parent would be consulted, thus overlapping with the sub group of sixty-two companies mentioned below.

following are typical of many replies in this group. The first firm is small and was established in Canada early in the fifties, the others are large firms and have been in Canada for decades.

> Entire responsibility is decentralized and rests with Canadian company. Major matters are cleared with parent for reasons of information and benefit of experience only.
>
> Responsibility and decision-making with respect to operations and policies of the Canadian company are highly decentralized. Generally speaking, the operation of the Canadian company is the responsibility of its own Board and senior officers. When it is apparent to the senior officers of the Canadian company that they could benefit by the previous experience of the parent company in any field, the opportunity is taken to consult the parent company. When major capital expenditure programmes are contemplated, the parent company is consulted.
>
> The Canadian operating committee makes all its own decisions subject to consultation with the parent on major policy.

Another example may be cited from the interviews, where the president of one large firm noted that autonomy in his case meant that he and his resident executives initiated major proposals and then tried to persuade those associated with the parent to accept them, especially if they impinged in some way on the overall firm — for example, in the need for funds. They also protested any action or inaction on the part of the parent or its affiliates which they believed to be detrimental to the interests of the Canadian company. In this case, it may be added, the degree of decentralization was probably related to, among other things, the existence of a closely-held minority stockholding and the fact that the resident managers had world-wide experience and were accustomed to independent action under varying circumstances.

A number of the firms in this group added that the major constraint on their decision-making powers was simply that the rate of profit earned by the Canadian firm over time must be acceptable to the affiliate. Still other types of response indicated a more regular procedure for joint consultation or decision-making at the level of major policies. In some cases the president of the Canadian company is a member of an operating committee for the international firm, which sets overall general policies. In other cases one or two representatives of the parent on the Canadian board, along with one or two representatives of the management of the Canadian company, will serve as a liaison committee between the firms. The most frequent procedure, however, is direct contact between senior executives of the two companies, both at board meetings and less formally.

A further group of sixty-two companies in this general category listed quite specific qualifications to their generally decentralized status, either as an exception to a general statement on degree of decentralization or by spelling out in detail the division of responsibilities between the firms. In the great majority of cases the specific qualification was either financial policies or capital expansion or both; six companies listed financial policies as the sole exception, sixteen gave capital expansion, and a further twenty-one gave both as the only exception. Twelve of the remaining companies gave the introduction of new products as the exception, with six of them listing capital expansion with it. Many of the companies in the group indicated that the specific qualification applied only if a major change was contemplated.

The senses in which the generally decentralized status of the subsidiary was qualified may be seen from the following examples, which are typical of various types of replies in this category. These firms cover each of the four asset sizes by which firms are classified in this study, and age distributions from roughly one to six decades.

> The only two aspects of the operation of the Canadian companies which are subject to approval by the English affiliate are capital expansion, and some very major financial policies.

> Only limits on Canadian President are in regards to obtaining approval on major capital expenditures and major market innovations. Canadian President has generally autonomous control with a responsibility for return on capital invested.

> Briefly, this company is almost completely self-sufficient in regard to every day management and in the formulation of general policy. The main exception is in the question of major capital expansion, and it is quite reasonable that such expenditures should require approval by the top officers of the parent corporation in view of the fact that the capital involved is 100 per cent owned in the United States.

> Production planning — completely decentralized. Financial Policy — chiefly responsibility of Canadian Management. Major items only referred to Parent Company if additional capital required. New Products and techniques — largely responsibility of Canadian Management who will avail themselves of facilities of Group Research and Development Centre. Marketing and Labour Relations — completely decentralized.

> The parent company takes a direct interest only in matters affect-

ing the overall financial policy of the Canadian company, such as capital and/or corporate expansion or the embarking on major new ventures. Even in these areas, executives of the Canadian company carry a large degree of responsibility, although final decisions must be made by officers or board of directors of the parent company. On all other matters (eg. production planning, new products or techniques or markets, marketing, labour relations) responsibility lies entirely with persons associated with the Canadian company.

Primary responsibility rests with the Canadian company, with the parent company being contacted for concurrence on matters of major financial policy or capital expenditure.

Since parent and subsidiary market the same production in essentially the same kind of markets, there is, of course, close co-ordination in major advertising and new product introduction programmes. Otherwise responsibility and decision making are, in great part, decentralized.

In a third group of eighteen firms there was operational freedom within centralized policy determination. In some of these firms the degree of decentralization may not be greatly different from some in the second group above, judging by operational freedom or policy constraints. In these cases the distinction was drawn on whether there appeared to be any process of consultation in determining the policies applicable to the Canadian firm. In those grouped here there did not appear to be such consultation to any significant extent, so far as one could judge from the material available.

In a fourth group of nineteen firms, finally, there was a substantial degree of centralization of both operations and policies, judging by the replies to the question noted above. In one or two cases there were such unqualified statements as "Responsibility and decision making in hands of Affiliate."[31] In some cases the local manager is responsible for production, but other matters are either centralized ("Production planning independent. Remainder handled from U.S. office") or there is very close and frequent liaison with parent executives about them. Again one must note that the group inevitably involves companies which vary in the degree of centralization. In some cases the local manager will decide when to refer a wide range

---

[31]Both of the firms referred to in this paragraph were small. One of them was quite new and the other was established just after World War II. It may be noted in passing that the parents own all of the voting stock of the firms whose replies have been quoted, in part or whole, in this section, with the exception of two firms in the second group above.

TABLE 14

DEGREE OF DECENTRALIZATION OF RESPONSIBILITY
(Number of companies)

Decentralization by groups	Country of control			Asset size in $ millions	
	All Countries	U.S.	Overseas	25 and over	10-24.9
1. Fully decentralized, no explicit qualification beyond board	37	30	7	9	4
2. Substantial decentralization, qualified on major policy and finance	111	92	19	16	14
3. Policies centralized, operations decentralized	18	17	1	1	2
4. Largely centralized	19	13	6	2	—
Replies not classified because unclear*	26	16	10	3	2
No reply to question†	69	59	10	4	2
Total	280	227	53	35	24

* Twenty-three replies were too brief or unclear for classification in this table. Three others included here gave replies on the degree of supervision which were at the opposite extreme to those on the degree of decentralization. † For high non-response in some tables, see page 35.

of matters to the executives of the affiliate for a decision, and he will have some day-to-day discretion on production problems, labour relations, and sales. In others, centralized bookkeeping, handling of payments, and direction of domestic sales effectively relieve local managers of all but local technical and personnel matters. The branch or company is rather similar to a selling agency in some cases, except for the fact that assembly and production are involved.

Judging by replies to this question the degree of decentralization is not generally different for firms owned overseas compared with those owned in the United States. The only difference is that there are relatively fewer firms in the overseas category in group three above and relatively more in group four, but the numbers are so small that this may not be significant. While some firms owned overseas have an unusually high degree of decentralization, there is no general support in the data for the view sometimes heard that, because of distance and differences in the business setting, responsibility is more decentralized in the typical case in subsidiaries owned by overseas firms. A full test of this view would require both a more precise definition of decentralization and a sufficiently large number of firms to permit adequate statistical analysis. It might be noted in passing that for some of the Canadian companies owned in the United Kingdom the differences in distance, technology, and institutions are more apparent than real, since part of the supervision which is exercised comes not from the parent firm in the United Kingdom but from an affiliate of the parent in the United States.

The larger firms cover the entire range of decentralization noted above. The firms with assets of $10 million or more tend to be represented relatively less frequently among groups three or four, although this should be qualified by the small numbers involved and the overlapping of categories at the margin which was noted earlier. Firms with assets of $25 million or more accounted for seven of the twelve explicitly indicating they were responsible only to their own board and/or officers and those in the size group $10 - 24.9 million accounted for two more.

Conclusions drawn from the material presented here must be guarded, as noted earlier. What does stand out is the very wide degree of decentralization involved in practice, ranging from firms which are virtually autonomous to firms whose operations and policies are minutely controlled centrally. In particular, the term *control* can have a wide variety of meanings as applied to these firms, ranging all the way from the minute regulation of production scheduling and a variety of other day-to-day operations from the centre all the way to the desire of the centre simply to be informed about the degree of success of the operation. In the great majority of cases "a high degree of controlled autonomy" seems best to describe the situation.[32] By this is meant that persons primarily associated with the subsidiary have most or all of the operational responsibility, subject to reporting and review as noted below, and also the main responsibility for initiating and planning changes in policy for the areas indicated earlier. The parent company's executives in the typical case must be consulted in some way or other on major policy changes, particularly those involving financial changes or capital expansion. This is not surprising, given the investment interest of the parent and the fact that financial changes may require direct

---

[32]This term is used by Dunning, *op. cit.*, p. 109. It may be noted that, using a somewhat different approach, Dunning concludes in Chapter 4 that one third of the American-owned firms he studied in the United Kingdom were negligibly supervised, one third partly, and one third extensively. The approaches used here and in the next section have turned up somewhat smaller proportions at the two extremes.

financing from it or affect the dividend.[33] The control of financial changes is a key one, of course, and impinges in one way or another on many other areas of policy.[34]

It is evident from the replies to this and other questions that the parent firms of most of the subsidiaries in this study require either that capital budgets be submitted or that major capital expenditure be approved. In some cases this requirement takes effect where specified limits for the president and (usually a higher one) for his board are to be exceeded; in others, it will take place as a matter of course for major expenditures, without such specification. No doubt the overall policies of the parent play an important part in the outcome. Yet it would be a mistake to conceive of these as fully predetermined and inflexible, requiring full conformity by the subsidiary. For it is also evident from most of the replies that the officers of the Canadian firms typically do not play a passive role even here but plan and propose changes which they believe justified, and as such play a

---

[33]Fayerweather's view is worth noting in this connection as regards controls on subsidiary companies: "In virtually all cases, however, there is agreement that three vital areas of authority should be retained by the home office, and, if judiciously used, controls in these areas provide a large measure of direction over the whole pattern of operation of foreign units. The three are basic policy decisions, major allocations of funds, and selection of key executives." See Fayerweather, *op. cit.*, p. 367.

[34]The logic of control on capital has been put graphically in the following comment: "The importance of capital expenditure is that much of it is medium or long term in character and, therefore, it determines the directions in which the business is going to move for some time to come. You can compare it to laying down the permanent way of a railway. Once the track is laid, those in immediate charge of operating the line may, within reason, experiment with different types of rolling stock and, if they guess wrong, their mistakes can be corrected without much difficulty. But if the track has been laid in the wrong direction to start with, the venture will never pay and it is a terribly expensive matter to have to pull it up and start all over again. We try to prevent this kind of thing happening in Unilever by controlling capital expenditure throughout the business both by means of annual budgets and by requiring individual items above certain limits to be submitted for approval." Comment by the Chairmen of Unilever Ltd. and Unilever N.V. in describing the management structure of the firm, on p. 11 of *Anatomy of a Business*, published by Unilever Limited, London, 1962. This is given here as typical of the views of many senior executives, rather than as a justification for the close watch over capital spending. One might add that some of the parent companies exercise an unusually close check in the area of capital purchases. Some firms with assets in the $1-4.9 million category, for example, reported that the senior resident officer required authorization to purchase individual capital goods if they exceeded $1,000 in value. This figure is well below that for other firms in the same size category, and also often well out of line with the discretionary limits available to the same officers in regard to other purchases and in arranging for or extending credit, decisions which could have an equally important effect on the firm's future. Perhaps the economist and the accountant have overstressed the importance of capital formation.

role of varying degrees in the process of overall decision-making as it affects the subsidiary. The impact they may have will vary with circumstances to be noted below on the determinants of decentralization.

The Degree of Supervision

In the main body of the questionnaire the companies were asked: "In general, do you consider that the operations and/or overall policies of the Canadian firm are supervised extensively, partly, or negligibly by your affiliate?" This question has the virtue of permitting a brief and largely unqualified response for those who would be unwilling to answer a more detailed question, such as that noted above on the degree of decentralization. It permits some relatively simple relationships to be drawn with other questions in what is necessarily a complex area. All but twenty-three of the 280 firms replied to this question.[35] On the other hand the question is clearly a very subjective one, since criteria for various degrees of supervision were not given.

It will be noted that about 50 per cent of the firms chose the word "partly" to describe the degree of supervision, a sizeable minority of 32

TABLE 15

EXTENT TO WHICH OPERATIONS AND POLICIES ARE SUPERVISED BY THE AFFILIATE
(Number of companies)

	Country of control			Asset size in $ millions			
	All Countries	U.S.	Overseas	Under 1	1 - 4.9	5 - 24.9	25 and over
Extensively	45	37	8	24	11	6	3
Partly	122	98	24	38	44	22	11
Negligibly	80	65	15	36	24	7	13
Other*	10	7	3	4	2	1	3
No reply†	23	20	3	2	1	7	5
Total	280	227	53	104	82	43	35

* Most of these indicated their operations were supervised negligibly but policies partly or extensively.
† With regard to the relatively high proportion of no replies for the two largest groups of firms, here and elsewhere, see footnote 3, Chapter 2.

[35]Few firms drew a distinction between operations and policies in their replies. It might have been more revealing to ask the question separately for operations and for policies, although the experience with the replies on degree of decentralization in this respect suggests that the distinction is not always easy to make.

per cent claimed that supervision was "negligible," and a still smaller group of about 18 per cent that it was "extensive," neglecting those which did not answer this question or gave a combination of categories. As with the question on degree of decentralization there does not appear to be a marked difference between companies owned in the United States and those owned overseas; in fact, the percentages for the various degrees of supervision are almost identical in each case with those just noted for all firms together. Firms with assets under $1 million are somewhat more heavily represented in the extensively supervised groups than those over this size. The small numbers in some size groups and the rather erratic patterns in the other categories suggest that further conclusions on the relationship between degree of supervision and absolute size should be guarded ones.

The question on degree of decentralization of responsibility and decision-making is not precisely on the same matter, nor phrased in the same way, as that on the degree of supervision exercised by the affiliate. Nevertheless, the questions are sufficiently related to suggest that a comparison of the replies to them is useful. To the extent this is valid it will permit the personal experiences and views of executives, as expressed in their replies to this question, to qualify our own classification of their more detailed replies to the question on degree of decentralization. The comparison has been made only for those which replied "negligibly" or "extensively" to this question and also answered that on the degree of decentralization.[36] All of those replying "negligibly" to the degree of supervision fell neatly into the more decentralized groups one and two with regard to the degree of decentralization, except for two which fell into group three and five which were among those whose replies to the question on decentralization could not be classified. However, eleven firms classified in group two by the degree of decentralization are extensively supervised by this set of replies, though several of them qualified this by stating that it was only their policies which were extensively supervised. Subject to qualifications on the relationship between the questions, it appears that some of these eleven firms listed in group two might, with more detailed replies, have been classified as group three. Finally, it should be noted that fully seventeen of the forty-five firms which replied that supervision was extensive failed to reply to the question on degree of decentralization, while eighteen of the eighty firms which indicated it was negligible failed to answer the other question.

---

[36]As noted earlier, the replies to these questions were classified independently except for the deletion of three firms which were at opposite extremes in their answers to the two questions.

To the extent that the questions are related, this may suggest that among the firms which did not answer the question on degree of decentralization the distribution by groups may be more towards groups three and four than is the case for those which did answer the question.

An attempt was made to determine whether the involvement, whatever it was, of the parent company in the operations and policies of the Canadian subsidiary differed markedly from that in the case of other comparable foreign subsidiaries, on the one hand, and other comparable domestic subsidiaries of the parent, on the other. The quality of response here must be judged particularly low, given that the respondents will have rather differing knowledge of the parent's affiliates outside Canada, and given also the variety of interpretations which can be placed on the words "markedly" and "comparable." A very large number of executives did not reply to the question at all, many simply indicating they did not know. Another large group indicated explicitly that the question was inapplicable because the parent had no other foreign affiliates or no comparable foreign or domestic affiliates. Those which did or could reply indicated the involvement was either not markedly different or less in Canada, compared with other foreign affiliates of the parent, in the ratio three to one respectively. Relative to comparable domestic affiliates of the parent, the involvement was either not markedly different or less in the ratio of two to one. Only one or two companies believed there was more involvement in the Canadian company in either case. A few more suggested that proximity to the parent and more integration of equipment led to somewhat closer supervision than for overseas affiliates in certain areas of operations, but in general believed the supervision was not markedly different.

It should be emphasized that these answers cut across very different sets of companies. They give us only a subjective view of what is the case but do not tell us whether national location as such, as distinct from variables such as the nature and size of the firm, is reflected in the degree of supervision. The qualifying adjectives used were an attempt, no doubt of limited success, to modify this difficulty. One can only speculate, moreover, on the reasons for these results, since these were not asked. The smaller degree of supervision involved for Canadian subsidiaries compared with other foreign subsidiaries may reflect in part the availability of more qualified managers in Canada, at least when compared with some less developed countries. The greater similarity of Canadian institutions with those of the main foreign lenders may work both ways. Less supervision is in fact necessary in order to achieve the overall objectives of the international firm, while proximity to the United States and important economic and other similarities may tempt parent company officials to assume that decisions made for the parent can be extended to Canada with minor modifications. At the same time, there is sufficient difference in institutional and other respects to help account for the fact that some Canadian firms receive less supervision than the domestic subsidiaries of the parent companies. The main point to emerge, however, is that the officers of most of the subsidiaries who answered these questions believed that the degree of supervision was not markedly different from that received by both domestic and foreign affiliates in comparable circumstances.

TABLE 16

COMPARATIVE DEGREE OF INVOLVEMENT BY PARENT COMPANY IN OPERATIONS AND POLICIES OF CANADIAN COMPANY
(Number of companies)

	Relative to comparable foreign subsidiaries of parent		Relative to comparable domestic subsidiaries of parent	
	All companies	U.S. companies	All companies	U.S. companies
More supervision for Canadian company	2	2	1	1
Not markedly different	75	55	66	53
Less supervision for Canadian company	26	18	30	24
Not applicable	92	83	54	45
No reply or unknown	85	69	129	104
Total	280	227	280	227

NOTE: The size distributions are not meaningful given the great variation in proportions by size in the last two categories. As noted in the text many did not think comparable subsidiaries existed or did not know what supervision they received.

The degree of supervision accorded to a subsidiary by the officers of the parent at any given time is determined by an extremely complex set of factors. To disentangle these somewhat, two different approaches have been used. In the first place, the firms were further cross-classified by their stated degree of supervision and their answers to other questions, such as age of firm and nature of product. While the question on degree of supervision is a subjective one, it does yield some interesting results when these degrees are classified by other characteristics. The other approach was simply to ask the firms to indicate any circumstances which affected the degree of supervision in their case and changes in supervision over time. It is well to emphasize that these approaches are quite different, though some of the major conclusions are broadly similar. The cross-classifications will be considered first, and some of the more interesting ones are shown in table 17.

If size is interpreted as size of assets relative to the affiliate when looking at the three degrees of supervision, the most significant difference is at the extremes. The firms which were smallest relative to the affiliate (defined as one per cent to five per cent of the latter's assets) had the smallest percentage of those reporting they were supervised negligibly. The firms which were largest (defined as 20 per cent or more of the parent's size) had the smallest percentage of those reporting they were extensively supervised. The difference in the extremes persists if one considers it within three groups of firms classified by absolute size.[37] Other differences among relative size groups are less striking or erratic.

The group which reported a negligible degree of supervision did not vary greatly with the age of the firm, measured by the date when the firm was acquired or established by the present foreign owner. Those which reported extensive supervision did decline significantly as the age of the firm rose. Both these patterns are confirmed when the data are examined within three size groups. It is possible to take this a step further by re-examining the concept of age of firm. Those firms which were purchased by their present owner, and hence had a previous history, can be compared with those which were established by the present owner.[38] At first sight it appeared that this made no difference to the degree of supervision, since the proportions reporting the three degrees of supervision were just about the same for the two sets of firms. When grouped by absolute size of assets, however, a quite distinct pattern appeared. In the two smallest size groups the firms which had been acquired rather than established were relatively larger portions of the extensively supervised than of the partly supervised, and larger portions of the partly supervised than of those negligibly supervised. In other words, they tended to get more supervision than

---

[37]It will be recalled that for purposes of these cross-classifications the absolute size groups used are under $1 million, $1-4.9 million, and $5 million and over.

[38]The latter category in the estimates includes some firms purchased by the present non-resident owner from other non-resident owners, or from both resident and non-resident owners, but these are not frequent enough to change the results.

those established anew by the parent. The reason might well be that greater supervision was necessary, at least for some time, in order to ensure conformity to the parent's operating procedures. On the other hand in the largest size group the situation was the reverse, in that the firms established by the parent were much more likely to receive greater degrees of supervision than existing firms acquired by the parent. Further analysis of the data indicated that the difference in this respect between these two groups of firms was not due to systematic differences among them in other characteristics, such as types of business or product, size, or age.

Turning to type of business, the processing and manufacturing group conforms with and determines the overall pattern: thus 29 per cent of this group reported supervision was "negligible," 54 per cent replied "partly," and 17 per cent "extensively," disregarding those not answering this. The few extractive firms reported that a relatively high proportion of their number was extensively supervised, while higher proportions of the integrated firms and of those making semi-fabricated products were in the negligibly supervised category than was the case for the other groups. Analysis of these differences, particularly within various size groups for the firms involved, is limited by the few firms in most categories. The greatest differences regarding degree of supervision classified by the range of products compared to the affiliate, when examined either within three size groups or overall, are consistently between the firms at the extremes. Those which have a wider product range than the parent reported the lowest percentage of firms with extensive supervision, while those which had comparatively few products—almost all of which indicated they produced fully processed or manufactured goods—reported the highest proportion of firms with extensive supervision. The differences are not negligible; the firms whose range was wider than their affiliates' reported in half the cases that they were negligibly supervised and in the remainder that they were partly supervised, while in the case of those producing only a few of the affiliates' products over half were partly supervised and one fourth were extensively supervised.

When these data are considered by sixteen major types of products they tend to follow a broadly similar pattern. In fourteen of the sixteen industry groups used in this study the percentage of the firms which indicated the degree of supervision was negligible fell within a range of 20 per cent to 40 per cent of the firms in the industry. Similarly, in twelve of the sixteen industries the percentage of the firms which indicated the degree of supervision was extensive fell within a range of zero to 20 per cent of the firms in the industry. Moreover, there does not appear to be any difference in degrees of supervision among primary and primary manufacturing on the one hand and secondary manufacturing on the other, broadly defining the former as indicated earlier. The degree of supervision does differ, but only moderately, when the data are classified by the nature of the subsidiary's products, compared to the products of the affiliate. In view of small numbers in some categories the firms whose products are identical with those of the affiliate should be combined with those reporting marginal differences, and similarly for those reporting products which are substantially modified and those which are not comparable. The first two groups combined reported 31 per cent of their number was negligibly supervised as against 42 per cent for the second two groups combined. The first two groups together reported 18 per cent of their number extensively supervised, as against 13 per cent for the latter two groups. These differences remain when considered within the three size groups of firms. Finally, there is a tendency for more supervision where the Canadian subsidiary is the only foreign subsidiary or one of a few. Thus the proportion of firms which is extensively supervised declines as one moves from situations where the parent has only the Canadian subsidiary to those where there are subsidiaries in up to five other countries and to situations where there are more than five other subsidiaries. These distinctions stand out quite clearly when the data are considered within three size groups.

The second approach to the determinants of the degree of supervision is to note the circumstances surrounding it, and changes in it over time, as reported by the respondents themselves in approximately 125 separate and relevant observations in another part of the questionnaire.[39] One of the factors mentioned as determining the degree of supervision is the recentness of establishment of the company in Canada, and about thirty replies referred to this. It is a common pattern with an entirely new subsidiary to send a number of senior management and technical personnel to Canada to establish and supervise administrative and production processes and to help train

---

[39]Two related questions were asked. Less than one-third of the respondents reported there were special circumstances affecting the degree of supervision now accorded to the firm, while close to half indicated there were no such special circumstances. In a separate question less than one-quarter indicated that there had been a significant change over time in the degree of supervision, many of them indicating the reasons for the change, while half of the respondents indicated explicitly that there was no such change. A substantial portion of the remainder in both questions gave replies which simply affirmed the degree of decentralization. For present purposes the relevant responses to these two questions have been combined where information was given on the reasons for the degree of supervision, or of changes in it, after deleting a number of replies which were unclear or not directly relevant.

Canadian personnel.[40] After the initial period of establishment and operation these may be withdrawn except for a chief executive officer and perhaps one or two others to assure continuity of procedures in line with parent policies. In a few years these persons may also return to the parent firm or go to another subsidiary while Canadian officers take over their positions, although some of them settle in Canada for their entire remaining careers. Thus the difficulties of the initial period of operation, and the inexperience of local management with regard to the technical processes or to the general administrative policies of the parent, may lead to close contacts in the early years. About one-quarter of the responses used in the present context indicated that supervision was extensive currently because of this, or had declined over time as these circumstances changed. Many of these replies emphasized the growing confidence over time of parent company executives in the resident officers as the experience and skills of the latter increased.[41]

Equally prevalent were replies which emphasized the policies of parent company executives toward decentralization of responsibilities in general. In most cases this appeared to be a deliberate response on the part of these officials to other factors, such as the growth in the size and complexity of the domestic and foreign operations, a corresponding belief in the need for more flexible administration to meet quite different local needs and problems, and the good fortune to have, or the wish to attract, competent management. Some company officials believed no such rational process was

---

[40]This is by no means the universal procedure. A number of both large and small firms in this study began operations with Canadians in the executive positions. Sometimes these persons were working in the international firm when appointed to Canada, at other times they had no connection with it. Management and technical liaison is likely to be close in the early years, nevertheless, particularly where processes are complex and the difficulties of establishment great.

[41]It need hardly be emphasized that not all of the new firms are closely supervised nor all of the older ones negligibly supervised. The following comments from different parts of the questionnaire from one of the respondent firms, which had been in operation for only a few years, will make this point clear: "U.S. policy clearly states that the Canadian subsidiary is to be as independent as possible regarding policies and product. No U.S. citizen to be a member of the executive staff operating the company. The (non-resident) president is an exception on a temporary basis. . . . Parent company executives are available to act in a staff capacity to render advice only. There are no specific written reports required. Information is requested and given at a frequency of approximately five such requests per year. Responsibilities are defined fully and are so written as to infer independence. . . . Decentralization is at a maximum. Financial control is based on an annual budget for capital expense. Control of operating expense is in the (Canadian) company's hands entirely. This control applies to all items listed with the exception of capital expansion which requires a meeting of both the Canadian and U.S. boards of directors."

TABLE 17
DEGREE OF SUPERVISION CLASSIFIED BY SELECTED CHARACTERISTICS

Characteristic	Degree of supervision			Number of replies*
	Negligible	Partly	Extensively	
		(% distribution by rows)		
Age				
1 — 10 years	30	43	26	119
11 — 21	43	47	10	30
22 — 41	34	51	15	59
42 and over	29	66	6	35
Total	33	49	19	243
Type of business				
Assembly	32	46	21	28
Extractive	20	30	50	10
Semi-fabricated products	54	21	25	24
Fully processed or manufactured	29	54	17	165
Integrated	42	58	—	19
Total	33	49	18	246
Product compared with affiliate				
Identical	30	51	19	146
Marginally different	32	51	17	65
Substantially modified	40	40	20	15
Not comparable	44	50	6	16
Total	32	50	17	242
Range of products compared with affiliate				
Wider	50	50	—	20
About the same	36	43	21	77
Majority	23	62	15	66
Minority	38	35	28	29
Only a few	21	54	25	24
Total	32	50	19	216†
Number of other subsidiaries of parent				
None	34	40	26	80
One to five	29	56	15	82
Over five	34	56	10	62
Total	32	49	18	224

* The shortfall from 280 reflects thirty-three firms which did not reply to the question on degree of supervision and a varying remainder which did not reply to the other questions. In calculating percentages these non-replies were disregarded. The actual non-replies by most sub groups are available in other tables in this volume.

† Excludes sixteen firms replying that products were not comparable or giving other replies.

involved in their case: as one put it, the parent company's officials were simply too busy to pay much attention to the subsidiary, so that decentralization had come "by default." It was also clear in some cases that pressure from officers of the subsidiary had helped to establish a decentralized operation, though in several of these the related evidence indicated that there was some real basis for it, such as quite different market situations. It should be added that, while policies tending toward decentralization predominated, international firms with centralized policies of international administration were not rare. For example, in most cases where responsibility exists by divisions in Canada to the corresponding division in the parent company it gives way in time to centralization of responsibility within a Canadian head office.[42] Some firms have reversed this process, however, in an attempt to exercise more direct supervision by the parent's central executive staff on functional divisions both in their domestic and foreign operations; for example, to ensure more uniform procedures and informational checks and, it is hoped, increase profitability. Some of the international firms where owner and management interests are closely linked or identical appeared also to involve a more personal and often a more extensive supervision of subsidiary operations than was the case for many firms where ownership of the parent is dispersed.

In sixteen further cases the respondents believed that the existence of a substantial minority and, on occasion, equal resident ownership was a key circumstance in minimizing the degree of supervision. In all but three or four of these the minority or equal resident ownership was concentrated completely or largely in a firm or a few individuals. In effect, these were joint ventures. Only a few firms with an unconcentrated minority shareholding drew attention to this as a special circumstance minimizing the degree of supervision, usually by indicating that the freedom of action which existed before a partial takeover had carried over to some degree afterwards. It was much more common to point to a concentrated minority shareholding, and strong directors representing it, as a factor in minimizing supervision. In a number of cases, in fact, the active supervision of the subsidiary was by the minority or equal stock-owning resident firm, within an agreed framework of policies between the two parent companies.

---

[42]Few of the firms in this study indicated that the departments or divisions of the Canadian firm were reporting to particular product departments or divisions of the parent firm. Technical liaison with such divisions might be very close, but on general policies they reported to their Canadian central management. Where the Canadian units were largely responsible to product divisions of the parent they appeared usually to be relatively new and tightly-controlled operations.

Another factor which was noted as reducing the degree of supervision was special or different products and processes in the subsidiary for part or most of the output. One consequence of a different product range or different technical requirements is that the production and related skills are developed only or mainly in Canada.[43] A more important result in the context of the present section is the fact that the firms are non-competitive to at least that extent, with the result that actual and potential conflicts of interest are reduced. Conversely, a number of companies referred specifically to the need for integration of machinery and equipment, for close quality controls, for special skills and complex techniques available only from the parent; that is, to the need for close liaison because of identical and highly engineered products. The importance of this can be stated in another way by referring to the experience of several firms included in the interviews. These had acquired many of the attributes of "autonomy" in the fifties, including completely resident and Canadian personnel, large public stock issues and formal decentralization of decision-making. Because of very similar products and processes, however, and the highly technical nature of the products, the ties with the parent were as close as ever. Altogether, eighteen companies mentioned the nature of the product as a key to the degree of supervision. Twelve other respondents stated that the profits and general performance of the Canadian firm were instrumental in determining the degree of supervision. In most of these the degree of supervision had been reduced or was small because of favourable results, in several the reverse had occurred because of losses.[44] The remainder of the 125 replies represented a variety of situations. In four, for example, heavy spending programs combined with the need for capital from the parent had led to increased supervision for the time being; only three firms mentioned distance from the parent as a factor in the degree of supervision; some referred to a closer interest by the parent because of major market changes; and still other firms mentioned other particular situations which, in the view of the respondents, significantly affected the degree of supervision.

This is probably as far as one should push these replies reflecting the

---

[43]A difference in product alone may not be a sufficient guarantee of decentralization. Several primary resource producers, for example, noted that integrated policies and operations were required between the firms since the parent was wholly dependent on the Canadian firm as a source of supply.

[44]The danger of emphasizing single-variable explanations is evident from the fact that executives of the parent companies in two cases took a greater interest in the affairs of the subsidiary *because* its profit position improved, and in one of these cases a greater degree of supervision was definitely involved!

views and experience of the respondents. Some of these groups of reasons clearly overlap, some are perhaps closer to effect than to basic causes, and some firms gave some minor reasons as well as major ones in explaining the degree of supervision. Certain broad conclusions can be drawn together by way of summary, and their implications explored.

In the first place, the actual degree of supervision at a point of time will reflect a complex of variables which are not easily separated and weighed. In addition, the degree of involvement by the officers of the parent will ebb and flow as circumstances change. For example, a substantial and continuing financial loss can lead to more direct management and technical involvement, whether invited by the subsidiary's officers or not, and possibly some changes in the management of the subsidiary, until the loss is corrected or the firm wound up or sold.

Second, if one can speak of a trend factor here subject to what has just been said, it would be in terms of a reduction of the parent's involvement. Those replies which indicated a significant decrease in the parent's involvement over time exceeded very considerably those which indicated that the reverse had occurred.[45] There is a marked preponderance of decreases even if one deletes the relatively new firms which are experiencing more freedom of operations after the close supervision usually found in the early stages of operation. This may seem like a surprising conclusion in view of the major advances in management control techniques, communications, the gathering and analysis of information, and other developments which might be expected to lead to increased centralization. It can only be suggested that some of these factors may be offset by other developments such as more experienced resident officers and increasing size and complexity of both parent and subsidiary operations. It is also well to repeat that the subsidiaries generally remain accountable to their major or sole shareholders, at least on major policy. The reduction in the degree of direct parental supervision and involvement will not end varying degrees of conformity on major policy in most cases, as noted in the discussion on degrees of decentralization, as well as the technical ties not yet discussed here.

Third, purely human factors necessarily play a significant role in inter-management relationships. The relationships worked out in geographically

---

[45]It should be recalled that most firms replied that no significant change had occurred over time in the degree of involvement by the parent in the operations and policies of the subsidiary. In most cases, however, these were already subject to a negligible or partial, rather than extensive, degree of supervision as judged by replies to an earlier question.

decentralized international firms are likely to be particularly important. Nor should one underestimate the fact that the personal stature and ambitions of the officers of the firms involved may often be a key factor in decentralization. It is not difficult to find situations where the degree of decentralization exists partly because of the particular lack or availability of competent executives for the subsidiary, and, considering the exodus of talent to the parent, for the centre as well. One should not discount such human factors. Indeed, the generally decentralized status of some aspects of the operations of subsidiary companies reflects diseconomies of scale with respect to management, in the sense that personal supervision cannot effectively be extended beyond certain broad policy areas because of human limitations. More generally, increasing attention has been given in economic theory to the importance of managerial discretion with regard to the operations of the large corporation. One result has been a smaller emphasis on the influence of market forces generally and more emphasis on the personal and group objectives of the executives.[46] Yet it must also be emphasized that the interview and questionnaire responses to questions on the degree of supervision suggest strongly that the particular situation in which the subsidiary finds itself in terms of its environment is also highly important. Enough evidence is given in this chapter and what follows to suggest that such factors as the recentness of establishment of the firm, the technical nature of its products, the market and cost situations it faces, and the overall size and complexity of the international operation, as well as the management philosophy of the parent, are important in assessing the scope which the resident management may have in determining the affairs of the subsidiary.

Fourth, it will be clear that no particular degree of decentralization of decision-making will suit all subsidiary-parent situations in any given period of time. The degree of involvement by the parent at any given time is largely a means to profitable operation of the subsidiary, not typically an end in itself. As such, it is one of the key imports associated with direct investment. Whether through executive and board contacts on policy, technical liaison, training programs, and in other ways, the skills and experience and contacts of the parent are transmitted to the subsidiary and, in varying degrees,

---

[46]See, for example, Oliver E. Williamson, "Managerial Discretion and Business Behavior," *The American Economic Review*, Vol. LIII, No. 5 (December, 1963), pp. 1032-1057. The problems of co-ordination in the large managerial firm, particularly in the relations between different levels of management, are emphasized in R. Joseph Monsen, Jr. and Anthony Downs, "A Theory of Large Managerial Firms," *Journal of Political Economy*, Vol. LXXIII, No. 3 (June 1965), pp. 221-236.

to the economy generally. Succeeding chapters will give further details on aspects of these transfers.[47] This transfer of skills is not costless, of course, since management fees of various kinds, royalties for use of patented knowledge, and ultimately profits are returned to the parent firm. Much more will be said about this later.[48] What needs to be emphasized in the present context is that no one pattern of decentralization will suit the best economic interests of all subsidiaries or of the Canadian economy. The close involvement of the parent is often advantageous in the early stages of such investment: it may be advantageous at some later stages when, for example, the subsidiary has suffered a string of losses or when it is about to embark on major developments regarding which the parent already has some experience. In this context, so long as the improvement in the position of the subsidiary is not offset by an equal loss elsewhere in the economy, as would happen where the improvement involved the establishment of a long-term monopoly position, it is difficult to see how the domestic economy would suffer by such involvement. The only point of substance which has been raised in this respect is that the supervision of the subsidiary necessarily involves the resolution of conflicts of interest where products or markets overlap, and that such resolutions may minimize domestic growth while still being consistent with the maximization of the position of the international firm. Usually the explicit or implicit view here is that ownership as such makes a difference in resource use; this view will be examined in various places in this book but especially in Chapter 9. It has also been suggested that the given degree of centralization in decision-making on major policy necessarily removes from the officers of many Canadian firms the opportunity to develop their skills at the highest level of management. No doubt there is something to this, but it should be offset against the fact that much of the decision-making is joint rather than purely one-sided and that there are rather substantial gains from the import and training of managers.

Finally, while stressing the fact that a significant degree of decentrali-

---

[47]For an unusually thorough and revealing study of the impact of American managerial techniques, in this case on British industry, see Dunning, *op. cit.*, Chaps. 4-9.
[48]While profits earned and dividends paid by direct investment companies are available and will be presented in Chapter 8, less is known about other types of payments. *The Corporations and Labour Unions Returns Act, Report for 1962*, pp. 40-41, shows payments to non-residents by *all reporting corporations* whether owned by residents or non-residents as follows: management and administrative fees, $61 million; salaries, fees and other remuneration to officers and directors, $14 million; royalties of all kinds, $58 million; and payments for research and development, $35 million. Other types of payments are also involved.

zation is involved in many cases and that there has been an increase in decentralization over a period of time, it is well to recognize the limits to this process. The limits are only partly inherent in the fact that ownership of capital is involved. They lie also in the fact that, as much of this book makes clear, direct investment is an extension of management and technical skills. Neither the owners of capital nor their managers in the parent are likely to surrender the right of review of major decisions in most cases, however much they may encourage the local managers to plan and initiate proposals and to participate in parts of the review. The desire to protect the investment, and in this process to bring into play the influence of centralized managerial resources in maximizing the return to the overall firm, will ensure this is so. Even without much direct supervision the use of the parent's products and techniques will often necessarily continue to exert a strong indirect influence on the actual range of choice open to local management. It is not our intention to deny the influence of the many environmental factors, both private and public, which condition the operation of the subsidiary in its Canadian setting. It is necessary to point out, however, that beyond certain limits the case for a maximum degree of decentralization of decision-making at the national level becomes essentially a case against direct investment as such. The case for or against this must rest in part on the actual results of the decisions made in the context of the direct investment firm. The ensuing chapters are devoted to an analysis of the decision-making process and its results in a number of key economic areas.

4
The Exports of
Subsidiary Companies

Direct investment is closely bound up with foreign trade. The original investment by the parent firm often results from barriers to imports imposed by the recipient country, particularly in the case of manufactures. This forces the foreign parent to cease shipments of its products in whole or in part and to manufacture or assemble them in a subsidiary or branch. Direct investment then becomes, in effect, a necessary alternative to exports. In these circumstances it should not be surprising that the parent will continue to export components and finished goods to the subsidiary wherever the legal barriers and economic costs of so doing permit such export. This trade is likely to be relatively one-sided in aggregate, at least for assembly and manufacturing subsidiaries. Where a subsidiary has been created because of tariffs or such economic forces as transport costs, it is unlikely to export for some time after its establishment, if ever. The fact that it requires legal or natural protection against imports in itself may mean it cannot enter foreign markets on a competitive basis, in contrast with the parent which may have been exporting to this and other markets for some time. This point raises the much larger one of the relative efficiency of parent and subsidiary, a point which will be considered in Chapter 7. To the extent that some specialization of production is possible between the parent and subsidiary, a two-way trade between them becomes possible even at a very early stage. Moreover, comparative advantage is not a static phenomenon. A subsidiary which is initially unable to export competitively may with time develop some advantage with regard to some portion of its product, leading to export. A more obvious example of the relationship between direct investment and foreign trade occurs where the parent company establishes a foreign subsidiary to supply it with a raw material necessary to its production process. It should be added that there is no necessity for the foreign trade of the subsidiary to remain concentrated in the parent and its affiliates, however much this may have been a factor in developing it. Contacts with suppliers and customers of the foreign affiliates, or with firms having no connection with them, may spread the foreign trade of the subsidiary. One of the major purposes of this chapter and the next is to explore the extent to which subsidiary companies engage in foreign trade and the directions which such trade takes. Exports and imports as a percentage of output, the area distribution of such trade, and the extent to which it is with affiliates will all be considered. Some aspects of the organization for foreign trade in such companies will also be considered. A number of questions or assumptions about the foreign trade of such companies should be clarified in the process.

One of the key questions or assumptions has aroused substantial controversy in Canada over the past decade. Put briefly, it is very frequently alleged that the subsidiary company, *because* it is foreign-owned, tends to export less and to import more than it might. Since some firms export a very substantial volume of primary or semi-fabricated products the argument is usually put in terms of exports of manufactures not directly related to a significant natural resource base. If such allegations are correct there could be a significant built-in tendency to trade deficits in the Canadian economy, a barrier to efficient industrial expansion and to the implementation of commercial policy, and resource misallocation which is analogous to that resulting from cartel arrangements between independent firms. In brief, there would be a considerable offset to the gains from foreign investment if only because it would reduce the optimum size of the Canadian firm. The analysis below will deal with exports but much of it applies to related questions regarding imports.

The view that foreign-owned firms are biased against exports, particularly of manufactures, has found growing expression in Canada over the past decade particularly as a result of views expressed to and by the Royal Commission on Canada's Economic Prospects. This view has steadily and frequently been echoed by the members of successive governments since that Report.[1] It was explicitly advanced as part of the reason for the changes in the withholding tax in 1963 and 1964 which were noted in

---

[1]It would be tedious to list the literally scores of speeches by Ministers, beginning particularly in 1957, in which the allegedly poor export and import performance of subsidiary companies is mentioned. This theme occurs particularly frequently in the speeches of the Ministers of Finance, Trade and Commerce, and Industry.

Chapter 1. The expectation from such legislation was that some firms now wholly or largely owned by non-residents will avoid the higher taxes applicable to them by meeting the requirements of the act, and that the effect of a significant minority shareholding and of a minimum number of resident directors will be to encourage the use and development of domestic production and other facilities, including export capacity.[2] At least one federal government department has collected some data on the export interests of subsidiary firms (among others) and is engaged in a campaign to encourage such firms and their parents to increase exports from Canada.[3] The question of export-import relations of parent and subsidiary companies has also come up in a number of policy contexts. The export incentives for automobiles and parts introduced in the early sixties, for example, appear to involve, among other things, an assumption that parent companies are not interested in specialization of output within the international firm given both the fact of foreign ownership and the legal and economic obstacles involved, and that they require a substantial financial inducement to achieve this.[4] Again, at the aggregative policy level, there has some-

---

[2]This, presumably, in spite of the fact that the enforced sharing of profits from exports with minority shareholders would tend to have the opposite effect insofar as the establishment of new capacity is concerned. The same result occurs if the non-resident owned firms with existing capacity do not meet the requirements of the act and continue to pay dividends abroad: the prospective net rate of return on such assets based in Canada is reduced by the legislation, and hence so is the expansion of export capacity in Canada.

[3]See, for example, the statement by the parliamentary secretary to the Minister of Trade and Commerce as reported on the editorial page of the *Financial Post* for June 6, 1964. What may be a not entirely hypothetical example of the procedures of the Department of Trade and Commerce in this respect can be found in the example contributed by Gordon Huson, pp. 547-554 of Fayerweather, *op. cit.* Note also the following statement by the Minister of Trade and Commerce for Canada: "In the ordinary course of its trade activities the department has a continuing interest in knowing what are the export policies of the Canadian companies which seek assistance and where control of these policies lies. This information is requested in the questionnaire which must be completed before a company can be included in the department's confidential exporter's directory. Before we undertake assistance in promoting exports for the subsidiary of a foreign manufacturing company we have to seek an understanding, and readily obtain as a rule any needed assurance that the assistance which we extend will not be diverted to the benefit of production and employment in some other country, but only used for the benefit of Canadian industry." This was in response to an earlier statement by Mr. Harold E. Winch on the subject of restrictions on exports of subsidiary firms. See Canada, House of Commons, *Debates*, June 25, 1959, pp. 5188-5189 and July 15, 1959, pp. 6095-6096.

[4]The legislation was intended to improve the balance of payments and to create employment, and to give producers of automobiles and of parts an incentive to achieve more specialization, longer runs, and lower costs. The basic tariff was 17½

times been an attempt to relate the slower economic growth of the late fifties to, among other things, the assumed limitation of the market horizons of foreign-owned firms.[5] Finally, there have been external pressures on the parent-subsidiary relationship in an attempt to affect the volume and direction of parent-subsidiary trade. The most widely discussed cases have been pressures by the United States government or its agencies in connection with trade with the Peoples' Republic of China, and the "guidelines" to American-owned subsidiaries designed to improve the balance of payments of the United States.

The evidence on both export and import policies and practices of foreign-owned companies is very limited. The existing analytical and empirical evidence will be considered briefly before considering the material from the present study. It is perhaps well to emphasize again that the great preponderance of firms involved here is in manufacturing and/or assembly, as indicated in table 5. In various places the number of firms whose operations are largely in the primary or semi-fabricated stages of production is given so that the effect of these firms on the results may be clearer. The industrial distributions may also aid in this regard.

---

per cent on vehicles or parts though some important components, including engines and automatic transmissions, paid 25 per cent. A long list of parts not made in Canada entered free, thereby increasing the effective protection of dutiable components. The policy introduced in 1962 and extended in 1963 provided unilaterally that for every extra dollar of Canadian content of increased exports for automobiles and parts above the level of such exports for the year ending October 31, 1962, the Canadian automobile manufacturer earned remission of duty on a dollar of imported automobiles or parts. The 1965 agreement with the United States eliminated the United States duty on cars and most parts for all importers and the Canadian tariffs on imports for qualified automobile manufacturers. Both countries attached content provisions, with the Canadian producers also agreeing to raise the value added in Canadian manufacturing of automobiles and parts so as to increase the Canadian share of the North American market. For a full discussion of these policies see Harry G. Johnson, "The New Tariff Policy for the Automotive Industry" in *Business Quarterly*, Vol. 29, No. 5 (Spring, 1964). See also Johnson's article "The Bladen Plan for Increased Protection of the Canadian Automotive Industry," and the "Comment" by Neil M. MacDonald, in *The Canadian Journal of Economics and Political Science*, Vol. 29, pp. 217-238 and pp. 505-515. See also H. E. English, "Automobility—Predicament or Precedent," *The Canadian Banker*, Vol. 72, No. 2 (Summer, 1965), pp. 23-35.

[5]See the article by Roger Dehem, "The Economics of Stunted Growth," in *The Canadian Journal of Economics and Political Science*, Vol. 28, No. 4 (November, 1962), pp. 502-510. Dehem generally blames the tariff and lack of growth orientation to economic policy for the slower growth, but suggests also that the affiliated status of subsidiary companies usually prevents them from entering world markets and serves therefore to limit the impetus to growth generally.

The Evidence on Private International Trade Restriction

The impression that foreign-owned firms do not have the freedom to sell or buy wherever it is most profitable to do so arises from the fact of the existence of affiliates abroad. As members of the same international firm the various affiliates may well look to one another for markets or supplies, insofar as the degree of vertical integration and other characteristics permit, and may also expect or demand that open competition not take place between them. Such is certainly a widespread assumption in the literature about such firms.[6] Nor is it entirely illogical that this is so given the financial, technical, product, personnel and other relationships between the affiliates. The existence of such intra-enterprise arrangements in markets is not in doubt. What needs to be asked is their prevalence, the reasons for them, what the effects are in both short and long periods on Canadian exports, and whether the effects are only the result of foreign ownership as such.

Fundamentally two assumptions are involved in the criticisms of foreign-owned firms. The first is that there is a conflict between national and international interest when considering the social desirability of private economic action. Such a conflict may arise because, from the strictly national point of view, only the direct and indirect effects on the welfare of residents would be taken into account, while from the international point of view the gains or losses to non-residents should also be considered.[7] The second assumption is that the locus of ownership of the national firm will have an effect on the result. It is assumed that non-resident owned Canadian firms will be more likely to overlook the national interest in making private economic decisions than would their resident-owned counterparts, because they must take international interests into account at least to the extent that these are represented by their affiliates abroad.

The first assumption need not detain us here, except to note that its modern application has generally been to the foreign trade and investment relations between economically developed and underdeveloped countries. Specifically, it is suggested that foreign investment from the former in export-oriented natural resource industries in the latter leads to a form of

---

[6]See, for example, the case of the "Carmen Manufacturing Company," by E. R. Barlow, in Fayerweather, *op. cit.*, pp. 554-558. Kingman Brewster repeats this theme frequently in *Antitrust and American Business Abroad*, McGraw-Hill, New York, 1958; see pp. 182, 184, and 213 for example.

[7]The point is developed by Tibor Scitovsky, at the end of his article, "Two Concepts of External Economies," *The Journal of Political Economy*, April, 1954, pp. 143-151.

development where benefits accrue largely to the developed countries because of unfavourable changes in terms of trade over time between exports of manufactures and of primary products. Moreover, it is suggested that internal development is not aided by such foreign investment and trade because the resulting stimuli cannot penetrate the large non-commercial sectors of many economically backward countries, and indeed may even be hindered by the diversion of resources from potential manufacturing industry.[8] Whatever relevance such views may have for the problems of economically backward countries their literal application to Canada is limited by the fact that much foreign investment has gone into manufacturing and because the essential assumption of a dual economy, of commercial and non-commercial sectors, is missing. Indeed, there is a growing literature which suggests that international private investment between relatively developed countries under competitive conditions may tend to be excessive from the point of view of the national economic welfare of the lending country, partly because the general developmental benefits which go with capital largely accrue to the borrowing country.[9] Nevertheless, the juxtaposition of a large and small country with close economic ties which inevitably influence the smaller country relatively more, the natural advantage of primary resource-oriented production in Canada, and questions about where the developmental benefits actually accrue, have all created a variant of the position noted.

It is a frequent complaint in Canada that foreign investment has tended to concentrate in industries closely related to natural resources, and to export these in a raw or semi-manufactured state. The argument is heard most frequently when the rate of unemployment rises, but it is combined with a desire for more secondary manufacturing and the external economies assumed to come with it, and at times with a desire for the increased political independence assumed to result from a reduced reliance on exports or on primary exports. The argument appears to overlook the very large foreign investment in secondary manufacturing industries as noted in Chapter 1 above, as well as to underestimate the extent to which foreign

---

[8]There is a considerable literature on this, particularly in the past decade or so where it merges into other questions of development such as external economies and balanced growth. An early presentation appears in H. W. Singer, "The Distribution of Gains Between Investing and Borrowing Countries," *Papers and Proceedings of the American Economic Association*, Vol. 40, 1950, pp. 473-485. Its relationship to foreign trade theory is more explicitly developed in the last section of the paper by W. Arthur Lewis, "Economic Development with Unlimited Supplies of Labour," *The Manchester Review*, May, 1954.

[9]See footnote five in Chapter 1.

tariffs and other legal barriers inhibit the development of more processing of primary products for export. In any case, the present analysis will concentrate on exports of manufactures where the exporter has affiliates abroad. Not only do the present data lend themselves better to this case, but the question of primary product exports involves special factors and has received far more attention in the literature on Canada.[10]

The second assumption noted above was that the locus of ownership of the national firm will affect the outcome.[11] It will be assumed that the international firm is interested in maximizing its profits in its overall operations over time, within the context of demand and cost considerations and the framework of law, domestic and foreign, within which it operates. In such circumstances it can be demonstrated that the case for private export restriction is at best a short-run case. Assume that facilities for producing identical or almost identical manufactures exist in the Canadian subsidiary and in the parent abroad, facilities established in Canada because of (let us say) natural or tariff obstacles to the movement of goods. It will also be assumed that the parent's unit cost of production is below that of its Canadian subsidiary, for in Chapter 7 this will be shown to be the most frequent case. Finally, it will be assumed that major decisions on plant expansion, product development, and marketing in third countries are effectively subject to the veto of executives of the parent firm. Unless distribution costs are lower from the subsidiary, or unless it enjoys a tariff or similar legal preference in third markets, the parent will continue to export to third markets in order to maximize its overall profit. Should distribution costs or tariff preferences change so as to favour the subsidiary, the subsidiary should export if the parent is to maximize its overall profit. The

---

[10]For a discussion of the history and problems involved in controlling exports of pulp, nickel, petroleum and natural gas, see Hugh G. J. Aitken, "The Changing Structure of the Canadian Economy, with Particular Reference to the Influence of the United States," in Aitken (ed.) *The American Economic Impact on Canada.* He concludes that Canadian policy in securing more processing for export has succeeded only where it reinforced other locational advantages which affect business costs, and where it has accelerated a transfer of processing facilities that would have occurred anyway, albeit more slowly. For a discussion of the problems of foreign investment in natural resources as seen from the point of view of the investors, see the *Report* of the President's Materials Policy Commission chaired by William S. Paley, Washington, D.C., 1952, Vol. 1, Ch. 12. There is a good general discussion of the issues regarding foreign investment in raw materials in Chandler Morse, "Potentials and Hazards of Direct International Investment in Raw Materials," in Marion Clawson (ed.), *Natural Resources and International Development,* Johns Hopkins Press, 1964.
[11]In some, but not all, respects the analysis of the next few pages follows that developed with the aid of the present writer in Brecher-Reisman, *op. cit.,* pp. 140-145.

same is true where taxation differences between the two countries dictate that more of the overall firm's profits should be generated in Canada, at least in the first instance. If the above is granted, then the same is true of a clear and continuing advantage in production costs which the Canadian firm develops over time, either because of differential changes in production costs in the two countries over time or of greater efficiency in handling special runs. The same is true if the parent or subsidiary develops in time any design advantages more suitable to the different mix of production factors of the subsidiary. The overall firm maximizes its total net income, assuming an efficient operation, when the rate of return on its different parts is the same at the margin. Activity in each part should tend to be carried to the point where the last unit of investment in each part is yielding the same return, discounted for risk of capital loss. The same principles apply to entry by the subsidiary into the parent's own market because of improvements in its production or distribution costs, including tariff changes in the latter term. There is no difference in principle between a subsidiary entering the parent's markets in third countries and entering its domestic market.

Such would be the result if the parent were interested in maximizing its profits for the international firm over time. In the short run, that is, while existing assets have not been fully depreciated and where there may not be alternate uses for given plant, the result may be somewhat different. Except to the extent that it can find alternative uses for existing facilities, the parent may delay the construction of new facilities in Canada designed to serve the existing markets in third countries or the parent's domestic market. The logic of such a delay is clear if one recognizes that the parent has incurred fixed costs, not yet fully depreciated, which may not be compensated by the increased return it receives on exports from its subsidiary. If the projected average total cost of production of the new facilities in Canada is below the average variable cost of production of existing facilities in the parent, it will pay overall to construct new facilities in Canada to serve the foreign market even if the facilities there have just been constructed themselves and even if there is no return on them in alternative uses. Other things being equal, the transfer of facilities to Canada should be faster where fixed costs are not large relative to variable costs, the plant is divisible into a number of relatively small units, alternate uses are available for the parent's facilities, excess capacity does not exist more generally, and/or the overall market for the product is expanding.[12]

---

[12]Clearly it is difficult to generalize on the point of time at which existing assets may be scrapped or be considered worth replacing, given not only such factors as those

The same considerations will apply in the case of an industry, dominated by foreign-owned firms, in which Canada achieves some clear and continuing advantage in production or distribution, including tariff and similar legal changes over time. Much of the industry should tend to shift to Canada, including production for export, subject to the qualifications about time and other variables noted above.[13] One significant addition emerges when one considers the level of the industry rather than the firm, namely, that competition expedites the change. New entrants to the industry will enter at the point where average total cost of production falls below expected market price, and where the return is better than for alternate uses of capital. In any case, since they are new entrants, they will not have to weigh the desirability of new investment against assets already held by them in the industry.[14]

The analysis so far points to the conclusion that any delay involved in the location of economically justifiable plant in Canada to serve the export market would be a function not of foreign control as such, but rather of the lack of effective competition including any barriers to entry to the industry.[15] It is worth emphasizing that the argument regarding fixed costs is simply a reflection of the fact that plant has already been built elsewhere, and that it is strictly a short-term hindrance to development of economically justifiable facilities in Canada. Nor would a resident-owned firm deviate from this. It could not escape the necessity of having an economically justifiable cost and demand situation in the first instance. It

---

noted in the text but also the degree of competition, the age of the existing equipment, or simply the inertia and institutional obstacles to change. Economic literature deals with this point in various contexts; for example, in the question whether the existence of older capital equipment is a handicap to rapid current economic growth. For the recent literature on this and a specific analysis from British economic history, see C. P. Kindleberger, "Obsolesence and Technical Change," *Bulletin of the Oxford Institute of Statistics*, August, 1961, pp. 281-297.

[13]In addition, it should be noted that eventually all of the industry would shift if unit costs were decreasing or constant, but part only if they were increasing, assuming barriers to entry do not prohibit expansion.

[14]No doubt they will run into serious competition from existing producers, especially if demands are relatively stable. The existing producers have nothing to lose, so long as operating costs are covered, by cutting prices below average total cost to meet or block such competition. There may also be other effective barriers to entry.

[15]It should be added that some United States judicial decisions may reinforce this conclusion, insofar as they suggest that market restriction within the international firm may be illegal under United States law in certain circumstances, particularly where the subsidiary is not wholly owned by the parent. For a discussion of the cases and probable limitations on the doctrine of intra-enterprise conspiracy, see Kingman Brewster, *Antitrust and American Business Abroad*, Ch. 8.

could, as a new entrant, avoid the problem of having to take into account
its own fixed investment, but so can new entrants which are foreign-owned.
Neither could escape the competition which is likely to come from existing
producers anxious to protect existing overheads and to block or meet
potential entrants to the industry. Finally, if a resident-owned firm had, or
was considering, investment abroad, it would face a similar set of choices
on the location and timing of expansion. One should not underestimate the
time lags involved in absolute or relative shifts of an industry where investment is lumpy, particularly where important auxiliary facilities or services
develop in proximity to it. Nor should one underestimate the barriers to
entry to an industry given established producers, specific barriers such as
patents, the financial investment necessary, and so on. Nevertheless, the
analysis suggests that the economic efficiency of Canadian production, the
problems of distribution (including foreign tariffs), and the degree of competition are the determining criteria for the actuality and the speed of any
transfer to Canada for export, and not the nature of the ownership of the
firm. Even where competition is not effective the parent firm will delay the
transfer to Canada only in the short run.

For the parent firm which is maximizing its international profits, private
export restriction makes sense only in the short run. It is important to note
also that the protection for higher-cost facilities works both ways. The effect
of such private trade restrictions is also to give temporary protection to the
Canadian subsidiaries from their foreign affiliates, when competition from
outside the international firm permits. Too often the assumption in discussions on this point in Canada is that the protection runs only in the
reverse direction, an assumption which would be true only if the unit costs
of the subsidiaries were generally lower than those of the affiliates.[16]

16An example of how the parent may itself be limited with regard to exports to
Canada which would compete with its subsidiary's lines is given in the *Report of the
Commissioner*, Combines Investigation Act, *Rubber Products*, p. 172 (Ottawa, 1952).
Admittedly, the restraining factor here in part was the regulations of the Canadian
industry association with regard to imports. The relevant part of the letter to the
parent company dated May 1, 1947, follows: "The information given in your (export
division of the parent company at Akron, Ohio) letter of April 25th is disturbing to
us, from an Industry viewpoint, as we shall have to explain this shipment to other
interested parties, if it comes up, and we expect it will come up. We have had an
understanding, for many years, that no Mechanical Rubber Goods products would
be shipped into Canada, that can be made in Canada by any of the companies who
make Mechanical Rubber Goods. Fire hose is made in Canada by 4 companies
besides ourselves. We shall explain this shipment of 1,500 ft., 2-½" Double Jacket
Fire Hose to the other interested parties, if it comes up, but we must have assurance
that our policy and arrangements with the Industry in Canada are understood by the

In practice it is not difficult to see why private export restrictions exist. There may be some logic to them in the short run in order to protect sunk costs, particularly if competition from other firms is not effective. Moreover, the concept of profit maximization assumes knowledge of costs and demands, present and prospective. It is not at all unlikely that ignorance or errors will lead to decisions on expansion and capital allocation which are wrong from the point of view of the firm itself, and which commit it for a time at least to a course of action it would gladly reverse if that were possible. Such problems are obviously magnified in enterprises covering many firms in many different countries where, nevertheless, some rational central long-term policy of allocation of funds and of expansion of the parts is attempted. There are institutional barriers to profit maximization which have the same effect, such as pressures by various governments, labour unions, and other groups in the respective countries of operation, sometimes requiring different investment decisions or different timing of investment decisions than the firm might make simply to maximize its profits. From the point of view of management relationships within the international firm, moreover, it may be administratively convenient to share markets among members of the corporate family in an attempt to maintain a non-competitive peace, even at the cost of foregoing some profit opportunities. Where the parent firm is involved in collusion on markets or other factors with unrelated firms, the agreement may be extended to cover the foreign subsidiaries, by informal understandings if possible, by abuse of patent and other legal rights if not. Even where the firm acts or is permitted to act knowledgeably and rationally from its point of view over time, it will usually insist on consultation between its domestic and foreign parts when traditional sales areas are to be disrupted.

No doubt there are problems here from the point of view of the subsidiary. The ability to exploit opportunities for new products and new markets is partly a function of whether companies are actively seeking such

---

Export Department and the Domestic Mechanical Sales Department in Akron. We feel sure that this is, as you say, an unusual circumstance, and an exceptional case and we trust it will not be repeated with any other Mechanical Goods, but we should like confirmation that we shall have the fullest cooperation from Akron or otherwise our selling arrangements over here will be greatly disturbed." It might be noted that there is even more direct evidence in the report that the marketing rules of the industry association in Canada frequently outweighed the wishes of officers of the parent companies; see pp. 73-74 and 104 of the report, for example. There were exceptions, of course, as noted on p. 326. It should be added also that other parts of the report make clear that the agreed prices were based on those of the parent firms, adjusted by a formula. See pp. 54-57, for example.

opportunities on a continuing basis, consistent with changing cost and market considerations and the firm's particular capacities to exploit them. A subsidiary may enjoy a good many advantages from the parent's export organization, yet, particularly if its own ability to export is improving rapidly, feel hampered by market or other constraints designed to avoid unregulated competition among the different parts of the international firm. It is also a common complaint in geographically decentralized operations that the central management, busy with its domestic market, is uninformed about or simply uninterested in foreign opportunities. Where it makes overall decisions suitable to its own market and applies these without adjustment to the different circumstances of the subsidiary, the result is to delay or inhibit the development of the subsidiary.[17] One can readily find what appear to be examples of such decisions, sometimes accompanied by comments from executives of the parent firms about the inability of officers of the subsidiary to take account of the overall needs and resources of the international firm. Such problems, enhanced in the giant international enterprise, should not detract one from the position that firms are unlikely to persistently disregard known and continuing opportunities to enhance their profitability. Too much of the empirical evidence of this book suggests broadly rational economic decision-making for it to be suggested that firms will knowingly and deliberately eschew profit opportunities, unless coaxed or coerced by governments and private groups to do so. At the worst, the lack of competition will delay their exploitation of such opportunities.

In the above it was assumed that the decision on export was made centrally, in order to see the result of foreign control most clearly. Certainly it is common for the subsidiaries to at least consult with the parent before considering invading its market or that of other affiliates, apart from any restrictions due to formal market division reinforced by such things as allocation of patent rights. It is well to add that a significant minority of firms, judging by the interviews and by other studies, operate in a quite independent way with regard to changes in international marketing. In these firms open competition is encouraged among the subsidiaries and the parent in one another's markets, without even the requirement for prior consultation. There are many reasons why the decision to export and where to export is left fully to the officers of the subsidiaries in these cases: sometimes the products or the stages of production are different in the main so that substantial competition with the parent is not involved, sometimes

---

[17]See Fayerweather, *op. cit.*, pp. 359-361 and the reference to Smith, *op. cit.*, footnote 26 in Chapter 3 above.

the Canadian firm has had a past history of independent operation and its executives are able to use this to operate relatively freely, in other cases the parent's executives cannot be bothered much with the affairs of the subsidiary, at least while such competition is marginal. Perhaps most frequently, however, the parent encourages direct competition within the international firm as a matter of policy in order to have an automatic check on the efficiency of the subsidiary and the initiative of its officers. This type of policy is particularly meaningful where the different subsidiaries are at the same stages of production, produce similar products, and do most of their own financing with little recourse to the parent. It is probably less relevant where the parent is expected to supply financing and is unwilling to permit unlimited duplication of facilities, and where problems associated with consumer acceptance of a given trademarked product (for example, where almost no variation in quality could be tolerated) limit the area of competition possible by varying the product.

All of this weakens the case for believing private export restriction is widespread *over time,* a case which is based essentially on informational and institutional problems and one which persists even then only if competition from outside the firm is lacking. To the extent this is so, it identifies the most important barriers to specialization and export in the international firm as the underlying cost situation of the subsidiary, the tariff and other obstacles to the maximum size of its market in Canada and abroad, and the degree of competition between firms in those markets.

That the above simplified analysis is consistent with the broad tendencies of investment decisions in international firms is apparent from a good many actual case studies. The historical shift of the newsprint industry to Canada is an outstanding example of non-resident owned firms, among others, shifting output from the parent land. This process was accelerated, however, by the removal of the United States tariff on newsprint and by provincial restrictions on exports of pulpwood.[18] That economic decisions are involved for manufactures also is evident from the substantial imports of automobiles into the United States in the late fifties even though, in this case, competition from the domestic industry eventually reduced the import flow. In the late fifties about one-quarter of the large imports of automobiles and parts into the United States was manufactured abroad by firms owned or controlled in the United States.[19] The shift to Canada for a few years of the entire

---

[18]See the industry case studies by Aitken in footnote 10 of this chapter.
[19]See, for example, U.S. Department of Commerce, *U.S. Business Investments in Foreign Countries,* p. 114.

automotive division of an American firm in the early sixties is another example of what can happen in an international firm for economic reasons even when the loss of facilities is in the parent market.[20] Needless to say, such changes can be expedited by tariff adjustments and other government incentives, as the recent automobile agreements between Canada and the United States indicate. More generally, there has been a substantial investment in manufacturing facilities by United States firms in overseas markets as well as in Canada since World War II, in response to a combination of factors among which lower costs of production abroad and tariff and other barriers to export from the United States are very important.[21] One effect has been to restrict direct exports of finished goods from the United States below what they might otherwise have been, although there are offsets to this in the balance of payments through exports of components and through dividend and royalty receipts. Moreover, the parent firms involved might well have lost the markets involved if direct investments had not been made. What needs emphasis here is that these tendencies, quite beyond the control of the firms involved, have also reduced exports from Canadian subsidiaries to overseas markets for the same cost and tariff reasons. In many of the interviews it was clear that the Canadian subsidiaries had enjoyed substantial exports to overseas markets in the twenties and thirties and just after 1945, but, like the United States parent, had found these reduced because relatively lower costs abroad and exchange shortages along with greater legal obstacles to exports led to the creation of affiliates abroad to serve the overseas markets. The pattern was not entirely dissimilar to that in the earlier decades of this century when Canadian tariffs combined with lower wage costs and some other factors to restrict imports from the United States and to lead to the establishment of many subsidiary firms.[22]

---

[20]Late in 1963 Studebaker Corporation decided to close down its automotive division in the United States, which was suffering losses, and switched its production for the United States and overseas markets to its Canadian plant, where lower manufacturing costs and favourable tariff and currency arrangements prevailed. See the *Globe and Mail*, December 9 and 12, 1963 and the *Financial Post*, December 14, 1963, p. 25. In March 1966, however, the company decided to cease automobile production permanently.

[21]See the article "Business Moves Abroad," in the *Economist*, December 5, 1959. That Canadian-owned firms have also been caught up in this process is evident from the statement by the Chairman of Massey-Ferguson Ltd. referring to a major expansion of the company's facilities in Europe and noting that relatively high costs prevented establishment of some of the new facilities in Canada. See the *Financial Post*, April 2, 1960, p. 19.

[22]See Marshall et al., *op. cit.*, Chapter 4 for the key role of the tariff in locating many direct investment manufacturing firms in Canada. Note also the following: "The

Finally, as will be noted below, there is considerable evidence in the present study of specialization and trade between affiliated firms, and of export patterns which reflect different unit costs between affiliates.

It might be thought that the logic of the above would suggest a much greater degree of specialization among affiliates than the data indicate. If profit maximization globally is the objective, why not go all the way to full specialization of production of components by subsidiaries, and substantial exports and imports for assembly in local markets? There are examples of such complete or substantial specialization.[28] The obstacles to it are partly economic and partly legal. In terms of economics, transportation costs, rapidly rising unit production costs with greater volume, and the need for local adaptation may limit the degree of specialization. In terms of legal barriers continuing tariff and other legal obstacles to exports and imports may be noted.

The evidence on private export restrictions is particularly difficult to unearth. Also one may not know for any specific case whether and how much it actually restricts exports, or would do so only if the subsidiary became competitive, or how long it might take to be freed of the restriction in such a case given that the sales of the affiliates are affected. In brief, one does not know the extent to which, at any given time, such restrictions adopted for administrative convenience and similar reasons may not also correspond broadly with the competitive capacities of the affiliates. The only general study of this in Canada was as part of a larger study of international cartels

company had a large plant at St. John's, Quebec, which had been sending about 80% of its production to Latin America. The shift to local production in Brazil and Mexico had reduced the volume of its exports. Singer had been frustrated in its development of the Latin American market by exchange and import restrictions. While the economics of local production were not favourable, it had been forced to set up plants in Brazil and Mexico to maintain itself in these markets." Fayerweather, *op. cit.*, p. 585, in a case study of The Singer Manufacturing Company based in large part on an article in *Fortune*, January and February, 1959.

[28]Many firms in the interviews and questionnaires gave examples of specialization and trade for parts of their output, but relatively few (apart from primary resource firms) for most or all of their output. Examples of such specialization from published sources include the case of Ernest Leitz (Canada) Ltd., which specializes in the production of lenses only for world-wide distribution and exports about 80 per cent of its production. See the *Financial Post*, June 6, 1964. A well-known case is that of International Business Machines, where substantial specialization of production between affiliates has been achieved. See the article by John E. Brent, "International Business Machines, World Trade Corporation," in International Management Association, Inc., *Case Studies in Foreign Operations*, Special Report No. 1 (New York, 1957), pp. 11-17. See also the *Financial Post* for October 10, 1964, p. 15. The recent automobile agreements have as a major objective the greater specialization of production between Canada and the United States.

published in 1945.[24] One phase of this enquiry sought information on private international trade agreements by means of letters to about 300 Canadian firms. In its specific examples and general discussion there is the clear implication that parent-subsidiary relationships are particularly conducive to restrictive trading arrangements, whether informal and formal, since restrictive agreements involving the parent and third parties are often made to apply to the Canadian subsidiary. The enquiry suggested this can occur even without the active participation or even knowledge of the subsidiary. Unfortunately, the report presents no data on the incidence of such private trade agreements whether overall or as they relate to parent-subsidiary relationships. Almost the entire discussion of this subject by the Commissioner, apart from mention of specific foreign-owned companies in its chapter on examples, consists of two pages in which it classifies four situations with regard to exports. These involve situations where the subsidiary is left free to determine its own policy (a relatively rare case in the Commission's opinion), where the subsidiary is confined definitely to the Canadian market, where it is allocated certain export territories, and where products of the subsidiary must be exported through a separate export sales organization affiliated with the parent. The Commission states that market sharing within the international firm has the same restrictive effects on Canadian exports as the division of markets under a cartel agreement. It goes on to recommend that the government secure more information on the financial interests which persons or corporations outside Canada have in Canadian enterprises, and how such interests are exercised.[25] The Commission went on to note that the use of patent rights to restrict production and trade forms the basis for many restrictive private trading arrangements and that inter-governmental co-operation will be required to deal with the restraints imposed thereby on exports and imports. It warns that market allocation by restrictive private agreements of all kinds can effectively thwart commercial policies designed to increase either exports or imports.[26]

It may be of interest to record here some information available on the export franchises of Australian companies with overseas affiliations, whether direct investment companies or linked by a licensing agreement.[27]

---

[24]*Canada and International Cartels, Report of Commissioner*, Combines Investigation Act, Ottawa, 1945. See especially part 2 of Chapter 1, and Chapters 2 and 6.
[25]*Ibid.*, p. 43-44. The first part of the Commissioner's recommendation (also given on p. 67) was met by the *Corporation and Labour Unions Returns Act of 1962*, 17 years later.
[26]*Ibid.*, Chapter 3 and p. 66.
[27]See H. W. Arndt and D. R. Sherk, "Export Franchises of Australian Companies

Of the 650 Australian firms so affiliated with American firms about 275 recorded an interest in exports. About 100 of the latter were restricted to certain areas in their exports. The export interest of the 560 Australian firms similarly connected with British firms is not known, but about seventy had a limited export franchise. While the extent of restriction is interesting to note, it is also, unfortunately, the case that the data are not sufficiently refined for economic analysis: subsidiaries are likely to have wider export franchises than companies operating under a licensing agreement, since the overall firm gains the profits of the subsidiary; nothing is known about the franchises of firms not interested in exports; and a firm may have an export interest without being able to exercise it competitively in non-franchise areas.

The Export Pattern of Direct Investment Companies

Before considering the percentages of output exported by the particular firms in this study, it is well to note the absolute values of production and of exports for all American-owned firms in Canada.[28] The detailed census data for 1957 collected by the United States Department of Commerce indicate that American-owned enterprises in Canadian manufacturing, mining, and petroleum industries had overall sales of U.S. $10.7 billion. Fully 20 per cent of these sales were for export, namely, $1.4 billion to the United States and $0.7 billion to other countries. Export from Canada originating with these direct-investment companies accounted for about 50 per cent of total Canadian exports of manufactures (including pulp and paper) in 1957, while for petroleum and other minerals and metals combined the proportion was over 85 per cent. These proportions are higher than the proportion of capital invested in Canadian industry which was

---

with Overseas Affiliations," *Economic Record*, Vol. XXXV (August, 1959), pp. 239-242. The material is from a survey by the Industries Division of the Department of Trade, Government of Australia. It is interesting to note that, contrary to what was suggested above, the authors believe the parent has nothing to gain by competition from its Australian subsidiary in its home or third markets, except where the sale might otherwise be lost to unrelated parties.

[28]The absolute figures for 1957 are from U.S. Department of Commerce, *U.S. Investments in Foreign Countries*, A Supplement to the Survey of Current Business (1960), pp. 68, 110-111 and 114. Ownership and control ratios were derived from D.B.S., *The Canadian Balance of International Payments, 1960*, pp. 82-83. Data for 1963 and 1964 are from U.S. Department of Commerce, *Survey of Current Business*, November, 1965, pp. 19 and 24. The data shown in this section were given for American-owned companies only in my article, "The Exports of American-Owned Enterprises in Canada," Papers and Proceedings, *American Economic Association*, Vol. LIV, No. 3 (May, 1964), pp. 449-458.

owned and controlled by residents of the United States at that time, as defined and measured by the Dominion Bureau of Statistics. At the end of 1957 residents of the United States owned 39 per cent and controlled 43 per cent of the capital of Canadian manufacturing industries, while American ownership and control of capital invested in petroleum and mining combined were 53 per cent and 63 per cent respectively. These estimates suggest that, on an aggregative basis, the American-owned sector of the industries involved is more oriented to exports than are the other sectors. No comparable detailed census has been made for recent years. Data collected on a sample basis show that in 1963 and 1964 the total sales by American-controlled manufacturing firms in Canada had risen to $10.2 billion and $11.5 billion respectively, of which $0.8 billion and $1.2 billion respectively were exported to the United States and $1.0 billion and $0.9 billion respectively to overseas countries. American-controlled mining affiliates in Canada had total sales of $1.0 billion and $1.3 billion in 1963 and 1964, of which only $0.2 billion and $0.3 billion was sold in Canada. No data are available for the petroleum industry beyond 1957, an industry

TABLE 18

PROPORTION OF SALES IN CANADA, CLASSIFIED BY SIZE OF ASSETS OF COMPANIES
(Number of companies)

Percentage of sales in Canada	Asset size in $ millions				
	Under 1	1-4.9	5-24.9	25 and over	All companies
100	75	45	4	0	129
95-99	18	24	20	15	82
70-94	5	10	12	7	37
Below 70	5	2	3	9	20
Not available or no response to question	1	1	4	4	12
Totals above	104	82	43	35	280
	Averages for above data (percentages)				
First quartile	100	100	99	96	100
Median	100	100	95	92	99.5
Third quartile	99	97.5	90	21	95

most of whose capital has been supplied from the United States and which has become a major exporter.

Such aggregative comparisons from different sources, which are comprehensive for only one year, are open to a number of objections on statistical grounds. It is also well known that a few large firms in a few primary resource-oriented industries dominate the absolute values for exports. Thus $1 billion of the total of $1.4 billion exported to the United States in 1957 by American-owned firms consisted of metals and minerals and newsprint and pulp. The analysis of typical export patterns requires finer breakdowns.

In this study the data on exports were requested for the year 1959 or for "an average of recent years" where 1959 was not typical. It is important to note that the export data consist entirely of frequency distributions of the percentage of the output of individual firms which is exported. In order to emphasize typical patterns these percentages have not been weighted by the value of exports for the firms involved or in any other way, although distributions by the size of the firms' assets are shown. The data presented here give some information on three points, namely, the proportion of companies exporting and the proportions of output exported, the geographical distribution of exports, and the portion of exports which represented trade with affiliated companies outside Canada.

Almost half of the 280 firms in the present study did not export in 1959. Exports accounted for five per cent or less of sales in over one-quarter of the firms, while one-fifth of the firms indicated exports in excess of five per cent of total sales. There is a marked increase in the ratio of exports to total sales as the size of the firm increases; the proportion of firms with no exports falls from 72 per cent for those with assets under $1 million to 55 per cent for those with assets from $1 million to $4.9 million, 9 per cent for those with assets from $5 million to $24.9 million and zero for those with assets of $25 million and over.[29] This point can be seen more clearly if one uses averages for the proportion sold in Canada by size groups. Quartiles and medians are most appropriate for this purpose since they are not subject to extreme values as is the arithmetic mean. The first quartile, above which one-quarter of the observations lie, is at 100 per cent of sales in Canada. The second quartile or median, on either side of which half of the observations lie, is 99.5 per cent of sales. The third quartile, below which one-quarter of the observations lie, is 95 per

---

[29]Each of the four firms with assets of $25 million and more, for which precise data were not available, had some exports in 1959.

cent. It will be noted that each of these measures falls (i.e. the proportion of sales abroad rises) as one moves to larger sizes of firms. The sharp fall in the third quartile for the largest firms, which are few in number, warrants a further comment.[30]

The method used here diminishes the role of the few very large exporters of primary-resource products in order to show typical export patterns. It may be of interest to note also the distribution in table 18 of those 13 per cent of the firms which indicated their type of business was mainly extractive or the production of semi-fabricated goods.[31] These firms comprised nine of the twenty exporting over 30 per cent of output and dominated the firms in this group with assets of $25 million or more. They comprised only one-sixth of those exporting from 5 to 30 per cent of output and did not predominate in any size-group. They comprised about 10 per cent of each of the other groups shown and were concentrated in the two smaller size-groups in these cases. A further refinement should be made here in order to understand the nature of the data. A distinction is often drawn in the literature on direct investment between market-oriented firms in manufacturing which export little or nothing and supply-oriented firms in primary industries which export most of their output. The eleven firms in this study which indicated their type of business was largely extractive, or extractive and some other category, conform to this pattern, as the data in table 20 make clear. All but one of these firms are in the two larger size groups in table 18. The twenty-six firms mainly producing semi-fabricated products, however, do not fit this pattern. While there are some large firms producing semi-fabricated goods mainly for export, most of these firms are in the two smaller size groups and produce largely or wholly for the domestic market. Extensive analysis of the purely extractive firms is obviously precluded by the small numbers involved in this study; nor can one assume that the hundreds of smaller extractive firms in the population at large conform to the characteristics of the few large ones included here.[32]

---

[30]It may be noted that if asset size is taken relative to that of the parent, rather than in absolute terms, there is a much less marked variation in proportion of sales sold abroad. Firms which are 16 per cent or more of the size of the parent have a smaller proportion of their number in the group selling only in Canada, and a higher proportion in the group selling over 30 per cent of sales abroad. In the smaller relative size groups the pattern is erratic.

[31]The types shown here should not be confused with the distinction sometimes made between primary and secondary manufacturing. It should be added that some awkward matters of definition are raised by all such classifications, particularly where multi-product firms and various degrees of vertical integration exist.

[32]It bears repeating that some large producers of primary and semi-fabricated goods which do not have parent firms abroad have been excluded from this study even

The most frequent destination of exports is the United States. Fully 71 per cent of those firms with exports had some exports to the United States, while only 34 per cent and 40 per cent of those with exports had some exports to the United Kingdom and other sterling area countries respectively. Fully 46 per cent of the firms with exports sent 70 per cent or more of their exports to the United States. A similar table in the Appendix indicates just about the same results for the American-owned firms only. The view that American-owned firms are more likely to export to overseas markets than to the United States, because of tariff preferences or because of restrictions on exports to the parent's market, seems to be contradicted by this material.[33] Nor is there much support for the view that the exports are simply "captive exports" in the sense that they usually export to the parent or its affiliates abroad when they do export. The most likely export destination was to non-affiliated entities, whether in the United States or elsewhere: 77 per cent of the firms with exports reached such destinations, while fully 62 per cent exported 70 per cent or more of their exports to such destinations. Companies with exports very frequently found markets with their affiliates abroad, however. Almost half reported some exports to their parent company, in fact, over one-quarter of those with exports sold between 30 and 100 per cent of their exports to the parent. A smaller portion also sold to affiliates of the parent in third countries. The table in the Appendix broadly confirms this pattern for American-owned firms taken alone. A similar Appendix table for firms owned overseas indicates very much the same patterns, namely, a marked tendency to export most frequently to the United States and to non-affiliated parties wherever they are located.[34]

---

though their stock is largely owned abroad. About 20 per cent of the firms owned in the United States and those owned overseas exported over 5 per cent of their output. Thirty per cent of the former exported 1-5 per cent of their output, as against 40 per cent of the latter. This difference is probably not significant in view of a somewhat different distribution by industry and the consequent effect on the small number of overseas firms included.

[33]Note, for example, the following qualified statement from p. 391 of the *Final Report* by the Royal Commission on Canada's Economic Prospects: "In some cases, Canadian subsidiaries of United States parent companies are permitted to export their products to the markets of Commonwealth countries because of preferential tariffs, but are prohibited from competing with their parent companies in the other markets of the world. In most cases, there may be little possibility of Canadian companies being able to compete successfully with much larger American companies including their own parent concerns but this may not always be so."

[34]Neither of the major conclusions in this paragraph is upset if one deletes the largely extractive firms, since they are too few to change the conclusions noted. In any case they follow the pattern of the other firms by exporting most frequently to the United States but very largely to non-affiliated parties.

What can one tell about the proportion of sales to the domestic market, or conversely the proportion of output which is exported, when classified by other characteristics? There does not appear to be any clear tendency for older firms to export more of their output than those acquired or established recently. It is true that a higher proportion of the firms established or acquired before 1939 have some exports than have those set up since, but this and other comparisons by age tend to disappear when considered within three size groups; in other words, the observed differences by age would appear to be due actually to the differences by size of assets which were noted earlier.

TABLE 19

DESTINATIONS OF EXPORTS, RESPONDENT NON-RESIDENT OWNED COMPANIES WITH EXPORTS
(percentages by each destination)

Percentage of exports to destination indicated	Distribution of responses by each destination							
	Area				Affiliation			
	U.S.	U.K.	Other sterling area	Other	Parent	Other foreign affiliates of parent	Own subsidiary abroad	Other
100%	28	2	11	8	10	5	0	38
70-99	18	2	3	10	9	1	3	24
30-69	12	5	3	13	8	5	0	7
1-29	13	25	23	16	21	9	2	8
0	29	66	60	54	52	63	15	23
Not relevant	—	—	—	—	—	17	81	—
	100	100	100	100	100	100	100	100

NOTE: The data should be read by columns, which total 100 per cent except for rounding. The cases shown as not relevant refer to companies with exports but where the parent companies had no other foreign affiliate or the Canadian company did not have a subsidiary outside Canada. About 115 companies are involved in each column of this table (after excluding those with exports in table 18 which could not give destinations) of which nineteen indicated their type of business was extractive or semi-fabricated products. Eight of the nineteen were largely extractive in their operations.

By types of business, the eleven extractive firms in this study clearly differ from the rest in that they all export significant portions of their output. The integrated producers are somewhat more oriented to exports than are the other three types. Each of the other three types of business show quite large portions of firms with no exports at all. It should be noted again that manufacturing firms dominate the classification by type of business, with the result that rather few firms are involved in the other categories. When considered within three size groups the difference of extractive and integrated types of firms from the other three types persists. It should be noted that the extractive and integrated firms are largely concentrated in the largest size groups, a factor which is not unrelated to their clearly superior export performance. It is in considerable part because such firms can export, and meet import competition effectively, for a variety of other reasons that their size tends on the average to be in excess of those of the other firms. These differences are related in part to the classification of sales by types of product. Primary mining and smelting, and lumber, pulp and newsprint, were the only major industry groups in which all firms reported that over 30 per cent of their output was sold abroad. No other major industry group had half of the firms selling over 30 per cent of their output abroad, in fact, in fully twelve of the sixteen major industry groups less than 10 per cent of the firms reported they sold over 30 per cent of their output outside Canada. In six major industry groups — textiles, paper products, metal fabrication, electrical products, chemicals and miscellaneous — at least half of the firms in each case reported no sales abroad whatsoever in 1959. It is true that these results may not be representative in some industry groups given the few firms involved, and it is also true that analysis of exports requires more refined industry breakdowns than is possible with this material. The concentration of exports by industry does stand out, nevertheless. It may be well to note also that a distinction between primary and secondary manufacturing, made rather crudely as indicated earlier, yields the expected difference in export performance. The primary manufacturing industries show eight firms with 100 per cent of sales in Canada, and twelve, six, and fourteen firms respectively in the categories with 95-99 per cent, 70-94 per cent and under 70 per cent of sales in Canada. The remainder show 117, sixty-seven, twenty-nine and six firms respectively in these sales categories. The differences in export performance are obvious at the two extreme categories. Finally, these differences in export performance persist when the data by type of product are examined within three asset size groups. The type of product, in other words, is clearly an important determinant of export performance even after differences in size of firm are taken into account.

It is also of interest to note how the destination of sales varies when the subsidiary's product is compared with that of the parent. Firms which reported their products were generally identical with those of the foreign

TABLE 20

PER CENT SALES TO CANADIAN MARKET CLASSIFIED BY SELECTED CHARACTERISTICS

Characteristic	Percent sales to Canadian market				Number of replies*
	100%	95-99% (% distribution by rows)	94-70%	Under 70%	
Type of business					
Assembly	65	26	10	—	31
Extractive	—	—	36	64	11
Semi-fabricated products	58	25	8	8	24
Fully processed or manufactured	50	32	14	5	181
Integrated	28	44	17	11	18
All firms	49	30	14	8	265
Type of product					
Petroleum products	11	44	44	—	9
Primary mining and smelting	—	—	—	100	6
Foods and beverages	36	43	14	7	14
Rubber products	—	80	20	—	5
Textile and clothing	75	13	13	—	8
Wood and furniture	29	29	—	43	7
Paper products	57	43	—	—	7
Primary metals	29	43	14	14	7
Metal fabricating	57	32	7	4	28
Machinery (excl. electrical)	49	33	13	5	39
Transportation equipment	45	30	20	5	20
Electrical products	56	28	15	—	39
Non-metallic mineral products	43	43	14	—	7
Chemicals	55	27	18	—	33
Pulp, lumber, newsprint	—	—	—	100	4
Miscellaneous	69	19	8	4	26
All firms	48	31	14	8	259

Nature of products compared with affiliate

Identical	58	26	11	5	151
Marginally different	41	39	16	4	69
Substantially modified	31	56	6	6	16
Not comparable	37	5	21	37	19
All firms	50	30	13	7	255

Range of products compared with affiliate

Wider	63	26	11	—	19
About the same	55	29	13	4	77
Majority of affiliate's products	42	37	14	7	71
Minority	58	30	6	6	33
Only a few	44	24	24	8	25
All firms	51	31	13	5	225†

*, † See footnotes to table 17.

affiliate also reported a higher proportion of their number with 100 per cent of sales in the Canadian market. In the case of those reporting that the products were not comparable to those of the parent, the difference to the other firms shows up in the greater proportions exporting over 30 per cent of output, which is clearly related to our findings above on Canadian firms engaged in extractive industries. If one concentrates on the differences among the other three types, the firms which reported that their products were substantially modified appear to have a higher portion of their number in the group selling up to 5 per cent of their output abroad but not beyond this point. These results are broadly confirmed if the data are considered within three size groups, though it is well to add that the analysis of sales by comparative nature of product is hampered by the fact that there are relatively few observations in some categories. The portion of sales in Canada was also classified by the range of the subsidiary's products compared with that of the affiliate. Those reporting a comparatively wider range had the largest portion of firms selling 100 per cent of output on the domestic market: indeed, not one of these firms sold less than 70 per cent of their output in Canada. Those producing a majority of the affiliate's products, and those producing only a few, reported the smallest proportion of firms with 100 per cent of sales in Canada. The latter reported a larger proportion of firms with less than 95 per cent of sales in Canada than did any other group.[35] Again these findings are confirmed when examined within three asset size groups.

In the early part of this chapter it was noted that it was partly the existence of competing assets abroad which has led to the suggestion that the foreign-owned firm may be biased against exports. It might then be thought that the more the foreign affiliates of the parent the less likely is the Canadian subsidiary to enter export markets. This is a proposition which can be tested broadly with the present data since both the exports of the subsidiary and the number of foreign affiliates of the parent are available for 238 of the firms in this study. For the eighty-four firms which reported that the parent had no other foreign subsidiary, 73 per cent reported no exports, 12 per cent reported up to 5 per cent of output was exported, 10 per cent that from 6 to 30 per cent of output was exported, and 6 per cent reported that over 30 per cent of output was exported. The eighty-six firms whose parents had from one to five other foreign subsidiaries or branches reported 42, 35, 13 and 11 per cent of their number respectively were in the export categories just noted. The sixty-eight firms whose parents had six or more other foreign affiliates reported 31, 45, 18, and 6 per cent of their number were in the export categories noted. These results are confirmed broadly when examined within three size categories of firms. They are not definitive since other variables affect export performance also. In addition, as will be noted below, there are some specific limited problems affecting export performance adversely. In themselves these overall data do not suggest any tendency for firms with more affiliates abroad to have less export orientation. If anything, they suggest the reverse.

The Nature of the Export Sales Organization

A firm may use one or more of many forms of organization to facilitate exports, depending on such things as the nature of its product and its market, the significance of exports, and the existence of affiliates abroad. In table 21 the point emphasized is the degree to which the direct investment

---

[35]It is of interest to note that, for firms with assets of $5 million or more, those firms with a wider range of products than the parent reported three with exports of 5 per cent or less of output and one firm with exports over five per cent of output, those firms reporting the range was about the same indicated eight and four firms in these export categories, those producing a majority reported sixteen and seven firms, those producing a minority reported three and three firms, and those producing only a few reported three and six firms. It is well to note that we have excluded from the present comparisons those firms whose products were not comparable to those of the affiliate: they are much more oriented to sales abroad than any of the groups noted under range of products in table 20.

companies used their own export organizations or those of their affiliates. A large number of firms indicated there was no export sales organization. Many others left the question unanswered: most of these had no exports in the late fifties. It will be noted also from the accompanying table that these two groups are very largely accounted for by the two smallest groups of firms. The great majority of the firms with export sales organizations export either solely through their own organization or solely through those of the parent. Only twenty-two of the 117 firms with export organizations take advantage of both their own and their affiliate's export organization. This is perhaps a rather surprising result. It is true that generalizations about export organization are hazardous without more detailed knowledge of the situation with which the firms are faced regarding export. Nevertheless, somewhat greater use of both organizations might have been expected if only to broaden the market contacts of the firms involved. The pattern was the same both for firms owned in the United States and those owned overseas, though the latter exported more frequently solely through their own organizations rather than solely through those of their affiliates. Even the larger and medium-sized firms, which are more often involved in export, in most cases export only through one or the other organization.

TABLE 21

LOCUS OF THE EXPORT SALES ORGANIZATION
(Number of companies)

	Companies controlled in		Asset size in $ millions			
	All Countries	U.S.	Under 1	1-4.9	5-24.9	25 and over
Firms exporting only through own organization	44	32	10	14	8	9
Firms exporting only through affiliate's organization	46	40	5	12	18	7
Firms using both organizations	22	15	3	1	9	7
Special situations*	5	4	0	0	1	4
No export sales organization	91	75	51	29	5	5
No explicit reply to question†	72	61	35	26	2	3
Totals	280	227	104	82	43	35

*Pooling arrangements in Canada for exports.
†In 50 of these there were no exports.

Where the subsidiary used its own export sales organization, either solely or along with that of its affiliate, the most popular form was export through agencies, sales representatives, brokers and the like. Fully forty-three firms reported such uses, while another fourteen appear to sell directly abroad without the use of such intermediaries.[36] Twenty-five additional firms reported some form of export sales organization in the Canadian firm, and ten of these twenty-five explicitly mentioned an export division, export subsidiary, or international sales corporation of the Canadian firm. Some of the remaining fifteen may have had such: judging from replies to this and other parts of the questionnaire and from the interviews, however, most had designated an export manager in the Canadian firm — sometimes a person with other duties — or used part of the domestic sales force, but had no formal organization as such. Five firms indicated they exported through their licensee or their producing subsidiary abroad, that is, that these were their export sales organization.

Where the subsidiary used the export sales organization of the parent, either solely or along with its own, the most popular form of export sales organization was the parent's export department, export subsidiary, or international sales corporation — thirty-four firms reported such methods. It may be noted in passing that the international sales company of the parent is not necessarily located in the parent country. Several gave Switzerland as the location and a few are located in Canada. Another twenty-two reported exports through some form of export sales organization in the parent without specifying its precise designation: these likely include both the formal types of organization just noted as well as less formal arrangements for export in the parent firm. A further thirteen firms reported exports through the parent's agencies, dealers, and other representatives abroad. In eleven cases the firms gave exports to the parent or to its affiliates as the reply to the question on export organization and in five other cases the export organization is, in effect, through other foreign affiliates of the parent.[37]

These few comments cannot do justice to the very extensive export organizations maintained by some of the firms in this study. A few of the

---

[36]There is considerable double counting in the figures in this and the next paragraph, since firms listing more than one export technique are included in more than one category.

[37]In assessing this it must be recalled that a much larger number of companies sold something to the parent or its affiliates. Six of those which gave this reply in response to the question on export organization sold most or all of their exports to affiliates. Four of the eleven mentioned only this form of export sales organization.

larger Canadian firms in particular maintained unusually extensive international sales organizations involving an extensive network of international sales corporations, foreign subsidiaries, agents, sales offices, and licensees. This type of extensive international distribution system was very common among the parent firms, and often of considerable advantage to those Canadian firms which had access to them on a competitive basis. The qualification is important and will be considered shortly.

Examples of replies classified in the first three categories of the table follow. All but two of the companies are producing highly manufactured products, three have assets under $5 million and three have assets of $25 million or more.

Our local sales organization handles export sales. We have agents in various countries who report enquiries to us and through whom we generally quote.

Sales organization consists of three vice-presidents — sales:
1. Domestic (includes all North America for commercial products).
2. International – for commercial products. Each Vice-President is assisted by managers, representatives and agents located throughout the world.
3. Military sales — world wide responsibility.
The above organization is completely independent of affiliate organization.

We have a licensee in U.S.A. assembling our product and several jobbers.

Parent's international sales corporation (located in Switzerland, not in parent land, U.S.A.) now handles all exports except to U.S. dependencies.

We are using the dealership organization of the parent company only.

Canadian company's export sales are handled through parent company's export division which in turn is represented by agents or brokers in many foreign countries.

All export transactions are with affiliated companies or offices in foreign countries and as such are not direct dealings with customers.

Parent company sells for us in Eastern U.S. An agent represents us in Western U.S. Foreign (i.e. overseas) sales through an export agency in New York. Some direct foreign sales by ourselves.

U.S.A. — Wholly owned subsidiary of Canadian Company covers sales areas of North and South America. Elsewhere — Sudsidiaries of Parent U.K. company cover sales areas.

Does exporting via the parent organization confer any specific advantages or disadvantages on the subsidiary? In theory it would appear to confer advantages by widening market contacts and knowledge via affiliates and their distribution system abroad, subject to the assumption that the subsidiary is free to take advantage of these aids to the extent it can economically do so. It will be noted below that some are not free to do so, at least in the short run, and some others which export through the parent's export sales organization face export allocation systems which put them at a disadvantage. Only detailed case studies could satisfactorily answer this, but some general observations are possible from the present data. On the overall statistical level, the data permit only limited analysis of this point in view of the fact that a very large number of firms do no exporting. This, plus non-response to these particular questions, leaves only just over a hundred firms using a Canadian or parent export sales organization or a combination of the two. If one considers the export performance of these by type of export organization, it does not appear that those exporting solely via the parent export organization show a worse export performance than those exporting solely via the export sales organization of the Canadian firm. In both cases about 60 per cent of the firms report exports at 1-5 per cent of output, about 30 per cent report exports at 6 to 30 per cent of output, and about 10 per cent report exports at over 30 per cent of output. On the other hand, 35 per cent of those which reported they used both types of export outlets also indicated that exports were one to five per cent of output, 35 per cent that they were 6 to 30 per cent of output, and 30 per cent that they were over 30 per cent of output. Given more firms one could refine the data by testing it after allowance for such important export determinants as type of product and size of firm. What little we have been able to do in this respect does not show significant differences beyond that just noted. An additional piece of evidence exists in the responses made to the question noted below on the effects of affiliation on exports by those firms which export only through the parent's export sales organization. Sixteen of these forty-six firms replied that affiliation had a favourable effect, six that effects were unfavourable and the rest either did not reply or believed that there was little or no effect. In three of the six the unfavourable effect arose from the construction of new subsidiaries abroad by the parent, thus eliminating an export market for the Canadian firm — something the latter might not have been able to avoid as an independent firm in any case. This limited evidence does not suggest any widespread disadvantage associated with export through the parent's export organization as such. On the contrary it suggests that such access may help more companies than it hinders, while not guaranteeing exports since, as many pointed out, the firms must be competitive in any case to win orders through the parent's export sales organization.

Apart from direct export of its products or services a firm may export through the establishment of a subsidiary or branch abroad or by granting a license to a foreign firm to make its products or use its processes. These types of export techniques are infrequent in the firms in this study. Only nineteen firms indicated they had branches or subsidiaries abroad, excluding from these the purely selling or servicing agencies abroad.[38] These firms had forty-six subsidiaries or branches abroad, with eleven of the nineteen indicating they had only one branch or subsidiary abroad. Five of these subsidiaries were located in the United Kingdom while the rest were almost equally divided among the United States, sterling area countries other than the United Kingdom, and all other countries as a group. In ten of these nineteen firms the investment in the Canadian companies' subsidiaries and branches outside Canada was five per cent or less of that in the Canadian company. Sixteen of the nineteen were American direct investment firms in Canada. Thirteen had Canadian assets in excess of $5 million and seven had assets in excess of $25 million. Not only were such subsidiaries and branches few in number but their trade with the Canadian parent was rather the exception, as indicated in table 19.

Nor were licensing agreements with foreign firms particularly widespread. Only fourteen firms reported they had such agreements, amounting to thirty-five agreements in all.[39] Twelve of these firms were American direct investment companies. Apparently the relatively smaller firms find this more attractive as an export technique; eight of the fourteen firms had assets under $5 million. About half of the thirty-five agreements were with

---

[38]It is of interest here to note the following from p. 50 of D.B.S., *Canada's International Investment Position, 1926-54:* "Although the capital involved is large, the number of Canadian companies or groups of Canadian investors with direct investments abroad is only slightly over 300, and many of these Canadian companies are themselves controlled by non-residents." This number includes subsidiaries of both non-resident and resident-owned firms and also other than commodity-producing industries. Thirty-seven firms did not explicitly answer our question. Internal evidence on the questionnaire as well as public sources of information on some of the firms suggests few if any of these had subsidiaries abroad.

[39]Fully fifty of the responding firms did not answer this question. The statement at the end of the previous footnote also applies here. It may be noted that the questions preceding this one which dealt with the destinations and sources of exports and imports had significantly lower non-responses, although they are at least as difficult to answer.

licensees in the United States and almost all the rest were with licensees in the United Kingdom and other sterling area countries.

The characteristics of the firms granting licenses or with subsidiaries and branches abroad are of some interest. The firms involved are both United States and United Kingdom direct investments, roughly in proportion to their overall numbers in the study, and they cover most types of industry. There is a very decided concentration among them by type of product and by relative costs, however. Firms with products substantially modified or not comparable, when compared with those of the affiliate, are a significantly higher proportion of this group than they are of all of the respondent firms in the study. Similarly, firms with unit costs which are lower than or equal to those of the affiliate considerably exceed those with unit costs higher than those of the affiliate, while the reverse is true for all of the firms in this study. These results are broadly consistent with what one might expect from the attempt to maximize profits over time over the international firm as a whole, rather than simply within its parts. The considerable number of exceptions which remain in the data by the tests just used might well be lessened if more detailed analyses over time were possible.

The Effect of Affiliation on Exports

One of the larger questions appended to the end of the questionnaire asks "In what ways, if any, has the fact of affiliation with companies outside Canada discernibly affected the volume, nature, and direction of your exports; for example, guaranteed purchases by affiliates, assignment of markets to be served, contacts with potential customers?" The question is both general and subjective, and by itself does not permit analysis of the many ways, both direct and indirect, in which affiliation may affect exports. It does permit, however, a summary evaluation of the total effect of affiliation on exports as seen by the respondents.[40]

---

[40]In view of the substantial non-response to this question among those returning the questionnaire it is well to ask whether there is any pattern to the non-responses. Specifically, did those firms which omitted this particular question export a smaller or larger portion of their output relative to those which answered the question? It is possible to examine this since, in another part of the questionnaire, the proportion of sales to the Canadian market (and thus to exports) was given. When considered by the four size groups used in this study the quartiles and medians for the proportion of sales in the Canadian market were virtually identical for the two sets of firms, that is, for firms answering the question on the effect of affiliation and those not answering it. The only exception was in the largest size group, where the export performance of the respondents to the question on the effect of affiliation was better than that of non-respondents. There are so few firms in this category that a small shift among the two groups could change this result. See also page 35.

Almost two-thirds of the respondents answered this question in ways which indicated that affiliation had little or no effect on exports or that the question was not applicable. The latter group consisted of replies such as those indicating the product was not an export product because of freight and other economic obstacles to exports or that the company was new and the question not yet answerable. Thirty-nine firms indicated the effect was favourable, often highly favourable, not only because of guaranteed purchases by affiliates and contacts with potential customers but for a wide variety of other reasons. Many firms pointed out that the exports enjoyed by the subsidiary basically reflected such factors as the established name of the parent, the quality of the parent's products, the expensive research and development it undertakes, and the large sales organization it maintains. A few quotations from replies may help to give an idea of their nature for this group of companies. All of these firms had assets of $5 million or more, and the first and last of them were engaged in producing primary products or in primary manufacturing.

> Large effect due to established quality of affiliate's products, international reputation, and large and concerted research and sales efforts by affiliate.
>
> When products are identical, arbitrary division of export volume between plants in Canada, U.S.A., and abroad. Has given Canada assured markets for a substantial percentage of production.
>
> We have probably gained markets we would not otherwise have been able to contact by virtue of our affiliate's selling organization. This method has not kept us from markets in which we would otherwise have been able to compete.
>
> Affiliation has increased our exports. The parent company is our largest single customer and has given us access to world-wide export through its own export organization to an extent which we could not otherwise afford.
>
> Affiliation with outside companies guarantees by contract the sale of a minimum production of product. Affiliate's contacts with other customers probably could not be duplicated in Canada.

The other side of this is the twenty firms whose answers suggest that the effect of affiliation may have been unfavourable. Included here are ten firms which indicated that they were restricted to specific countries or areas, either with or without a reference to decreased exports as a result, and ten firms which stated that exports were reduced or non-existent because of the existence or establishment of affiliates abroad. Several of the replies in this group must be considered marginal to the group at best, particularly three firms which indicated the diminution of exports reflected the establishment by the parent of subsidiaries abroad which may have had lower costs than the Canadian firm. In other words it cannot be assumed in all of these cases that the firms would have been able to avoid export declines as independent firms. Three of the replies in this group of firms follow. All three firms are in secondary manufacturing industries. The first two had assets under $1 million.

Only influence is that we are limited in exports to sterling area countries.

Affiliation with the English company very definitely affects the policy of the Canadian company so far as exports are concerned. The old established English company has traditional markets throughout the world which of course it wishes to maintain and the policy has therefore been established of confining the Canadian company to Canada, the U.S. and Mexico with the possibility of entering other markets only after it has been established that they do not conflict with the parent company's business. With regard to guaranteed purchases by the affiliated company these do not exist; business between the two companies is always conducted on the basis that each company will purchase from the most economical source and the affiliated companies therefore are expected to be competitive.

Our parent company having a world wide operation has numerous distributors around the world thus restricting the availability of our exporting. The parent company serves the Western hemisphere whilst the English subsidiary (of the parent) serves Europe, Africa and Asia.

TABLE 22

EFFECT OF AFFILIATION ON EXPORTS OF CANADIAN COMPANY
(Number of companies)

	Companies controlled in		Asset size in $ millions			
	All Countries	U.S.	Under 1	1-4.9	5-24.9	25 and over
None or very little	74	55	30	22	10	10
Not applicable	38	26	19	13	2	3
Favourable	39	32	10	4	11	13
Unfavourable	20	17	6	9	1	2
Effect uncertain or varies	10	8	1	2	2	2
No reply to question	99	89	38	32	17	5
Totals	280	227	104	82	43	35

Ten replies have had to be left unclassified because the effect on exports as such is uncertain. These are mostly cases where the subsidiary explicitly notes both favourable and unfavourable effects as regards exports but does not give the net effect; for example, it cannot enter a specific market or export a specific product, but it also has substantial help in entering other markets.

There appears to be no significant difference between firms owned overseas and those owned in the United States with regard to the effect of affiliation on exports when account is taken of the differences in numbers of firms involved. There is a significant difference in replies by size of firms. In both absolute and relative terms a greater proportion of firms reporting favourable effects are concentrated in the two larger size groups. When weighted by size of firm, in other words, the balance swings even more toward favourable effects.[41]

The overall effects of affiliation on exports would appear to be either non-existent or favourable except for a small minority of cases. This analysis must be enlarged in two further directions, namely, the method of allocating exports within the international export organization and the effect on exports of the allocation of patent rights. Regarding the first point an attempt was made to ascertain how sales were allocated by the parent's export sales organization among the various affiliates, where the parent's export sales organization was used by the Canadian firm. There is considerable variety here.[42] The question clearly does not apply to the great

---

[41]These results are not affected much by the eleven extractive firms noted earlier. The favourable responses among the two larger groups of firms would probably have been significantly greater if more of the eleven purely extractive firms, most of which export substantial amounts, had replied. Only four of these answered this question, three indicating favourable effects and one no significant effect yet but an expectation that the parent's contacts abroad would be valuable shortly.

[42]One well-known example occurs in the *Report of the Commissioner*, Combines Investigation Act, *Rubber Products*, pp. 202 and 177-180. One of the firms had to forward all export orders for mechanical rubber goods to the parent's export company and filled export orders under the direction of the latter. Another firm reported it sold only to the parent's export company and only by assignment from it, at cost plus a fixed percentage of the profits of the parent's export company. Both these firms exported substantial portions of their output in 1946-1948, varying from 11 to 18 per cent per year, while the latter had exported a third of its output before the war. The Commissioner was critical of the fact that these firms could not promote export sales but added that "it cannot be known how the export sales Canadian companies might have obtained by their own efforts would have compared with what they obtained through the orders passed to them by their American parent companies." It might be added that the one large Canadian-owned producer of mechanical rubber goods was exporting a little less than these two firms as a percentage of output just after the war, a large firm owned overseas was exporting very little, and the other American-owned firm was not exporting at all.

majority of firms, which either do not export or do not export through the parent's export organization. Nor can one assume that the question applies to all of the sixty-eight firms which are shown in table 21 as exporting through the parent's sales organization: some of these firms indicated there was no allocation as such even though the parent export company refers occasional orders to them or although some of their exports go through various parts of the parent's sales organization. Thirty-six companies gave information in sufficient detail that a rather rough classification can be attempted of the methods of allocation used in the export sales organization. In addition, for a number of these firms, more detailed comment from interviews was also available on this point. In one group of six firms the allocation can only be described as more or less arbitrary. The various affiliates share export orders according to either some fixed division of markets to be served or the size of the firm as regards identical products, but usually with less restricted arrangements where products differ. In three of these cases the Canadian firms appear to have a preferred position on exports.[48] In seven companies broadly economic factors are listed as the basis of allocation, such as location in relation to customers and the specialized products or capacities of different parts of the international firm.

The remaining twenty-three firms are classified separately because they not only emphasized economic variables but gave more explicit information. For most of these it appears that some form of bidding on price occurs within the international firm on the basis of specifications set out by the export company. The decision on which firm receives the order is decided on this basis adjusted, where necessary, for such factors as the requirements of exchange control systems and the local availability of financing for the export. In perhaps a third of these firms it appears that bidding as such does not take place. The Canadian firm has a fixed export price with the parent's international corporation, on the basis of which the latter allocates orders depending on such factors as the profit margin involved for the different affiliates, tariff preferences, freight costs, and delivery dates. Presumably the parent export corporation accepts the source which maximizes its potential netback, including the profit margin, since it will thereby increase its chances of securing the order or, if already secured, making the largest return on it. It may not matter which system is used where the costs of the Canadian firm are well above those of its affiliate and are likely to remain

---

[48]The allocation technique for one or two of these may not be as arbitrary as present information suggests, since there is some indication that costs may be lower for part of their output.

so with increased business. The method of allocation does matter to those subsidiaries which, given permanently increased volume and larger and/or different productive facilities due to export orders, may find themselves equalling or going below the costs of their affiliates. Distributive costs would also have to be taken into account, of course, including tariffs. Where such possibilities exist the method of allocation just noted could be a hindrance to the achievement of an economic export volume. Presumably in such cases the subsidiary's officers can raise the matter with the parent's executives, thereby proposing to upset traditional marketing arrangements but with a good case in terms of the profitability of the overall operation.[44] A second point works in the same direction. Some of the firms which quote fixed prices to the export corporation are also not permitted to solicit export business on their own. This may inhibit the exploitation of any particular advantages which they have or believe they can develop with the expectation of larger volume. One cannot assume that the officers of the international export corporation necessarily know better than executives of the subsidiary what the potential for the latter may be.

A second area where difficulties may arise for some direct investment companies which become competitive in the international market is with respect to industrial property rights. The assignment of patents and trademarks raises difficult legal and economic issues which cannot be dealt with adequately here. The relevant point in the present context is that such assignment can and often does carry a market restriction, which is either actual or potential depending on the relative costs of the firms involved. The owner of the patent, for example, if it is the international firm rather than its subsidiaries, can effectively restrict each subsidiary to its own national market by assigning each of them the patent and trademark rights to that market only. This appears to be a quite legal restraint of trade within the international firm, although its legality may depend on the specific circumstances of ownership and some other factors.[45] The effects

---

[44]The case is presumably relevant where the limited size of the Canadian market of itself prevents the full development of internal economies of scale. For the view that this may be an insufficient criterion for such development, and that external economies have probably already been largely realized as part of an international firm, see S. Stykolt and H. C. Eastman, "A Model for the Study of Protected Oligopolies," *Economic Journal*, Vol. LXX (June, 1960), pp. 336-347.

[45]See Kingman Brewster, *Antitrust and American Business Abroad*, Ch. 8. That there are some serious questions about the legality of such restrictions in the minds of executives of the parent firms is apparent from comments in U.S. Department of Commerce, *Factors Limiting U.S. Investment Abroad*, Supplement to Part 2, pp. 185-190.

are similar to that resulting from an international market-sharing combine between independent firms insofar as the effect on exports from any given market are concerned.[46] Once again one must note that a parent firm is unlikely to indefinitely restrict the export of the subsidiary if the latter develops an advantage in exporting. To insist on continued market limitation in this circumstance is to reduce the profits of the international firm, taxation and other factors being equal. The point of the restrictions is to protect exports of the parent and the sales of its subsidiaries, that is, to prevent encroachments by non-related parties.[47] As before, it is well to recognize some short-run exceptions to this general principle so far as the competitive subsidiary is concerned; there may be ignorance or lethargy to contend with, a desire to avoid administrative problems which arise when one firm in the overall enterprise enters the markets of the others, and an attempt to shield other corporate assets in the short-run. Moreover, the parent may have licensing agreements with related or non-related firms which limit access for some period of time to given markets. These can mean a considerable delay before arrangements can be modified. One should add a further complication here in that the existence of minority shareholders in the subsidiaries abroad involves a sharing of income from export, hence often a reluctance to assign the international patent rights to that subsidiary. The very existence of such minority shareholders may require explicit assignment of patent rights in the first instance, where less formal arrangements may suffice with wholly-owned subsidiaries.

From the strictly Canadian point of view the issues raised here may have less to do with foreign ownership than with the problems raised by abuse of the international patent system. Such abuse is obvious where foreign-owned firms are required to conform to collusive arrangements entered into by their parents; it is equally obvious where the Canadian firms are not foreign-owned. For a country which is looking toward a significant increase

[46]For a discussion of the use of patents by combines to restrict exports see Combines Investigation Commission, *Canada and International Cartels*, Ch. 3. This report notes that imports to Canada can also be blocked if the foreign patent holder refuses to grant a license to make it abroad for export to Canada. Indeed, Canadian patent law itself militates against import of patented articles since it is an abuse of the exclusive rights under a Canadian patent if manufacture in Canada on a commercial scale is prevented by import. See Frances Masson and J. B. Whitely, *Barriers to Trade Between Canada and the United States*, Canadian-American Committee, Montreal, 1960, pp. 62-64.

[47]This was the primary objective of four-fifths of the firms studies by J. N. Behrman. See "Licensing Abroad Under Patents, Trademarks, and Know How by U.S. Companies," *The Patent, Trademark and Copyright Journal of Research and Education*, June, 1958 (11,2), p. 185.

in exports of manufactures one might reverse the argument about patent restrictions on exports from subsidiary companies. It is the financially unrelated independent Canadian firm, which, if it needs to borrow technology, is likely to find the terms both explicit and restrictive as to markets. Any gains made by a subsidiary and not spelled out, or inadequately spelled out, in a royalty agreement can be recouped by profits or dividend transfers to the parent, whereas they must be anticipated and spelled out in any arrangements with a financially independent firm. It is a moot point whether or not Canadian authorities would agree to removing by international agreement the actual or potential restrictions on exports which are applied by licensors. The counterpart of freer access to foreign markets would presumably be freer access to the Canadian market than now exists because of the exclusive licensing arrangements assigned to Canadian firms.

In a later chapter the nature and terms of access by the subsidiaries to the knowledge of the affiliate will be considered in some detail. It will be noted then that, for many of these companies, informal arrangements are involved rather than formal licensing agreements. Fifty-one of the firms involved in this study replied to a general question at the end of the questionnaire asking for information on the markets covered by the formal patent and trademark rights received from the parent. Ten of these firms merely indicated that the patents and/or marks owned by the parent were usually or always registered in Canada under the subsidiary's name; for perhaps five of these the reply can be interpreted to mean the subsidiary has the rights to the Canadian market only. Five firms answered the question simply by stating they owned the patents and/or trademarks and either assigned them to affiliates in some foreign markets or licensed other firms. The remaining thirty-six named the markets for which the rights available from the affiliate apply: in eighteen cases Canada was the only market, in six Canada and some other specified market, such as Commonwealth or worldwide except for the parent's country, and in twelve the rights were worldwide. Many of the firms went on to note that they had exclusive rights in the market or markets concerned where the market was not worldwide. A number pointed out these were valuable property rights owned by the parent and subject to its disposition, and that access to them at little or no direct cost was valuable even if only for the Canadian market. Several pointed out also that the rights to Canada, being exclusive, gave useful protection from firms within and outside the corporate family. Where the patents or trademarks were available for use outside Canada via exports, they often conferred substantial benefits on the subsidiaries since the parent's research and name was being used by the subsidiary. The parent, of course, hoped to reap its reward — by royalty in some cases, but more often by the eventual return on its investment in Canada. Finally, a number of firms noted that the limitation on extension of the rights to markets not now covered usually reflected not parental prohibition as such but the fact that prior legal arrangements made by the parent, with both related and unrelated firms, prevented entry to those particular markets.

It is interesting to note the characteristics of the thirty-six firms which indicated precisely the markets for which the rights applied, even though the numbers are small. They divide evenly into eighteen where the rights apply only to Canada and eighteen where they include part or the rest of the world. There is a significant difference in export performance between the two groups; thirteen of the first group export only one per cent or less of their output while six of the latter group are in this category. In part this must be related to the fact that firms in the latter group tend to be larger than those in the former and also include several firms where the product is substantially modified compared with the parent. None of the eighteen firms whose rights were limited to Canada produced to any great extent products which were more than marginally different from those of the parent. In one respect earlier expectations are confirmed; six of the eighteen firms with export franchises on patented goods had costs below those of their affiliates for a significant part or all of their output, while this was true of only two of the firms without such franchises. On the other hand, our earlier expectation is not confirmed with regard to the greater willingness to extend such franchises to firms which are wholly-owned; fifteen of those with no export franchise are wholly owned or almost so as against seven for those with such franchises.

A number of firms in a questionnaire to resident-owned companies had access to the patents and/or trademarks of non-affiliated firms located outside Canada. This questionnaire will be discussed further in Chapter 9. It is worth noting here that these were usually formal agreements involving specified royalty payments. Fourteen firms gave information on the markets to which these rights applied. In twelve of the fourteen the rights were available only for the Canadian market.

Finally, the question of private trade restrictions can be considered by bringing together in one place the different kinds of practices which might act as a restraint on exports. For present purposes this can be taken to include (a) all cases where patent rights apply to Canada only, (b) cases where the effect of affiliation on exports was stated to be unfavourable, and

(c) the cases where the subsidiary exports through the parent's export corporation but is not permitted to bid on exports. It must be emphasized that these are not necessarily actual restrictions on exports, deliberate or otherwise: they are simply situations where an impediment to exports might exist or might appear if the subsidiary was or became competitive. Thirty-eight firms are involved in this, after eliminating double counting where a firm appears in more than one category. Thus the total number of situations where actual or potential restrictions might exist, according to the information made available by the respondents, amounts to just under 15 per cent of the firms involved.[48]

The first thing that strikes one is that these restrictions must be largely potential rather than actual. Only three of the thirty-eight companies had unit production costs lower than the affiliate's on comparable products, and only two more had unit costs which were variable compared with those of the affiliate. Another six had costs which were about the same on comparable products, so far as production costs are concerned. The percentages of output sold by these firms in Canada is distributed almost exactly as in table 18 for all 280 firms. Nor, one might add, does it appear that one can trace the restrictions on these firms to the existence of relatively more affiliates of the parent in third countries; the parents of these thirty-eight firms have relatively fewer affiliates in third countries than is true of the other firms in this study. All in all, it appears that the private trade restrictions which might be involved are largely potential impediments for the majority of the firms at the present time, however much they may inhibit exports of some particular firms or of some particular products of those firms. These potential impediments to exports, it may be added, are concentrated in a relatively few industries. The machinery industries, electrical products industries, and some branches of chemical industries, which together represent 40 per cent of the firms in this study, accounted for almost two-thirds of the restrictions noted here.

The emphasis in this chapter has been on private trade restriction. It should be repeated that the question of the ability of the subsidiary to engage in exports competitively is another matter, one important aspect of which will be considered in Chapter 7. The evidence from the interviews suggests that for most of the companies the major problems regarding

---

[48]The data do not include the ten uncertain cases in table 22 where both positive and negative export effects were indicated, or the five cases where patent rights were available in some but not all foreign markets. There may be a case for including the latter for some purposes, thus raising the percentage to 15 per cent.

exports are the higher costs of production of the subsidiary compared with its affiliates, on the one hand, and barriers to trade such as distribution costs, tariffs, customs procedures, foreign exchange shortages, and the erosion of trade preferences on the other hand. Such developments have led to the establishment of affiliates in various foreign countries which can serve the local market more efficiently than either the foreign parent or the Canadian subsidiary. It was not rare in the interviews to come across manufacturing firms which had been exporting a significant portion of their output in earlier decades, but because of relatively greater cost increases or greater institutional barriers were exporting little or nothing by the time this study was made.

External Pressures on Foreign-Owned Firms

Up to this point exports from subsidiary firms have been considered in terms of the logic of the international firm acting in its own economic interest. At times factors external to this process dominate the outcome. In the context of the exports of direct investment firms the most significant example arises from the extra-territorial application of United States law.

The details involved are not as clear and full as one would like, partly because the matter quickly became a political issue in the federal election of 1958 and later and partly because of contradictory statements from the firms and governments involved. What seems clear is that at least one American subsidiary in the automobile industry may have refused to pursue the possibility of selling automobiles to the Peoples Republic of China because the Foreign Assets Control regulations of the United States Treasury make the parent company responsible for preventing such sales.[49] Whatever the precise details, it is not difficult to see how a conflict can arise. United States policy on China involves a complete denial of trade with that country for her nationals. It also involves an attempt to prevent firms abroad owned by nationals of the United States from circumventing the restrictions imposed on their owners by engaging in trade with China. Apart from this the regulations appear designed to ensure also that the ban on trade with the Peoples Republic of China applies equally to nationals, whether or not they happen to have subsidiaries abroad. The officers of the parent firms are subject to prosecution if the regulations are thwarted by their foreign subsidiaries. It is equally clear that the Canadian interest

---

[49]This and related cases are discussed at length in Kingman Brewster, *Law and United States Business in Canada*, part 4, Montreal, Canadian-American Committee, 1960.

in the matter is different from that of the United States. The Canadian government prohibits exports of strategic items to the Peoples Republic of China but permits other exports. Under Canadian policy a good many items produced by subsidiary firms could be exported to China. An economic issue is involved, particularly since the matter was first raised publicly in an industry suffering considerable unemployment at a time of weak general demand in the economy. The more fundamental issue is that firms domiciled in Canada must avoid commercial activity which is not illegal under Canadian law and regulations.

It is true that the Canadian and American governments reached an agreement which permits a Canadian subsidiary which is willing to trade with China to ask the Canadian authorities to request a specific exemption from the regulations as they apply to the parent. Little is known about the way in which this has worked, although the few known cases do not suggest it has been particularly effective in permitting exports to occur.[50] Some doubts also surround later instances of alleged refusal of parent companies to permit exports from subsidiaries to China, involving as they do contradictory statements by government officials, politicians, and executives of parent and subsidiary.[51]

The issue in such cases is not essentially an economic one, even if it be admitted that more may be involved economically than the few relatively small orders which have come to public attention. The issue involves, fundamentally, the question of sovereignty over the operations of firms which are legal residents of Canada and which are assumed to conform to Canadian law and regulation. Put thus, it is easy to see that the reticence of Canadian governments to clarify the issue sharply and fully with American authorities has contributed to the confusion surrounding the issue. Admittedly the issue has been a delicate one for Canadian governments, involving as it does an appreciation that United States prohibition of trade with the Peoples Republic of China could be thoroughly evaded by trade with subsidiaries, combined with an explicit recognition that Canadian policy toward that country does permit trade short of strategic goods. There is no way, however, in which a Canadian government can shirk its

---

[50]*Ibid.*, pp. 25-26, and the article by Walter Stewart, "Canada — A United States Colony," in the *Star Weekly*, February 5, 1966.
[51]See, for example, the announcement by federal authorities in Ottawa that automobile parts were shipped to China, accompanied by a denial from the parent firm of one subsidiary assumed to be involved, in the *Globe and Mail*, October 11, 1962. Further questions regarding automobile parts exports to China were rather evasively answered, as evident from reports in the *Globe and Mail* from March 24 to 26, 1964.

obligation to continue to insist on Canadian sovereignty in these situations, consistent with a carefully determined position on what serves Canada's long-term interests. Only if Canadian foreign policy were to be always identical with American — a quite untenable position for a nation — would the issue be avoidable. It is surely no part of the understanding of the liabilities involved when direct investment takes place that the firms will serve, however unwillingly, as vehicles for the implementation of the policies of foreign governments.[52] The issue needs to be resolved by a clear and firm agreement between the two countries. Should the decisions of United States regulatory agencies or courts significantly and persistently infringe Canadian sovereignty in this and other respects it is altogether likely, in spite of the difficulties it will cause, that a suitable statute may be necessary positively asserting jurisdiction over subsidiary firms in Canada.[53]

[52]Similar problems of extra-territorial application of United States law have arisen over antitrust decisions in the United States which have directly affected the structure and operations of subsidiary firms domiciled in Canada. See Brewster, *Law and United States Business in Canada*, parts 2 and 3; *Notes* for an Address by the Minister of Justice, The Honourable Davie Fulton, to the Antitrust Section of the New York State Bar Association, New York, January 28, 1959; and the *Financial Post*, December 13, 1958, p. 23. Unlike the trade cases, the political and economic aspects of the antitrust cases are not necessarily both opposed to the Canadian interest. The dismantling of private foreign trade restrictions by a United States court order, for example, may not be opposed to the Canadian economic interest however much it may infringe on Canadian sovereignty.

[53]See the reference to the speech by Davie Fulton in the previous footnote.

5
The Imports of
Subsidiary Companies

For many reasons the typical direct investment company will have a significant import of commodities and services, including in particular a substantial trade with the parent firm itself. The original investment by the parent firm often results from barriers to imports imposed by the recipient country, thereby forcing the foreign parent to cease shipments of its products in whole or part and to assemble or manufacture them in the recipient country. High or rising transfer costs for commodities, such as transportation costs, have the same effect. In such circumstances the parent will often continue to export some parts or equipment or materials to the subsidiary insofar as legal and economic obstacles permit, as well as some types of finished goods to be distributed by the subsidiary. If the establishment of the subsidiary is not the result of barriers to trade as such but of economies associated with decentralization of plant and/or distribution, there is still likely to be a substantial trade with the parent. This trade reflects the fact that it is often more economical to buy from the parent or its suppliers than any other source, if, indeed, the specific item is available anywhere else. To the extent that the subsidiary produces items identical to or marginally different from those of the parent there is a built-in incentive to buy from the parent, if it produces the components, or from its sources. The use of the parent's patents and trademarks, with the frequently related need to meet uniform specifications on quality and design, points towards a significant trade with the parent or with sources of supply developed by it to meet its specific needs. Everything from the capital equipment to the products produced and the ancillary services may reflect an inherent tendency for considerable trade with the parent or its suppliers. Frequently the plant and equipment will have been constructed or purchased with the advice of the parent's engineers, based on design for one of its other plants suitably modified for Canadian conditions. It is not surprising, therefore, if the executives of the subsidiary seek the experience and purchasing contacts of the parent when replacement and expansion become necessary. Many components in the production process will come from the parent or its developed sources simply because the subsidiary is selling products developed by the parent to its specifications; in the first instance, at least, the items are probably not available anywhere else in Canada or abroad or are not available at anything like the same terms. The various technical and other services available from or through the parent are at first an almost inevitable accompaniment of the transfer of capital and personnel. Not the least of these services is the advice, information catalogues and, on some items for some firms, the centralized purchasing which is available from the purchasing departments of the parent and its other affiliates. Familiarity with the personnel and procedures and products of the parent and its sources, combined with the costs of exploring or developing alternative sources of supply, may well enhance these effects.

There are, then, many compelling reasons for expecting a substantial import from the parent and its sources, except possibly in the case of firms engaged in purely extractive operations. There are equally convincing reasons for believing that there will be a substantial domestic content to the output of the subsidiary as well as striking differences among the firms in this regard. It was noted above that transfer costs and the sometimes associated economies of decentralization of production and distribution can lead to the establishment of the subsidiary, hence to domestic production. Many of the officers of the firms interviewed pointed to the Canadian tariff and related regulations as a key factor limiting their imports from the parent or other sources abroad, particularly where a specific Canadian content to production is required. Significant differences in requirements for the Canadian market can lead to production here, requirements ranging all the way from different government standards set for similar consumer products to differences in climate and tastes. Some materials cannot be transported far economically and tend to attract industry to them. The progressive development of economical alternative sources of supply in Canada as the volume required of the item expands is a potent force transferring purchasing to domestic sources. At the same time it is important to emphasize that the extent to which subsidiary firms rely on imports from the parent or its sources will vary considerably, in view of the differing extent to which the Canadian economy can supply various products competitively at a given time and over time, in view of the different stages of production and varying degrees of integration of subsidiary and parent firms, and in view of the different stages of development of the subsidiaries. It was a common experience of many of the firms in this study to import a component or commodity until the increase in the size of the Canadian market for it, the acquisition of the necessary skills of production, the development of domestic sources of supply, or a favourable change in some cost component — sometimes accompanied by an adjustment in the tariff — permitted its economical production or purchase in Canada. Clearly there are pressures working the other way as well, such as relative cost changes for given products which favour production elsewhere, competitive new products which do not suit existing Canadian resource patterns or locations, or downward adjustment in the tariff. The import pattern at any point of time will be simply the end result of these and similar forces, some of which can be delineated empirically.

In this chapter the purchasing pattern of foreign-owned firms will be considered with emphasis on the extent of Canadian content in their purchases and how this varies with certain variables. Some aspects of the policies followed with regard to purchases will be examined, particularly how the fact of affiliation affects the imports of subsidiary firms. Some of the considerations involved here are similar to the questions considered with regard to exports, for example, the question of how one shifts production within the international firm, and hence need only brief further comment. The distinctive difference is one of degree: the typical subsidiary in secondary manufacturing in particular is likely to be a much greater importer than exporter, since it is in part an extension of the parent's sales and techniques into markets which cannot be served by exports from the parent because of transfer costs and the related economies of partial decentralization of production.

The Import Pattern of Direct Investment Companies

Before considering the data collected for this study it is useful to look at the estimates of total imports by Canadian subsidiaries owned in the United States, as collected by the United States Department of Commerce for the year 1963.[1] The data presented here are restricted to the Canadian affili-

---

[1]See Samuel Pizer and Frederick Cutler, "U.S. Trade with Foreign Affiliates of U.S. Firms," *Survey of Current Business*, December, 1964. These data were first collected for the year 1962. They are based on a sample of parent companies, 256 in 1963, which has been expanded to the total universe of such firms by various techniques described in the article. For overall data on the exports of American-controlled companies see footnote 28, Ch. 4, and the accompanying text.

ates of United States manufacturing firms since detail is available for this group. These affiliates imported $1.7 billion from the United States in 1963. This consisted of $614 million for processing or assembly from parent firms, almost all of which was parts, components and similar manufactures, with crude materials accounting for only $24 million; $535 million for resale without further manufacture; $439 million of imports purchased directly by the affiliate from other sources in the United States; and $105 million of miscellaneous categories of imports. These imports can be compared with the total sales of the Canadian affiliates. They amounted to 15.5 per cent of such sales, as against 8.8 per cent in the case of Latin American subsidiaries of United States manufacturing firms, 4.8 per cent in the case of European affiliates and 8.7 per cent in the case of affiliates elsewhere. There is a considerable concentration of imports by industry in Canada as witnessed by the fact that transportation equipment alone accounted for $592 million, chemicals for $255 million, machinery for $291 million, and electrical machinery for $200 million. Such imports into Canada when compared with the sales of the Canadian affiliates were 2.5 per cent for food products, 3.0 per cent for paper and allied products, 18.0 per cent for chemicals, 9.6 per cent for rubber products, 5.4 per cent for primary and fabricated metals, 31.0 per cent for machinery (excluding electrical), 15.0 per cent for electrical machinery, 27.4 per cent for transportation equipment, and 15.3 per cent for all other products.[2]

These figures provide a revealing first view of the overall imports of subsidiaries of United States manufacturing firms in Canada, but they need to be considerably refined before they can be used for some purposes. Thus it may be of interest to exclude throughout the data the import of products which are resold without further processing or manufacture, that is, where the subsidiary acts as a distributor rather than a manufacturer. This makes up a very large portion of the data on imports which was just presented.[3] The data collected for the present study, which will now be considered, generally exclude such imports which are for resale without further processing or manufacture.

The considerable variation in the extent to which direct investment companies rely on purchases from suppliers in Canada is evident from table

---

[2]*Ibid.*, p. 24.

[3]In addition there is some doubt whether purchases from unrelated parties in the United States have been fully or evenly reported. Two-thirds of all such purchases were reported for Canadian affiliates. It is not known if this means that such direct purchases in the United States by other affiliates are small or whether there was better reporting for Canada. See p. 22 of the source in the previous footnote.

23.[4] About 30 per cent of those answering the question indicated that 90 per cent or more of their purchases were from suppliers in Canada, about 33 per cent that from 70-89 per cent of their purchases were from such sources, and the remaining group of just over one-third was below 70 per cent. There is a considerable difference in this respect between firms of different sizes, with the proportion of purchases from suppliers in Canada rising as the size of the firm increases. The difference between size groups is mainly between firms with assets under $1 million and the remainder, as the quartiles and medians make clear. It is well to recall here that the smallest size group of firms includes a greater proportion of more recently established firms, which may have a lower domestic content on average. It will be noted that the median for firms with assets of $25 million or more is eighty-five and the third quartile seventy. Only two such firms made less than 50 per cent of their purchases in Canada; for the seven which could not give a specific percentage no more than two, on further enquiry, were below this level. Comparisons with data available in Appendix A indicate there is also a significant difference between firms owned overseas and those owned in the United States, in that the former have a relatively larger number in the group purchasing less than 40 per cent in Canada; again, however, this may reflect the fact that relatively more of the firms owned overseas were established in the fifties.

About 220 firms were able to give details on the sources of their imports.[5] The imports of these firms are very heavily concentrated in the United States. Fully 42 per cent of them acquired all of their imports from the United States and another 32 per cent took 70 per cent or more of their imports from that source. Fully 58 per cent bought nothing at all from the United Kingdom and much larger proportions bought nothing from other overseas sources. The major source of imports is clearly the parent: only 13 per cent of these firms bought nothing from the parent while 21 per

---

[4]The question asked for the percentage of total purchases of the Canadian company (materials and parts, equipment, services) which was from suppliers in Canada. Note that imports of finished goods directly for resale by the subsidiary are excluded by this definition. It will also be recalled that firms which identified themselves solely as selling agencies were omitted from this study. In a subsequent question in the same section of the questionnaire the term services was defined to include such purchases as insurance, advertising, and accounting. Some firms gave the domestic content for part of their purchases only; these were listed in the tables as "not available." As in the case of percentage of sales to the Canadian market, the data were requested for 1959 or for an average of recent years if 1959 was not typical.

[5]The precise number varies by the source. Apart from about thirty-five firms which did not answer the question on overall purchases from Canadian sources, and seven which had no imports, another twenty or so could not distinguish sources precisely.

cent made all their import purchases from that source and another 28 per cent bought at least 70 per cent of their imports from the parent. The bulk of the remaining imports came from non-affiliated sources. Only 11 per cent bought anything from other affiliates of the parent (admittedly, 38 per cent of the firms with imports had no such other affiliates) while most of these firms do not have their own subsidiaries abroad. In 13 per cent of the firms non-affiliates supplied 100 per cent of imports and in another 16 per cent of them at least 70 per cent of their imports.

Details on imports by country of ownership of the subsidiary, presented in Appendix A, confirm that American-owned firms concentrate their imports heavily in the United States. The parent is the main source but non-affiliated sources are very important also. The firms owned overseas (in all but a few cases, in the United Kingdom) provide a rather interesting

TABLE 23

PROPORTION OF PURCHASES IN CANADA, CLASSIFIED BY SIZE OF ASSETS OF COMPANIES
(Number of companies)

Percentage of purchases in Canada	Asset size in $ millions				All companies
	Under 1	1-4.9	5-24.9	25 and over	
95 and over	13	11	3	4	32
90-94	10	12	10	6	40
80-89	17	17	6	6	47
70-79	11	12	6	5	34
60-69	10	9	2	5	29
50-59	7	3	2	1	13
40-49	3	3	2	1	9
30-39	11	6	0	0	17
Below 30	16	5	2	0	24
Not available or no response to question	6	4	10	7	35
Totals	104	82	43	35	280
Averages for above data (percentages)					
First quartile	85	90	90	90	90
Median	70	80	80	85	77
Third quartile	35	60	67	70	60

TABLE 24

SOURCES OF IMPORTS, RESPONDENT NON-RESIDENT OWNED COMPANIES WITH IMPORTS
(Percentages from each source)

Percentage of imports from source indicated	Distribution of responses by each source							
	Area				Affiliation			
	U.S.	U.K.	Other sterling area	Other	Parent	Other foreign affiliates of parent	Own subsidiaries abroad	Other
100%	42	5	1	1	21	1	0	13
70-99	32	5	0	4	28	1	1	16
30-69	11	4	1	3	23	2	0	21
1-29	8	28	4	18	16	7	0	27
0	7	58	95	74	13	52	8	24
Not relevant	—	—	—	—	—	38	91	—
Totals	100	100	100	100	100	100	100	100

NOTE: The data should be read by columns, which total 100 per cent except for rounding. The cases shown as not relevant refer to companies with imports, but where the parent companies had no other foreign affiliate or the Canadian company did not have a subsidiary outside Canada. About 220 companies are involved in each column of this table after excluding those with imports in table 23 which could not give sources.

example of how the many factors which lead to imports from the affiliate can be offset in part by costs, tastes, design and other considerations. It is true that the most frequent source of imports for firms owned overseas is the United Kingdom, and specifically the parent. Non-affiliated sources in the United States form a close second, however, as a source of imports to these firms. Finally, it should be noted that, whatever role Imperial tariff preferences may have played at one time in directing imports to sterling area countries, their influence today cannot be very great judging by the data given here. Only 7 per cent of the American-owned firms bought anything from such sources while, surprisingly enough, none of the firms owned overseas which answered these questions on import sources bought anything at all from sterling area countries.[6]

[6]One such firm did purchase some of its imports from sterling area countries. Since it could not give a precise breakdown of sources of imports it was classified for this purpose with those not replying to this question. It should be added that ten of the fifty-three firms owned overseas were unable to give a breakdown of imports by source: the comment in the text refers to the remaining forty-three firms.

The extent to which purchases are made from domestic sources can be classified usefully by certain other variables. There is a fairly widespread view that the newer direct investment firm imports relatively more than the older, well-established firms which have had time to build up their domestic content. This idea was used earlier in this section, in fact. It would appear from the present data that only that group of firms which purchase less than 60 per cent of their supplies in Canada unequivocally reflect a decrease in the proportion of firms involved as the age of the firms rises. Thus 32 per cent of the firms established or acquired in the fifties made less than 60 per cent of their purchases in Canada, a figure which drops steadily to only 16 per cent of the firms established forty-two years ago or longer. When one looks at the other groups which have been used to show the percentage of purchases from Canadian suppliers, the proportion of the firms which are involved moves somewhat erratically with age. It is quite true that the percentage of firms making 90-100 per cent and 80-89 per cent of their purchases rises as one moves from the firms established in the fifties to those established in the forties (and, conversely, the proportions fall for the groups with domestic content below 80 per cent) so that there is confirmation for the view expressed earlier to this extent. But there is no persistent change as one goes further backward in time except for the group with less than 60 per cent domestic content. If one looks at this material within three size groups for the firms involved, age and domestic content move together positively only for the firms with assets under $1 million, a group where most of the firms founded in the fifties is concentrated. Beyond a certain minimum volume requirement probably related to the effects of the tariff and to technical aspects of production, the extent of specialization and imports by the typical firm appears to be related to factors other than age.

The effects of some of these factors can be seen if the data on purchases are classified by the type of business of the Canadian firm. There are very distinct differences in the proportion of purchases from the domestic market in this case, with the proportion rising as one proceeds from the assembly type of operation to firms producing semi-fabricated goods, to those producing fully processed or manufactured goods, and, finally, to the fully integrated and extractive firms which have the highest domestic content to their purchases. (It will be recalled that the extractive firms had by far the highest proportion of sales abroad: it now is clear that they also have by far the smallest proportion of purchases from abroad.) These differences cannot be ascribed to differences in the size of the firms involved in these groups. When type of business and locus of purchases are considered within three size groups, admittedly with rather few firms in some categories, the differences by type of business persist. The one exception is in the case of the integrated firms, which reflect a mixture of several types of business. This point can be made in a somewhat different way if one looks at the proportion of purchases in Canada classified by industry. Once again it should be noted that there are few firms in some groups and a variable response rate. It is quite noticeable, nevertheless, that five of the seven industries in which one-third or more of the firms have a domestic content which is over 90 per cent are those in which primary products or primary manufactures bulk large. These include petroleum and products, mining and smelting, wood and furniture, primary metals, and pulp, lumber and newsprint. On the other hand, those industries in which one-third or more of the firms have a domestic content under 60 per cent are generally more representative of highly manufactured products, namely, transportation equipment, electrical products, non-metallic minerals and miscellaneous industries. Only an approximate comparison of type of product can be made within size groups, but it does not upset this conclusion: indeed, for the firms with assets of $5 million or more, such a comparison fully confirms that type of product is an important determinant of the domestic content of purchases independent of any effect which size of firm has on this. Industry data for all firms which are affiliates of United States manufacturing companies, presented at the beginning of this section, tend to confirm these conclusions.

Two further classifications are of interest. Do firms which produce a relatively smaller range of their affiliates' products have a smaller or larger import content than those producing the full parent line? The data in table 25 do not suggest any consistent difference in the percentage of purchases which are in Canada when the firms are classified by the range of products compared with the affiliate. Once the data are examined within three size groups for the firms, however, there is a clear tendency for firms producing a minority or only a few of the affiliate's products to have a higher domestic content in their purchases than is the case for firms producing most or all of the parent's products. Similarly, the data presented here underline the earlier observation that the similarity of products between affiliated companies leads to heavy imports by the subsidiary. Firms whose products are generally identical with or only marginally different from those of the affiliate have a lower domestic content, in the main, than those whose products are substantially modified or not comparable. This observation is

TABLE 25

PURCHASES CLASSIFIED BY SELECTED CHARACTERISTICS

	Per cent purchases from domestic market				Number of replies*
	90-100%	80-89%	60-79%	Less than 60%	
	(% distribution of companies by rows)				
Age					
1-10 yrs.	30	15	23	32	116
11-21	43	20	13	23	30
22-41	26	24	29	21	58
42 and over	24	19	41	16	37
Total	29	19	26	26	241
Type of business of Canadian company					
Assembly	7	10	30	53	30
Extractive	78	22	—	—	9
Semi-fabricated products	23	18	14	46	22
Fully processed or manufactured products	33	21	27	20	165
Fully or largely integrated production	22	22	39	17	18
Total	30	19	26	25	244
Type of product					
Petroleum products	44	11	22	22	9
Primary mining and smelting	75	25	—	—	4
Foods and beverages	46	15	23	15	13
Rubber products	—	67	33	—	3
Textiles and clothing	29	14	29	29	7
Wood and furniture	43	14	29	14	7
Lumber, pulp, newsprint	100	—	—	—	3
Paper products	29	29	29	14	7
Primary metals	57	14	—	29	7
Metal fabricating	33	29	21	17	24
Machinery (except electrical)	32	13	29	26	38
Transportation equipment	17	6	39	39	18

Electrical products	13	24	26	37	38
Non-metallic mineral products	17	—	33	50	6
Chemicals and allied products	20	30	30	20	30
Miscellaneous industries	29	17	21	33	24
Total	29	19	26	26	238
Range of products compared with affiliate					
Wider	24	29	24	24	17
About the same	29	18	30	23	73
Majority of affiliate's products	21	24	29	26	66
Minority of affiliate's products	33	10	30	27	30
Only a few	35	13	17	35	23
Total	27	19	28	26	209†
Nature of products compared with affiliate					
Identical	28	18	26	28	141
Marginally different	24	18	30	27	66
Substantially modified	27	40	20	13	15
Not comparable	44	22	17	17	18
Total	28	20	26	26	240

* † See footnotes to table 17.

confirmed when the data are examined within size groups. It should be added that these findings go well beyond the few extractive firms in this study to include a number of firms in other categories, as the numbers in the table make clear.

Policy and Organization with Regard to Purchasing

In the great majority of cases the responsibility for policies regarding purchases of materials and components, capital equipment, and services lies with the officers of the Canadian company. Only eighteen firms indicated that the officers associated with the parent were responsible for such policies. In nineteen further cases the responsibility was a joint one, usually for major equipment purchases but sometimes for the purchase of a major raw material. Almost all of the firms with assets over $5 million reported that the responsibility for purchasing policies lay with the Canadian firm.

It is important to add that in thirty-five of the cases where the locus of responsibility for purchasing policies was identified as the Canadian firm the replies were qualified. The qualifications in these cases were about equally divided among two groups. In the first group the qualification was usually to the effect that the Canadian firm was responsible for purchasing within its overall budget or subject to approval or to consultation on major capital purchases. In the second group the qualification was to the effect that certain services or commodities were purchased jointly with or through the parent in order to achieve lower costs. The purchase of various kinds of insurance was particularly frequently mentioned here, although advertising was also referred to and a few examples of both capital equipment and raw materials were given. All of the thirty-five companies involved mentioned that the responsibility for purchasing policies lay with the Canadian firm but for the exceptions noted. The exceptions are important and warrant further comment. One cannot conclude that joint purchases with the parent involve a surrender of decision-making on purchasing to the parent. Some of the firms involved made it clear that they were engaged in joint purchases for strictly economic reasons and could break away from them if it appeared to the advantage of the Canadian firm to do so. It is not difficult to find in the interviews and questionnaires a number of cases where this had happened. The interest of both parent and subsidiary is likely to coincide here in both the short and long run to the extent that the purchase is from an unrelated third party. More will be said on the extent and nature of joint purchases in a subsequent section. More important is the fact that the responsibility for purchasing must be considered in the context of the overall degree of decentralization of policy between parent and subsidiary. In Chapter 3 this was dealt with in detail, noting that most firms consult officers of the parent on major policy and major financial and capital items in particular. It was also noted that similarities of product, specification of standards, and similar factors necessarily lead to considerable purchases from the parent or its sources of supply. It is within the context of these qualifications that it is correct to say that the great majority of the Canadian firms exercise responsibility for purchasing policies. Indeed, one can go further and note from table 26 that in all but a few cases the Canadian firms use their own organization for making purchases rather than that of the parent. This is so even for most of the small and frequently relatively new firms.

About 70 per cent of the firms also supplied information on their policy,

TABLE 26

POLICY AND ORGANIZATION ON PURCHASING
(Number of firms)

	Country of control			Asset size in $ millions			
	U.S.	Overseas	All Countries	Under 1	1-4.9	5-24.9	25 and over
Locus of responsibility for purchasing policies							
Canadian company*	156	39	195	60	58	38	29
Affiliate	16	2	18	14	3	1	—
Both companies	15	4	19	7	8	1	1
No reply to question	40	8	48	23	13	3	5
● Total	227	53	280	104	82	43	35
Policy regarding country of purchase							
Purchase in Canada†	90	20	110	50	28	16	10
In Canada, depending on specific terms also	26	3	29	7	6	2	12
Other countries	3	3	6	4	1	1	—
Depends on terms or no policy as such	37	13	50	15	15	14	5
No reply to question	71	14	85	28	32	10	8
Total	227	53	280	104	82	43	35
Organization which does the subsidiary's purchasing							
Own organization	182	45	227	78	70	37	31
Affiliate's organization	6	1	7	5	1	—	—
Both organizations	11	3	14	7	1	3	1
No reply	28	4	32	14	10	3	3
Total	227	53	280	104	82	43	35

* Thirty-five of these firms, while indicating that the Canadian company was responsible for purchasing policies, stated this was in the context of overall financial policy or referred to specific joint purchases. See also the accompanying text.
† Fifteen of these stated some general qualification to this policy as noted in the text.

if any, regarding country of purchase.[7] Fully 110 indicated that they had a policy of buying in Canada. A number of these firms have tried to develop Canadian sources of supply even at the cost of initial disadvantages in purchasing in terms of price or other considerations. It is not difficult to find reasons for such policies in the interviews and questionnaires: the domestic content requirements of the tariff, the need for supplies suited to Canadian conditions of production, the greater certainty sometimes accompanying sources which are close at hand or which avoid customs and currency problems, and the desire to improve customer and public relations, all tend to favour domestic purchases. Fifteen of these firms added some general qualification to the effect that the policy was to buy in Canada whenever feasible, available, or possible, and more might have done so or added the qualification noted below if the question had been phrased more precisely. These particular firms shade into another twenty-nine which also stated they favoured Canadian sources but in all cases added some specific qualification to the effect that this depended also on the terms. In other words, these firms favour Canadian sources only if the terms are equal or in some cases at the cost of a small initial premium price or other disadvantage. Six firms reverse this process to favour the country of the parent. In fifty others there was no policy regarding country of purchase or such purchases depended unequivocally on the terms of purchase.

The firms which stated they had a policy of favouring Canadian purchases did not necessarily actually buy more of their supplies in Canada than did those which had no such policy. Many factors influence the domestic content of purchases, and not simply the policy regarding country of purchase. About the same proportion of the two sets of firms (the groups of 110 firms and of fifty firms in table 26) bought 90 per cent to 100 per cent of their supplies in Canada. The distinctive difference between them was that a somewhat *larger* proportion of the firms whose policy was to buy strictly on the basis of the terms was in the category buying 80-89 per cent of their supplies in Canada, and a correspondingly smaller portion was in the category buying less than 60 per cent of their supplies in Canada. This may be related to the fact that the firms with a buy-in-Canada policy tended to be somewhat more heavily concentrated in the smaller firms which have a relatively larger proportion of recently established firms

---

[7]One would have more confidence in the overall replies to this question if the response rate had been higher. Such a low response within the body of the questionnaire may reflect the fact that it was combined with another question which was partly related to it.

among them which are still rapidly raising their domestic content. It is important to add that all categories of size of firm are well represented in the group with such policies, as is evident from the tables.[8]

The Effect of Affiliation on Purchases

As with exports an attempt was made to get an overall evaluation of the effect of affiliation on purchases. Specifically, the question was "In what ways, if any, has the fact of affiliation with companies outside Canada discernibly affected the nature, sources, and costs of your purchases: for example, joint purchases with affiliates, contacts with potential suppliers, commitments to particular sources of supply?" This again was one of the questions at the end of the questionnaire inviting a more general response than most of the others. It was answered by 192 firms.[9] The replies, which varied in length and quality, are even more difficult to classify than in the case of exports, particularly with regard to whether the effects are favourable or unfavourable from the point of view of the subsidiary.

Half of the respondents believed that affiliation had no effect or a very limited one, or that the question was not applicable to their circumstances. It is not difficult to understand why many firms should be in this category; a number noted, for example, that affiliation had little effect because the tariff required that they purchase domestic supplies largely, or, in the groups replying "not applicable," that their type of business differed from that of the parent. It would be going too far to say that affiliation had no effect at all, even indirectly, on the purchases of these firms. Some of their purchasing practices might be influenced by those of the parent, and similarities of product could lead in some cases to purchases of components from the parent or its sources. A more detailed study would no doubt have led to more detailed replies on such points. The relevant point here is that

---

[8]Examination of the data within three asset size groups, however, again showed no tendency of the firms with a buy-in-Canada policy to buy relatively more in Canada, but rather a tendency for the reverse.

[9]In view of the substantial non-response to this question among those returning the questionnaire it is well to ask whether there is any pattern to the non-responses. Specifically, did those firms which omitted this particular question import a smaller or larger portion of their purchases relative to those which answered the question? It is possible to examine this since, in another part of the questionnaire, the proportion of purchases from Canadian suppliers, and thus from imports, was given. When considered by the four size groups used in this study, the quartiles and medians for the proportion of purchases from Canadian suppliers did not differ systematically for the two sets of firms, that is, for firms answering the question on the effect of affiliation on purchases and those not answering it.

such effects are small enough or indirect enough that they are not mentioned, and, more specifically, that the three particular effects noted in the question do not exist. Most of the largest firms were in this category.

In forty other cases the reply was that affiliation led to joint purchases with the parent, contacts with suppliers, and other effects. The common characteristic of all of these was that they were explicitly described as helping the subsidiary in its purchasing programs. In addition, so far as could be determined from this and other questions, the subsidiary was responsible for its purchasing policy subject only to any overall financial constraints such as those on major capital items. Joint purchases were most frequently mentioned; the effect of these was to secure lower prices for the subsidiary because of the volume involved in such purchases, to the extent that this practice did not contravene anti-trust laws and Canadian customs regulations, and sometimes earlier delivery as well. Contacts with potential suppliers were also important, reflecting in part the fact that the parent had developed supply sources for its materials, components, and capital equipment which the subsidiary could use to its advantage because of knowledge of what is available, lower prices than domestic suppliers could quote or local production would involve, or known standards of quality. Other favourable effects were noted by some companies, for example, the advice of the parent's purchasing department and the use of the credit of the parent in purchases from third parties.

The two replies below, from a medium-sized new firm and a large old one, are typical of replies in this group.

> Joint purchases with other affiliates in group have brought cost advantages.
>
> Purchases to meet requirements of Canadian company are carried out by personnel of Canadian company on the basis of the economic factors prevailing in Canada and other potential supply sources. Similarity of products and process as with those of the parent results in liaison with the purchasing department of the parent regarding potential U.S. suppliers and on a few occasions the advantages of the parent's contracts have been extended to the Canadian company. There is no commitment to particular sources of supply and in substantially all cases purchase negotiations are carried out by the Canadian company buying in Canada wherever economically possible.

In eleven other firms various tied arrangements were noted as the result of affiliation. These involve joint purchases of parts or raw materials from which the affiliate is not free to depart, or central buying by the parent for all of its affiliates with the same restriction, or tied purchases from the parent or its affiliates. It should be noted that these firms were usually given responsibility for purchases beyond the specific item noted, though in several cases the specific item was a large part of their total purchases. One example may suffice, from one of the large older firms:

> Our purchases of major materials, with one exception, are the responsibility of our own Purchasing Department. The one exception is a major raw material ingredient which is manufactured by a domestic U.S. division of our parent company, which is the largest supplier of this commodity in the world and policy dictates that we purchase from them. On the other hand, benefits do accrue to us in the services of the Corporate Purchasing Department and those in other U.S. divisions in regard to our purchases of many other materials.

In thirty-four other cases it was stated that affiliation led to significant purchases from the parent firm itself. Half of these firms stated explicitly that the subsidiary was free to secure the supplies or components elsewhere if it was to the subsidiary's advantage to do so. The others made no reference to this but simply stated that affiliation led to significant imports from the parent, adding, in some cases, that this was to the subsidiary's advantage. Some of these may in fact be tied purchases; the rationale underlying restrictive arrangements on purchases between affiliated firms will be discussed below. As already noted, some of these purchases are likely to be the result of other factors. It is not surprising to find substantial purchases from the parent: not only similarity in product, but frequently lower costs from this source, the fact that the parent may be the only producer of some components in design-oriented products particularly, familiarity with the parent's supplies, and inertia combined with the cost of seeking new sources will all contribute to this result. Some of the answers classified here may be of interest.

> Many finished and sub-assembly items and parts purchased from parent where it is less costly than manufacturing in Canada. Otherwise complete freedom to purchase is given.
>
> No particular effect except many purchases made from parent that could conceivably be made to advantage elsewhere if value analysis carried out by engineering and purchasing. This has been done in isolated cases with beneficial results.
>
> Large buyer of parts from parent. Canadian company can buy parts elsewhere if price is less than landed price from parent, but it is difficult to beat parent's price. Products are highly specialized.

In this connection a brief further comment is called for on a problem discussed earlier. It has frequently been suggested that the international firm limits the development of local sources of supply because of requirements that the subsidiary purchase its parts and materials from the parent or its other affiliates, insofar as these produce them. In particular it is suggested that, in deciding whether the subsidiary will buy from non-affiliated sources or continue to import from affiliates, it is not enough that the price from the former simply be lower than that from affiliates. The price from non-affiliates must be low enough, it is argued, to compensate the international firm for the contribution which the sale to the subsidiary was making to the overhead costs, plus any profit mark-up, of the international firm.[10] This argument is clearly similar to that considered earlier to the effect that the Canadian firms will not be allowed to export to markets served by the parent, whether to third markets or to the parent's domestic market, since facilities may already exist for this purpose. One can therefore repeat the conclusions in considering the case of imports from affiliates abroad. To the extent that the question is relevant because of vertical integration and because the international firm is maximizing its profits globally, the argument applies only in the short run when existing facilities in the parent have not been depreciated, and where equally rewarding alternative uses for existing capacity are not available. It does not apply, even then, if the total cost per unit in securing the item from the subsidiary or some non-affiliated source is below the average variable cost of the parent. Other things being equal, the transfer of sources to the subsidiary or to non-affiliates is faster where fixed costs are not large relative to variable, plant is not lumpy, excess capacity does not exist, and the overall market is expanding. Of great importance also is the degree of effective competition in the industry; the move will be expedited if and to the extent that competitors take advantage of the lower cost source or plan to do so. Once again it must be added that ignorance of costs and inability to freely search for and develop sources of supply may cause problems for some subsidiaries and non-affiliated sources for a time, where the parent intervenes in the pur-

---

[10]It has been stated, for example, that parent automobile firms cannot allow wholly-owned subsidiaries to buy parts on the basis of the subsidiaries' out-of-pocket costs alone, since the parent must consider the worldwide corporate profit generated from the sale of the part to the subsidiary by the parent. It has been pointed out, however, that this view reflects either a short-run situation or the presence of unexplained oligopolistic influences. See Neil B. MacDonald, "A Comment: The Bladen Plan for Increased Protection for the Automotive Industry," and Harry G. Johnson, "The Bladen Plan: A Reply," in *The Canadian Journal of Economics and Political Science*, Vol. 29, No. 4 (November, 1963), pp. 505-515 and 515-518.

chasing decision. Nevertheless it is the relative efficiency of Canadian production and distribution and the degree of competition within given tariff and other barriers to trade which will eventually determine the sourcing of supplies, as in the case of the Canadian-owned firm. The qualification to this, and it can be an important one, is that where design is important the parent may continue to be a unique source of supply for some time.

One might go further and suggest that the issue raised here is similar to that within a resident-owned firm, in terms of decisions on making the product within the firm or buying from outside it.[11] It, too, will favour its given facilities in the short-run because of the contribution to overheads and/or its profit mark-up. In the longer-term, subject to the pressures noted, it can hardly avoid shifting to the most efficient source of supply if it is to remain competitive. One might argue that there is a bias to domestic purchase in this case since the original facilities are located in Canada. This should be no more than a short-run factor. If it reflected a situation favouring production in Canada on a continuing basis then, as noted above, the result should be similar for the foreign-owned firm intent on maximizing its global profit. This point will be considered again in Chapter 9 when the purchasing pattern of independent Canadian firms is compared with that of foreign-owned subsidiaries.

The direct empirical evidence available on this point is limited. It stems mainly from some of the interviews, where in nineteen cases the point was discussed in enough detail for an opinion to be given here. In five of these cases it was quite clear that, in deciding whether an import from the parent should be produced in the subsidiary or bought from non-affiliated sources, the question of the loss of the contribution to the parent's overhead or profit was quite explicitly considered. Two of these added that this had not made much difference over long periods as witnessed by the gradual but substantial decline in the proportion of purchases from the parent. Nevertheless this consideration was significant for some purchases in the short run (in one or two cases a rather long short-run) especially where other factors led to vertical integration of considerable degree. In fourteen other cases the officers reported that the subsidiaries disregarded such considerations even in the short term. In most cases they emphasized that the subsidiary has the responsibility for its purchases; some added this was short

---

[11]The problem arises frequently in business literature. For an examination of the issues involved see, for example, Carter C. Higgins, "Make-or-Buy Re-Examined," *Harvard Business Review*, Vol. XXXIII, 2, (March/April, 1955), pp. 109-119.

of major capital purchases, which may not be from the parent in any case. In effect, in these firms the parent has sacrificed whatever short-run opportunities there are for maximizing global profit from directing some subsidiary purchases to itself or its other affiliates, presumably because the long-run interests of the overall firm are better served by permitting the subsidiary to control its own purchasing and thereby to maximize its own profit.

There is much more to be said on this issue as reflected in the discussion on the similar problem regarding exports. The two problems merge at some point: for example, the replacement of imports by local production in the subsidiary may in fact be for, or lead to, exports. If such exports are to affiliates abroad the same considerations arise but in reverse. Moreover, the more general questions about exports from Canada arise, including relative competitiveness of costs and distribution, barriers to exports, and so on. As with exports also, imperfect competition in the sense of one or a few buyers or sellers, of the abuse of legal monopolies through patents and other devices, and of actual collusive arrangements between producers, can seriously hamper for varying periods of time the access of the subsidiary to the lowest-cost supply and hence adversely affect the wider interests of the country.[12] One should not diminish the importance of such obstacles to maximizing welfare, wherever the firm is owned, nor the need to develop effective public policies in this regard. The more important point by far is the overwhelming extent to which the direct investment firm, in the context of legal and natural barriers to trade and for reasons of access to lower-cost supplies, has led to the development of Canadian sources of supply. This, surely, is what stands out from the data on sources of purchasing which were noted earlier. The more relevant question then becomes not only the contribution to the development of local sources but the efficiency of the direct investment firm as a means of supplying Canadian demands. Some aspects of this will be considered in Chapter 7.

As with exports, at times the agencies of foreign governments may attempt to directly affect the imports of subsidiary companies. In December of 1965 Canada was included in the balance of payments "guidelines" used by the United States government as part of its "voluntary" program for reducing the deficit in the international accounts.[13] The nature of the guide-

12Examples of restrictions of these types and their effects on imports from the United Kingdom have been examined by G. L. Reuber in *Britain's Export Trade With Canada*, University of Toronto Press, 1960, Ch. 5.
13See the address by the Honourable Eric W. Kierans, Minister of Health for Quebec, entitled "The Economic Effects of the Guidelines," to the Toronto Society of Finan-

lines and their effects on financial ties between parent firms and their subsidiaries abroad will be dealt with in Chapter 8. While the main and direct intent of the guidelines is to reduce on a global basis the net outflow of capital to the subsidiaries, including increased transfers of income and idle balances from the subsidiaries, there is, nevertheless, a potential foreign trade effect of considerable importance to Canada. This was the suggestion to those parent companies to whom the regulations applied that they give some attention to increasing exports of components and raw materials to their subsidiaries abroad in order to aid the United States balance of payments. In effect, the companies were being asked to make decisions about trade between affiliates other than those they would make on economic grounds, in order to suit the objectives of the balance of payments program. This brought them into conflict with the stated objectives of the provincial and federal governments of Canada which have been to encourage firms to increase their domestic content in manufacturing (and to increase exports) in order to reduce the substantial deficit on current account. Some of the financial aspects of the regulations have also been criticized in Canada as interference with the operations of the subsidiaries. At the moment of writing it is not clear what economic and political consequences the regulations will have or even how long they will be in force. As in the case of exports to China, however, the entire issue raised once again the question of extra-territorial application of United States law, and it did so in a context where Canadian interests do not necessarily coincide with those of the United States. It will be noted in Chapter 8 that the United States authorities have indicated they do not expect the companies to depart from their normal business practices, but the guidelines, which appear to require such departure, remain in effect. As noted at the end of Chapter 1 the Canadian government has issued its own set of guidelines in response to those of the United States, urging subsidiary companies among other things to do more of their purchasing in Canada.

---

cial Analysts, February 1, 1966 (largely reprinted in the *Globe and Mail*, February 2, 1966); the statement by the Honourable Mitchell Sharp, Minister of Finance for the Government of Canada, House of Commons, *Debates*, January 27, 1966, pp. 322-327, and the interview with him printed in the *Financial Post*, February 12, 1966, pp. 17-18; and the issues of the *Globe and Mail* for February 4, 8, 9 and 18, 1966.

6
The Transfer of Knowledge

The transfer of knowledge through direct investment may often dwarf the transfer of capital in importance so far as the recipient country is concerned. In this chapter the extent and the terms of transfer of the research, development and other knowledge of the parent firm to the subsidiary will be considered. In addition, the extent to which the subsidiary firms undertake research and development will be examined. Both of these have important implications for the recipient nation.

There is a growing amount of information on expenditures on research and development and the results thereof. Nevertheless, both statistically and analytically this must be regarded as a relatively underdeveloped area of economics. Few countries have the wealth of data now available for the United States, for example, and even that is of relatively recent origin.[1] There is room for dispute regarding the determinants of research and development and their impact on the economy. There has been only limited information and analysis on these points in Canada.[2]

Organized large-scale industrial research is a relatively recent development everywhere. The amount spent on systematic research and development in the United Kingdom at the turn of this century was probably not over £1 million per year. In the United States it was not until the same period that an industrial firm organized research as a separate and continuing activity.[3] The state of affairs in Canada just half a century ago was

[1]See the series of reports prepared for the National Science Foundation by the United States Department of Labor, entitled *Science and Engineering in American Industry*, and the National Science Foundation's *Review of Data on Research and Development*.
[2]For a brief analysis of the role of industrial research in Canada, see H. Edward English, "Growth — The Implications of Institutional Factors," in *Growth and the Canadian Economy*, mimeo., Carleton University, Ottawa, 1965.
[3]As stated by Dunning, *op. cit.*, p. 164.

summarized by a scientist describing the results of the first census of industrial research in Canada in 1917. "Only about thirty-seven firms in this Dominion appear to have research laboratories, the majority of these have, each, only one research man employed. There are about seven or eight that employ four or more, something like four that employ two or three, and in some of them the work is purely routine, for although called research, it is not research at all, it is simply making analyses of raw materials to ascertain whether they are up to standard."[4] According to the National Research Council it was not until World War II and after that Canada experienced growth in industrial research and development similar in relative terms to that experienced in the United States during and after World War I.[5] Expenditures for industrial research and development have risen considerably in recent years. Nevertheless, there is much dissatisfaction with the amount of spending on research and development by Canadian industry, partly because much of it is the result of direct government financing rather than any conviction by industry of the benefits of such spending, and partly because the spending by Canadian industry is comparatively less than that by the United States, United Kingdom, and several other industrial countries. In addition to continuing assistance from a number of provinces the government of Canada has undertaken to stimulate industrial research by several means since 1962. Most significant in this connection have been programs in which 50 per cent of the cost of approved research projects can be shared by the National Research Council or the Defence Research Board, and the permitting of an extra 50 per cent charge against taxable income, beyond the usual 100 per cent charge, for corporate expenditures on scientific research for industrial purposes in excess of those in the base year 1961.[6]

Estimates presented by the National Research Council, which are shown

---

[4]*Proceedings* of the Special Committee Appointed to Consider the Matter of the Development in Canada of Scientific Research, Parliament of Canada, 10 George V, Appendix No. 5, p. 18, King's Printer, 1919. For reference to and discussion of the Canadian surveys of industrial and other research, see George T. McColm, "Canadian Surveys of Research and Development," in National Science Foundation, *Methodology of Statistics on Research and Development*, Washington 25, D.C., 1959.
[5]See National Research Council, *Thirty-ninth Annual Report, 1955-56*, Queen's Printer, 1956, pp. 11-12.
[6]The 150 per cent deduction expires in 1966. In the budget of March, 1965, it was announced that it would be replaced by some form of direct subsidy. The programs are summarized and discussed in articles in the *Financial Post* for January 27 and April 14, 1962, February 15, 1964 and February 6, March 20 and May 8, 1965. Their effectiveness is measured in a study by the National Industrial Conference Board, entitled *Scientific Research in Canadian Industry*, Montreal, September, 1963.

TABLE 27

COMPARATIVE DATA ON RESEARCH AND DEVELOPMENT EXPENDITURES, CANADA, UNITED KINGDOM, UNITED STATES, 1959*

	In millions			As % of GNP		
	Canada	U.K.	U.S.	Canada	U.K.	U.S.
Total expenditures†	$251	£478	$12,430	0.72	2.11	2.58
Performed by:						
Federal government	120	159	1,780	0.34	0.70	0.37
Industry	97	280	9,438	0.28	1.23	1.96
Financed by:						
Federal government	154	320	8,030	0.44	1.41	1.67
Industry	78	144	4,075	0.23	0.63	0.85
	In billions					
Gross National Product	$34.9	£22.7	$482.1			

* From the **Forty-Fourth Annual Report of the National Research Council, 1960-61**, pp. 17-18.
† Including government, industry, universities and other institutions.

in table 27, indicate the relatively smaller role of research performed by industry in particular in Canada. Various interpretations can be placed on the data depending on the question being considered. In particular, it is not at all evident that a country need have the same percentage of its resources devoted to industrial research as do others in order to maintain its competitive position or rate of growth relative to them. In the first place, the statistical evidence on the relationship of spending on research and development to these other variables is not convincing.[7] Secondly, the country's particular circumstances will have much to do with its optimum spending in this area. For example, defence spending plays a greater role in the United States economy than in Canada and defence-oriented research (which is very large) plays a correspondingly greater role. Moreover, since research varies greatly by type of industry there will be significant national differences in research spending simply because the structure of industry varies. Thirdly, it is well to note that international comparisons of research and development spending are very greatly affected by differing definitions of what is being measured, for example, with regard to such important parts of the total as those involved in experimental production of aircraft.

[7]See, for example, the article by J. Jewkes, "How Much Science," in the *Economic Journal*, Vol. 70 (March, 1960), pp. 1-16.

Finally, a country need not actually perform research in a particular area in order to enjoy access to it; the relevant question with regard to economic welfare then becomes the terms of access to the research or the products of the research.

For present purposes only one explanation of these international differences in spending on research will be noted, an explanation which has gained widespread acceptance in Canada. It is that the extensive foreign ownership of Canadian industry militates against the performance of industrial research in Canada, since subsidiary firms tend to rely on the large research facilities of the parent rather than to undertake research in Canada. It is recognized that there are some advantages to this ready access to some of the greatest research laboratories in the world. Many persons, nevertheless, regret the assumed lack of industrial research in Canada because of such reasons as the possible competitive trading disadvantages which may result, the need for adaptation to Canadian circumstances, and the lack of opportunity for scientists. The following are rather typical comments in this regard:

> There are two main factors which have affected the development of industrial research in Canada. In the first place in a pioneer country primary industries develop first and secondary industries came rather late into the picture. As a result good facilities for research in agriculture and in mining developed long before industrial research as such got going at all. This is the normal course of the development of research in a country as it becomes industrialized. The second factor is that because of the proximity of Canada to the United States and because of the financial relationship between Canadian and American (and British) firms, most Canadian plants are essentially branch plants and research is normally done by the parent organization outside the country. As a result Canadian industry has been largely dependent on research in the United States and in Britain. The result of this is that, by comparison with the United States or Britain, relatively little industrial research has been done in Canada *by* industrial organizations while a great deal has been done by Government agencies *for* the industry.[8]

> The scientists also deplore the fact that many subsidiaries of U.S. companies either are forbidden to do their own research, or must

---

[8]See *Canadian Research Expenditure*, a submission by Dr. E. W. R. Steacie, President of the National Research Council, to the Royal Commission on Canada's Economic Prospects (Exhibit 262, Ottawa, March 8, 1956). See also pp. 8821-8839 of the transcript of evidence by Dr. Steacie on that data to the Commission, for further discussion on this point.

hand over their successful research projects to U.S. parents for development outside Canada. . . . There is no denying, of course, that in many cases (nearly all) Canadian subsidiaries are run from head office so far as research and development are concerned.[9]

This non-resident control provides a ready access to research results abroad and tends to limit the amount of research and development performed in Canada.[10]

Some of the criticism of direct investment companies has come close to suggesting that a country should not take advantage of access to the very extensive and expensive research and development which is done abroad since this inhibits the development of local research and development. This view can be challenged on *a priori* grounds. It is not evident that a country is better off to use its resources to duplicate research-development which is done abroad and is available at relatively low cost to it. The qualifications are important: the research-development must be available quickly at low cost and the firms involved must be free to exploit it commercially. If such is the case, and given that scientific resources are scarce, the country in question is presumably better off to invest its existing research skills in areas not covered by what is easily and cheaply available from abroad.

One can also challenge the implicit assumption that the subsidiary will not undertake research, or will do very little of it, where access to it is easy. There is a superficial case to be made in this respect. Where much larger parent companies are already undertaking expensive research, expenditures for which will often total as much as the entire sales of the subsidiary, it may be asked why the parent would permit duplication of such costs among its affiliates. The answer lies partly in the economies of decentralization of research-development in some industries and partly in the specialization of research-development, rather than duplication of effort, among the affiliates. Some of the executives who were interviewed insisted that decentralization of research in their industry would be impossibly costly and wasteful. Economies of scale were such that none of the many

---

[9]This is from the lead article in the *Financial Post* for January 28, 1961, outlining criticisms by senior government scientists of the lack of industrial research and replies by businessmen. The same charge about subsidiary firms is made in an article in the *Financial Post* for February 15, 1964, on p. 3, in an attempt to explain the apparently limited response by industry to the provision for sharing of the cost of projects with National Research Council or Defence Research Board. An interesting aspect of the latter article is that the firms which had made arrangements up to that time for sharing of costs are listed by name; roughly half of them are subsidiaries of foreign companies.

[10]McColm, *op. cit.*, p. 63.

international affiliates did very much research-development apart from the parent, which made its findings available quite fully, and often at little direct cost, to its affiliates. A number of others believed basic research could not be decentralized to the same extent as the applied research; in many cases not even the parent was doing much basic research, which both in Canada and abroad tended to be concentrated in universities and/or government agencies. The relevant question then becomes whether it is available through publication and otherwise, and how fully and quickly. In addition, not all firms are suited to research-development on any large scale, either because of the stage of development of the firm or because of the nature of the product. Not all of the parent companies, for example, are extensively engaged even in applied research. On the other hand, there are many good reasons why subsidiary firms often undertake research: economies of scale do not appear to exist with regard to some kinds of research in some industries, adaptation to local conditions may be required, the smaller Canadian firm may be a better place in which to test certain ideas before applying them in the international firm, and in some industries it is necessary to do research and development as part of the production process itself. A substantial number of the executives who were interviewed indicated the Canadian firm was engaged in research, sometimes specialized in a product or process which did not duplicate the work of its affiliates. They also indicated that there were many advantages to research within an international firm. Access to the research of the affiliate saved a good deal of time and cost in their own research, for example. Several pointed out also that once they had invented a process or product they could often use the skills of the affiliate in the difficult job of development and production on a volume basis, often to the considerable profit of the subsidiary.

In view of the many criticisms of the research effort of subsidiary firms, and in view of the importance attached to such expenditures, it is remarkable that no comprehensive study has been undertaken of them. The official studies of industrial research have never broken out the data by country of ownership of the firm. Even a brief glance at the overall data, nevertheless, would suggest that some care must be exercised in advancing the above reason for the relative lack of industrial research, for they suggest that most of the research which is performed within Canada tends to be rather heavily concentrated in the foreign-owned sector of Canadian industry. This can be seen from table 28 where the $97 million of industrial research performed within Canadian companies in 1959 is shown by industry. About 57 per cent of the total is concentrated in three industries whose capital was heavily owned by non-residents. The transportation equipment industry can be broken down into automobiles and parts where 89 per cent of the capital was owned by non-residents in 1959, and other transportation equipment in which 58 per cent of the capital was foreign-owned. Indeed, fully 24 per cent of industrial research-development expenditures in 1959 was in one sector of this, aircraft and parts, whose capital is mainly owned abroad. In electrical apparatus and supplies 74 per cent of the capital was owned by non-residents. In chemical products 61 per cent of the capital was owned by non-residents in 1959.[11] Some of the other major industrial spenders on research and development also have a substantial degree of foreign ownership of capital, such as the pulp and paper industry, non-ferrous metal products, and mining and petroleum. It is true that in electrical apparatus and transportation, particularly the aircraft sector, a substantial portion of the expenditures shown represents funds supplied by government. This reflects the requirements of defence. In any case, these two industries financed more research from their own funds than did any of the others shown, except chemicals.[12]

Such data must be treated with care in assessing the performance of firms by ownership of capital. One would want to know which firms in each industry were undertaking research, for example, since it is theoretically possible that the resident-owned firms in the above industries are doing more research than their non-resident owned counterparts; and whether, given product-mix, size of firm, and other characteristics, there was a difference in research performance. The only available data on industrial research do suggest quite clearly, however, that the research-oriented industries tend generally to be the ones where foreign ownership is relatively high.

The Performance of Research by the Respondent Companies

No part of this study is more likely to reflect problems of definition and measurement than the present chapter. It was quite evident from the interviews that extreme care had to be exercised in asking and interpreting questions on this subject given the variety of meanings ascribed to research

---

[11]See table 3 in Chapter 1 for these and other ownership ratios by industry. The classifications in these two tables are not closely comparable but the broad point made here should not be vitiated thereby.
[12]Government supplied $14 million to the transportation equipment industry and $6.4 million to the electrical apparatus industry, amounting to 96 per cent of funds supplied directly to industry through prime and procurement contracts. For detail on sources of funds see table 4 in the publication noted in table 28.

TABLE 28

INDUSTRIAL RESEARCH-DEVELOPMENT EXPENDITURES IN CANADA BY INDUSTRY, DONE WITHIN THE REPORTING COMPANY, 1959

Industry	Expenditures for research-development ($ millions)	Number of firms involved
Mining, quarrying, oil wells	4.9	30
Manufacturing		
Foods and beverages	1.8	25
Rubber products	1.2	7
Textile products	1.4	8
Wood products	0.2	12
Paper products	6.6	26
Iron and steel products	5.6	64
Transportation equipment	25.6	24
Non-ferrous metal products	5.9	13
Electrical apparatus, supplies	15.9	51
Non-metallic mineral products	1.4	17
Products of petroleum and coal	3.8	5
Chemical products	14.1	47
Other manufacturing	3.0	21
Transportation, storage, communications		
public utilities	2.8	5
Other non-manufacturing	2.6	12
Total	96.7	367

SOURCE: Dominion Bureau of Statistics, Industrial Research-Development Expenditures in Canada, 1959, Tables 1 and 13. Data refer only to firms conducting research-development within the company. An additional $2.6 million was spent for research performed in Canada but outside the firm and $22 million for research done in other countries. This last figure is unlikely to be an accurate measure of the receipt of research and development from outside the country in view of what is said below about the charges for research between subsidiary and parent firms.

and development by the officers of companies in different industries. The line between research and development on the one hand and production on the other is often an imprecise one, and some firms may confuse relatively routine functions with research. Beyond the basic or fundamental research which few firms are likely to do one must allow for a wide range

TABLE 29

COST OF RESEARCH AND DEVELOPMENT AS A PERCENTAGE
OF TOTAL ANNUAL SALES*
(Number of firms)

Research-development as % of sales	Done within the Canadian company	Purchased from affiliates outside Canada	Purchased from other firms or organizations	Total cost of research-development
0%	129	153	191	93
Up to 0.5	23	21	7	19
0.6 – 1.0	22	9	1	21
1.1 – 2.0	26	9	—	33
2.1 – 5.0	16	10	—	26
Over 5.0	3	1	1	6
% unspecified†	19	23	7	36
No reply to question	42	54	73	46
Total	280	280	280	280

* There is duplication among the first three columns in the sense that any single firm could theoretically answer all three questions. The fourth column reflects the total research effort included in (up to three of) the previous columns.
† These firms indicated they were doing research-development as defined but did not give the percentage to sales. Many of them indicated the research effort was small, probably under one per cent of sales.

of applied research in order to encompass the situations in widely different industries.

As it happened there was a simple way out of the dilemma involved in dealing with a complex issue within a short list of questions. This was to use the definition of research and development which is used by the Dominion Bureau of Statistics. The advantage of this approach, apart from the merit of the definition itself, is that the firms would have already answered questions on this subject using the same definition. In addition, the present data would be directly comparable with the overall data for Canada.[13] The definition follows, as adjusted for our purpose:

For present purposes, the term "research and development" comprises activities directed to pure or basic research (i.e. to programs

[13]For a discussion of the D.B.S. definition see *Industrial Research-Development Expenditures in Canada, 1959*, p. 31 ff. A useful discussion of the problems of measurement is available in *Estimates of Resources Devoted to Scientific and Engineering Research and Development in British Manufacturing Industry, 1955*, published by the Department of Scientific and Industrial Research of the United Kingdom in 1958. See also the publications listed in footnote 1 of this chapter.

not primarily committed to specific product or process applications) and also to conceiving and developing new products, new processes and major changes in products and processes, and bringing them up to the stage of production. Such activities as market and sales research, process and quality control, and geological and geophysical exploration, should be excluded. If in doubt, please use your normal definition and briefly specify its nature.

With this definition in mind the results of the present survey can be considered. It will be noted that 109 of the firms did some research and development, as defined, within the Canadian company. Fully 129 did no research and development within the Canadian firm, while forty-two did not answer the question. A smaller group of seventy-three firms reported purchases from affiliates outside Canada, including forty-three which were doing research-development within the Canadian company. Many more receive such research without direct payment, as will be noted shortly. Only sixteen purchased research from all other firms or organizations.[14] In terms of the total research effort it will be noted that 141 firms make direct payments for research-development performed within the firm, by affiliates abroad, or by other firms or organizations while ninety-three make no such payments.[15]

There is no significant difference in the extent to which firms owned overseas and those owned in the United States undertake research and development within the Canadian company, as indicated by a comparison of table 30 with data for American-owned companies presented in Appen-

[14]Only sixty-five of all the firms in Canada in 1959 paid for research-development done outside the firm (but within Canada), to the amount of only $2.6 million. See *Industrial Research-Development Expenditures in Canada, 1959*, tables 1 and 13.

[15]The non-response to this set of questions was higher than for almost all other questions within the body of the questionnaire. A number of the firms answering the questionnaire stated that the definition of research-development was so restrictive as to exclude their work in this area. The evidence from other questions having to do with research and development strongly suggests, however, that many of the other firms which did not respond to this set of questions were not doing research-development as defined. The replies to other questions also suggest that most of the fifty-four firms which did not here answer the question on purchases from affiliates abroad were receiving the results of the affiliates' research without any direct payment, that is, they may belong in the group marked zero per cent.

It is of interest to compare these results with those for American-owned firms in the United Kingdom. Only 25 per cent of the firms in Dunning's study had no separate research-development department, 56 per cent did some applied and development research, while 19 per cent did some basic research. It should be noted that Dunning concentrated exclusively on firms employing more than 100 workers in 1953. See Dunning, *op. cit.*, p. 168.

TABLE 30

**RESEARCH AND DEVELOPMENT DONE WITHIN THE CANADIAN COMPANY,
BY SIZE OF COMPANY**
(Number of firms)

Asset size in $ millions

Research-development as % of sales	Under 1	1-4.9	5-24.9	25 and over	All companies
0%	60	41	13	10	129
Up to 0.5	5	3	3	11	23
0.6 – 1.0	8	6	6	1	22
1.1 – 2.0	6	9	6	5	26
2.1 – 5.0	5	7	1	3	16
Over 5.0	1	—	1	1	3
% unspecified	2	5	6	1	19
No reply to question	17	11	7	3	42
Total	104	82	43	35	280

**Averages for above data
(% of sales)**

First quartile	0	0	0	0	0
Median	0	0	0.23	0.23	0
Third quartile	0.50	1.00	1.14	1.35	1.00

dix A. There appears to be a distinct relationship between size of company and research-development as a percentage of sales in the sense that the larger companies are more likely to do research.[16] Thus 58 per cent of the respondent firms which had less than $1 million in assets reported no research-development expenditures within the Canadian company, as compared with 50 per cent for those with assets in the range of $1–4.9 million, 30 per cent of those with assets in the $5-24.9 million range, and 29 per cent for those firms with assets of $25 million or more. The median and quartiles in table 30 bear this out. On the other hand, for those firms which

---

[16]In the following comparisons by groups it is well to remind the reader once more that there are variable rates of non-response to particular questions by those firms answering the questionnaire. These non-responses are shown throughout so that the reader can judge whether the data can support the particular interpretations put on them. It will be clear from what follows that we have implicitly assumed the non-responses are randomly distributed across the responding groups.

are doing some research-development in the Canadian company there does not appear to be any marked variation by size of firm in the percentage which research bears to sales, once one gets beyond the smallest size category of firms. The median and third quartile do tend to rise but the rise is moderate and not uniform.

It will be noted from table 31 that relatively few of the firms in certain industries are engaged in research-development. There was no difference between primary industries and primary manufacturing on the one hand and secondary manufacturing on the other, as distinguished very roughly earlier; just over half of the firms in each group did no research and development at all. Unfortunately, one must note that comparisons by industry are plagued by too few firms for the sixteen industrial categories used and by significantly different non-responses for some categories. A test of the relation between size of firm and research-development as a percentage of sales, within sixteen industry groups, was made by combining the resident-owned and non-resident owned firms in this study which gave sufficient data on research expenditures, size of firm, and industry group. The 136 observations thus available, when considered within four size groups by industry, indicate a slight tendency for research-development as a percentage of sales to *fall* within industry groups as the size of firm increases. The test is a very rough one in view of the limitations noted.[17] Small numbers also must qualify another approach to this question, namely the relation to type of business of the Canadian firm. The firms engaged in producing fully-processed goods do appear to have a greater orientation to research, as do the fully integrated firms. This is particularly noticeable if one considers those with research expenditures in excess of one per cent of sales. The differences by type of business broadly persist when examined within classifications by absolute size of firm.

The research performance within the Canadian subsidiary appears also to be related to certain characteristics of the industry relative to the affiliate. There is a marked relationship between research-development as a percentage of sales and the size of the Canadian firm relative to the affiliate. Thus 30 per cent of those firms with assets one to five per cent as large as those of the affiliate did research, but this proportion rises steadily to 72 per cent for those firms whose assets were over 20 per cent in relation

[17]Some credence is given to the result noted here by the results of the D.B.S. study, which show a tendency for smaller firms to do more research-development as a percentage of sales when grouped by industries, as well as overall. See *Industrial Research-Development Expenditures in Canada, 1959*, table 5.

TABLE 31

**RESEARCH AND DEVELOPMENT EXPENDITURES WITHIN THE CANADIAN COMPANY
CLASSIFIED BY SELECTED CHARACTERISTICS**

By asset size relative to affiliate	Research as a Percentage of Sales			Number of replies*
	0%	0.01-1.00%	Over 1.00%	
	(% distribution of companies by rows)			
1% to 5% of affiliate	70	15	15	54
6% to 10%	64	14	22	83
11% to 15%	55	20	25	20
16% to 20%	31	31	38	16
Over 20%	29	48	24	21
Total	58	20	22	194
By general nature of products compared with affiliate				
Identical with comparable products of affiliate	74	15	11	128
Marginally different	38	36	26	58
Substantially modified	23	31	46	13
Not comparable	22	28	50	18
Total	57	23	20	217
By range of products compared with affiliate				
Wider than affiliate	44	39	17	18
About the same	66	19	15	67
Majority of affiliate's products	60	22	18	60
Minority of affiliate's products	54	13	33	24
Only a few	68	18	14	22
Total	61	21	18	191†
Type of Product				
Petroleum products	90	10	—	10
Primary mining and smelting	33	50	17	6
Foods and beverages	46	46	8	13
Rubber products	—	67	33	3
Textiles and clothing	60	40	—	5
Wood and furniture	71	29	—	7

Lumber, pulp, newsprint	20	40	40	5
Paper products	66	17	17	6
Primary metals	20	60	20	5
Metal fabricating	70	18	12	17
Machinery (except electrical)	59	18	24	34
Transportation equipment	53	29	18	17
Electrical products	53	13	34	32
Non-metallic mineral products	67	—	33	6
Chemical and allied products	63	17	20	30
Miscellaneous industries	63	16	21	24
Total	58	22	20	220
Type of business of Canadian company				
Assembly	80	12	8	25
Extractive	64	27	9	11
Semi-fabricated products	63	26	11	19
Fully processed or manufactured products	55	24	21	150
Integrated	37	16	47	19
Total	58	22	20	224

* † See notes to table 17.

to those of the affiliate. Similarly, the proportion of firms spending on research from 0.01-1.00 per cent of sales rises as one moves to higher size groups relative to the affiliate, and the same tendency exists for those spending over one per cent of sales on research. If one re-examines this data classified by *absolute* size of the Canadian firm, the relationships persist. In other words, the observed relationship between size of Canadian firm relative to the affiliate and the propensity to do research-development in Canada does not appear to result from any observed relationship between absolute size of the Canadian firm and its performance of research.

There is a marked relationship between the research performance of the subsidiary on the one hand and the nature of its products compared with those of the affiliate on the other. Where the products are generally identical with those of the affiliate 26 per cent of the firms did research. The percentage doing research rises to well over half of the firms in each of the categories where the products are generally differentiated from those of the parent firms, and it tends to rise with the degree of differentiation.

involved. Taking these differentiated groups together to get around the problem of small numbers, it turns out that only 32 per cent of the firms did no research in the three groups whose products are differentiated to some degree. This difference is not due to differences in size of firm within these categories. Within each of the three size groups used to test such differences (under $1 million, $1-4.9 million, $5 million or more) the firms with products generally identical to those of the parent ranked very substantially below each of the other three categories of product differentiation shown in table 31. The present techniques and data do not show a relationship betwen the range of products compared with the affiliate and the research performance of the Canadian firm. If the five groups shown in table 31 are compared the results for research performance appear to be erratic. If the first two and last two groups are combined there is virtually the same proportion of firms doing research in each category. Further analysis within size groups leads to results which are ambiguous at best.

The Nature of the Canadian Research Programs

There were facilities of some specific kind in the company in ninety-two of the firms in this study. Some others did research-development but had no facilities as such devoted to such work. The facilities would vary a good deal in terms of organization, distinction from other operations of the firm, and program. Nor was it always clear to these firms, particularly to some of the older and more complex ones, just when facilities for performance of research in the firm had advanced to the point where specific personnel, equipment, and plant were assigned to this function. Nevertheless, the recentness of establishment of most such facilities stands out strikingly for the seventy-six which gave precise information on year of establishment. Only thirteen of these firms had research-development facilities as such before 1940.[18] It is in the period since the second world war, and especially in the fifties, that the great majority of such facilities have been established. Thus fourteen firms indicated they had established such facilities in 1940-49, and forty-nine in 1950-59. Both the large and the small firms reported in most cases that the facilities had been established recently. Fully fourteen of the thirty firms in this group with assets of $5 million or more reported their facilities had been established from 1950 to 1959, and another eight that they had been established from 1940 to 1949.

---

[18]At most another five of the sixteen which could not give precise dates could have had such facilities prior to 1940, judging by the date these companies were established. All but one of the five were in the two largest size groups.

The reasons for establishing such facilities in Canada varied a good deal. The major factors which led to the establishment of such facilities, or to a major expansion in them, were outlined by seventy-three of the ninety-two firms which reported the existence of facilities for research and development in the Canadian company. One of the most frequently mentioned reasons was the need to meet Canadian conditions. This included the need to meet Canadian standards which are sometimes different from those specified elsewhere, as in the electrical industry; the need to modify the affiliate's product or develop some new ones to suit Canadian tastes, weather, the requirements of industrial customers, and other market requirements which were different from those in the country of the affiliate; and the need to modify the parent's production techniques or develop entirely new ones, as in the supply of certain raw materials. Twenty-six of the seventy-three firms explicitly gave this type of reason for establishing or greatly enlarging their Canadian research facilities. Another twenty-six gave a variety of reasons which can most simply be characterized as product development, namely, the development of new products in order to round out the product line, to compensate for obsolescence of existing products, to meet customer requirements including those involved in government defence contracts, and similar reasons. Also included here are a few cases where the development of a major process, usually associated with the establishment of the firm itself, led to the establishment of research facilities. There is some overlap between this group and the first one since some product development, such as that designed to meet customer requirements, may involve adaptation to peculiarly Canadian circumstances. The line of demarcation used for the two groups is simply that this was explicitly stated to be the case in the first group. In a third group of twelve firms the Canadian facilities were established or greatly enlarged to meet competition. In several of these it was the need for quality control (which, by itself, was excluded from the definition of research-development) which led to the establishment of facilities designed to improve products or processes. Finally, nine firms gave a variety of reasons including several which listed growth in the size of the market as the major reason. It is interesting to note here that, taking those few which explicitly referred to growth in the size of the market and those companies in other groups where this reason might be inferred, only about seven firms gave this as the major reason for establishing or greatly enlarging research-development facilities. This refers to simple expansion in size of market with given products and processes and not to changing product or process requirements which often go with overall growth of the market. The point should not be over-stated since the firms with facilities were not asked to make this distinction as such and the many firms without research facilities obviously were excluded entirely from the analysis of this question. It does raise questions about the existence or scope of economies of scale with regard to research-development in some industries at least.

The companies which had research programs in Canada were asked to describe briefly the nature of the Canadian program and how it compared with that of the parent. The analysis below is restricted to 122 firms consisting of ninety-two firms which indicated they had research facilities in Canada, a further twenty-six which had no formal facilities but gave data on expenditures on research and development as defined which was performed within the Canadian firm, and four additional firms which satisfied neither criterion but purchased research from non-affiliated firms or organizations.[19] It will be noted below that some other firms which do not perform research-development as defined do have some form of research underway and indicated its nature in response to this set of questions. These were excluded from the present comparisons. All of the firms included here met the definition of research and development and either had formal facilities or some spending on research-development within the Canadian firm, with the four exceptions just noted. If the subsidiary's research program consisted only of the purchase of research-development from affiliates abroad, it was excluded from the analysis for present purposes.

In half of the 122 firms both the improvement of present products and processes and the conceiving and developing of new products and processes were significant parts of the Canadian program. In a further twenty-six firms only the former was significant, and in eight other firms only the latter. In thirteen firms there was, in addition to programs such as those just noted, a significant amount of research devoted to programs not primarily committed to specific product or process applications.[20] These conclusions must be qualified by the fact that no standard for the use of the term "significant" was used. Moreover, the interviews indicated clearly

---

[19]It will be noted that the first two figures add to 118 firms as against 109 in table 29 reporting they were doing research-development within the Canadian firm. The difference represents firms which reported they had just established such facilities but did not yet have a full year's expenditures to report and firms with facilities which failed to give data on expenditures.

[20]Eleven of the thirteen indicated all three types of research activities were significant while two indicated that entirely new products or uncommitted activities were involved.

that the definition of what is included in the various programs varies a good deal between companies. It is particularly likely that the category of uncommitted research bears some relation to the search for new products and processes in the case of some of these replies, but only intensive case studies could clarify this further. There are no striking differences by country of control or by size of firm in the nature of these research programs, taking account of differences in absolute numbers of firms involved.

TABLE 32

NATURE OF CANADIAN RESEARCH PROGRAMS

(Number of companies)

Program	Country of control			Asset size in $ millions*	
	U.S.	Overseas	All Countries	Up to 4.9	5 and over
Improvement of present products and processes	21	5	26	14	11
Conceiving and developing new products and processes	5	3	8	5	3
Combination of above programs	53	9	62	32	25
Above programs plus programs not primarily committed to specific product or process applications	12	1	13	8	5
No reply or not available	7	6	13	6	5
Total	98	24	122	65	49

* The total for all countries includes eight firms which could not be classified by size of assets.

Seventy-nine of the firms which indicated the nature of the Canadian research-development program also gave information on that of the affiliate. The results can be summarized briefly by noting that in thirty-nine of the parent companies both the improvement of present products and processes and the conceiving and developing of new products and processes were significant parts of the research programs, while in twenty-six others both of these activities plus programs not primarily committed to specific product or process applications were significant. Seven other firms indicated simply that the subsidiary's programs were less extensive, less directed to fundamental research, and so on. These figures, when compared with the data for the subsidiaries, indicate clearly the relatively greater orientation of programs in the affiliates to uncommitted or basic research in particular and to some extent to conceiving and developing new products and processes as well. It is worth adding that the search for and the development of new products and processes was a significant part of the research programs of most of the subsidiaries which had such programs.

The 122 companies which performed research in Canada were also asked whether the programs of parent and affiliate were largely co-ordinated or significantly different. This turned out to be a badly phrased question since it involves two different ones on the similarity of programs and the degree of co-ordination. One should treat the replies with considerable reservation since companies will have emphasized the two parts somewhat differently depending on their particular interpretation. What they chose to reply in essence was that in twenty-nine firms the programs were different, in six there was no co-ordination, and in fifty-one more (along with eight of the first group) the programs were largely co-ordinated. Firmer data are available in comparing the expenditures of the two sets of companies on a relative basis. It is worth recalling that the present comparisons apply only to those 122 firms which are doing research in Canada, or more precisely to the proportion of these which answered the questions comparing their programs to those of their affiliates. Of the ninety-six firms which gave such comparisons, sixty-nine subsidiaries were spending considerably less on research-development than were their affiliates on a relative basis, twenty-two spent roughly the same, and five considerably more. The experience with the interviews suggested that further questions on the actual range of difference would be unlikely to yield extensive or precise replies.

Before leaving this topic it is well to refer to forty-four firms which have been excluded throughout the discussion of the 122 firms which do research-development in Canada. These forty-four indicated they did not do research-development in Canada as defined, or they did not answer the questions requesting information on expenditures or on the establishment of research facilities. Nevertheless, they went on to answer some of the questions on the nature of research-development programs which have just been analyzed. They have been excluded from the analysis of research programs at

TABLE 33
COMPARISONS WITH RESEARCH PROGRAMS OF PARENT COMPANIES
(Number of companies)

	Country of control			Asset size in $ millions*	
	U.S.	Overseas	All Countries	Up to 4.9	5 and over
Nature of program of affiliate					
Improvement of present, and conceiving and developing new, products and processes	36	3	39	26	10
Above programs plus those not primarily committed to specific product and process applications	23	3	26	5	19
More extensive or basic than subsidiary	7	—	7	3	4
Other replies	3	4	7	6	1
Not applicable and no reply†	29	14	43	25	15
Total	98	24	122	65	49
Relationship between programs of two companies‡					
No co-ordination	3	3	6	3	3
Significantly different	18	3	21	13	7
Largely co-ordinated	44	7	51	32	16
Different but co-ordinated	7	1	8	4	4
Other replies	3	—	3	3	—
Not applicable and no reply†	23	10	33	10	19
Total	98	24	122	65	49
Relative expenditures compared with affiliate					
Roughly the same	17	5	22	12	8
Considerably less	58	11	69	38	27
Considerably more	5	—	5	5	—
Not applicable, not available, no reply†	18	8	26	10	14
Total	98	24	122	65	49

* The figures for all countries include eight firms which could not be distributed by size of assets.
† For six firms the question was not applicable, usually because the parent had no research-development program.
‡ The material in this section must be treated with some reservation since the groups of replies shown are not mutually exclusive. See accompanying text.

the risk of excluding a few which could not give precise data but had research-development as defined, and others which, had it been possible to do a more intensive study of research-development, might have been included. The great majority of these firms indicated that they were engaged in improvement of their products or processes though some indicated they had developed a new product or process. It is probable that in most cases this involved relatively minor changes in products and processes, changes closely related to and sometimes indistinguishable from the production process as such.

Access to the Parent's Knowledge

It was clear from the interviews that access to the parent's store of knowledge, as embodied in everything from its research and management skills to its production techniques and the products themselves, is at the heart of the process of direct investment. The emphasis so often given to the transfer of monetary capital, important as it is at the establishment of the firm and in periods of rapid expansion, frequently pales by comparison. In fact, the transfer of monetary capital is frequently simply a direct and immediate accounting counterpart to the transfer of knowledge embodied in equipment and services from the parent.

It was also clear from the interviews that no part of this study would lend itself less to exploration by brief questionnaire enquiries than the nature and effects of access to knowledge. The relations between parent and subsidiary on this score are so ubiquitous and varied and the consequences so great that they defy full unravelling and analysis except by the most detailed and rigorous statistical and theoretical techniques.[21] The opportunity could not be permitted to pass without at least an exploratory look at these ties, particularly since information about them is even scarcer than for many other aspects of parent-subsidiary relationships. Accordingly, several questions were inserted on the last page of the questionnaire as part of a set of general questions requiring more qualitative or more extended replies. The material is presented below briefly and with qualifications to indicate the limitations of the present approach to this complex issue.

The transfer of knowledge is most directly and importantly effected by the transfer of personnel. This was dealt with in the chapter on the man-

---

[21]Dunning, *op. cit.*, is the most successful statistical work in this area which has come to the writer's attention. For the more limited area of licensing agreements, including both affiliated and independent firms, see the references to Behrman's work in footnote 24 of this chapter.

agers and their powers, partly in terms of the movement of senior personnel and partly in terms of the methods of contact. The present discussion is restricted to transfer of research-development and related techniques, and patents and trademarks.

There can be no question about the extent of access to the parent's knowledge. In response to the question — "What access do you have to (i) the research and development and (ii) the industrial and other know-how of your affiliate? Please describe the nature of the agreement" — fully 187 of the 215 firms which answered the question explicitly indicated that the knowledge of the parent firm was fully available to them. In another eighteen cases this was not made explicit but the answers, indicating the agreement was formal or informal, implied some degree of access. Many firms outlined broadly what was transferred to them by this process. This included not only the results of the parent's research and development as defined above, but also, what was often more important, a vast range of other information and skills with respect to production, marketing, administration, and physical investment in plant and equipment. Only ten firms did not have such access to the parent's knowledge; in some of these the question was really inapplicable since the parent firm was not engaged in the production of commodities or was in a totally different line of business. Information on the nature of the agreement was explicitly given by only a third of the firms answering this question, so that the results cannot be given much weight: for what it is worth, these replies suggest that only a fifth of these firms had formal agreements with the parent covering the exchange of such information with the rest relying on informal arrangements.[22] Formal agreements were relatively more common among the larger firms, namely those with assets of $5 million or more and especially those with assets of $25 million or more. This is likely to be related in part to the fact that a higher proportion of the larger firms have minority shareholders whose interests can be defined often only by means of formal agreements on the allocation of various costs between the two firms. It should be added that differences in degree of access and nature of agreement were small when considered by country of control of the subsidiary.

The terms of payment for access to this knowledge varied all the way from no direct payment of any kind to the full cost to the parent. There was no direct charge in eighty-two cases out of the 182 replying to a question on the terms of payment. It is probable that many of the firms not answer-

[22]This information cannot be derived in full from table 34 since it covers some categories not shown separately in the table.

TABLE 34

EXTENT OF ACCESS TO THE KNOWLEDGE OF THE PARENT
(Number of companies)

	Country of control			Asset size in $ millions	
	U.S.	Overseas	All Countries	Up to 4.9	5 and over
Access to research-development and know-how					
Fully available	112	26	138	92	37
Fully available, informal or no agreement	32	10	42	24	17
Fully available, formal agreement	5	2	7	2	5
Degree of access not clear, but exists	14	4	18	10	7
Not applicable, no access	8	2	10	7	3
No reply	56	9	65	51	9
Total	227	53	280	186	78
Access to patents and trademarks					
Both fully available	92	14	106	74	29
Patents only available	17	2	19	10	9
Trademarks only available	2	3	5	3	2
Degree of access not clear, but exists	11	2	13	8	5
Not applicable	21	14	35	19	16
No reply	84	18	102	72	17
Total	227	53	280	186	78

ing this question also received such information without charge, as suggested in the footnote to table 35. In a further twenty-five cases the charges were nominal. Still another twenty-three firms paid a fee measured as a fixed percentage of the subsidiary's sales. Most of these fees ran from about 1 per cent to 5 per cent of sales. These payments as a percentage of sales are considerably higher than those noted for all firms making payments in table 29 above. This can be partly accounted for by the fact that the payments being discussed here involve more than the results of research and development. They are also likely to reflect the fact that, when terms of payment are formally negotiated, they are likely to reflect something closer to their market value. In another thirteen cases the subsidiary was assessed the full cost or, what amounted usually to the same thing, a charge related to the specific service performed in each case for the subsidiary. The remaining thirty cases reflected a variety of techniques of charging the subsidiary. The most frequently noted technique was to base the fee on the percentage of the subsidiary's sales or production or capitalization in relation to that of the parent and its other affiliates. In other cases the fee was included in the cost of the products sold to the subsidiary or prorated on the basis of such sales. In still others the fee was negotiated on the basis of a number of variables including some which can only be described as gamesmanship. The larger firms were more likely than the smaller ones to be charged something beyond purely nominal charges. Both those firms whose capital was controlled in the United States and those controlled overseas were heavily concentrated in the categories with no charge or a

TABLE 35
TERMS OF PAYMENT FOR RESEARCH, DEVELOPMENT, AND INDUSTRIAL AND OTHER KNOW-HOW
(Number of companies)

Terms	Country of control			Asset size in $ millions	
	U.S.	Overseas	All Countries	Up to 4.9	5 and over
No charge	61	21	82	62	16
Nominal payment	22	3	25	9	15
Fixed per cent of sales of subsidiary	18	5	23	16	7
Full cost or related to specific projects	13	—	13	5	8
Other methods of charging	27	3	30	14	12
Not applicable	7	2	9	6	3
No reply to question*	79	19	98	74	17
Total	227	53	280	186	78

* Forty-eight of the ninety-eight firms which did not answer this question indicated in the body of the questionnaire (under section V) that no payments were made to the parent for research and development. Thirty-two firms answered neither of these questions on payments to the affiliate. It should be noted that the payments in this table cover more than research and development. See also page 35 for the high non-response to the questions covered by Tables 34, 35 and 36.

nominal charge, with those controlled overseas slightly more heavily concentrated in this group.[23]

There is an obvious relation between transfers of research-development and technical assistance and transfers of patents and trademarks. The information involved in the former is often necessary to make the latter useful, while patents and trademarks may be necessary in order to get access to the results of past research and development. Unfortunately, it proved more difficult to get information on patents and trademarks. Access to them is widespread, though not quite as much as in the case of information which has not yet been embodied into formal property rights. Fully thirty-five firms of the 178 which gave information stated that the question was not applicable. Reasons were not always given in such cases, but those given covered such situations as the fact that the parent's operations did not yield usable patents or trademarks, or for a variety of reasons their transfer had not been negotiated by the firms involved. Another 106 firms replied that patents and trademarks were fully available, though not all of these made use of them, nineteen replied that patents only were available, and five that trademarks only were available. Thirteen other replies gave insufficient information on this particular aspect to warrant classification for present purposes beyond the fact that some patents and/or trademarks were available. Too few companies gave information on the nature of the agreement to permit generalization here. All that can be said is that formal licensing agreements on patents and/or trademarks and quite informal arrangements were both prevalent among those replying.[24]

With regard to payment for access to patents and trademarks the responses fell off drastically to less than a hundred firms, apart from the thirty-five for which the question was not applicable. In about two thirds of

[23]Dunning found that 57 per cent of the companies in his study of American-owned companies in the United Kingdom paid something for access to the parent's research and development while 43 per cent made no direct payment. Of the former, 10 per cent paid a specific fee, 30 per cent paid an agreed percentage of sales, while in the remainder the sum was nominal or was a lump sum related to specific information. The actual payments in 1954 averaged 2-3 per cent of sales of the subsidiary, though in some cases they were much higher. Dunning, op. cit., p. 174.

[24]Behrman found that while licensing of independent companies was more frequent than licensing of affiliates, most of the latter were also licensed. See his "Foreign Investment and the Transfer of Knowledge and Skills," Ch. V of Raymond F. Mikesell, U.S. Private and Government Investment Abroad. See also J. N. Behrman, "Licensing Abroad under Patents, Trademarks, and Know-How by U.S. Companies," The Patent, Trademark and Copyright Journal of Research and Education (The George Washington University, Washington, D.C.), Vol. 2, No. 2 (June, 1958), pp. 181-277, and especially pp. 187 and 245-246.

these there was no direct charge or a purely nominal charge, while the remainder indicated access to patents and/or trademarks was available for everything from a fixed per cent of the sales of some or all of the subsidiary's products to quite sporadic levies. One suspects that the free access to patents and trademarks for some of these firms reflects the fact that limited use was being made of them at the time. In any case the low response to the question on payment for access to patents and trademarks suggests that not much reliance can be placed on this set of replies. The whole area of licensing agreements between independent as well as affiliated firms requires a detailed study of its own.[25]

It may be of interest to note two replies from among those used to derive information on the access to the knowledge of the parent. Both are large firms which have been operating in Canada for long periods, the first since the twenties and the second since before World War I. Both conduct research in the Canadian firm.

All the know-how of our parent company's Research and Development staff, Industrial and other Engineering staff and of other departments including top management is freely available to us. There is no agreement, formal or informal and the only payment made is for specific work done at our request by Corporate personnel. The reason there is no payment other than as above is that no provision was made at the time the company was formed for any such payment and this condition has been maintained ever since. However, in recent years, discussions have taken place as to whether or not we should negotiate a management fee to cover such services. These discussions have arisen because of the growth of the economy and the increased amount of know-how etc. that is being made available to us. U.S. owned patents and trademarks are applied for in Canada and registered in our name. The only cost to us is the legal expense involved in searching the register and applying for the patent or trademark.

In the field of research and development the Company's relationship with the parent company is in the nature of two independent companies who have agreed to undertake an exchange of technical information in selected areas. This arrangement is formalized in a technical information and patent license agreement. The agreement provides for a net technical fee, the amount of which reflects differences in contribution taking account of size. This fee is subject to renegotiation each year. Since in general our Company benefits from the larger

---

[25]For comment on the markets for which these patent and trademark rights apply, see the fourth section of the chapter on exports.

programs of our associates in the United States who are in a better profit and economic position to undertake a higher percentage of supporting work, we consider the fee as a payment for outside research. It is so indicated in this questionnaire. The companies license each other non-exclusively in connection with patents resulting from research programs which each company may wish to utilize. In the event our company undertakes manufacture in a new area of activity compensation for know-how is negotiated as a business proposition for each individual case. This applies equally to know-how generated in the Canadian company involving information not scheduled between the two companies. The result of this system is encouragement of independent action yet utilization to the fullest of information available from the affiliate in the United States.

The fact of access without charge to all kinds of information and property rights by so many subsidiaries requires some further comment. To many of the firms this question of payment seemed artificial. It has already been noted that there are different ways of charging for such access without attaching a specific payment to it; for example, by including the cost of research-development in the price of the product to the subsidiary. Moreover, the knowledge and skills of the parent are transferred through a great many personal contacts between officers and technical personnel of the two firms, or by transfers of personnel as such, in ways which would be difficult to evaluate for purposes of charging fees. In any case, and this is the heart of the matter, affiliated companies will often not consider charging such fees explicitly, except possibly in the case of transfers of patents and trademarks. The parent firm, after all, receives the profits of the subsidiary or sees the value of its foreign assets increased if profits are retained. This reasoning is particularly prevalent in many wholly-owned subsidiaries since in such cases there is no need to distinguish claims to profits by the minority shareholders as distinct from the parent. A number of companies, in replying to these questions on payments for research-development and industrial and other know-how in particular but also regarding patents and trademarks, gave replies similar to the following:

There is no payment involved as an expense item; we are a wholly-owned subsidiary of our parent and consider effectively that we are a single company operation as opposed to two companies working independently from this point of view. (This firm had complete access to its parent's knowledge, patents and trademarks, and vice versa.)

It will be apparent that the *quid pro quo* for this availability of patents and brands as between all (affiliated) companies is the profit or expectation of profit of the basic stockholders on their investment.

The results of research and development conducted at the head office and incorporated into sales of (improved) products and methods of operation are available to the Canadian company in the ordinary course of operations without charge. There is no agreement as such, but the exchange of information etc., is made through day to day contacts.

The effect of all of this is to qualify the findings on payments for the parent's knowledge as reported both within the body of the questionnaire (see table 29) and in this section. These payments greatly understate the value of the access simply because it is not customary in many affiliated firms to charge for them explicitly or to charge anything but a nominal price. In some cases the rationale for this is the reverse flow of knowledge from the subsidiary to the parent, although, as noted below, this is in most cases quite limited by comparison with what the subsidiary receives. In some cases it is an initial subsidy to a new firm or to a firm which is making only sporadic and limited use of the access. The basic rationale is simply that the easy access to knowledge between affiliated firms is difficult to measure for purposes of charging; that an unrestricted exchange of information among related firms carries obvious advantages to the international firm, and, indeed, is in some respects the essence of such a firm; that the major policy decisions of the subsidiary, hence its need for the knowledge of the parent, are typically reviewed by the parent's officers; and that the net benefits derived by subsidiaries in such an exchange are eventually recaptured by the parent firm via profits. Income tax considerations are unlikely to be raised so far as the Canadian authorities are concerned since the effect of the practices involved is to yield more profit for tax purposes in Canada. In fact, one may suggest that the prevalence of nominal or zero direct charges for access to the parent's knowledge may be related also to differential rates of corporate income tax in Canada as compared with the countries supplying most of her direct investment capital. So long as the rate of taxation is lower in Canada there is a temptation to throw more of the profit to Canada through low charges and in other ways in order to increase overall income net of tax, at least in the first instance.[26]

---

[26]See the article entitled "Canadian Subsidiary 'Shows' U.S. Parent" in the *Financial Post* for March 8, 1958. Note particularly the following: "Originally the parent company thought that a management fee should be charged to the Canadian company. That is eliminated since this fee becomes an expense in Canada and a profit in the higher tax area. As long as the federal corporate tax in Canada is 47% as compared with 52% in the U.S. it is desirable to have a profit show in the Canadian operation where we can retain more of it."

Much the same sorts of considerations apply to the access by the parent to the knowledge of the subsidiary, allowing for the fact that in many cases the Canadian firm has much less to offer. Of the 169 firms which commented on the reverse flow of knowledge forty-seven indicated the question was not applicable. Sometimes the reason was that the products or lines of business were dissimilar but usually there was nothing to offer the parent.[27] In 106 firms there was full access to the knowledge of the subsidiary: a dozen of these explicitly stated that, in practice, little was available to offer. Only five firms reported that the affiliate did not have access to the knowledge of the subsidiary. Another eleven gave miscellaneous replies, most frequently that the parent had not yet requested such access. It was very common to report that, where the subsidiary had something to offer, there was full access both ways among the firms involved.[28]

The importance to the subsidiary of the access to the parent's knowledge cannot be measured with precision given the varied and complex help available and the informal arrangements for receiving it which frequently exist. Many firms could not even give a qualitative assessment of the importance of such access. A broad qualitative assessment is all that can be attempted, as indicated in table 36 covering 135 firms which did answer. Fully thirty-two stated flatly that the subsidiary could not exist without such access, and, in what were sometimes closely related answers, a further forty-four indicated such access was highly important to the operation of the subsidiary. A further eleven specified such access was important, while eighteen more indicated it was beneficial in various specific ways but failed to note the degree of importance. In most of the latter cases it was stated that it would have cost much more to perform or otherwise acquire the knowledge received from the parent. Only seventeen firms considered such access, where applicable, was of no importance. Both the smaller and larger firms place great value on such access: relatively more of the smaller

---

[27]Many of those which did not answer this question did not spend anything on research-development in Canada, judging by the section of the questionnaire dealing with this. They may have had some know-how in particular to exchange, however.

[28]Most of the firms which gave information on access to the subsidiary's knowledge did not give information on the precise terms of access. The few which did do so covered situations involving both access without charge and a variety of negotiated charges, with the former predominant. Given the much smaller flow of knowledge to the parent, the arrangements for access are frequently even more informal than is the case with the flow to the subsidiary. It is when the subsidiary has acquired a substantial body of knowledge, and particularly when easily identifiable property rights such as patents are acquired by the subsidiary, that more formal arrangements are usually made.

ones considered it indispensable but a greater proportion of the larger ones, including one-third of those with assets of $25 million or more, stated such access was highly important. Relatively more of the firms owned in the United States considered such access to be important than did firms owned overseas. All of this needs to be greatly qualified by the fact of an unusually low response to this question.

TABLE 36

IMPORTANCE TO SUBSIDIARY OF ACCESS TO KNOWLEDGE OF AFFILIATE
(Number of companies)

Importance	Country of Control			Asset size in $ millions	
	U. S.	Overseas	All Countries	Up to 4.9	5 and over
Indispensable	28	4	32	24	7
Highly important	39	5	44	17	26
Important	8	3	11	2	7
Various specific benefits	14	4	18	15	3
Little or no importance	13	4	17	13	4
Not applicable	9	4	13	8	5
No reply, cannot assess	116	29	145	107	26
Total	227	53	280	186	78

Some further information is of interest with regard to the seventy-six firms which considered such access to be indispensable or highly important. This group of firms was analyzed by age, by industry, and by research done within the Canadian company. The importance of such access extends over all age groups but does not appear to be relatively greater among the newer firms. If anything the reverse is the case, suggesting that the older firms are able to make better use of the knowledge of the parent. Thus 25 per cent and 18 per cent respectively of the firms which had been established or acquired from one to ten years ago and eleven to twenty-one years ago replied that access was indispensable or highly important. The corresponding percentages for those established or acquired twenty-two to forty-one years ago and forty-two or more years ago were 31 per cent and 39 per cent. Firms involved in secondary manufacturing industries tended to give such access a greater valuation than those engaged in producing primary products or primary manufacturing. About one-third of the respondents in each of the following industries indicated the access to the knowledge of the parent was indispensable or highly important: rubber products, paper products, metal fabricating, machinery, transportation equipment, electrical products, and chemicals. At the other extreme, none of the firms in the wood and furniture industry, primary metals, and the lumber, pulp and newsprint industry group gave access to the parent's knowledge such a high general rating, though some did consider it important in specific ways. The value of such industry comparisons is limited by the small number of reporting firms in some industries, but the results are approximately what one would expect from the general nature of the industries involved.

The degree of importance of access to the parent's knowledge may depend in part on the extent to which the Canadian firm is itself engaged in the production of knowledge. One aspect of this was considered by examining the Canadian research-development programs of the seventy-six firms which gave a very high rating to access to the parent's knowledge. There is no difference in this respect between the group doing no research-development in Canada and those spending up to one per cent of sales on research-development: in each case 28 per cent of the firms in these categories replied that access to the parent's knowledge was indispensable or highly important. Interestingly enough, 36 per cent of those firms spending more than one per cent of sales on research-development in Canada rated access to the parent's knowledge this highly. Differences of this magnitude are probably not statistically significant when a relatively small number of firms are involved. They do suggest that highly important access to the parent's knowledge is not a bar to the establishment and expansion of research-development facilities by the subsidiary. On the contrary there is much evidence in the interviews and questionnaires of the considerable assistance by technical and other personnel of the parent firm in helping to establish and to encourage the research-development of the subsidiary.

A few examples from both small and large firms will illustrate the types of replies for firms which found access to the knowledge of the parent of some importance and indicate also some of the benefits derived. The first two firms were established in the fifties, the last two in the thirties. All are in secondary manufacturing. Only the fourth had assets in excess of $5 million.

> Most important since it is the basis of our quality and breadth of line.
> Our company depends for its success on the ability of our parent company to develop, production engineer, develop merchandise programmes etc. on new products. At the present time we would have a

great deal of difficulty existing without our affiliation with our parent company.

It may be of interest to note that even a product such as ours could not be made available to Canadian consumers at the price paid were it not for the facilities of the U.S. organization. Laboratory, Art Department and Engineering, to name a few, present costs which could not be absorbed by our operation in Canada. Without the techniques provided through our affiliate, our product could be made, but the average Canadian wouldn't find it comparable to that he now enjoys.

It helped make us the acknowledged leader of our industry. As a wholly-owned subsidiary, we benefit by research and product development, free to us. As we developed the Canadian market for a particular product, we expanded facilities to produce it here — practically every product developed in our industrial field for the past fifty years is that of our U.S. parent — now almost all copied by other Canadian fabricators.[29]

The great importance to the subsidiary of access to the parent's knowledge has been noted. In many ways this is the essence of direct investment — a continuing transfer of knowledge, as embodied in a variety of skills and products, from one firm to another. There is no question of their importance to the subsidiary, but the degree of importance to the recipient land is something else again. That depends in very large part on two questions. First, are these benefits available in other more efficient ways? For many industries production in Canada was the only economic way of acquiring these products and services at given qualities and prices. For many others, import of the products embodying this technology was or would be a feasible alternative in the absence of legal barriers to trade. In the latter case there is some substantial offset to the gain from foreign investment. All that can be stated here is that Canada would have had the worst of both worlds if tariffs had not been accompanied by foreign direct investment. Given the tariff, so that production domestically will take place, a country is economically better off to have the production accompanied by the widest possible access to the knowledge of international firms engaged in those areas of production. As emphasized earlier, the knowledge must be available fully and at low cost, and the country be permitted to exploit it com-

---

[29] This firm went on to suggest vividly one aspect of the relation between lack of payment and degree of ownership as follows: "If our parent company was required by law to open part of share ownership to others, it would cost us heavily for our share of research and other benefits — making us less competitive, and probably reduce our ability to grow and employ more Canadians."

mercially wherever economically feasible. The second point is that these gains are available to the community at large, as distinct from simply enhancing the profits of foreign capital, to the extent they are widely dispersed through these and other firms, thus lowering prices, bringing further improvements in quality of product or services, and so on. This is related to a further point, the considerable competitive advantage of the subsidiary not only because of access to the knowledge of an international firm but also because its accounts usually show much less than full charges, if any, for such access. The competitive pressure of this is evident from the replies on this point by resident-owned firms, which will be considered in Chapter 9. These firms have met this competition by product improvement from their own resources, through licensing agreements with foreign firms, by pooling of research and similar methods. It is probable also that they have concentrated more of their effort in areas of production where the advantages of the subsidiary in this respect do not loom as large. The consequences are not always easy for the resident-owned firm to absorb. The results are to expand the economy in an efficient manner, to the benefit of the public and of industry, in the price and variety and quality of the commodities and services involved.

7
Comparative Costs of Production

Throughout the earlier chapters the question of the efficiency of the direct investment firm has been only touched upon. It is time to consider it, as well as to look at the larger question of the environmental determinants of the efficiency of the firm. Attention here will be focused on comparisons with the parent firm. In a succeeding chapter the economic performance of the subsidiaries will be compared in certain respects with their resident-owned counterparts.

Unit Production Costs Compared with Affiliates

There are various ways in which one can measure the efficiency of the subsidiary relative to its parent. The question which was asked in this respect is not as inclusive as some others which might have been asked, but it has the merit of being easily comprehended and therefore was more likely to be answered and to be answered correctly. The companies were asked, as part of the larger questions at the end of the questionnaire, to compare their unit costs of production for their major comparable products with those of the parent company abroad, at the current rate of exchange and at normal volume of operations.[1] It will be noted that costs of distribution are not included here, nor is it known what returns are associated with these costs; there will be a comment on the latter point in the next chapter. The data are accordingly only of limited value in answering questions about the allocation of resources within the international firm.

---

[1] One question which immediately arises is whether these typical unit cost comparisons for major comparable products can be taken to be representative of the overall output of the firms involved. It is reasonably certain that they are fairly representative, given the data presented below on the similarity of products of parent and subsidiary and the range of products produced.

Two-thirds of the firms returning the questionnaire answered the most general form of the questions on unit costs. In 57 per cent of these cases unit costs on major comparable products were typically higher than those of the affiliate, in 20 per cent about the same, in 11 per cent typically lower, while in the remaining 12 per cent the unit costs varied or the products were not generally comparable. In firms owned overseas there was a relatively larger group in the higher cost category, though the difference is probably not large enough to be statistically significant in view of the numbers of firms in the various categories. There is a marked difference between the largest size of firms and the others: only 18 per cent of those with assets of $25 million or more had unit costs higher than those of the affiliate, while the corresponding percentage for each of the smaller size groups was about 60 per cent. The largest firms also have a greater proportion of cases where relative unit cost varies or the products are not comparable, but even if one excludes these two groups throughout the comparison the largest size category of firms has a considerably smaller proportion of its number in the higher cost group.

Companies with unit costs which were typically higher or lower than those of the affiliate were asked to indicate the approximate average difference. Not unexpectedly, the response rate fell further here. Of the fifty-nine companies with higher costs which answered this question, twenty-one had unit costs ranging up to 10 per cent in excess of those of the affiliate and a further twenty-four had unit costs from 11 to 20 per cent higher than those of the affiliate. The seven companies indicating the extent to which their costs were lower were all within 15 per cent of the affiliate's costs. For the 103 precise observations on unit cost differences (including thirty-seven which reported unit costs were about the same) one-quarter were in excess of 16 per cent above the unit costs of the parent, the median was 3 per cent over that of the parent, and the third quartile was among those indicating costs were about the same. The range of cost variation is not substantial in general, it would appear, though one would feel more secure in this conclusion if the question had been answered by more of those firms which returned the questionnaire. The only other recent study on this, covering fewer companies but much more intensively, arrived at conclusions similar to these on the relatively narrow range of variation of costs between American parent firms and their Canadian subsidiaries.[2]

---

[2]See Theodore R. Gates and Fabian Linden, *Costs and Competition: American Experience Abroad*, The National Industrial Conference Board, 1961, especially Ch. 2 and Ch. 7.

TABLE 37

UNIT COSTS OF PRODUCTION RELATIVE TO AFFILIATES, ON MAJOR COMPARABLE PRODUCTS
(Number of companies)

	Country of control			Asset size in $ millions			
	U.S.	Overseas	All Countries	Under 1	1-4.9	5-24.9	25 and over
Typical unit cost							
Higher	80	28	108	47	33	18	5
About the same	29	8	37	15	13	4	5
Lower	18	2	20	9	5	2	4
Varies	10	0	10	1	1	3	5
Not applicable	8	5	13	1	1	3	8
No response and not available	82	10	92	31	29	13	8
Total	227	53	280	104	82	43	35
Approximate average percentage difference							
Higher by:							
Over 25%	1	7	8	6	1	1	—
21-25	4	2	6	2	4	—	—
16-20	12	2	14	6	3	3	1
11-15	8	2	10	6	3	—	1
6-10	10	1	11	5	3	2	—
Under 6	10	—	10	6	2	1	1
About the same	29	8	37	15	13	4	5
Lower by:							
Under 6	4	—	4	2	1	—	1
6-15	3	—	3	2	1	—	—
Varies	10	—	10	1	1	3	5
Not comparable	8	5	13	1	1	3	8
No response and not available	128	26	154	52	49	26	13
Total	227	53	280	104	82	43	35

Firms owned overseas tend to have higher unit costs relative to their affiliates than is the case, by and large, for firms owned in the United States, judging by the limited number of observations in the present study. It is important to note that in the two larger size categories a higher proportion of the firms reported their unit costs varied by product (i.e. they named two or three of the three categories used here) or that the products were not comparable. In other words, these firms have a significant part of output which is produced at the same unit costs as the parent (or in some cases at lower unit cost) or in which products are generally not competitive with those of the parent. It is particularly interesting to record that all but three of the twenty-two largest size of firms replying to this question were in these two categories. If this data is representative the relative *production* inefficiency of Canadian industry in its foreign-owned sector extends only to part of the output of the larger firms and more generally to the output of smaller firms. Even in the latter case the cost differences are generally not very great.

What accounts for these differences in unit production costs? The major reasons for the higher or lower costs in their particular cases, where cost differences existed, were given by 110 firms.[3] Since thirty-nine gave two or three reasons there are 157 observations in all. Lower wage rates in Canada made up twelve of the twenty-one observations for firms with lower unit costs. These lower wage rates were in all cases relative to the United States and were spread through all size categories. The remaining reasons for lower costs were a mixture: three firms mentioned lower raw material costs, two had lower overheads, and others mentioned various specific reasons. Three of the four firms with lower costs in the largest size group referred to lower raw material costs, the fourth to more modern plant. The 136 observations for companies with higher unit costs were concentrated in a few categories. The largest group was sixty-four observations to the effect that production runs were shorter, or volume was lower, or that these, in turn, led to relatively less tooling and mechanization, and similar replies. These replies are obviously closely related. This group of reasons was more likely to be noted by firms owned in the United States than those owned overseas, and it was mentioned by a substantial proportion of each size group. In twenty-three cases the reply was that wage rates for labour were higher in Canada; almost all of these replies were from firms owned overseas. Fifteen firms, in this case all owned in the United States, replied that

---

[3]It will be noted from the table on unit costs above that the question was not relevant for sixty firms whose unit costs were the same as those of the parent or varied, or where the products were not comparable. Presumably some of the group which did not answer this question were also in these categories.

duties on imports were the major reason for the higher unit costs of the subsidiary relative to the parent. Higher costs for raw materials and components in Canada were given as the major reason for cost differences in twenty cases; this group is in part related to the preceding one since several of these involved imported items.[4] It is of interest to note that only three or four firms stated that costs were higher because the quality of labour as such was lower, that is, as distinct from other factors which affect productivity.[5]

Here as elsewhere one must be careful to note that the interpretations placed on the replies to such broad questions depends in turn on other considerations. The widely observed phenomenon of shorter production runs, for example, is correctly reported here. One does not know from this *why* production runs are shorter. The larger questions of industrial environment and public policy which surround this issue will be considered briefly later, but here it is well to emphasize how much of the problem of relatively higher costs for direct investment firms is concentrated in two areas, especially in the case of American-owned firms. Those areas are the problems of shorter runs and of higher costs of materials and components. The latter was often related to tariffs, as noted above, and the former is the result of tariffs in part as will be noted below.

Do differences in unit production costs in fact lead to differences in the performance of the subsidiary in relevant respects? Only a limited reply can be given to this question. If one is looking at exports and imports, for example, production costs are not the only relevant variables: the commodities involved face quite different tariff and other obstacles to trade, distribution costs will vary, and there are other variables to take into account as shown elsewhere in this study. Given the importance of production costs, it is of interest to ask whether there is any tendency for those with lower production costs to have a higher portion of their sales abroad and a greater portion of their purchases in Canada. The data suggest that such tendencies exist but also that other variables are important. Thus in 74 per cent of the firms with higher costs 98 per cent or more of their sales

---

[4]Gates and Linden, *op. cit.*, place major emphasis on the relatively higher costs of materials and components in Canada when noting reasons for higher costs of subsidiaries relative to their American parents.

[5]For data on the quality of labour in United States parent firms and their affiliates abroad, see Mordechai E. Kreinin, "Comparative Labour Effectiveness and the Leontieff Scarce-Factor Paradox," *The American Economic Review,* Vol LV, No. 1 (March, 1965), pp. 131-139. He shows 71 observations for Canada which, on average, show equal labour effectiveness between United States parent firms and their subsidiaries.

TABLE 38

MAJOR REASONS FOR DIFFERENCES IN UNIT PRODUCTION COSTS BETWEEN SUBSIDIARY AND ITS PARENT
(Number of companies)

Unit costs lower in Canadian firm because:	Country of control			Asset size in $ millions			
	U.S.	Overseas	All Countries	Under 1	1-4.9	5-24.9	25 and over
Wage rates lower	12	—	12	5	2	2	2
Other	7	2	9	4	1	—	4
Total	19	2	21	9	3	2	6
Unit costs higher in Canadian firm because:							
Shorter production runs	9	2	11	5	4	—	2
Lower volume	33	2	35	12	10	6	3
Lower volume and less mechanized	14	4	18	6	6	6	—
Labour rates higher	4	19	23	12	5	4	1
Cost of materials and components higher	14	6	20	11	5	2	1
Customs duties	15	—	15	8	4	2	—
Other	9	5	14	10	2	2	—
Total	98	38	136	64	36	22	7
Overall number of observations	117	40	157	73	39	24	13

NOTE: 110 firms with higher or lower unit costs gave major reasons for these differences. Since thirty-one gave two reasons and eight gave three, there are 157 observations. The question was not relevant for at least sixty firms whose costs were the same as those of the parent or were variable, or the products were not comparable.

went to the Canadian market; the corresponding percentage for the firms with costs which are the same, lower, or variable relative to the affiliate was 57 per cent. At the other end of the scale, 3 per cent of those with higher costs sent less than 70 per cent of sales to Canadian purchasers, as against 12 per cent for the other group. It is well to emphasize the concentration of firms at the point where 100 per cent of sales are to the Canadian market. Half of the firms giving data on unit cost are at this

TABLE 39

CLASSIFICATION OF SALES AND PURCHASES IN CANADA BY UNIT COSTS RELATIVE TO AFFILIATE

	Unit costs compared with affiliate		
Percent of sales to **Canadian market**	Higher	Lower, about the same, varies (percentages)	Total number of firms involved (number of firms)
100 %	55	43	85
98-99	19	14	29
95-97	9	15	19
90-94	6	8	11
80-89	4	8	9
70-79	4	—	4
Below 70	3	12	11
Total	100	100	168*
First quartile	100	100	
Median	100	99	
Third quartile	97	90	
Percent of purchases from **Canadian market**			
95% and over	8	13	16
90-94	11	17	21
80-89	26	17	35
70-79	14	17	24
60-69	13	8	18
50-59	4	8	9
40-49	3	7	7
30-39	9	5	12
Below 30	11	8	16
Total	100	100	158*
First quartile	85	90	
Median	75	75	
Third quartile	50	50	

*The remaining firms did not answer one or both questions, mainly the one on unit costs, or did not give a sufficiently precise answer for present purposes.

point, including many whose unit costs are close to their affiliate's for part or all of their output. A scatter-diagram for comparative unit costs and percentage of sales in Canada is rather like a right-angled triangle, showing a positive relationship (with percentage sales in Canada tending to rise as unit costs rise) but terminating in a cluster of observations on a vertical unit-cost line at the 100 per cent level for sales in Canada. The medians for the two groups are only one percentage point apart. The third quartile, beyond which one-quarter of the firms lie, is 97 per cent of sales for firms with higher costs and 90 per cent for other firms.

In the case of purchases from the Canadian market the differences between the two sets of firms are concentrated almost entirely in the groups making 80 per cent or more of their purchases in Canada. A smaller portion of those with higher unit costs made 90 per cent more or of their purchases in Canada but this difference is fully reversed in the group buying 80-89 per cent of purchases in Canada. Below the 80 per cent level for purchases in Canada there is little difference between the two groups. The medians are identical but the first quartile is 85 per cent of purchases in Canada for the firms with higher costs and 90 per cent for the others.

It has been emphasized that there is concentration in both sets of firms at certain points, particularly at 100 per cent of sales in Canada. Nor are some of the differences just noted particularly striking. The most that might be said is that, in terms of the direction of the results, the data are not inconsistent with the view that competitive ability as measured in this limited sense is a factor in performance.[6] Other factors are obviously very important as determinants of performance, particularly for those many firms

---

[6]This conclusion is considerably strengthened for exports and moderately for imports if one considers the data in detail, using individual observations for each firm, and thus taking account of the spread from the comparatively lowest cost firms to the comparatively highest cost ones. The concentration at certain points already noted and the low response for unit cost together limit the meaningfulness of correlation techniques. For similar reasons it is not possible to examine statistically classifications between unit costs and some variables used in earlier chapters, such as range of products and nature of product compared with affiliate. Because so many firms tend to be miniature replicas of the parent in a number of respects, there are few firms left in some of the categories of immediate interest for comparisons with unit costs; for example, there are relatively few firms producing a minority or only a few of the affiliate's products, or where products are substantially modified compared with the affiliate. In addition, where such is the case, a comparison with unit costs of the parent was often not possible because the products differed. Finally, the response to the question on unit costs was low with the result that few firms are involved in some of our groups. In such circumstances the observed similarities or differences and their relation to unit costs are particularly likely to reflect the paucity of data rather than meaningful results.

where production costs alone are not a barrier to higher exports or lower imports.

It does not appear that age of firm makes much difference in reducing the spread of unit costs relative to the affiliate judging by the very few observations which are available. The proportion reporting higher costs is 65 per cent for the age group one to ten years, 61 per cent for those where the Canadian firm was established or acquired eleven to twenty-one years ago, 51 per cent for the twenty-two to forty-one age group, and 69 per cent for the forty-two and over age group.[7] The differences in unit costs relative to the affiliate persist once established, presumably in part because many cost-reducing changes are applicable to both sets of firms thereafter. The relative inefficiency of the foreign-owned sector of Canadian industry will not disappear with time, if this is any guide, but rather with changes in the structure of industry which lead to more specialized production, particularly in areas of industry where some comparative advantage accrues to Canadian industry or can be introduced.

Broader Issues Regarding Efficiency

These considerations raise the broader question of motives for direct investment. The most extensive early study of this was made in the early thirties.[8] It placed major emphasis on the tariff as the reason for direct investment in Canadian manufacturing, particularly in the case of firms established after 1909. Its general conclusion was that "In the absence of tariffs the remaining barriers would be insufficient to explain the establishment of many — probably the majority — of the plants now in existence."[9] A significant number of the firms also mentioned Empire tariffs as an additional motive. Other significant factors in the decision to manufacture in Canada were the adaptation of products to Canadian demands, including here, however, the preferences for local goods created by campaigns to buy Canadian products, economies in transportation, and after-sales servicing of various kinds. Labour costs and raw material costs were not found to be

---

[7]These percentages refer to totals reflecting seventy-seven, twenty-eight, forty-one and twenty-six firms respectively. The rest did not give unit cost observations.

[8]Marshall-Southard-Taylor, *op. cit.* Approximately 170 replies were received in each case from questionnaires mailed separately to the Canadian subsidiaries and to the parent United States companies, making 300 companies when duplication of replies was taken into account. Fully 102 of the 170 replies from officers of Canadian companies reported the tariff was an important factor in the decision to manufacture in Canada. It should be noted that essentially manufacturing firms were involved, hence the absence of replies indicating Canada was a source of raw materials.

[9]*Ibid.*, p. 209.

significant factors in the decision to manufacture in Canada. Some more recent studies tend to give importance to the tariff also.[10]

The present study concentrated on the reasons for establishment in Canada for those firms which began production here in the period after World War II. This was a general question at the end of the questionnaire which simply asked for the specific reasons in approximate order of importance. Of the 150 firms which have been established since 1945, 109 answered the question. A number listed more than one reason, but these additional reasons follow very closely the pattern outlined below derived from first reasons only. It must be stressed that the quality of these responses was generally rather low, and the information given in many cases was so general that only broad classifications, which probably overlap, could be attempted. In over one-third of the replies the expansion of the Canadian market or the expected expansion of that market for the product or products involved was given as the primary reason for the establishment of production facilities in Canada. In about one-fifth of the replies the Canadian tariff was given as the first reason with some of these adding that savings on transport costs were also involved. Another fifth gave the need for better servicing of individuals and of industry as their first reason as compared with direct export to Canada, licensees, agencies, and other techniques which had usually been tried and found wanting. Less than one in ten emphasized the need to expand the parent company's volume as the main reason, while a similar proportion were established basically to secure a source of raw materials. The remainder gave a wide variety of reasons.

It is tempting to conclude from a comparison of this and the earlier study noted above that the tariff has been less important in the establishment of direct investment companies since 1945 than was the case for the inter-war period. This much might reasonably be inferred also from the history of changes in the incidence of tariffs and of administrative protection between the fifties and the inter-war period. It would be an error, however, to take the data presented here as a full indication of the role of the tariff in recent years in attracting direct investment firms to Canada. It is true that, even if one examines reasons beyond the first one given, the proportion

---

[10]See, for example the article entitled "Canada: An Expanding Market," in National Industrial Conference Board Inc., *The Conference Board Business Record*, Vol. XV, No. 1 (January, 1958). This study of 110 manufacturing companies with subsidiaries in Canada gives the elimination of payments for tariff duties as the main reason for production rather than direct sales to Canada, with preferences for locally-manufactured goods also given as a frequent reason.

of firms involved which explicitly refer to the tariff rises to only 25 per cent of the total. It will be recognized, however, that some of the firms in the largest category in particular (expansion of the Canadian market) might well have indicated the tariff was a factor in their decision to locate here had a more intensive investigation been made of this point. The conclusions which may be suggested are that the tariff is probably less important than it was as a factor in locating direct investment in Canada but that its recent impact in this respect, while significant, is uknown.[11]

A related question regarding efficiency is the actual extent of fragmentation of the Canadian market for manufactures. This can be suggested indirectly for the foreign-owned firms in this study by bringing together data referred to earlier.[12] In the first place, it has been emphasized that most of these firms produce items very similar to those of their parents. Fully 59 per cent of the respondents reported the Canadian company, in general, was producing products which were identical with those of the affiliate, and another 28 per cent reported the products were only marginally different. Only 13 per cent reported that their products were substantially modified or not comparable. It is true that the larger firms have a greater proportion in the differentiated categories but the majority of even the largest size group of firms indicated their products were, at most, only marginally different from those of the affiliate. Secondly, about two-thirds of the respondents indicated they produced at least a majority of the affiliate's products in Canada: 8 per cent produced a wider range, 31 per cent about the same range, and 28 per cent a majority of the affiliate's products. The firms owned overseas tended to be more limited in their range of products relative to the affiliate than were those owned in the United States, possibly because relatively more of them had been established in the fifties and had not yet had the time to round out their product lines. Again one finds that in all four size categories the majority of the firms are producing at least a majority of the affiliate's products: in three of the four size categories about 60 per cent of the firms are producing at least a majority of their affiliate's products while in the $1-4.9 million range fully 84 per cent are in this group. Finally, this similarity of product and of product-range must be considered in the context of Canadian firms which are very much smaller

---

[11]This is one question which, in retrospect, required much more exact phrasing and possibly a list of alternative replies. The Marshall-Southard-Taylor study gave such a list, headed by the avoidance of tariffs, but in the context of the thirties made no reference to expansion of the Canadian market.

[12]The comparisons, it will be noted, are all at the level of the firm. No data were collected for Canadian plants as such though in many cases they will coincide.

TABLE 40

COMPARISON OF PRODUCTS AND SIZE OF CANADIAN FIRM RELATIVE TO ITS FOREIGN AFFILIATE
(Number of companies)

	Country of control			Asset size in $ millions			
	U.S.	Overseas	All Countries	Under 1	1-4.9	5-24.9	25 and over
Nature of products compared in general with affiliate							
Identical with comparable products of affiliate	128	28	156	66	51	16	16
Marginally different	61	12	73	27	20	13	9
Substantially modified	13	4	17	4	6	4	2
Not comparable	14	5	19	5	5	4	5
No reply	11	4	15	2	0	6	3
Total	227	53	280	104	82	43	35
Range of products compared with affiliate							
Wider than affiliate	17	3	20	7	8	3	2
About the same	67	12	79	29	34	4	9
Majority of affiliate's products	64	8	72	22	21	15	9
Minority of affiliate's products	28	9	37	18	6	6	3
Only a few	17	12	29	14	3	7	4
Not comparable, other	13	3	16	6	3	3	4
No response to question	21	6	27	8	7	5	4
Total	227	53	280	104	82	43	35
Percentage size relative to affiliate*							
1-5%	55	12	67	27	21	9	7
6-10	86	19	105	44	30	15	13
11-15	15	5	20	4	10	4	1
16-20	15	6	21	8	6	3	2
Over 20	23	3	26	10	6	3	6
No response	33	8	41	11	9	9	6
Total	227	53	280	104	82	43	35

* The comparisons were usually given in either sales or assets.

on average than are their foreign affiliates. Almost three-quarters of the Canadian firms are one-tenth or less of the size of their foreign affiliate, and fully 28 per cent of the Canadian firms were only 5 per cent or less of the size of their affiliate. Even more striking is the fact that this was generally true regardless of the absolute size of the Canadian subsidiaries. Among those with assets of $25 million or more, for example, six were at least one-fifth of the size of their foreign affiliate but twenty were one-tenth or less of the size of their affiliate.

To the extent that economies of scale are likely to occur beyond the size of company implied here, the closeness of unit production costs may seem surprising. The closeness of costs reflects, of course, the closeness of many factor costs of production. The crucial point to note here, however, is that the foreign-owned company is in a position to escape some of the penalties of small scale because of the specialized commodities and services which it can secure from its foreign affiliate. Many instances of such access were given earlier with regard to research and development, exports and imports, and in the access to management and technical help, often at less than full cost. The resident-owned firm, on the other hand, can acquire these goods and services only if specialized firms exist to supply them either by direct purchase or by royalty agreements. To the extent that neither of these alternatives is feasible or desired and they are built into the resident-owned firm itself, it will have to be larger than its foreign-owned counterpart in order to achieve that scale of operations at which all economies of large-scale operation are available to it.[13] This point will be considered again when comparisons are made between the two sets of firms in Chapter 9. It will suffice to point out here that the available evidence suggests that the resident-owned firms which are in industries in which the foreign-owned firms are concentrated are no larger than the latter, while if all commodity-producing industries are considered the resident-owned firm tends to be smaller than the non-resident owned firm.

It is important to emphasize, therefore, that the meaning to be attached to the questionnaire responses shown earlier which referred to the limited

---

[13]This analysis of the two types of firms has been made by Stefan Stykolt and H. C. Eastman, "A Model for the Study of Protected Oligopolies," *op. cit.*, especially pp. 338-339. They note that the minimum optimum size of plant is the main determinant of the minimum optimum size of firm (the size at which all economies of large-scale operation are attained) but that the former probably sets only the lower limit to the latter. See also H. C. Eastman, "The Canadian Tariff and the Efficiency of the Canadian Economy," *Papers and Proceedings of the American Economic Association*, Vol. LIV, No. 3 (May, 1964), pp. 437-448.

volume of operations depends on broader considerations with regard to the economic environment and public policy as they affect the companies involved. As emphasized in the introductory chapter, it is obvious that the findings of this study generally are within a given context of factor costs and demands, industrial structure, and government policy on tariff, exchange rates, and other variables. It is frequently stated in the writing on this subject that the small size of the Canadian market for many manufactures results in a scale of plant and of firm which is too small for lowest-cost production. This is often coupled with the observation that the United States tariff and transport costs maintain the small size of market.[14] This view has been demonstrated to be an oversimplification by more systematic research which has shown the relation of the Canadian tariff and oligo-polistic market structures to the inefficient scale of production. Such research has pointed to the need for reorganization of existing market structures through competitive forces, including tariff reduction and effective anti-combines administration, as key aspects of the approach to speciali-zation of output and the overcoming of the relative inefficiency of many Canadian manufacturing industries.[15]

It is clear even from our very limited data that the relative efficiency of foreign-owned industry varies a good deal. The data on comparative unit costs of production are very limited because of a high non-response to this question on the part of firms returning the questionnaire. Comparisons by industry, where few firms are involved in some groups, can be quite mis-leading, but when used with care one or two general points may be war-ranted. What stands out here is, first, that the firms producing primary products or engaged in primary manufacturing are in a relatively strong position *vis-à-vis* their parents, either because the unit costs of much or all of their output are the same as or lower than those of the parent or because the products are not comparable. In Chapter 2 these firms were assumed with some oversimplification to be most closely represented by petroleum products, primary mining and smelting, wood and furniture, lumber, pulp and newsprint, primary metals, and non-metallic minerals. One finds five

---

[14]Such is the emphasis, for example, in D. H. Fullerton and H. A. Hampson, *Cana-dian Secondary Manufacturing Industry*, Royal Commission on Canada's Economic Prospects (Ottawa, 1957). See especially Chapter 4.

[15]The theoretical reasoning has been developed most thoroughly in Stefan Stykolt and Harry C. Eastman, "A Model for the Study of Protected Oligopolies," *op. cit.* For empirical studies see H. Edward English, *Industrial Structure in Canada's International Competitive Position*, The Canadian Trade Committee (Montreal, 1964) and H. C. Eastman, "The Canadian Tariff and the Efficiency of the Canadian Economy," *op. cit.*

firms in this group with costs higher than the affiliate and seventeen with costs the same, lower, or variable by major products. The remainder include 103 in the former category and forty-eight in the latter, a very different and opposite proportion.

The second point to note is that about one-third of the firms in this second group, very largely in secondary manufacturing, have unit costs close to those of their affiliates for their typical products. All too often the foreign-owned firm in secondary manufacturing is dismissed as inefficient relative to its parent or simply the creation of the tariff. One must clearly distinguish types of secondary manufacturing, much of which enjoys unit production costs similar to those of the parent.[16]

It remains a fact, nevertheless, that most firms in secondary manufacturing have higher unit production costs. They must also surmount transport, tariff and other costs if they wish to export, and their higher production costs mean often that they face significant import competition in spite of transfer costs inward. It is very likely that, *within the given structure of industry,* many such firms will never be able to reduce costs enough relative to the parent and to other firms abroad to be able to export or to capture a much larger share of the domestic market.[17] To achieve a more efficient structure of Canadian industry it is clearly going to be necessary to concentrate relatively more of Canadian resources in industries where comparative advantage exists or can be developed, and in addition to achieve more specialization by firm within such industries. Canadians have all too often put themselves in the contradictory position of attracting industry to the country by the tariff in areas of manufacturing where it could not otherwise exist, then expecting it to compete on the export market or to raise its domestic content further as if it was efficient by world standards. In some cases, as noted earlier, they have also gone on to suggest that the lack of exports or continuation of imports for many firms must be proof of restraints by parent firms. These points were considered in detail earlier. Here it is important to emphasize that relative changes in the concentration of Canadian resources by industry and in specialization by firms in such industries will be needed if the objectives of better economic performance by industry, as defined throughout this book, are to be achieved. This is the

---

[16] More refined detail by product and product mix would demonstrate considerable differences within many industry groups as regards unit costs. The fewness of replies on unit costs, combined with the fact that detail on specific products would reveal the identity of some firms, prevents such presentation.

[17] Some, of course, are domestic products and do not enter foreign trade because of heavy transfer costs.

TABLE 41

UNIT COSTS OF PRODUCTION RELATIVE TO AFFILIATE, CLASSIFIED BY TYPE OF PRODUCT

(Number of companies)

Type of product	Unit costs relative to affiliate	
	Typically higher	Same, lower, or varies
Petroleum products	—	5
Primary mining and smelting	—	2
Foods and beverages	6	—
Rubber products	3	2
Textiles and clothing	3	1
Wood and furniture	—	2
Lumber, pulp, newsprint	—	2
Paper products	4	—
Primary metals	3	1
Metal fabricating	13	5
Machinery (except electrical)	17	11
Transportation equipment	11	4
Electrical products	16	11
Non-metallic mineral products	2	5
Chemicals and allied products	18	8
Miscellaneous industries	12	6
Total	108	65

most important way in which Canada can benefit from her favourable resource base and also cultivate the skills needed to ensure she will be at the forefront of some at least of the major industrial developments internationally. It is well to add that this is not the only aspect of efficient production. Not all plants will face equal market sizes, even where industry structure is efficient, so that it becomes important that plant and equipment be adapted to the particular size of market. There are many examples of such adjustments in foreign-owned Canadian industry. A number of the executives who were interviewed pointed out that while unable to compete on some items where specialization and very long runs were necessary to achieve minimum costs, on other items the economies of scale were not great or they enjoyed specific cost advantages.[18]

Two final points should be made on the direct investment firm itself in this process of adjustment. While emphasizing in this chapter the relative inefficiency of some foreign-owned industry, it is important to emphasize the cause. The firms are not comparatively inefficient *because* they are foreign-owned: their relative inefficiency may reflect the fact that legal or economic barriers to trade often require local production while their demand and cost situation does not permit as efficient production. This conclusion would be upset, and the relative inefficiency could be ascribed in good part to the foreign-owned firm as such, only if it could be demonstrated that the performance of resident-owned industry is better in similar circumstances. This will be considered in Chapter 9. Second, it has been emphasized in various places that the direct investment firm often brings with it at least potential advantages in research contacts, supply and market contacts, administrative skills, and so on. A nation intent upon achieving an important international industrial role may well have a significant advantage here, if it can learn to encourage the economic exploitation of that potential to the fullest.

---

[18]For cases of international specialization see footnote 23, Chapter 4. An example of efficient adaptation of machinery to shorter runs can be found in the case of Reynolds Aluminum of Canada Ltd. as described in the *Financial Post* for November 9, 1963.

8
The Pattern of
Ownership and Finance

No characteristic of direct investment firms in Canada has raised more questions than the pattern of ownership. The fact that in most of the firms the voting stock is wholly-owned by the parent has been a source of continuing criticism over the past decade.[1] Canadian governments have used tax incentives in recent years in an attempt to induce such firms to issue shares to the public and appoint more resident directors. A Canada Development Corporation has been under consideration for some time, one of whose major purposes would be to provide capital to larger or new firms which might otherwise sell a controlling interest to non-residents.[2]

In this chapter the ownership and financing practices of the firms involved will be considered, including closely related areas such as dividend policies. Before doing so, a brief comment is required about a group of firms which have been excluded from this study. In Chapter 1 reference was made to the fact that four more or less distinct categories of ownership exist among companies classified as direct investment in the official Canadian data. These categories are unincorporated branch plants, wholly-owned incorporated subsidiaries, subsidiaries whose stock is partly owned by a firm abroad, and firms where there is no corporate parent abroad but at least half of the voting stock is held by residents of a foreign country

---

[1]Much of this criticism stems from the hearings of the Royal Commission on Canada's Economic Prospects and its *Final Report*. One of the most extensive submissions to the Commission on this point was the *Brief* Submitted to the Royal Commission on Canada's Economic Prospects by the Security Analysts' Association of Toronto, Exhibit 172, February, 1956.

[2]For an analysis of this proposal see E. P. Neufeld, *The Canada Development Corporation — An Assessment of the Proposal*, Canadian Trade Committee, Montreal, 1966.

and it is believed that non-residents have control.[3] Two additional points should be made here. A small number of firms in the second and third categories are really joint enterprises in that two or more firms own part or all of the voting stock of the Canadian subsidiary. Sometimes the parent firms are related themselves. In other cases the parent firms consist of two unrelated foreign firms which have undertaken a joint venture in Canada or an independent Canadian firm which has undertaken such a venture in co-operation with a foreign firm. Six firms in this study indicated that all of their voting stock was held by two or more firms abroad; these were treated as if their voting stock was wholly-owned by a single parent. In addition, eight firms included in this study indicated that their voting stock was held by a Canadian and a foreign firm, usually on a 50-50 basis. There are too few firms here for separate analysis, and one cannot be sure that all such joint enterprises have been indicated.[4] Study of these eight firms has been combined with another group, namely firms which indicated in response to a specific query that the voting stock not held by the parent was closely held. Of the seventy-two firms in this study which had issued more than one per cent of their stock, twenty-eight replied that the minority stock was closely held (whether by another firm or individuals), twenty-seven that it was widely held, and seventeen did not give information on this point.

The second point to be noted is that this study excludes a number of firms which are included in the official definition of direct investment, namely those firms which have no corporate parent abroad but 50 per cent of whose voting stock is owned in one foreign country and where control is believed to reside with non-residents. There are not a great many firms in this group but since some large firms are involved the total value of direct investment excluded is quite significant. At the end of 1960, for example, these firms accounted for perhaps as much as $1 billion of the $8 billion of direct investment which was involved for firms with an individual investment of $25 million or more.[5] Since this type of international

---

[3]For a discussion of the types of financial organization of American-financed firms in Britain, and the determinants of such organization, see Dunning, *op. cit.*, pp. 97-106.
[4]A thorough study of such firms can be found in Wolfgang Friedmann and George Kalmanoff (eds.), *Joint International Business Ventures*, Columbia University Press, 1961.
[5]See footnote 19 of Chapter 1 and the accompanying text. The overall investment in these "other companies," including both Canadian funds and long-term funds from abroad, was $2.1 billion out of a grand total of $11.2 billion for all firms with an individual investment of $25 million or more.

firm very often occurs in mining, any interpretation of the official data on direct investment in mining should take due note of this point. One wonders whether some of these firms are not sufficiently different from parent-subsidiary types of relationship, in their patterns of ownership and organization and management, as to raise questions about whether they should be included in data on direct investment for many purposes. Some rather awkward decisions about changes in the data may have to be made when, for example, the active and widespread international trade in the stock of many such firms shifts their ownership in one country below or above the 50 per cent level — unless, of course, one is certain of both his concept of control and where it rests.

A number of these firms answered the questionnaire prepared for this study, or as much of it as they could. It will be appreciated that, since they do not have a distinct corporate parent abroad, they had considerable difficulty in answering some of the questions and were unable to answer others. After further correspondence and interviews with a few of them, and consideration of the material supplied, it appeared best to exclude them entirely from this study. The fact is that these firms do not fit easily in a number of respects the concept of a parent-subsidiary relationship which is at the basis of this study. Some of the firms have become so fully international, in effect, that strictly national delimitations of ownership and control can be misleading. Some other firms included in both the non-resident owned and resident-owned companies covered in this study approach these international companies in some respects. The line separating the two becomes a thin one at some point reflecting various degrees of internationalization of ownership and of management, particularly in the case of primary mining. The distinction between the two seemed rather arbitrary for the group noted, at least in terms of some of the questions posed in this study, hence their exclusion.[6]

The Ownership of Voting Stock[7]

Several overall studies of the ownership of voting stock of direct investment companies are available. The Dominion Bureau of Statistics prepared

[6]This group should not be confused with Canadian firms producing commodities whose stock is held by a financial holding company abroad. These are included in this study as direct investment firms.

[7]Unfortunately, information cannot be given on the distribution of non-voting stock and debt between the parent, other non-residents and residents. The questions on this were not framed to take sufficient account of the nature and complexity of these other forms of financing. For example, very large proportions of the firms reported there

TABLE 42

STRUCTURE OF OWNERSHIP OF INVESTMENTS IN ALL FOREIGN-CONTROLLED ENTERPRISES IN CANADA, END OF 1960

(Percentages)

	Country of control			
	U.S.	U. K.	Other	Total
Ownership of investments by residents of:				
Country where parent located				
Branches	10	6	6	9
Canadian corporations	69	52	65	66
Sub-totals	79	58	71	75
Canada				
Debt	9	18	16	11
Equity	9	16	7	10
Sub-totals	18	34	23	21
Other countries	3	8	6	4
Totals	100	100	100	100

SOURCE: D.B.S., The Canadian Balance of International Payments, 1961 and 1962, p. 84.

data for the end of 1953 showing the range of Canadian minority participation in the common stock equity of United States direct investment firms. Data gathered under the Corporations and Labour Unions Returns Act yield similar estimates for all but the smallest firms. The data were presented in summary form in table 6 above and compared with the firms in the present study. It is quite clear from this material that the common stock of the great majority of direct investment firms in Canada is wholly owned by the parent. Also available are data on the ownership by residents and non-residents of the debt and equity of all direct investment firms, as reproduced in table 42. It will be noted that firms whose parents are in the

---

was no other stock or debt, and the term "debt" was subject to a variety of interpretations. One consequence was that the non-response rate was unusually high. It appears that preferred stock for all direct investment companies in Canada with individual assets over $25 million amounted to only $578 million at the end of 1960, compared with common stock of $6,694 million. Fully 68 per cent of the preferred stock was owned in Canada. At that time 11 per cent of the assets of all foreign controlled firms were in the form of debt held by residents. See D.B.S., The Canadian Balance of International Payments, 1961 and 1962, pp. 84-89.

United Kingdom have outstanding in the hands of residents a larger proportion of their overall capital, both debt and equity, than is true of firms whose parents are in the United States. Investment from third countries in direct investment firms in Canada is also larger for firms controlled overseas than for those controlled in the United States. Where direct investment firms with assets over $25 million have issued shares, however, about the same proportions of their common stock were held by residents in 1960. Thus residents owned 20 per cent of the common stock of partly-owned American subsidiaries and 22 per cent of the common stock of Canadian subsidiaries partly owned by overseas firms. In the case of Canadian corporations without foreign parents, but the majority of whose stock was held outside Canada, the corresponding proportions for resident ownership of common stock were 36 per cent and 39 per cent.[8]

Data collected for the present study permit some aspects of the ownership of direct investment firms to be analyzed in much greater detail than this although only for a portion of the population. Table 43 confirms what is already known on the preponderance of wholly-owned firms: 71 per cent of the firms in this study fall into this category. It will be noted that there is almost no difference in this respect between firms owned in the United States and those owned overseas.[9] There is a difference if one looks at parental ownership of voting stock by size of firm. Those firms with assets of $25 million or more have a distinctly smaller proportion of wholly-owned companies among them and a correspondingly greater proportion of cases in which the parent owns 51-75 per cent of the voting stock. This difference may in turn be related in part to the fact that some of the largest foreign-owned firms are producing primary products or are engaged in closely related primary manufacturing processes, forms of production where some financing by the public or by independent Canadian firms may be more common than in secondary manufacturing.

There was ownership of voting stock by non-residents other than the affiliate in only thirty-seven companies, some of which may consist of joint

---

[8]D.B.S., *The Canadian Balance of International Payments, 1961 and 1962*, p. 89. See pp. 84-89 of this publication for details on the structure of ownership of capital for such firms.

[9]Our data refer to only a portion of the firms, by *number* of firms, while the data published by D.B.S. referred to in the preceding paragraphs refer to all direct investment firms and to the overall *value* of the stock held by residents. It is of interest to note that, on the average, American companies held 85 per cent and British companies 40 per cent of the ordinary shares of their subsidiaries in Australia. See E. T. Penrose, "Foreign Investment and the Growth of the Firm," *Economic Journal*, Vol. LXVI, No. 262 (June, 1956), p. 227.

TABLE 43
OWNERSHIP OF VOTING STOCK
(Number of companies)

	Country of control			Asset size in $ millions			
	U.S.	Overseas	All Countries	Under 1	1-4.9	5-24.9	25 and over
Parent company*							
99-100%†	163	37	200	69	65	31	20
76-98%	21	6	27	13	7	4	3
51-75%	24	6	30	8	6	6	10
50% and less	13	2	15	9	2	2	2
No reply or not available	6	2	8	5	2	—	—
Total	227	53	280	104	82	43	35
Non-residents other than affiliates							
25% and over	9	4	13	6	1	1	5
10-24%	10	1	11	3	2	3	3
2-9%	12	1	13	2	2	4	5
0-1%‡	190	44	234	88	75	35	22
No reply or not available	6	3	9	5	2	—	—
Total	227	53	280	104	82	43	35
Residents of Canada‡							
25% and over	27	5	32	13	7	6	6
10-24%	16	4	20	9	3	2	6
2-9%	11	5	16	5	4	4	3
0-1%	167	36	203	72	66	31	20
No reply or not available	6	3	9	5	2	—	—
Total	227	53	280	104	82	43	35
Parent company*	(Percentage distribution)						
99-100%†	72	70	71	66	79	72	57
76-98%	9	11	10	13	9	9	9
51-75%	11	11	11	8	7	14	29
50% and less	6	4	5	9	2	5	6
No reply or not available	3	4	3	5	3	—	—
Total	100	100	100	100	100	100	100

* Unincorporated branches are included in the category where 100 per cent of voting stock is owned by the parent. This category also includes six firms in which 100 per cent of the voting stock was held by two or more firms located abroad.

† The firms were asked to exclude directors' qualifying shares. In order to ensure these were excluded, all firms with 99 per cent ownership by the parent have been classified as wholly-owned.

‡ In five firms the distribution between residents and non-residents other than affiliates could not be given. These were classified as if all this stock was held by residents (and under zero for other non-residents). One of the percentages so classified under residents was in the 2-9 per cent group, the remainder in the 25 per cent or over group.

TABLE 44
PARENT OWNERSHIP OF VOTING STOCK CLASSIFIED BY SELECTED CHARACTERISTICS

	Parent ownership of voting stock			Number of replies*
	99-100%	75-98%	0-74%	
	(% distribution of companies by rows)			
Age				
1-10 years	69	7	23	121
11-21	68	26	6	34
22-41	79	11	11	66
42 and over	77	11	11	44
Total	73	11	16	265
Type of business of Canadian company				
Assembly	74	13	13	31
Extractive	36	9	55	11
Semi-fabricated products	71	17	13	24
Fully processed or manufactured products	77	11	13	184
Fully or largely integrated production	67	5	29	21
Total	73	11	15	271
Type of product				
Petroleum products	30	10	60	10
Primary mining and smelting	50	—	50	6
Foods and beverages	93	—	7	15
Rubber products	83	17	—	6
Textiles and clothing	86	14	—	7
Wood and furniture	100	—	—	6
Lumber, pulp, newsprint	80	20	—	5
Paper products	43	43	14	7
Primary metals	57	29	14	7
Metal fabricating	89	4	7	28
Machinery (except electrical)	87	8	5	38
Transportation equipment	67	14	19	21
Electrical products	71	12	17	42
Non-metallic mineral products	88	—	13	8
Chemicals and allied products	59	9	32	34
Miscellaneous industries	73	15	12	26
Total	74	11	15	266

* See footnote to table 17.

enterprises rather than public holdings. There was a resident shareholding in 24 per cent of the firms in this study, fairly evenly divided between shareholdings of 25 per cent and more and under 25 per cent of the firms' voting stock. In fifty-one of the seventy-eight firms with assets of $5 million or more residents held one per cent or less of the voting stock.

The degree of ownership of common stock by the parent has been classified by several other variables in table 44. Once again it should be noted that each of these cross-classifications was also made by three size groups (under $1 million in assets, $1-4.9 million, $5 million and over) to determine whether any observed co-variation between ownership and some other variable existed within size groups also. These distributions by size groups, which are not shown here, suffer because of too few firms in some categories. It will be noted that the firms established or purchased in the last two decades have a higher proportion of cases with shares outstanding than do firms in either of the earlier age groups. When the firms were classified within three size groups, however, there was no longer any such pattern insofar as the two smaller size groups were concerned. The largest size group did show a distinctly higher proportion of the firms established in the last two decades (and especially in the fifties) with a share issue, compared with the older firms.

Analyses of classifications by type of business and of product are limited by the small numbers in some categories. This is so, for example, in the case of the extractive industries, where seven of the eleven firms had a minority share issue. In any case, once allowances are made for the size of firms, the differences in share issue by type of business disappear completely. In the case of classification by type of product it will be noted that in five industries 40 per cent or more of the reporting firms had issued stock, namely, petroleum, primary mining, paper products, primary metals and chemicals. In the first two of these industries almost all of the firms with stock issues had issued 25 per cent or more of their stock. It may well be that the nature of financing in parts of some of these industries is such as to require more recourse to equity capital.[10] In eight other industries 20 per cent or less of the respondent firms had issued stock. Very rough tests by size of firms within industry groups suggest that these differ-

---

[10]In mining, for example, a minority issue will often arise as the prospectors, owners of rights, promoters and others are given stock in the process of putting together an operating concern. Moreover, the highly speculative nature of the initial phases often requires use of considerable equity financing and its distribution among a number of persons or firms.

ences by industry are not in general due to differences of size of firms by industry. The present data do not permit an adequate test of the relation between industry and share issue within size groups, particularly because all firms with assets of $5 million or more have had to be grouped without further size distinction for this test. Finally, the majority of firms in both the primary and primary manufacturing industries and the secondary manufacturing industries had no minority share issue; two-thirds of the former and three quarters of the latter were wholly-owned by their parent firms.

Further evidence on the attitude of the parent firm toward ownership of the voting stock of the Canadian company is available from analysis of the changes which have taken place in ownership since the relationship between the two firms was first established. Data on changes in the parent company's ownership were secured from 242 firms. In 188 of these no change had taken place in ownership of stock since the relationship was first established. The remaining fifty-four firms included thirty-two cases in which the parent had increased its ownership of the voting stock of the Canadian company after the latter was established and twenty-two cases where decreases had occurred. The meaning of these figures is brought out more clearly if they are put another way. Potentially, all of the 242 firms giving information on this point might have shown a decrease in the parent company's ownership of voting stock — only twenty-two did so. Most of these decreases were from the 100 per cent level of initial ownership by the parent, a situation in which 172 of the 242 firms began their affiliated status. These findings must be qualified in two important respects. In seven of the twenty-two cases the decreases were under 5 percentage points. In nine of the remaining fifteen firms the resulting minority stock issue was described as closely held; in other words, another firm or firms or a small group of individuals held the stock. Only a few of the 242 firms have issued stock which was widely held, subsequent to their initial entry into Canada. On the other hand, of the 242 firms involved only seventy could have shown an increase in parent ownership of stock since the remainder began with 100 per cent initial ownership. Thirty-two of these seventy firms showed increases in ownership of the Canadian firm by the affiliate up to 1959, in nine cases to the 100 per cent level. All but five of the thirty-two increases were in excess of 5 percentage points. The same patterns appear if one concentrates on the sixteen firms with assets of $25 million or more which showed changes in ownership by the parent. Eleven of the sixteen showed increases in ownership by the parent and five showed decreases; if changes under 5 percentage points are eliminated the figures are respectively eight and four.[11]

The increases which have occurred in the affiliates' ownership reflect their desire to achieve a greater investment for various specific purposes, the willingness of the minority owners to sell their shares, and sometimes the lack of alternative buyers for these shares. It may be of interest to state briefly the reasons given by the officers of the subsidiaries, recognizing that in some cases a variety of motives may have been involved at the time even though a major or sole one is given subsequently. In five firms of the thirty-two showing increases the change reflected the eventual exercise of options to buy which were established at the time of initial investment by the affiliate. These cases are similar in some respects to those which reported no change in ownership. In six cases the purpose of the increase in ownership was to provide funds for the subsidiary; this includes also cases where the affiliate took shares not desired by the minority share-holders, and situations where full ownership was achieved because it was believed it would be less complicated thereby to supply new capital to the Canadian firm. In four cases the retirement or death of the resident owners supplied the occasion for the increased ownership by the affiliate, some-times helped by the need to raise succession duties. Less frequent reasons for the increased ownership by the affiliate were the failure of the Canadian firm, the wish to increase ownership as the involvement of the affiliate in the subsidiary increased in other respects, a desire to exchange technical information more freely than appeared possible with minority shareholders, and simply in order to benefit more than would otherwise be the case from an expected high return on the Canadian firm's operation.

As for the twenty-two firms which showed a decrease in parent company ownership, in three cases the stated reason was to achieve some degree of public investment in the subsidiary. Three other firms gave employee or executive participation in ownership as the reason and three indicated the decrease was the result of a merger with, or acquisition of, another Cana-dian firm. Other reasons given for a reduction in the affiliate's ownership

---

[11]According to the *Corporations and Labour Unions Returns Act, Report for 1962,* p. 37, nine of the 138 corporations in mining and manufacturing with assets in excess of $25 million, at least half of whose stock was owned by non-residents, issued voting shares to the public in the five years 1958 to 1962. Nine of the seventy-nine com-parable corporations, at least half of whose stock was owned by residents, also issued stock. The eighteen corporations offered shares to the public which would represent about 15 per cent of the equity at the end of 1962. No distribution is given for these issues, and it is not stated whether these larger companies repurchased stock.

included the desire to raise funds, changes in the control of the affiliates which led in turn to reductions in their ownership of the Canadian subsidiaries, and situations where shareholders of the parent were given a direct ownership interest in the Canadian subsidiary.

Another way to look at the pattern of ownership is to consider all of the firms which had minority share issues, beyond directors' qualifying shares, at the end of 1959, whether these issues were made after the affiliate had acquired control of the voting stock of the Canadian firm or existed at the time the relationship between the two firms was first established. This analysis is related to that just made above but is more inclusive since it covers situations where a minority stock issue existed from the beginning of the parent-subsidiary relationship as well as situations where a stock issue was made subsequently.[12] At the end of 1959 all of the voting stock was held by the parent in all but eighty-five of the firms in this study. In thirteen of the eighty-five, one per cent or less of the stock had been issued, cases which have been classified as wholly-owned by the parent in the tables. It cannot be assumed that the minority stock issue of the remaining seventy-two firms was readily available on stock exchanges. In twenty-seven cases the minority stock issue was described as widely held but in twenty-eight other cases it was closely held, while in the remaining seventeen the degree of dispersion of the minority shares was not indicated. In the case of the twenty-seven firms whose minority stock issue was widely held the most important reason given for the "establishment" of the issue was simply the fact that it was there at the time the present parent bought out the previous Canadian (or foreign) majority owners. Sixteen of these firms fall into this category. Only four firms indicated they had established a minority share issue in order to achieve public participation in share ownership. A few had issued stock mainly to secure funds. It may be that the fact that these twenty-seven firms continue with a widely held minority issue is proof enough of their desire for Canadian stockholder participation. This inference should be made with care in view of the fact that in fourteen of the twenty-seven firms involved the parent has increased its share of ownership of the voting stock since the original affiliation was established.

As for the twenty-eight firms whose minority stock was closely held, the most frequent reason for the existence of the minority issue was the fact that the firm was established as a joint venture. In other words, the firms were set up to secure both foreign and Canadian skills and capital. At least

---

[12]It cannot be reconciled perfectly with the earlier analysis partly for this reason and partly because the response rate to the two questions was different.

eight of these firms fall into this group. In six cases employee and executive incentive plans were the reason for the establishment of a closely-held minority share issue. In a few cases the minority issue resulted from the merger with an independent Canadian firm after the subsidiary had been established in Canada. Again only one or two firms explicitly mentioned a desire to permit public Canadian participation in ownership as the reason for the share issue.

How satisfactory has the relationship with minority shareholders been from the point of view of the development of the Canadian company and its relations with its affiliate? Forty-one of the fifty-five firms which gave information on the degree of dispersion of their minority stock issues commented also on this point. In thirty-five cases the answer was that the relationship had proved satisfactory. Frequently the answers indicated that it had been highly so insofar as the respondents to the questionnaire (in almost all cases, the management of the Canadian firm) were concerned. Only two firms stated unequivocally that the experience had been quite unsatisfactory. Four others indicated problems of varying intensity had arisen, generally with regard to the position of minority shareholders relative to that of the affiliate as the subsidiary expanded its financial base. Some important qualifications must be added to these replies. In the first place, fully half of the firms which reported satisfaction with their minority share issue also reported the shares were closely held. Their satisfactory experience with such a share issue reflects a situation where a few individuals or another firm formed the minority stockholders, and not the general stockholding public. Second, these findings relate only to firms which had a minority share issue at the time of reply to the questionnaire. As noted earlier, a number of parent firms have bought out (and some have issued) minority shares in the subsidiary since the subsidiary was established, presumably indicating some dissatisfaction with (or a willingness to entertain) minority shareholders. Finally, the question of share issue can be explored more broadly with the help of the interviews, during which it received some attention.

It was noted that most of those firms in the study which had issued shares considered the relationship with the minority shareholders to be satisfactory. There are exceptions, of course, and one must emphasize that the interests of a dominant corporate shareholder and of public minority shareholders are not always reconcilable. The former can often afford to take a longer view with regard to the financial policies of the subsidiary than can the minority shareholders, with consequent dissent over financial policy, dissent which will be resolved usually in favour of the dominant owner. In spite of such sources of friction there are some advantages to the parent firm in having a minority share ownership in the subsidiary, apart from any addition to the firm's capital which results. It is sometimes an aid to sales if the firm sells directly to a mass market, and it helps in the acceptability of the firm in a country where government has expressed a distinct preference for a share issue. A number of the firms in this study emphasized that the parent firm deliberately followed a policy of issuing shares in its subsidiary companies in Canada and elsewhere, particularly in the interest of harmony with local governments and public but also for the other reasons just noted. The changing attitude toward this was described as follows by one British businessman:

> It used to be thought that the most satisfactory arrangement was that an overseas enterprise should be a 100 per cent subsidiary of the British parent company. Failing this, it was regarded as necessary to have at least *de jure* control, i.e. more than 51 per cent. Today I believe this concept is outmoded, certainly in so far as 100 per cent ownership is concerned. Countries are nowadays inclined to resent their inability to invest in their own industry. . . . Moreover there is not an unlimited amount of capital available in the United Kingdom, and as a business expands it is generally found desirable, if not necessary, to tap the local market.[13]

At the same time the evidence given above on the fewness of such firms and on the number of firms which have tried to buy out minority shareholders suggests that most firms are reluctant to issue shares in the subsidiary.[14] The reluctance to issue shares in the subsidiary warrants some further comment particularly since it has been the reason for a good deal of recent Canadian criticism and law with regard to direct investment companies. One might argue that this reluctance stems simply from a desire on the part of the foreign owners of successful subsidiaries to retain the earnings of the firms they have developed or acquired, insofar as govern-

---

[13]Val Duncan, "Meeting the Industrial Challenge," *Investors Chronicle*, London, November 18, 1960.

[14]One may note here also the submissions by the Montreal Stock Exchange and the Canadian Stock Exchange to the Royal Commission on Banking and Finance as reported in the *Financial Post* for September 22, 1962, p. 36. Apparently ninety-four of the largest direct investment firms without a minority issue were approached by the Montreal Stock Exchange regarding a share issue. Sixty-four replied, only one of which said it planned such an issue. The others cited a variety of problems including possible conflicts of interest between majority and minority interests, little financial need, low profits or losses, and tax laws which are said to favour debt financing.

ment taxation permits, that this attitude is by no means peculiar to foreign-owned firms, and that no more need be said about the subject in this context. In fact, however, the issue goes much deeper and permits some further insight into the nature of the international firm.

It has been emphasized that the structure and operating characteristics of subsidiary Canadian companies vary a good deal, hence the logic of public share issues varies a good deal in terms of the interests both of the firm and of the investor. The foreign-owned firms which do not issue shares vary all the way from the small new firm with one or two products or processes, not far removed from a purely assembly operation or even selling agency, to the large well-established firm producing a wide range of products largely based on domestic supplies. A share issue for many of the small firms or the firms which are simply specialized adjuncts of the parent may be as unsuitable for them as for their many resident-owned counterparts.

Moreover, under Canadian federal law a firm with fewer than fifty shareholders is not required to report financial information.[15] Since a parent firm is counted as one shareholder the wholly-owned firm is able to maintain secrecy regarding its overall financial results. No doubt its competitors, trade unions, and other interested groups can make fairly informed guesses about the financial position of the firm but only at some cost and perhaps at times without precision. It would seem to be strongly in the public interest to require all firms to publish a minimum amount of data, since it is hard to see how rational investment and other decisions can be made in the industry if some firms in it are permitted to hide even the overall results of their operations. The federal government now requires financial disclosure under the Corporations and Labour Unions Returns Act but the details of the companies' financial results are not being released to the public under the Act. Thus the wholly-owned firm is still able to maintain secrecy about its financial results, in contrast with firms which have fifty shareholders or more. It must be added that this particular position against a share issue did not appear to be held strongly, judging by the comments on it during interviews.[16]

A more compelling reason why international firms try to retain full ownership is the flexibility it permits them in their dealings with the subsidiary relative to the rest of the global operation. It is far simpler to make

---

[15]See J. E. Smyth, "Financial Disclosures by Subsidiaries," *Queen's Quarterly*, Vol. LXV, No. 3 (Autumn, 1958).

[16]On these points see also Lindeman and Armstrong, *op. cit.*, pp. 40-48.

decisions about the location of plant to serve various markets, the financing of such additions to capacity, and the exchange of information and skills in all their variety, when the various affiliates are wholly owned. The reason is clear enough: in any given setting the firms can make such decisions on the basis of the maximum probable return over time (or whatever other objective is set, such as the maximum rate of growth consistent with a minimum profit constraint) without having to worry about the reactions and the interests of the minority shareholders. With minority shareholders a whole new set of circumstances must be taken into account, particularly when rapid change or growth in the circumstances of the subsidiary may be called for. This is so even though minority owners are at the mercy of the majority owners by law in most circumstances. The affiliate is not as free, for example, to assist a rapidly expanding subsidiary with new injections of capital, or a subsidy via accelerated transfers of information and skills, or a new market abroad. The new capital may dilute the interests of the minority: the question arises of raising a proportionate amount from the minority or, failing that, perhaps raising the parent's ownership. The new injections of information and skills (as, indeed, the old) must be transferred at a suitable price to ensure that the shareholders of the parent do not subsidize the minority shareholders of the subsidiary. An arms-length price must be set on the export to ensure that neither set of shareholders subsidizes the other.[17] It can no longer be assumed that exports of a particular product will tend to be located, given the transfer costs, demands, and the political climate, in the subsidiary where significant and persistent cost advantages appear. Such decisions are not always clear cut and local management may often have a considerable role to play in developing and pressing for such expansion: but, particularly if the parent is asked to finance the expansion, it must necessarily take into account the fact that the prospective return from a particular subsidiary must be shared with minority owners, while elsewhere it accrues entirely to the global firm and its ultimate owners. There may be an even more compelling reason for preferring complete ownership in these and other cases where arrangements on foreign trade are being considered, since such arrangements with a partly-owned subsidiary are more likely to be subject

---

[17]Since such prices affect profits and therefore taxes paid, one could assume that the tax authorities in each country would ensure that full arms-length pricing takes place in order to avoid a tax subsidy to the other country. Information presented earlier on the extent to which the knowledge of the parent is transferred without explicit charge suggests one should be wary about making such an assumption.

to United States anti-trust law than where they take place with a fully-owned foreign subsidiary.[18]

It must be recognized that this line of reasoning implies that the decisions made in the context of the international firm may at times go against any particular subsidiary's expansion, or even reduce its scope, because of a better alternative available within the international firm in another country. This has already been discussed in the chapter on exports. Whether this is desirable from a national point of view depends on whether in fact the particular demand and cost situations favour it relative to other locations and, if they do not, whether any different results might be expected from a resident-owned firm in the same circumstances. Eventually, from the nation's point of view, the answer depends on how much international specialization a country considers to be in its interests. The point being emphasized here is that the preference for complete ownership reflects in part the relative flexibility of decision-making it confers on the international firm. It should be added that this freedom to decide on change is more likely to be the case when substantial changes have occurred in the usual forces dividing markets, forces which often confer a certain distinctiveness to the subsidiary's operations, or in firms which have already specialized and also integrated their operations internationally. It was noted earlier that a significant number of manufacturing firms have achieved a considerable degree of integration both ways in trade with the foreign affiliates. Some of these in particular voiced strong opposition to minority shareholders in the subsidiary for exactly this reason, in the belief that consideration for minority interests and pressures for local production and diversification would reduce the degree of specialization to the detriment of both firms.[19]

---

[18]The judicial decisions are not entirely clear on this. See Brewster, *Antitrust and American Business Abroad*, Ch. 8; and pp. 5-8 of his *Law and United States Business in Canada*.

[19]It should be added that maintenance of the parent firm's interest in the subsidiary's operations need not mean 100 per cent ownership of the latter. Some firms have raised their ownership of the subsidiary to the point where the financial stake was taken to be closer to the degree of integration involved but stopped well short of 100 per cent ownership by the parent. As one firm put it, "While the holding of voting stock by Canadians is considered desirable, the maintenance of a significant majority holding by the parent is considered essential to facilitate exchange of technical information and know-how." See also the increase in ownership of Ford of Canada as described in the *Financial Post*, October 7, 1959, and the *Toronto Globe and Mail*, August 24, 1959. For a discussion of the reasons for and implications of increased or full ownership of several United States-owned firms in the United Kingdom see the comments in the *Economist* for 1960, pp. 803-805, 907, 1018, and for 1959, pp. 276 and 560.

Finally, there are a number of specific technical reasons for the attitudes toward full ownership. Part of these have to do with the timing of any such move. Those firms which did not object to such an issue for the reasons cited, nevertheless pointed out that it would have to come at a time when the firm needed capital and believed it could get it relatively cheaply in this fashion. Quite a few firms believed it would be a serious mistake to issue shares during the initial phases of rapid expansion of the firm, and a few were able to say this from experience. During such a period the firm may have losses or an erratic earning record. In part this also reflects the need for flexibility of operations including substantial but perhaps intermittent net financing by the parent and an irregular dividend payment, if any, as an accompaniment. It reflects also the widespread belief among business-men in such firms, whether correctly held or not, that a regular dividend policy should accompany a minority share issue, and that this and other aspects of a rapidly growing and changing firm considerably complicate the problem of determining the initial price of the stock. Apart from matters of timing there is a considerable problem for many firms in determining the charges to be made to the subsidiary for various services supplied by the parent, in order to ensure that the minority shareholders of the subsidiary are not subsidized by the shareholders of the parent or vice versa. Since the return to the parent will eventually occur in some form or other it is common in many wholly-owned firms to account with less than full precision for a number of inter-company transactions. Many of these must now be measured and charged with some degree of precision. Some of the officers of subsidiary firms believed that a full charge for the considerable informa-tion received in some highly technical fields, particularly in the early years, would cause a good deal of difficulty for the subsidiary. Assuming that the information is not otherwise available via imported products, or as cheaply, this could be a loss to the community as well, since a fixed annual payment is being substituted for an indeterminate future return based on prospective profits accruing to the parent.

Sources of Funds

As with resident-owned firms, the typical foreign-owned firm receives most of its funds from internal sources. The access to the foreign affiliate for funds is of vital importance to the newly established subsidiary, how-ever, and may again become important in subsequent periods of rapid expansion of the Canadian firm. For the period 1957 to 1964 data are available on the sources of funds for all United States direct investment

TABLE 45

SOURCES OF FUNDS, ALL UNITED STATES DIRECT INVESTMENT
COMPANIES IN CANADA, 1957-1964
(Percentages)

	1957	1958	1959	1960	1961	1962	1963	1964	1957-64
Funds from the United States	26	25	20	21	13	10	8	5	15
Funds from Canada outside the subsidiary*	13	14	11	—1	12	15	14	17	12
Net Income	35	32	39	45	41	43	45	49	42
Depreciation	26	30	30	35	34	32	33	30	31
Total	100	100	100	100	100	100	100	100	100

* Includes funds from other countries and some small miscellaneous sources.
SOURCE: Calculated from data in U.S. Department of Commerce, **Survey of Current Business,** November, 1965, October issues 1960, 1963, and September, 1961. Data refer to all United States direct investment firms in Canadian manufacturing, mining and petroleum industries.

companies in Canada. These funds were used to finance additions to property, plant, equipment and other assets and to pay out income. During these years the firms involved secured 73 per cent of their funds from net income and depreciation. A further 12 per cent was secured largely from other Canadian sources, with only 15 per cent secured from sources in the United States (mainly the parent firm). Sources in the United States supplied a much higher proportion of the overall funds used by the Canadian subsidiary firms during the years 1957-60 than subsequently; indeed, the absolute figures involved fell steadily throughout the period shown in table 45. This was due no doubt to a variety of reasons. Relatively tighter money in Canada compared to the United States for part of the late fifties would encourage such firms to rely more on the parent and other United States sources.[20] In addition, direct investment inflows to the petroleum industry

---

[20]It is of interest in this connection to note the following, from pp. 87-88 of the *Report* of the Royal Commission on Banking and Finance, Ottawa, 1964. "It is sometimes contended that direct-investment companies, by reason of their ready access to foreign funds, are more immune to domestic credit restraint than are Canadian-controlled concerns, a particularly important point given the large share of capital outlays made by such companies. However, in general we found that large firms, whether domestic or foreign-controlled, had easy access to foreign sources of funds. Firms in all size ranges also made increasing use of international trade credit in times of monetary restraint. Nevertheless, small, independent Canadian-owned firms appear to have more difficulty at all times in obtaining long-term finance than do those

and mining industries were relatively greater, compared with manufacturing, in the earlier part of the period. Mining and petroleum tend to rely somewhat more heavily than manufacturing on funds from the United States in most years.[21] Major specific events, such as the exchange rate disturbances of 1962, would also affect comparisons over short periods. The size and persistence of the absolute as well as the relative declines suggest also some diminution in the relative attractiveness of Canada as an outlet for investment of this kind.

The 280 companies in the present study supplied details of their sources of funds for the period 1950 to 1959 (or for a shorter period if established after 1950) classified by the five categories shown in table 46. It should be noted that all of the data were supplied in terms of the percentage distribution between the various sources, not in absolute values. It will be clear that any particular firm which answered the question would list from one to five sources totalling 100 per cent so that any particular firm can appear in up to five of the sources listed in the accompanying tables. Once again the emphasis in the tables and text is on the typical pattern of financing among the firms involved, that is, how many firms fit each particular sub-category. It should be noted also that too sharp distinctions cannot always be drawn between some sources of financing. It is possible that non-affiliated sources of financing abroad may at times have some relation to the foreign affiliates, though we have no direct evidence on this. Some firms had difficulty in giving clear-cut distinctions between categories, as shown in footnotes to the tables.

---

which are subsidiaries of large and well-financed Canadian or American corporations. The problem of the small firm was discussed in Chapter 3 but it is interesting to note that more than a third of Canadian-controlled firms with assets of under $1 million reporting to a Canadian Manufacturers' Association questionnaire reported sources of long-term capital as inadequate. This compared to one out of twenty-nine non-resident firms in the same size category. The limited size of the sample and the lack of follow-up make it difficult to rely heavily on these results, but they do suggest that the small Canadian firm with no strong parent to fall back on encounters extra difficulties in long-term financing. This, however, is an argument for improving Canadian financing facilities for small firms rather than for discriminating against foreign-controlled companies."

[21]See the source noted in table 45, which gives a breakdown of sources of funds by these industries. In 1957-1964 the United States-owned firms in the Canadian mining industry received 19 per cent of their funds from the United States. The corresponding proportions for United States-owned firms in Canadian petroleum and manufacturing were 22 per cent and 9 per cent respectively. It will be noted that the overall decline in funds from the United States occurred well before the American program encouraging international companies to finance more abroad, a program which was introduced in 1965 and extended to Canada in 1966.

Fifty-three per cent of the firms in this study which answered these questions received funds from the parent or other affiliates abroad during the fifties.[22] Over one third of the firms received 50 per cent or more of their funds from this source. As one would expect, the firms receiving a large proportion of their funds from affiliates abroad were very heavily concentrated among those which were newly established or acquired by the parent during the fifties. Eighty-seven of the 123 firms which received funds from affiliates during the fifties were established or acquired during that decade. Sixty-three of the eighty-one firms which received 50 per cent or more of their funds from their foreign affiliates during the fifties were established or acquired during that decade. Put still another way, there were 115 firms established before 1950 which gave details on sources of funds; fully eighty-one of these received no direct funds at all from their affiliates abroad in the fifties. Older firms can become reliant on their foreign affiliates for financing, of course, as other sources of funds become unavailable or unusual expansion takes place. Moreover, the retention of earnings in Canada has yet to be discussed. Nevertheless, the data support the view that in most cases the foreign affiliates prefer that the subsidiaries acquire their funds from other sources than direct transfers from the parent, beyond the initial years of the subsidiaries' operations.[23] There is a striking difference between firms owned in the United States and those owned by overseas investors in this connection. Fully 72 per cent of the latter received funds from foreign affiliates during the fifties compared with 48 per cent of the former. Almost half of the firms owned overseas received 50 per cent or more of their funds from foreign affiliates compared with about one-third of the firms whose stock was owned in the United States. In large part this

---

[22]The percentages disregard those which answered the questionnaire but did not answer these particular questions. The number of such firms involved is shown throughout the tables.

[23]This view of the direct investment firm finds support in the study by the U.S. Department of Commerce noted earlier, and in the work of J. N. Behrman. See the latter's article, "Promoting Free World Economic Development Through Direct Investment," in *Papers and Proceedings of The American Economic Association*, Vol. L, No. 2 (May, 1960), pp. 271-281 and the Discussion, and his chapter entitled "Foreign Associates and their Financing," Ch. IV of Raymond F. Mikesell (ed.), *U.S. Private and Government Investment Abroad*. Behrman suggests that the minimization of equity investment in foreign subsidiaries by the parent may be due in part to a desire to minimize tax liabilities. Particularly if large early returns are expected, parent loans (often interest free) may reduce overall tax payments of the international firm compared with dividends paid on equity. A repayment of debt is not "income" under the U.S. tax code. See pp. 272-273 and 298 of the first source noted here and pp. 105-106 of the second.

TABLE 46
SOURCES OF FUNDS, RESPONDENT COMPANIES, 1950-1959*
(Number of companies)

Specific source as per cent of all sources	Country of control			Asset size in $ millions			
	U.S.	Overseas	All Countries	Under 1	1-4.9	5-24.9	25 and over
Net financing from parent or affiliates abroad							
100%	24	10	34	22	7	1	1
75-99	8	6	14	9	4	1	—
50-74	28	5	33	21	8	2	2
25-49	14	7	21	6	3	6	6
1-24	16	5	21	6	4	4	7
0	98	13	111	27	47	20	14
No reply and not available	39	7	46	13	9	9	5
Total	227	53	280	104	82	43	35
Net financing from other sources abroad							
100%	—	—	—	—	—	—	—
75-99	—	—	—	—	—	—	—
50-74	2	—	2	—	—	1	1
25-49	3	2	5	1	2	—	2
1-24	6	6	12	4	1	—	7
0	177	38	215	86	70	34	20
No reply and not available	39	7	46	13	9	8	5
Total	227	53	280	104	82	43	35
Net financing from Canadian sources							
100%	6	2	8	3	3	2	—
75-99	1	—	1	1	—	—	—
50-74	8	1	9	7	2	—	—
25-49	16	9	25	15	6	2	2
1-24	23	7	30	7	5	4	14
0	134	27	161	58	57	27	14
No reply and not available	39	7	46	13	9	8	5
Total	227	53	280	104	82	43	35

Net income

100%	35	3	38	14	19	3	1
75-99	24	5	29	6	13	7	2
50-74	29	2	31	6	11	8	6
25-49	29	3	32	11	6	6	9
1-24	20	15	35	12	8	5	10
0†	50	18	68	42	16	5	2
No reply and not available	40	7	47	13	9	9	5
Total	227	53	280	104	82	43	35

Depreciation and depletion

100%	—	—	—	—	—	—	—
75-99	1	—	1	—	—	—	1
50-74	7	1	8	—	4	2	2
25-49	40	11	51	8	11	16	16
1-24	48	11	59	19	21	10	8
0	91	23	114	64	37	6	3
No reply and not available	40	7	47	13	9	9	5
Total	227	53	280	104	82	43	35

Other sources

100%	—	—	—	—	—	—	—
75-99	—	—	—	—	—	—	—
50-74	—	—	—	—	—	—	—
25-49	—	—	—	—	—	—	—
1-24	9	3	12	2	1	3	6
0	178	43	221	89	71	32	24
No reply and not available	40	7	47	13	10	8	5
Total	227	53	280	104	82	43	35

* Data include ten firms established before 1950 which gave statistics for a period shorter than 1950-1959. Firms established since 1950 would also cover a shorter period. Seventeen firms were unable to give a breakdown between certain sources of financing. We have arbitrarily assigned to financing from the parent five cases where the firm could not split financing between this source and net income; to financing from Canadian sources three cases where the firm could not split financing between this source and net income; and to net income nine cases where the firm could not split financing between this source and depreciation. In each of these seventeen cases 100 per cent of financing was involved, except one case of 13 per cent in the first type and one case of 90 per cent in the third.

† Including negative figures.

reflects the differing age structure of the two sets of firms, measuring age as the point at which the foreign affiliate established the Canadian firm or acquired a controlling interest in it. In fully two-thirds of the firms owned overseas the parent had established it or acquired control in the fifties; the corresponding proportion for the firms owned in the United States was 40 per cent. The firms with assets under $1 million dollars are clearly far more dependent on financing from their affiliates, partly because many were established recently and had not yet generated significant internal financing. The pattern of dependence by the larger size groups is not clear-cut, how- ever, and analysis is hampered by small numbers and a variable response rate by size to this question among the 280 firms. The medium-sized firms do not appear to be any more dependent on this source than the firms with assets of $25 million or more if one looks only at the numbers which had some access to funds from the affiliate during the fifties. Thus 64 per cent of the firms with assets in the $1-4.9 million range and 59 per cent in the $5-24.9 million asset range did not receive funds from their affiliates abroad in this period, compared with 47 per cent in the largest size group. As one would expect, the seventy-two firms with a minority share issue were less dependent on the parent for funds; only two of them received 75 per cent or more of their funds from the parent in the fifties, for example, compared with forty-six of the wholly-owned firms. Firms with assets of $25 million or more apparently had much easier access to other sources abroad than did the small or medium-sized firms as evident from the fact that almost a third of them received such financing during the decade. Very few of the small or medium-sized firms had financing from non-affiliated sources abroad.

About 30 per cent of the firms which answered the questions on sources of funds received financing from Canadian sources external to the firm during the fifties. In the great majority of these cases this source of financing accounted for less than half of the funds received by the firms involved; the firms which secured more than this proportion from such sources were almost all concentrated in the two smaller size groups. It is interesting to note that about half of the firms with assets of $25 million or more secured funds from such sources. In almost all of these cases, however, such funds accounted for less than a quarter of their overall funds. It is also worth noting that fully half of the firms receiving such funds were ones with a minority share issue, although they accounted for only about one quarter of the firms in this study.

About 30 per cent of the firms replying to these questions did not secure any of their funds from net income in this period. The proportion was closer to 40 per cent for firms owned overseas. As noted earlier, many of the firms in this study were established in the fifties; many of these would have no net income or would suffer losses in their initial years of operation. The smaller firms inevitably dominate this group. Nevertheless, this source of financing was the most important one for the generality of firms. In all size groups quite large proportions of the firms answering the question secured their funds internally: 29 per cent of those in the smallest size group got 50 per cent or more of their funds internally, as did 59 per cent, 52 per cent and 30 per cent in each of the succeeding size groups. Depreciation and depletion was a source of funds for half of the firms answering these questions. There is a marked positive relation between size of firm and proportion of funds derived from this source.

TABLE 47

DISTRIBUTION OF FIRMS BY SOURCES OF FUNDS, 1950-1959*
(Percentages)

Specific source as per cent of all sources	Sources of funds					
	Parent or affiliates abroad	Other sources abroad	Canadian sources	Net income	Depreciation and depletion	Other
100%	15	—	3	16	—	—
75-99	6	—	1	13	1	—
50-74	14	1	4	13	3	—
25-49	9	2	10	14	22	—
1-24	9	5	13	15	25	5
0	47	92	69	29	49	95
Total	100	100	100	100	100	100
No reply and not available as percentage of total	16	16	16	17	17	17

* The data should be read by columns which total 100 per cent. The actual numbers of firms in each category are available from the preceding table.

The data presented so far tell us what have in fact been the sources of funds, reflecting a wide variety of corporate financial circumstances and policies. In an effort to learn more about the latter some further questions on finance were asked. Specifically, the officers of the companies were asked to indicate any preferred policies and practices with regard to the form of capital and extent of financing from the affiliate (beyond the original investment in Canada) on the one hand and within Canada on the other. This was one of the more qualitative questions at the end of the questionnaire which usually elicited replies from a relatively small proportion of those answering the more quantitative body of the questionnaire; only 114 firms answered it. The phrasing of the questions was rather broad and so, consequently, were many of the replies. The results can only be suggestive, therefore. They suggest a preference for financing in Canada on the whole, beyond the original financing, with forty-eight firms so indicating, while twenty-four preferred to finance from the parent. The remainder were less clear cut on this point or without specific policies as such. Among the forty-eight classified as preferring local financing fifteen noted that the policy was to finance entirely by the retention of earnings, and this source was a large part of preferred sources of funds for a number of the remaining firms in

TABLE 48

**COMPANIES SECURING FINANCING FROM AFFILIATES ABROAD
IN 1950-1959, CLASSIFIED BY AGE**
(Number of companies)

Financing from affiliates abroad as percentage of all financing	Number of years in Canada*					
	1-10	11-21	22-41	42 and over	No reply on age	Total
100%	28	3	1	2	—	34
75-99	10	1	2	—	1	14
50-74	25	2	6	—	—	33
25-49	13	3	2	3	—	21
1-24	11	3	3	3	1	21
0	28	14	38	29	2	111
No reply and not available	12	8	16	7	3	46
Total	127	34	68	44	7	280
0 group as % of respondents†	25%	54%	73%	78%	—	40%

* Measured by date of establishment if a new firm, otherwise by year of acquisition by present owner.
† Excludes no reply and not available from total.

this group.[24] Eight of the remainder indicated a preference for financing from bank borrowing in particular, and several more referred to debenture issues and other debt instruments. In nine cases the reply was that financing by issuance of some of the stock of the subsidiary was planned, often with a qualification that the timing of the issue must correspond with financial needs and that the parent must maintain a controlling interest. Typical of replies in this group were the following:

Long term funds for basic establishment and expansion should be supplied by parent — but — when initial establishment is over and organization is firm then current funds should be supplied by Canadian Bank Loans. (A small firm established in the late fifties.)

Policy of the parent all over the world is to get the subsidiary started then leave it alone without further direct financing. The subsidiary borrows on local market if it can. (A large older firm.)

In twenty-four cases, on the contrary, there was an explicit preference for financing from the parent, beyond the original investment in Canada. In most cases these stated that the long-term capital needs in particular should be met by the parent. Eight of them stated that the policy was to not finance in Canada, particularly with regard to the issue of stock. In fifteen other cases it is difficult to classify the answers by the two categories of preferences noted above since explicit policy preferences were not given. Their answers suggest that perhaps seven might be classified as dependent on their own resources while eight were currently receiving significant additional financing from the parent. The remaining twenty-seven firms of the 114 which replied indicated they had no preferred policies as such; some of them noted that market conditions at any given time would be the determining factor.

Clearly such results are no more than suggestive since the categories are not defined sharply. They tend to support what was suggested earlier, namely, a preference for domestic financing beyond the original investment if this is defined particularly to mean reliance on retained earnings. Where substantial long-term capital in particular is required, however, a number of firms revert to the parent rather than seek local sources. This probably reflects the relative ease and cheapness of funds from this source, particu-

---

[24]Many other firms reported that the retention of part of their earnings was a matter of financing policy, usually along with some other policy. Only the latter policies have been recorded here in such cases in order to bring them out. The retention of earnings will be dealt with separately below. To this extent, retention of earnings as a policy is underestimated in this section.

larly where the parent is generating surplus funds itself or has easy access to low-cost sources of financing in more highly-developed money markets.

Payment of Dividends

Some of the overall data on income payments abroad will be of interest before considering the present findings. One measure of the burden of the foreign obligations Canada has acquired as a result of foreign investment is to compare interest and dividends paid abroad as a percentage of gross national product and of current account receipts. The evidence does not suggest that borrowing and the accompanying payment obligations have been excessive, at least by historical standards. Interest and dividends paid abroad as a percentage of gross national product fell sharply from 2.9 per cent in the late twenties and 6.4 per cent in the thirties to 1.9 per cent in the period 1957 to 1964 inclusive. As a percentage of earnings from the sale abroad of goods and services, earnings which are available to finance payments of all kinds abroad, the payments of interest and dividends have declined sharply from 16 per cent in the late twenties and 25 per cent in the thirties to 9 per cent in the period 1957 to 1964 inclusive.[25] These amounts must not be construed as the total return to the foreign owners. As indicated earlier, there are significant payments of royalties and fees of various kinds in return for patents and trade marks, management services and other transfers of knowledge. Frequently the payment of such fees is an alternative to the payment of interest and dividends. Unfortunately, no overall data have been published on such transfers by direct investment companies, although figures have become available recently for transfers by all firms in Canada except for the smallest ones.[26]

Because of the relatively greater role of dividends as compared with

---

[25]It is not implied here, in the context of discussion of long-term trends, that the heavy capital imports of the late fifties and early sixties were at a desirable level. On the contrary, it can be argued with considerable conviction that excessively stringent monetary policy led to excessive imports of debt capital in particular in some years in the late fifties. In the context of slow growth and considerable unemployment, capital imports of the size involved may well have been unnecessary and, indeed, exerted deflationary pressures given a flexible rate. The source of the problem, it should be noted, was the excessively stringent monetary policy.

[26]According to the *Corporations and Labour Unions Returns Act, Report for 1962*, payments in 1962 to non-residents were as follows: royalties of all kinds, $58 million; payments for production, distribution, sales franchises and similar rights, $18 million; payments for research and development, $35 million; administrative charges, $75 million. Canadian companies owned by residents as well as non-residents are included in those making these payments, however, so long as they are not exempted from the provisions of the Act because of size or other reasons.

interest in payments abroad, Canada is now in a much better position to avoid sharp increases in these ratios in the event of economic stagnation or decline. In the thirties the rigidity of interest payments abroad (indeed, their increase since some were payable in various currencies at the lender's option) was a source of considerable difficulty when production and international receipts declined. On the other hand, earnings on direct investment rise as the economy expands and to the extent that foreign-owned firms prosper.[27] Moreover, dividend payments are irregular in many firms and there is no necessary relation between earnings of any one year and payments of dividends for that year. It should be recognized that foreign-owned firms have created substantial exporting and import-competing sectors, as well as being able to draw on parent company financing, as made clear in other parts of this study. It should also be added that the problem of maintaining equilibrium in the balance of payments over any particular time should not be related simply to the foreign-owned sector: what matters here are the operations of this sector plus the resident-owned sector as a whole, in the context of suitable government policies directed to maintaining equilibrium in the balance of payments. Nevertheless, it is well to emphasize that the return to foreign direct investment is indeterminate and continues as long as the investment exists and is profitable, and that the dividend payments abroad associated with it are indeterminate and can be erratic. One would expect that in Canada, where much of industry is foreign owned and much of the foreign-owned industry is export oriented, the returns and the payments would tend to vary positively both with industrial production and with current account receipts over long periods of time. There is no good reason for a marked positive correlation over periods of up to several years at a time, however. In fact, the payment of deferred earnings at a point of time has in some cases loomed quite large in relation

---

[27]In this connection J. Knapp has criticized the use of net capital imports to measure the contribution of foreign capital to development, pointing out that net income payments should be deducted in order to measure the transfer of real resources. He has also suggested that excess borrowing abroad, namely borrowing which does not reflect a deficiency in actual or potential domestic saving in the borrowing country, is rather widespread — while indicating that it may be necessary at particular periods of history because of institutional factors such as the attitudes of domestic savers and monetary authorities. See J. Knapp, "Capital Exports and Growth," *Economic Journal*, Vol. LXVII, No. 267 (September, 1957), pp. 432-444; "Comments" by A. G. Ford and Knapp in the September issues for 1958, 1959, and 1960; the article by W. Rosenberg, "Capital Imports and Growth — The Case of New Zealand — Foreign Investment in New Zealand, 1840-1958," *Economic Journal*, Vol. LXXI, No. 281 (March, 1961), pp. 93-113; and the "Comments" by D. J. Delivanis, R. J. Ball, and Rosenberg in the issue for December, 1961.

to current international earnings. So long as the subsidiary is permitted to retain part of its earnings and so long as it continues to expand its operations, a contingent payment accrues which can have a significant impact on the current balance of payments situation should the circumstances of the parent or the subsidiary lead to its transfer. This point and its more general policy implications have been explored in an interesting article by E. T. Penrose.[28] The key point is that once a foreign-owned firm is established its continued growth is an increase in foreign investment. Penrose suggests that foreign investment increases more rapidly and continues longer when it depends on expanding existing firms compared with a situation where it depends on importing capital to new firms. All successful firms create new opportunities for their activities and plough back part of their earnings into growth. The point to note is that the foreign-owned firm on the one hand can call on the skills of a large operating parent concern as it creates or exploits opportunities, while an expansion of the firm in this process is at the same time an expansion of foreign investment. If earnings are retained while the growth of the firm proceeds the balance of payments impact of servicing the foreign investment is not really apparent; it becomes so only if and to the extent that retention of earnings slows down and dividends are paid. In such circumstances, if the change is a permanent one, a re-adjustment in the economy will be required to meet the need to transfer more income abroad; otherwise there are the usual requirements for flexibility in exchange rates, foreign exchange reserves or policies if it is a temporary change. Whether any necessary continuing re-adjustments are likely to be sudden or sharp will depend not only on the current international context but also on the extent to which the required changes in exports and imports have been anticipated by policy-makers and have been taking place in the combined foreign-owned and domestic-owned sectors.

Canadian data on income payments of interest and dividends for direct investment companies demonstrate some of the points discussed here. The Dominion Bureau of Statistics has prepared estimates of total earnings and of earnings paid abroad for all direct investment companies for the years

[28]See E. T. Penrose, "Foreign Investment and the Growth of the Firm," *op. cit.*, pp. 220-235. The article also describes the circumstances of a particularly large dividend payment by General Motors-Holden's Ltd., of Australia. The point has been explored further by Arndt, who argues that direct investment is likely to lead to a *long-run* balance of payments problem in the Australian case because its concentration in manufacturing does not create sufficient bias to exports or to import replacement to finance the growth in profit transfers. See H. W. Arndt, "Overseas Borrowing — the New Model," *The Economic Record*, Vol. XXXIII (August, 1957), pp. 247-264.

1946 to 1961. These show that the proportion of income paid abroad varied from an annual low of 38 per cent to a high of 63 per cent during this period. Moreover, changes in this proportion can occur over the space of a few years. Thus in the period 1955 to 1957 when economic expansion was rapid and relatively full employment existed the proportion of earnings paid abroad varied from 38 per cent to 42 per cent. In the next four years when growth had slowed and excess capacity prevailed the proportion rose to between 48 per cent and 58 per cent. One should add that total earnings declined after 1956-1957, but the point to be noted here is that earnings paid abroad generally continued to rise while there was a sharp diminution in the levels of undistributed earnings. As already noted, total earnings and earnings paid abroad need not correspond closely over short periods. Table 49 brings out another characteristic of direct investment which has been mentioned earlier, namely the growth of such investment by retained earnings. Insofar as the firms are successful and part of the earnings are retained, the total of foreign investment in the country grows without further capital inflows from the parent. The decision to retain earnings is, of course, equivalent to a decision to pay out and then to reinvest part of the funds paid out. The point is that retention of part of the earnings is virtually automatic in most firms; in foreign-owned firms this retention also has the effect of increasing the total foreign investment in the country. How important this is can be seen from the fact that just under half of the increase of United States direct investment in Canada from 1945 to 1954 represented the retention of earnings by firms which were in this direct investment group at the beginning of the period.[29] Retained earnings from 1946 to 1961 by all direct investment firms in Canada, including those by firms existing at the beginning of the period and also those by firms established or acquired later, amounted to about 40 per cent of the total increase in the value of direct investment during this period.[30]

It was clear from data on the 280 firms in this study that their most frequent source of funds has been net income: as noted earlier, 42 per cent of the firms received from 50 per cent to 100 per cent of their funds from this source alone. The extent to which the profits of the firm are available to it for financing is dependent on tax deductions and dividend payments. Over half of the firms which supplied information on dividends

[29]D.B.S., *Canada's International Investment Position, 1926-1954*, p. 25.
[30]The retained earnings of $4.3 billion are shown in table 49. The value of direct investment rose by $11 billion from the end of 1945 to the end of 1961. Because of problems of valuation, timing, and coverage, this must be considered a very approximate estimate.

TABLE 49

TOTAL RETURNS ON ALL FOREIGN DIRECT INVESTMENT IN CANADA, 1946-1961
(Millions of dollars)

Year	Remitted income	Allowance for withholding tax	Undistributed earnings	Total earnings	Percentage of earnings distributed abroad
1946	147	12	120	279	53 %
1947	183	15	125	323	57
1948	174	14	160	348	50
1949	233	19	155	407	57
1950	309	25	155	489	63
1951	272	23	200	495	55
1952	239	22	310	571	42
1953	215	22	325	562	38
1954	229	22	315	566	40
1955	282	26	365	673	42
1956	309	26	470	805	38
1957	335	24	460	819	41
1958	337	23	260	620	54
1959	365	24	370	759	48
1960	315	28	280	623	51
1961	405	57	240	702	58

SOURCE: D.B.S., **The Canadian Balance of International Payments, 1961 and 1962**, p. 22.

indicated they had paid no dividends at all in the fifties. Relatively more of the firms owned overseas and of the smaller firms paid no dividends. Sixty-nine more of the 228 answering the question indicated they paid up to 49 per cent of their net earnings as dividends, and only thirty-six that they paid over this amount. Only eleven firms of the entire 228 paid out 75 per cent or more of their earnings.[31] One must immediately qualify these statements by the fact that many of the firms in this study were founded in the fifties and thus might well pay little or nothing in the way of dividends

[31]These data on percentages of earnings paid as dividends may seem at variance with those for all direct investment companies presented earlier. It should be noted that the data for the 280 firms here is given by size of company. In other words, any approximation to the overall data for all firms must weight the different size groups. In addition, dividend payments by a few large firms with assets in the hundreds of millions can determine the level of dividends in any one year. There are no similar data at the level of all firms to determine whether the 280 are representative of the total in this respect.

TABLE 50

PERCENTAGE OF NET EARNINGS PAID AS DIVIDENDS, 1950-1959
(Number of companies)

Percentage paid	Country of control			Asset size in $ millions			
	U.S.	Overseas	All Countries	Under 1	1-4.9	5-24.9	25 and over
0	93	30	123	69	30	11	10
1-24	27	3	30	10	12	2	5
25-49	34	5	39	6	11	13	9
50-74	19	6	25	2	10	5	8
75-100	10	1	11	5	3	2	0
No reply, not available, not applicable	44	8	52	12	16	10	3
Total	227	53	280	104	82	43	35

because earnings were small or non-existent, or until the operation was well established in Canada. Thus the respondent from one small expanding firm established in the late fifties, which is wholly owned by the parent, stated, "Do not expect to declare a dividend before 1965. After that the indication is that dividends would not exceed 10 per cent of invested capital with a minimum net profit limit." It is more meaningful for some purposes to show this data by age of firm, therefore, as in table 51. It is at once evident that most of the firms established or acquired in the fifties paid no dividends at all in that period. New firms are generally supplied with some capital from the parent; in such circumstances the payment of dividends is often considered pointless, at least in the wholly-owned firm, since it would simply be returned to the subsidiary in the form of new capital from the parent. If the parent plans only a single investment concentrated in a few years it may still permit full retention of earnings for a time to finance the still expanding subsidiary before taking any return on its investment. It will be noted from the table that among the older firms a much smaller proportion is in the position of paying no dividends and that a higher and higher percentage of net earnings is paid for dividends as the age of the firm increases. Nevertheless, the flexibility of the direct investment company with regard to the payment of dividends must be emphasized. As financing demands require, and to the extent the parent can be persuaded to forego dividends for a time, the firm can retain its

earnings largely or wholly. It will be noted, for example, that quite significant numbers of the firms over ten years of age paid no dividends at all or
paid less than one-quarter of their earnings through the fifties.[32] The point
can be made more forcefully if one distinguishes those direct investment
firms which have minority shareholders from those which do not, and
particularly if a distinction is made between minority share issues which are
widely held and those closely held. Firms with a minority share issue,
particularly if it is widely held, may find it more necessary to pay dividends
(and to pay them more regularly) than the firm with a single corporate
stockholder. The data in table 51 show that among the 280 firms in this
study a higher proportion of earnings was paid as dividends in the fifties
by firms with a minority stock issue, particularly if it was widely held, than
by firms whose stock was wholly owned by the parent. This is an incomplete test since some other variables which could affect this result, such as
the level of earnings, are not known. It can be said that the differences in
average age of the firms among the different ownership groups, which could
affect this result, are not large enough to be significant.[33]

It will be appreciated that by indicating the proportion of income paid
as dividends for the fifties as a whole the full variability which is possible
in the dividend payments of direct investment companies has not been
shown. It seemed best to ask for dividends over a longer period in order to
be able to classify patterns of differences by certain other characteristics
more readily. A number of individual firms gave details of payments by
years which suggest that there is room for considerable annual variation.
The wholly-owned firm in particular is in a position to vary the dividends
paid considerably, subject to the general policy of the parent in this regard.
That policy may in fact give many of the subsidiaries considerable leeway
given the fact that their dividends are often a small part of the parent's
earnings, that the re-investment accrues to the parent's assets, and that
there are continuing returns, such as royalties and management fees, in
some cases. It was not unusual even among some of the larger, older firms

---

[32]It might be argued that this could reflect a lack of earnings for the firms involved
in the fifties. It is unlikely that such large proportions of the firms had little or no
earnings. In any case, by comparisons with the sources of funds in the fifties it is
possible to trace quite significant numbers of firms paying no dividends at all, or a
low percentage of their earnings as dividends, for which net income was a large
source of funds.

[33]It will be noted that a large number of wholly-owned firms did not answer the
question on dividends paid. They would almost all have had to pay no dividends in
the fifties to match the dividend performance of the firms with a minority issue
of stock.

interviewed to find wholly-owned firms which paid no dividends for five or more years of rapid expansion then paid a dividend equivalent to 100 per cent or more of earnings for several years. As suggested above, there are broad patterns which emerge when the firms as a whole are considered, particularly after the initial years of establishment of the firm. But the essence of the dividend on direct investment, particularly for wholly-owned firms, is that it is subject to variation as the opportunities and needs of the two firms dictate.

In companies owned largely or wholly by other firms the distinction between a payment of dividends and the withdrawal of capital, and between the retention of earnings and the inflow of capital, may become blurred at times. Partly in order to ensure that the data on dividend payments were not greatly affected by such withdrawals, and partly for its own interest, the firms in this study were asked whether there had been any significant net withdrawals of capital from Canada in the fifties. Close to 200 firms answered this question, with all but eight indicating there had been no significant net withdrawal. The circumstances of the net withdrawals varied greatly: the financial needs of the parent, the withdrawal of the initial capital investment in the subsidiary, and the sale of one division of the business were among those cited. One should add two qualifications here. In a different set of circumstances, such as prolonged economic stagnation in Canada, the withdrawals could be much larger. It is obvious also that only the successful, or at least operating, firms are included in this study: capital withdrawals in the fifties associated with unsuccessful ventures or simply the sale of the subsidiary are not included.

An attempt was made also to ascertain whether the subsidiary and/or the affiliate had any preferred policies or practices regarding the payment of dividends. A considerable number could not give a reply to this since the firm was established too recently for such a policy to be devised or there were as yet no net earnings to be disbursed. Given a high non-response to this particular question on policy as well, it was necessary to omit the usual detail on country and size of firm because of small numbers in some categories. An approximate classification can be given as follows. Thirty-two replies indicated that the preferred policy was to retain earnings to finance the growth of the firm. In twenty-four cases this meant no dividends were paid at all and in all but two of the remaining eight they were under one-quarter of earnings. (It should be added that many of these firms were not new companies; eighteen of the thirty-two had been established or acquired before the fifties and a further six in the first year or two

TABLE 51

**PERCENTAGE OF NET EARNINGS PAID AS DIVIDENDS, 1950-1959,
CLASSIFIED BY AGE OF COMPANY AND NATURE OF OWNERSHIP**
(Number of companies)

Percentage paid	Age in years*				Nature of ownership†			
	1-10	11-21	22-41	42 and over	Minority stock widely held	Minority stock closely held	All firms with minority issue	No minority issue
0	82	17	17	5	9	15	29	94
1-24	9	6	11	3	1	6	12	18
25-49	13	3	12	10	9	2	15	24
50-74	5	1	10	8	6	1	8	17
75-100	1	1	3	6	1	2	4	7
No reply, not available, not applicable	17	6	15	12	1	2	4	48
Total	127	34	68	44	27	28	72	208

* Excludes seven firms which did not reply to the question on age.
† The first two columns exclude seventeen firms with a stock issue which did not indicate its degree of dispersion.

of the decade.) Another fifteen firms indicated their preferred policy was to pay a fixed percentage of earnings. These were mainly medium-sized or larger firms which were well established: ten of them, in fact, had individual assets of $5 million or more. Four of these indicated the preferred rate was 25 per cent, three were in the 33 per cent to 45 per cent range, six preferred a 50 per cent rate, and two a 60 per cent rate. Another seven noted a variety of specific policies ranging from payment of a fixed absolute total per year to payment of the surplus above foreseen capital expenditures. Fully seventy-five indicated they had no policy. In thirty-two of these no dividends at all had been paid in the fifties. It must not be thought the seventy-five firms which indicated they had no policy on dividends were largely the relatively new and small firms as thirty-seven of them had been established before the fifties and forty-one had assets of $1 million or more. Finally, fully 151 firms did not or could not answer this question. In a few cases, such as unincorporated branch operations, the question was inapplicable. In sixty-three of these companies there were no dividend payments in the fifties, either because they were founded in the fifties (forty-one of them) and/or there were no earnings (thirty-seven firms). Another forty-five of the 151 companies neglected to answer questions on dividend payments as well as on dividend policies. It would be dangerous to attempt to draw any conclusions on policies regarding dividend payments when a large number of the companies neglected to answer the question. The very high non-response may suggest that the question was inapplicable. In other words, as indicated earlier, many firms whose stock is wholly owned or closely held by another operating firm or firms do not have to think in terms of a regular dividend payment in the sense in which publicly-owned firms often interpret their commitment to shareholders. A return to the parent must be made but it may be at distinct and often widely separated points of time. It is not difficult to find wholly-owned firms, particularly among the larger ones, which have a policy of declaring an annual dividend equal to a given percentage of net earnings, but most wholly-owned firms appear to have a more flexible approach to dividend payments.

The United States Guidelines Program

A country which relies heavily on imports of capital may from time to time be subject to substantial changes in the rate or direction of that flow. Such changes may reflect private decisions about a great variety of factors including, for example, changes in actual and prospective yields on capital and changes in the balance of payments situation which portend changes in the exchange rate. The stability of the capital flow can also be affected by specific government policies designed to affect the flow. It is well to emphasize that the pattern of financing of investment and payment of earnings can be changed both in the short-run and the long-run by such factors. The patterns shown above for the fifties, in other words, may be changed in the sixties.

One set of policies which is particularly likely to affect the rate and direction of international capital flows in the sixties is the measures used by the United States to correct the disequilibrium in its balance of payments. A number of measures were directed at capital flows but those dealing directly with the transactions of the international firm are particularly relevant in the present context. In February, 1965, the United States government announced a voluntary and temporary program involving private United States businesses with important direct investment transactions. These were asked to improve the balance on their international transactions on an average of 15-20 per cent in 1965 compared with 1964. A list of nine specific suggestions for improvement in their current and capital transactions was circulated to the firms but the emphasis of the program in 1965 was on permitting flexibility in the individual firm's approach toward meeting the overall objectives.[34] Quarterly progress reports were to be made by the firms involved, however. Three special situations were recognized. First, the program was not to inhibit direct investment in the less-developed countries. Second, the repatriation of short-term financial funds invested abroad was to be done in such a way as to avoid difficulties for countries subject to balance of payments problems. Finally, Canada was specifically exempted from the cutbacks in direct investment. It was suggested, however, that the short-term funds at the disposal of Canadian subsidiaries not exceed those required for their operating needs. It may be added here that Canada was also exempted from the 15 per cent interest equalization tax on new issues in the United States, beginning in mid 1963, on condition that this exemption not be used to increase Canada's reserves of foreign exchange beyond a target figure of $2.7 billion. Another exemption recognizing Canada's special dependence on the United States capital market was that from the "guideline" of December, 1965 limiting loans abroad by non-bank financial institutions in 1966 to 105 per cent of the amount at September 30, 1965, on condition that Canada's foreign exchange reserves not exceed a new target of $2.6 billion.[35]

In December of 1965 Canada's exemption from the guidelines program for international firms was removed. The decision apparently reflected the sharp increase planned in the investments of United States-owned subsidiaries in Canada, an increase in United States direct investment in Canada in 1965, and the feeling that the exemption of Canada created a loophole in the overall guideline legislation. The number of United States parent companies the program covered was raised from about five hundred to nine hundred. A new specific guideline was set with regard to direct investment permitting each parent corporation an average rate of direct investment abroad (including retained earnings) in 1965-1966 up to 135 per cent of its 1962-1964 average. Since direct investment as defined in 1965 was

---

[34]The specific suggestions were to expand exports, develop new export markets, accelerate repatriation of earnings, postpone direct investment in marginal projects, limit new direct investments made with funds raised in the United States, raise more funds in other developed countries, sell equities in foreign subsidiaries to residents of host countries, increase the use of American flag vessels and airlines, and minimize the outflow of short-term financial funds while repatriating funds previously invested abroad.

[35]See Bank of Canada, *Annual Report of the Governor to the Minister of Finance*, 1965, pp. 8-11.

higher than this, the guideline implied a reduction in 1966. In addition to this formula applied to direct investment flows plus retained earnings, the parent companies were encouraged to improve their net balance of payments situation in other ways as noted above. It should be added that the intent of the guidelines was to reduce the United States deficit by a given amount on a global basis rather than by any specific amount for any given country.

One aspect of this program, the suggestion that exports from parent companies to their subsidiaries be raised, was considered at the end of Chapter 5. Along with criticism of this point the Canadian government and a number of private persons have objected to the program's extension to Canada on the grounds that Canada is contributing on balance to the credit side of the United States balance of payments, and that the guidelines will make it even more difficult to maintain equilibrium in the Canadian balance of payments. Furthermore, while most persons concede that the United States can limit the new outflows of direct investment, the attempt to direct the degree to which earnings can be retained in Canada is seen as another case of extra-territoriality. In brief, one of the key Canadian objections is that the subsidiaries involved should not be required to make decisions other than those they would make for economic reasons, and that the attempt to force them to do so in these and other respects (as discussed with regard to exports and imports earlier) raises questions regarding Canada's sovereignty over the subsidiaries. These objections were presumably presented at a meeting of the Canada-United States Joint Committee on Trade and Economic Affairs in March of 1966. The statement issued at the end of the meeting said in part "The U.S. members made clear that the U.S. Government was not requesting U.S. corporations to induce their Canadian subsidiaries to act in any way that differed from their normal business practices as regards the repatriation of earnings, purchasing and sales policies, or their other financial and commercial policies."[36] This statement would seem to exempt Canada from the guidelines legislation which urges companies to forego their normal decisions on sources of financing, foreign dividend policy, and some aspects of foreign trade in order to suit the objectives of the balance of payments program. Yet Canada has not been officially exempted from the legislation. The entire situation remains in some doubt, as do the actual balance of payments consequences which

---

[36]See the *Globe and Mail* for March 7 and 8, 1966 and the reports on a talk by the Assistant Secretary for Economic Affairs in the U.S. Department of Commerce, March 3 and 4. See also the *Financial Post*, March 12, 1966, p. 25. For further comment on the guidelines, see also the sources listed in footnote 13, Chapter 5.

will not be known until the companies involved have reported. Some actual or potential effects of the guidelines have already had direct repercussions in Canada. The governor of the Bank of Canada in December, 1965 and January, 1966 informed the chartered banks that he expected them to look after their regular customers if they found themselves confronted with new applications for credit (i.e. from subsidiary companies) as a result of the United States guideline at a time of relatively tight credit.[37] Shortly after the above-mentioned meeting the Minister of Finance for Canada announced that well-known United States companies were issuing dollar securities for sale outside the United States. He asked Canadian investors not to acquire such securities or those issued by the non-Canadian (i.e. European) subsidiaries of United States parent companies. He also mentioned that the Bank of Canada and the Department of Finance had been discouraging the issue of securities in Canada by foreign borrowers. In doing so he pointed out that the demand for capital to finance investment was so great in Canada that purchase of such issues by residents would only lead to further borrowing in the United States.[38] Finally, as noted at the end of Chapter 1, the Canadian government issued its own set of guidelines to subsidiary companies early in 1966, including the suggestion that the firms retain sufficient earnings for growth after paying a fair return to the owners.

---

[37]Bank of Canada, *op. cit.*, p. 10.
[38]Canada, *House of Commons, Debates,* March 16, 1966, pp. 2755-2756. See also the *Economist*, March 26, 1966, pp. 1268 and 1271, and April 9, 1966, p. 174.

9
Nationality of Ownership and Performance of the Firm

Underlying much of the discussion in Canada of direct investment companies is the assumption that the results of their operations differ from those of their resident-owned counterparts. The difference, it is usually assumed, is in the direction of an inferior performance by the direct investment firm. The criticisms of their policies and results which were noted in the introductory chapter sometimes carry this assumption explicitly. Frequently the assumption is implicit in the fact that foreign ownership as such is considered the significant or sole determinant of the policy or result in question. These views have already been examined in this study in various connections, for example, in determining what are the actual policies and results of direct investment firms and some of the reasons for these. It is time to approach the issue directly.

In this chapter two approaches will be taken to this question. The 280 direct investment firms in this study contain some which are partly owned by residents and some which are wholly owned by non-residents. Do the former differ from the latter in significant aspects of performance and, if so, is this because of the different nature of ownership? It will be apparent that this is a limited test of the effects of ownership since the voting stock of all 280 of these firms is effectively controlled by non-residents. As direct investment firms they are all part of an international corporation and are all affected by this in ways already discussed. It is worth asking, nevertheless, if these effects differ in degree because of the varying extent to which their voting stock is held by the parent. A second and more direct approach is possible by comparing foreign-owned firms with resident-owned firms in similar circumstances.

Degrees of Foreign Ownership and Performance

One way to examine the effects of ownership on performance is to ask whether there is any difference in performance among the 280 foreign-owned firms in this study when they are grouped by degree of ownership by the parent. In the first chapter it was noted that when the withholding tax was lowered for firms with a degree of Canadian ownership, it was assumed that the performance of such firms would be improved in certain ways. Table 52 compares several characteristics of firms which are wholly owned by the parent, those in which there is a minority share issue of 25 per cent (the minimum specified by Canadian law in order to acquire the stated degree of Canadian ownership), and those in which a larger minority issue is involved. Too much should not be made of small differences between the categories since there is a concentration of firms in the 99-100 per cent parent ownership category and relatively few in the other owner-ship categories. It appears that significant differences between the cate-gories exist with respect to the nationality of the president, the proportion of directors who reside in Canada, and, less systematically, the degree of supervision exercised by officers of the parent firm. In other words, those firms which reported that the parent held less than 99-100 per cent of the stock also reported that a higher portion of their presidents were Canadian nationals, and that a higher portion of their directors resided in Canada. This was almost consistently the situation with regard to those firms in which up to 25 per cent of the voting stock was held by minority owners when compared with the wholly-owned firms, and as regards those firms with more than a 25 per cent minority ownership compared with those which had up to a 25 per cent ownership.[1] It also appears that a smaller proportion of firms which stated that they were wholly owned reported that supervision was negligible and a larger portion reported that they were partly supervised, at least when compared with firms with a minority ownership up to 25 per cent. There was no great difference, however, in these two degrees of supervision between the wholly-owned firms and

---

[1]These findings are consistent, in the main, with those reported under the *Corpor-ations and Labour Unions Returns Act, Report for 1962*, pp. 35-36. Data for manu-facturing and mining companies with assets over $25 million whose stock was half or more owned abroad in 1962 show that 47 per cent of the directors were residents of Canada when 95 per cent or more of the stock was owned abroad, and 63 per cent were residents in each case when 75-94.9 per cent and 50-74.9 per cent of the stock was owned abroad. The proportion of presidents resident in Canada with Canadian citizenship in these 138 companies rises from 40 per cent to 48 per cent to 56 per cent as the degree of foreign ownership of the firm falls by the categories just noted.

those with a minority ownership exceeding 25 per cent. The number of firms reporting extensive supervision declines as the minority share issue rises, but since only a few firms are involved in each of the minority share-issue groups this change may not be statistically significant. When these three sets of data are examined within three asset size groups for the firms involved the findings noted here are broadly confirmed. In other words, within the three asset size groups the firms which are wholly owned tend to have relatively fewer Canadian nationals as presidents and a smaller proportion of resident directors. They are also relatively less well represented in the negligibly supervised group in two of the three size groups.

In terms of economic performance, on the other hand, there does not appear to be any consistently significant difference between these firms when they are classified by the degree to which they are owned by the parent. The data on per cent of purchases from the domestic market give almost identical distributions when the firms are distributed by degrees of parental ownership. At first sight it appears that the proportion of output sold in Canada varies when classified by degree of ownership, since the percentage of firms selling 100 per cent of output in Canada is lower for those where the parent has 75-98 per cent ownership compared to cases where it has full ownership. For firms with parental ownership below 75 per cent, however, the proportion without exports is close to that for wholly-owned firms. A corresponding pattern occurs for other sales categories. Exactly the same thing occurs for research as a percentage of sales. On the other hand, there is no improvement in unit costs when one compares wholly-owned firms with those in which the parent owns 75-98 per cent of the subsidiary's stock, in that the percentage with unit costs which are typically higher than those of the affiliate is virtually the same for both groups. There is a drop in the percentage with higher costs if one looks at firms in which less than 75 per cent of the stock is owned by the parent. When these results on economic performance are measured within the three size groups of firms there is no consistent relation between performance and ownership. One must conclude that economic performance is not consistently related to ownership, unless one is prepared to suggest it can improve with minority ownership in one or two respects up to the 25 per cent level but not beyond, and also that this does not hold — or does not hold in quite this way — with other and not unrelated aspects of economic performance. It seems more logical to suggest, at least, that other variables are more closely related to economic performance than is ownership.

In view of the small numbers involved in the groups which are less than wholly owned, it may be as well to apply a test to determine whether these differences are statistically significant. In the last section of this chapter the chi-square test will be outlined and applied to the subsequent and major results of this chapter. Using that test on the differences noted above, it can be stated that at the 5 per cent level of significance the conclusions above are confirmed where the wholly owned firms are compared with all firms with a minority share issue. In other words the test confirms that there is a statistically meaningful difference in the case of the nationality of the president and the residency of directors but not in any aspect of economic performance. The test also suggests that the differences noted in the degree of supervision between wholly-owned firms and all those with a minority share issue are not statistically significant. If one uses chi-square to test the differences between the three degrees of ownership shown in table 52, a procedure which raises problems in some cases because of the small numbers involved, the conclusions just stated tend to be confirmed but not as consistently.

It was noted in the previous chapter that twenty-eight of the partly-owned firms reported that their minority share issue was closely held, but it is not known if the minority holders were individuals or firms. It seems worth asking whether or not closely-held minority shareholdings make a difference in performance since the voice of such shareholders ought to be stronger than that of scattered minority holders. The data can be summarized by noting how they compare with all firms. Percentage distributions of the performance of the twenty-eight firms with a closely-held minority share issue are very similar to those for all firms except for two characteristics.[2] Their performance is better in that a higher proportion of the twenty-eight firms have a Canadian national as president and a lower proportion have unit costs which are typically higher than those of the affiliate. The overall results with these particular data do not suggest that the existence of a closely-held minority interest results in a consistent and significant improvement in performance. In view of the small numbers of firms involved, however, these particular results may not be meaningful.

It can be concluded that the present data suggest that the nationality of the president and the residency of directors appear to vary systematically

---

[2]In one respect this evidence is not consistent with the views of executives as outlined in the last section of Chapter 3 above, where it was noted that some of them believed that a concentrated minority shareholding minimized the degree of supervision from the parent.

with the degree of parental ownership but that other variables do not change systematically with this. This test is limited in various ways, so a more direct examination of ownership and performance, such as that presented below, is in order. Before undertaking this, it may be asked whether the difference in performance relates not to the degree of ownership but to the extent to which the parent's executives exert their authority. Does performance vary with degree of supervision as measured earlier? It will be appreciated that this test is also limited because of the subjective nature of the question as discussed in Chapter 3 and by the fact that there are small numbers in some categories. Table 53 presents a summary statement classifying certain variables by the three degrees of supervision discussed earlier. Again it is true that firms which have a negligible degree of supervision have nationals of Canada as presidents, and resident directors on their boards, more frequently than do those with a partial degree of supervision. The latter, in turn, more frequently have senior Canadian or resident personnel as defined than do firms which are extensively supervised by the parent. Analysis within three asset size groups very largely confirms the results for the overall data. On the other hand, insofar as economic performance is concerned, classification by degree of supervision presents a mixed picture indeed. With regard to percentage of sales in Canada and percentage of purchases from abroad there is very little difference overall or within the three asset size groups when classified by degree of supervision and what differences there are do not appear to be significant. In terms of research as a percentage of sales, however, firms which have a negligible degree of supervision have a somewhat better performance than those partly supervised and a much better performance than those extensively supervised. The pattern just noted persists within each of the three asset size groups. On unit costs the situation is exactly the reverse. The extensively supervised firms have a lower portion of their number reporting unit costs which are typically higher than those of the affiliate. This difference is confirmed within the asset size groups except for the medium-sized firms.

All in all it appears that minority share ownership and/or less extensive supervision by the affiliate are associated with situations where there are relatively more Canadian nationals as presidents and relatively higher proportions of resident directors. No doubt the causation here can run either way depending on the specific situation in each firm. There are very few grounds for assuming any consistent association of economic performance with either the degree of ownership or the degree of supervision, in terms of the present set of data and present group of variables.

TABLE 52

EXTENT OF PARENT'S OWNERSHIP OF VOTING STOCK
CLASSIFIED BY SELECTED CHARACTERISTICS

Characteristic	Extent of parent's ownership			All firms
	99-100%	75-98%	Below 75%	
	(Per cent distribution of replies except for total number)			
Nationality of president				
Country of affiliate	57	50	32	52
Other (largely Canadian)	43	50	68	48
Total number of firms	160	22	40	222
Resident directors as proportion of total				
0-24%	21	4	8	17
25-49	30	35	14	27
50-74	36	43	57	41
75-100	13	17	22	15
Total number	137	23	37	197
Degree of supervision				
Negligible	29	54	36	33
Partly	52	32	53	50
Extensively	19	14	11	18
Total number	175	28	36	239
Per cent sales to domestic market				
100%	50	32	49	48
95-99	29	36	31	30
70-94	13	21	13	14
Under 70	7	11	8	8
Total number	191	28	39	258
Per cent purchases from domestic market				
90-100%	29	32	33	30
80-89	20	18	18	19
60-79	25	29	24	26
Under 60	26	21	24	25
Total number	177	28	33	238

Research development as per cent of sales

0%	60	43	54	57
0.01-1.00	24	14	26	23
Over 1.00	16	43	20	20
Total number	156	28	35	219

Unit costs compared with affiliate

Typically higher	64	63	52	62
About the same, lower, varies	36	37	48	38
Total number	127	19	25	171

NOTE: Where the total number of firms in the last column is not 280 the difference usually represents non-response to one or both questions by firms returning the questionnaire. In one or two cases the difference also includes a few special replies not relevant for present purposes. The second section excludes sixty-three firms which replied that their boards were inactive and eight which had no board.

The Nature of the Resident-Owned Firms in this Study

To compare non-resident owned and resident-owned firms it is desirable to have as wide a coverage as possible in order to be reasonably assured that any observed differences are statistically valid. The aggregative data available in this respect are few and not available in sufficient detail for present purposes. Official data on foreign trade, financial activity, research and so on usually do not give breakdowns by the country of ownership of the concerns involved. The few exceptions relate to comparisons of non-resident owned companies as a whole with resident-owned companies as a whole. Such comparisons are of interest in that they contrast the characteristics of predominantly non-resident owned industry with industry which is mainly resident-owned. Much more than a test of the effects of ownership is involved in such overall comparisons, however; differences in the nature of industry as such are important in the comparisons. The data on foreign-owned firms which were collected for the present study are rather heavily concentrated, of course, in industries where foreign ownership is large. It was decided to concentrate the comparisons with resident-owned firms as much as possible in the same industries, at least where resident-owned firms existed side by side with non-resident owned firms. This procedure would tend to minimize the effects of differences in industry and hence permit the effects of differences in ownership to appear. To achieve this, industries were examined at as detailed a level as the sources on degree of foreign

TABLE 53

THE DEGREE OF SUPERVISION CLASSIFIED BY SELECTED CHARACTERISTICS

Characteristic	Degree of Supervision			All firms
	Negligible	Partly	Extensively	
	(Per cent distribution of replies except for total number)			
Nationality of president				
Country of affiliate	38	53	83	53
Other (largely Canadian)	62	47	17	47
Total number of firms	69	99	36	204
Resident directors as proportion of total				
0-24%	12	16	36	17
25-49	19	33	36	29
50-74	49	36	23	39
75-100	19	15	5	15
Total number	67	93	22	182
Per cent sales to domestic market				
100%	51	49	53	50
95-99	31	30	22	29
70-94	13	14	13	14
Under 70	5	7	11	7
Total number	77	118	45	240
Per cent purchases from domestic market				
90-100%	32	25	29	28
80-89	16	21	22	20
60-79	26	28	17	25
Under 60	26	26	32	27
Total number	74	114	41	229
Research development as per cent of sales				
0%	49	58	85	60
0.01-1.00	20	23	6	19
Over 1.00	31	19	9	21
Total number	71	101	33	205
Unit costs compared with affiliate				
Typically higher	67	61	52	61
About the same, lower, varies	33	39	48	39
Total number	49	87	27	163

NOTE: See footnote to table 52.

ownership and on the identification of resident-owned and non-resident owned firms permitted.[3]

The second constraint was that this comparison was limited to firms with assets of $1 million or more in 1959. There are very large numbers of firms with assets under $1 million in each group of firms though accounting in each case for a relatively small percentage of the assets of all firms. Since these could not be adequately identified as to ownership or surveyed with any reasonable degree of inclusiveness with the available resources, they were omitted entirely from this comparison.

Eventually 284 resident-owned firms which were believed to meet these requirements were sent the questionnaire shown in Appendix B. A small portion of them, mainly the very largest ones, also received a second request. Of the 128 replies which were received twelve had to be abandoned because the firms were in service industries or turned out to be foreign-owned, or because the questionnaires were poorly answered. Another twenty are not included in this study since their assets were found to be under $1 million dollars each. Thus ninety-six firms are available for the comparisons with the foreign-owned firms. As in the case of the latter, each question-naire was checked in detail to ensure internal consistency of the replies to related questions, and to be certain that the questions had not been mis-interpreted, and so on. A detailed check was also made for some questions with publicly available sources. A limited amount of further correspondence was engaged in to clear up inconsistencies, insofar as this was possible. As with the material from the foreign-owned firms, the data was supplied on a confidential basis. Anonymous replies were accepted; in twenty-three cases the companies' officers chose not to identify the company on the question-naire. In most cases the data received refer to the year 1959.

It will be noted that the response rate to the questionnaire was con-siderably greater than for the foreign-owned firms, roughly 40 per cent as against about 20 per cent for the latter depending on how each is measured. This may reflect that fact that the response rate in such studies is usually better for medium-sized and larger firms, which comprised the bulk of the firms to which the questionnaire for resident-owned firms was sent, and also the fact that this questionnaire was much briefer and simpler than that

---

[3]The information on resident-owned firms was derived from the same sources as those listed at the beginning of Chapter 2. The list of firms owned by non-residents helped to delineate firms owned by residents. The detail on industries owned by non-residents goes well beyond that shown in table 3 above. See, for example, *Canada's International Investment Position 1926-1954*, pp. 43-44 and 92-93, and Brecher-Reisman, *op. cit.*, Appendix B.

to foreign-owned firms. The quality of the replies to the latter questionnaire was generally better, probably because the foreign-owned firms would be more interested in a questionnaire and a study which was more directly relevant to them.[4]

It will be evident from the above that industry and size of firm have been used as the key constraints for the comparisons between the two sets of firms. Size gave little difficulty since an effort was made in using the various sources to select large firms and, in any case, the respondent firms indicated their size in response to the questions, but the comparisons by industry are quite a different matter. Ideally, one should match pairs of firms in which the mix of products was close; then one could be certain that the effect of product differences on performance was largely eliminated and, to that extent at least, any differences in ownership isolated. Unfortunately it is not possible to make such a detailed comparison. The companies cannot be matched individually because their product mix is often dissimilar even when they fall into what appears to be a rather well-defined industry. Moreover, the companies were asked to give only the major products for purposes of industry classification, and some gave only the major industry group which described their output. One of the penalties of working at the level of the company or enterprise rather than the establishment — an unavoidable penalty if one is to study policy — is that industry classifications must be broader than one would like. Because of the relatively small number of medium and large firms (and of responses) in many of the finer industry groups, it is not possible to show such groups in detail without some risk of identifying the firms. Where data are shown by industry below, the major groups of the Standard Industrial Classification will be used and not the finer industry levels at which the material was collected.

As a check on the degree of similarity of the products of the two sets of firms a comparison was made of the ninety-six resident-owned firms and the 160 non-resident owned firms whose assets are known to be $1 million or more.[5] Where available, the products were listed in detail for the major groups of the Standard Industrial Classification, and were compared to

[4]For example, fifty of the 280 foreign-owned firms did not answer any of the set of general questions on the last page of the questionnaire, as against thirty-five of the ninety-six Canadian-owned firms. It must be admitted that more of these questions are likely to be inapplicable to the latter than to the former.

[5]It will be recalled there are 104 foreign-owned firms with assets under $1 million and sixteen which did not give information on asset size, or 120 in all to be deleted from the 280 direct investment firms for present purposes. The 160 firms studied in this chapter include 133 owned by residents of the United States and twenty-seven owned by residents of overseas countries.

ensure that they did not fall to any significant extent into quite different sub-groups in the major industry groups. Not unexpectedly, the products were largely concentrated in the same sub-groups; this result was inevitable given the fact that the resident-owned firms were selected, insofar as the sources permitted, from industry sub-groups where it was known that they co-existed with direct investment firms. There were one or two obvious exceptions, namely, industry sub-groups represented in the foreign-owned list where there are no Canadian-owned firms at all.[6] Since the number of firms involved is quite small these have very little effect on the overall results for 160 firms presented below. There are a number of industry sub-groups, of course, where one or the other group of firms predominates by number of firms, reflecting differences in Canadian and foreign ownership of the industry or in size of firm.

Some broad similarity in industries covered and in size can be claimed but it is well to emphasize that there are differences in detail which may affect comparisons of the performance of the two sets of firms. In the first place, the ninety-six resident-owned firms are older on average than the 160 non-resident owned firms. This is so even when the age of the non-resident owned firms is determined (where relevant) by the date at which they were established rather than the date at which the parent owner acquired the firm. If age leads to improved performance, the resident-owned firms as a group have an advantage in comparisons to be given below. Second, the differences between the two sets of firms in terms of size of assets is much less marked and probably not significant statistically, at least when measured by the intervals of size which are available.[7] There are a relatively larger portion of the non-resident owned companies in the smallest size group,

---

[6]These few firms might have been omitted here. Since the data have been prepared in detail for foreign-owned firms, including these, and since it made very little difference to the overall summaries presented here, it was decided to include them.

[7]These findings on comparative size of company appear to be contradicted at first sight by more inclusive series. Thus the *Report for 1962* under the *Corporations and Labour Unions Returns Act*, pp. 32 and 83-86, indicated that manufacturing companies, half or more of whose stock was owned abroad, accounted for 13 per cent of the total number when assets were under $0.5 million, 24 per cent when the assets were $0.5-0.9 million, 42 per cent when they were $1.0-4.9 million, and 57 per cent when they were $5 million or more. It will be noted, however, that the difference narrows considerably for the $1 million and over group, which is what concerns us here, and that these refer to *all* manufacturing industries while our data are concentrated in those where the two sets of firms co-exist. To the extent that the present data are representative of the latter group of industries, they suggest that in broadly comparable circumstances the two sets of firms do not diverge markedly in most cases in terms of size.

TABLE 54

SELECTED CHARACTERISTICS OF RESIDENT-OWNED AND NON-RESIDENT OWNED COMPANIES WITH ASSETS OF ONE MILLION DOLLARS OR MORE

	Resident-owned	Non-resident owned		Resident-owned	Non-resident owned	
		(numbers)			(percentages)	
Age distribution*						
1950-59	9	39	52	9	24	33
1939-49	14	24	19	15	15	12
1930-38	12	25	22	13	16	14
1919-29	23	27	28	24	17	18
Before 1919	38	43	37	40	27	23
Not given	—	2	2	0	1	1
Total	96	160	160	100	100	100
Asset size in millions of dollars						
1-4.9	41	82		43	51	
5-9.9	18	19		19	12	
10-24.9	17	24		18	15	
25-49.9	11	13		11	8	
50-99.9	3	10		3	6	
100 or more	6	12		6	8	
Total	96	160		100	100	
Type of business						
Assembly	2	11		2	7	
Extractive	16	10		17	6	
Semi-fabricated products	2	11		2	7	
Fully processed or manufactured	66	107		69	67	
Fully or largely integrated	8	20		8	13	
Not given	2	1		2	1	
Total	96	160		100	100	

* The first column under non-resident owned firms is based on the dates when the firms were established, while the second reflects the dates when the present major or sole shareholder acquired ownership.

$1-4.9 million, but this is fully offset in the size group $5-9.9 million. If it is taken that the resident-owned firms are no larger than their non-resident owned counterparts in the particular groups assembled here, and may be smaller if other data are accepted, this may mean the former are handicapped in their competition with the latter. It was noted in Chapter 7 that the resident-owned firms need to be larger in order to achieve the minimum optimum size of firm at which all economies of scale are exhausted, since the non-resident owned firm can acquire easily a variety of specialized goods and services from the parent.[8] The extent to which one or both sets of firms may have built beyond this scale for reasons other than those associated with economies of scale is not known. It will be shown later, however, that many of the resident-owned companies have made arrangements to secure specialized goods and services outside the company, thus reducing the size at which they can achieve all economies of scale. Third, the two sets of firms differ by type of business. They are both heavily concentrated in manufacturing and assembly, with almost three-quarters of each set of firms falling in these groups. The most distinctive difference is that the resident-owned firms are more heavily concentrated in extractive industries. This may affect performance in certain areas. Some of the data below will be given, accordingly, for the manufacturing industries alone.[9]

---

[8] See footnote 13, Chapter 7.

[9] In an earlier paper on exports a comparison was made of the two groups of firms using ten broad industry groups. See A. E. Safarian, "The Exports of American-Owned Enterprises in Canada," *Papers and Proceedings of the American Economic Association*, Vol. LIX, No. 3 (May, 1964), pp. 449-458, especially pp. 455-456.

Since this test involved only industries where at least four firms were available in each ownership category, it cut the number of firms involved to seventy and 113. This test has not been used here since it now seems that, particularly when compared by industry types, it implies a degree of comparability of data by industry sub-groups especially which cannot be claimed. In some industries, moreover, so few firms are involved that averages become meaningless. Results which are more consistent with the quality of the data are secured by comparing only manufacturing firms, as is done below. It may be of interest to list the ninety-six and 160 firms by major industry groups since this helps indicate the greater concentration of the non-resident owned firms used here in certain sectors of secondary manufacturing. The number of resident-owned firms is given first: petroleum and products industries, ten and ten; mining and smelting, eleven and six; foods and beverages, thirteen and ten; rubber, four and five; textile and clothing, three and four; wood and products, three and one; lumber, pulp, newsprint, six and five; paper products, nine and four; primary metals, eight and five; metal fabrication, six and fourteen; machinery industries, seven and twenty-five; transportation, four and thirteen; electrical products, three and twenty-two; non-metallic minerals, two and seven; chemicals, seven and sixteen; miscellaneous, and not classifiable by industry, zero and thirteen. It should be emphasized again that the resident-owned firms to be surveyed were selected at the level of industry sub-groups, not the major groups just noted, so as to correspond as closely as possible to the products of the non-resident owned firms.

Senior Personnel

The most important difference between the boards of resident-owned and non-resident owned firms is, of course, the fact that the locus of the owners is different. Directors identified with the owners form a much smaller portion of the boards of the former. In the larger non-resident owned Canadian firms about 40 per cent of the directors are associated with the foreign affiliates. In the larger resident-owned firms the significant owners form only 22 per cent of the membership of the boards. The difference is not made up by management representatives on the boards, who form just over one-third of membership in each case, but by the directors resident in Canada who are not associated with the firm except as directors. These outside directors form 17 per cent of the membership of larger non-resident owned firms and 38 per cent in the larger resident-owned firms. These differences reflect the fact that the immediate ownership of the typical non-resident owned firm is less diffuse than that of the resident-owned firm, in the sense that most of the former are wholly owned by a single foreign firm (whatever the ultimate stockholder interests of the parent firm may be) while most of the resident-owned firms are immediately owned by the ultimate stockholder interests. If one can make the assumption that the parent's representatives on the subsidiaries' boards are more likely to be management interests closely identified with the operations of the international firm rather than ultimate owners of the parent firm, then almost 80 per cent of the persons on the larger subsidiaries' boards represent management interests, whether of the subsidiary or its affiliate, as against only about one third for the larger resident-owned firms. Perhaps too much should not be made of this difference since not much is known about the characteristics of the owners and the outside directors of the resident-owned firms.[10] Fully three quarters of these last two groups would have to be closely connected with operations in the same line of business to match the proportions involved for non-resident owned firms, however — a circumstance which would seem unlikely.

The residency of the directors is related to the nature of ownership: 94 per cent of the directors of the boards of these larger resident-owned companies live in Canada as against 55 per cent for the larger non-resident owned companies. Twenty-six of the resident-owned companies had one or more non-resident directors, some of whom may be nationals of Canada, but in no case did non-residents exceed half of the directors. Among the

---

[10]Only four of the ninety-six resident-owned firms could not distinguish management and ownership groups, however.

TABLE 55

COMPOSITION OF BOARDS AND FREQUENCY OF MEETINGS, RESIDENT-OWNED AND NON-RESIDENT OWNED COMPANIES WITH ASSETS OF $1 MILLION OR MORE
(Number of companies)

Composition of boards	Number of directors or meetings per year*																				No reply to question	Not applicable†	Total companies	Total number of persons
	0	1	2	3	4	5	6	7	8	9	10	11	12	13	14	15	17	18	20	Other				
a. Non-resident owned companies with assets of $1 million or more:																								
Management of company		21	27	31	17	14	8	2			1										3	36	160	378
Associated with affiliates abroad	3	8	18	38	24	12	10	5	2												4	36	160	425
Resident outside directors	63	16	14	8	7	5	2	1													4	36	160	172
Other significant owners	109	4	3	2	1	1															4	36	160	25
Other	94	18	6	2																	1	36	160	36
Total number on board					1	22	11	16	18	19	12	8	5	2	4	3	2				1	36	160	1,036
Residents of Canada only	2	9	17	20	18	11	23	9	4	1	5	2	2								1	36	160	568
b. Resident-owned companies with assets of $1 million or more:																								
Management of company	1	16	20	25	14	7	3	2	1				1								1	5	96	274
Representatives of significant owners	14	16	11	5	6	2	1	1						1		1					3	5	96	181
Resident outside directors	13	6	3	2	2	9	6	16	15	7	9	8	7	2	2	1					3	5	96	307
Other	63	6	2	2	2	1															3	5	96	50
Total number on board‡								15	16	9	8	8	7	7	2			2	1			5	96	806
Residents of Canada only								14	20	15	7	6	4	3	4	3		2	1			5	96	757
Frequency of meetings																								
a. Non-resident owned companies:																								
With assets of $1 million or more	11	10	7	7	27	20	17	3	3	1	2	1	12							5	8	36	160	160
With assets of $25 million or more				3	3	7	6	2	1	1	2		7							3	2	3	35	35
b. Resident-owned companies:																								
With assets of $1 million or more	2		4	21	15	12	3	2	2	7	5		10	3					1	1	3	5	96	96
With assets of $25 million or more		1	4	3	1	1	1	1	3	4											1	1	20	20

* There were no entries under the numbers 16 and 19.

† In these firms the board was reported to be not active, except for one resident-owned firm where the reply was that there was no board. The composition for this group is not shown.

‡ The total for number of persons shown in the last column will not add vertically because of double counting of persons in the management and owner categories in four firms. This double counting does not exist in the figure for the total number of persons on the board.

larger non-resident owned companies residents did not exist for only two companies, they formed up to 24 per cent of the directors in eleven more companies, up to 49 per cent of the directors in twenty-seven other companies, from 50-74 per cent of the directors in sixty-one companies, and three-quarters or more of the directors in the twenty-two other firms with active boards.

It should be emphasized that in fully thirty-six of the 160 larger firms the board was described as not active, as against only five of the ninety-six boards of resident-owned firms. The composition of such boards has been excluded throughout. The active boards of the larger resident-owned firms met more frequently on average than those of non-resident owned firms, due mainly to a number of the latter which described themselves as "active" while meeting once or twice a year. One cannot say that either set of boards was notable for its activity, because only forty-one and forty-eight boards of the non-resident owned and resident-owned groups respectively met at least bi-monthly and only seventeen of either group met at least once a month. There is not much difference between the two groups of firms in frequency of meetings for those in the largest size group, that is, with assets of $25 million or more.

In spite of the differences in ownership, the nature of the management or executive committees of the two sets of companies is remarkably similar. About one third of each has no such committee, specifically, fifty of the non-resident owned firms and thirty-five of the resident-owned firms. For those with committees, in each set of firms the typical size of committee is from three to five members. The members of these committees in both sets of firms are largely residents of Canada — 80 per cent for the non-resident owned firms and 87 per cent for those owned by residents. Most of the firms gave information on the composition of their committees, the important difference being that different ownership groups are represented. The important similarity is that for each set of firms the management of the Canadian firm forms the preponderant group. The following estimates understate the extent to which management predominates on the committees of the two sets of firms, because they exclude twelve non-resident owned firms and eleven resident-owned firms which replied that the committees were entirely composed of management personnel but neglected to give the actual numbers involved: management of the Canadian firm formed 75 per cent of the membership of the non-resident owned firms and 59 per cent of that of the resident-owned firms; those associated with the parent abroad formed 12 per cent of the former while significant owners were 25 per cent of the latter; outside directors formed 10 per cent and 11 per cent respectively of the management committees of the two sets of firms; and other persons accounted for 3 per cent and 5 per cent respectively.

Marketing and Purchasing

In comparing the larger resident and non-resident owned firms used in this study, the extent to which they sell in Canada and abroad appears to be remarkably similar at first glance. About 30 per cent in each case sell only in Canada and in a further third or so 95-99 per cent of sales are in Canada. More of the resident-owned firms sell over 50 per cent of their output abroad. This difference is entirely concentrated in the firms with assets from $1-24.9 million. For the firms with assets of $25 million or more, the most significant difference is the fact that 40 per cent of the resident-owned firms do not export at all while all of the non-resident owned firms export something. A good measure of typical performance is the median and quartiles. These show identical first quartiles of 100 and almost identical medians of ninety-nine and ninety-eight. The third quartile is significantly lower for resident-owned firms, seventy-five compared with ninety for the non-resident owned firms. This difference, as just noted, is concentrated in firms with assets under $25 million. For the largest size group the measures just noted are all lower (i.e. export performance is better) for the non-resident owned firms. In the case of exports particularly the varying proportions of different types of business involved can affect these results. If one concentrates solely on the sixty-six resident-owned firms and 107 non-resident owned firms which reported their type of business as fully processed or manufactured products, the medians and quartiles are then almost identical.

As for the destination of exports, the market for both sets of firms is largely the United States and to virtually the same degree. One quarter of those with exports in each set of firms sent all of their exports to that market and about one fifth in each case sent 70-99 per cent of their exports to the United States. This contradicts the suggestion sometimes heard that foreign-owned firms are unlikely to export to the market in which the parent firm is located. Most of the larger foreign-owned firms in this study are in manufacturing or assembly operations and most are owned in the United States. In terms of *typical* performance as measured here they sell to the United States market to about the same extent as their resident-owned counterparts. In each set of firms over 60 per cent of those with exports sell nothing to the United Kingdom, and most of the remainder in each set sell under 30 per cent of their exports there. Relatively more of the resident-owned firms sell in other sterling area countries. These are interesting findings in view of the fact that many of the United States direct investment firms were at one time considered to have been established partly with sterling area markets in mind.

TABLE 56

PROPORTION OF SALES IN CANADA
RESIDENT-OWNED AND NON-RESIDENT OWNED COMPANIES
WITH ASSETS OF $1 MILLION OR MORE

Percentage of sales in Canada	All firms		Assets of $25 million or more		All firms		Assets of $25 million or more	
	R	NR (Number of firms)	R	NR	R	NR (Percentages)	R	NR
100%	29	49	8	—	30	31	40	0
95-99	32	59	2	15	33	37	10	43
90-94	3	13	1	3	3	8	5	9
80-89	3	12	1	2	3	7	5	6
70-79	4	4	3	2	4	3	15	6
50-69	3	2	—	—	3	1	0	0
Below 50	17	12	4	9	18	7	20	26
No reply	5	9	1	4	5	6	5	11
Total	96	160	20	35	100	100	100	100

Averages for above data (percentages)	All firms				Manufacturing only		
First quartile	100	100	100	96	100	100	
Median	99	98	97	92	99	99	
Third quartile	75	90	75	21	93	95	

NOTE: R means resident-owned, NR means non-resident owned.

By contrast with the similar overall markets of the two sets of firms a larger portion of the direct investment firms' purchases are from abroad than is so of their resident-owned counterparts. The difference is concentrated particularly in the firms which purchase 95 per cent or more of their supplies in Canada; fully 36 per cent of the resident-owned firms fall in this group as against 11 per cent of the non-resident owned firms. Similar proportions of the two sets of firms acquire from 80 to 94 per cent of pur-

TABLE 57

DESTINATION OF EXPORTS AND SOURCES OF IMPORTS
RESIDENT-OWNED AND NON-RESIDENT OWNED COMPANIES
WITH ASSETS OF $1 MILLION OR MORE
(Percentages)

| | Distribution of responses by: | | | | | | | |
| | Destination of exports | | | | Sources of imports | | | |
Percentage to destination (or from source) indicated	U.S.	U.K.	Other sterling area	Other countries	U.S.	U.K.	Other sterling area	Other countries
Resident-owned firms								
100%	25	2	14	2	38	—	—	1
70-99	23	2	0	8	34	—	1	3
30-69	12	8	14	16	19	10	5	10
1-29	10	25	29	29	7	41	4	15
0	31	63	43	45	1	49	89	71
Total	100	100	100	100	100	100	100	100
Non-resident owned firms								
100%	25	1	7	8	34	4	1	2
70-99	21	2	3	11	40	3	—	2
30-69	11	5	3	14	15	5	1	3
1-29	16	30	27	18	4	36	7	24
0	26	62	59	48	7	52	91	69
Total	100	100	100	100	100	100	100	100

NOTE: Data should be read by columns, which total 100 per cent except for rounding. In the case of exports about fifty resident-owned firms and about ninety non-resident owned firms are involved in each column after omitting those without exports or which did not give destinations. For imports, seventy-three resident-owned firms and about 130 non-resident owned firms are involved in each column after similar exclusions.

chases in Canada, while a larger portion of the non-resident owned group acquires less than 80 per cent of supplies in Canada. The same pattern appears if only the firms with assets of $25 million or more are considered. The medians and quartiles reflect the greater openness of the non-resident owned firm in this respect. These measures are lower — they reflect a greater proportion of purchases abroad — for the non-resident owned firms whether one looks at all those with assets of $1 million or more, at only the largest group with assets of $25 million or more, or at manufacturing only. These differences are unlikely to be due to other differences in the characteristics of the two sets of firms, such as the lower average age of the non-resident owned firms. (When the proportion of purchases in Canada was estimated only for firms established before 1950, for example, the percentage distributions of purchases turned out to be very similar to those shown in table 58.) They reflect rather the opportunity for greater specialization in supply *vis-à-vis* the parent and its sources abroad, and the fact that the direct investment firm is often a partial substitute for imports. The sources of imports of the two sets of firms are remarkably similar. Almost three-quarters of the firms in each group with imports buy 70 per cent or more of imports from the United States. About 90 per cent of each group buy less than 30 per cent of their imports from the United Kingdom, nothing at all from other sterling area countries, and less than 30 per cent of their imports from other countries.

Apart from direct exports a firm may export its products or services through the establishment of a subsidiary or branch abroad or by granting a license to a foreign firm to make its products or to use its processes. The number of foreign subsidiaries and branches of Canadian firms is known to be small (although the capital involved is large) and many of the Canadian firms are themselves owned by non-residents.[11] Among the ninety-six resident-owned and 160 non-resident owned firms considered here only a small minority use such export techniques. The non-resident owned firms use relatively fewer of either export technique, presumably partly because they gain access to some foreign markets via parent firms or affiliates of the parent. Twenty of the resident-owned firms in this study had forty subsidiaries or branches abroad compared with only sixteen of the non-resident owned firms with thirty-five subsidiaries or branches abroad. Over half of the subsidiaries of the former were located in the United States, while for the non-resident owned firms about a quarter were in the United States and almost half in the United Kingdom and other sterling area countries. In each case two-thirds of the firms with subsidiaries abroad reported that the investment in them was 10 per cent or less of that in the Canadian firm. It was noted in earlier chapters that most of the non-resident owned Canadian firms with subsidiaries or branches abroad did not export to or import from them at all. The same is true of two-thirds of the resident-owned firms with subsidiaries abroad. As for licenses, only eleven firms in each group had

---

[11]See footnote 38, Chapter 4. Since rather small numbers are involved here it may not be wise to infer much from the area or size breakdowns.

granted about thirty licenses in each case to firms outside Canada, including both affiliates and non-affiliates located abroad. In each case about half of the licensees were located in the United States. Most of the remainder were located in the United Kingdom and other sterling area countries.

TABLE 58

PROPORTION OF PURCHASES IN CANADA
RESIDENT-OWNED AND NON-RESIDENT OWNED COMPANIES
WITH ASSETS OF $1 MILLION OR MORE

Percentage of purchases in Canada	All firms		Assets of $25 million or more		All firms		Assets of $25 million or more	
	R	NR (Number of firms)	R	NR	R	NR (Percentages)	R	NR
95 and over	35	18	8	4	36	11	40	11
90-94	13	28	4	6	14	18	20	17
80-89	18	29	4	6	19	18	20	17
70-79	7	23	—	5	7	14	0	14
60-69	6	16	1	5	6	10	5	14
50-59	3	6	—	1	3	4	0	3
40-49	1	6	—	1	1	4	0	3
30-39	—	6	—	—	0	4	0	0
Below 30	2	7	—	—	2	4	0	0
Not available or no response	11	21	3	7	12	13	15	20
Total	96	160	20	35	100	100	100	100

Averages for above data (percentages)

	All firms				Manufacturing only	
First quartile	96	90	95	90	95	90
Median	90	80	90	85	90	80
Third quartile	80	64	86	70	75	65

NOTE: R means resident-owned, NR means non-resident owned.

In Chapter 4 the nature of the export sales organization of the non-resident owned firm was discussed. It will be noted from table 21 in that chapter that ninety of the 160 firms with assets of one million dollars or more were exporting through some form of organization — thirty-one through their own organization, thirty-seven through that of the foreign affiliate, seventeen through both, and five through pooling arrangements. Another thirty-nine had no such organization while thirty-one, most of which had no exports, did not answer. The corresponding figures for the ninety-six resident-owned firms were thirty-two with exports through some form of organization, forty-five with no such organization, and nineteen non-responses — of which all but three had some exports. The size and nature of the non-responses is such as to suggest caution in conclusions about the relative prevalence of export sales organizations in the two sets of firms. Moreover, a number of companies in both groups reported rather simple "organizations", such as a specific person or persons in the domestic sales force who served part-time as an export officer. Perhaps the safest conclusion is that about the same proportion of each set of Canadian firms, namely one third, had their own export organization. The distinctive difference between them is that many of the non-resident owned firms with their own organization, and some without, had access to the organization of the parent firm, broadening to this extent their contacts and sources of outlets for exports. As noted in Chapter 4, however, some of the non-resident owned firms indicated affiliation imposed certain market restrictions in the short-run at least.

In both sets of firms with assets of $1 million or more a very substantial group failed to give a clear answer on purchasing policy or did not reply at all. Many contented themselves with repeating the actual proportion of purchases from domestic and foreign sources, making us none the wiser concerning their policies. There are useful observations, consequently, for only fifty-one of the ninety-six resident-owned firms and only 110 of the 160 non-resident owned firms. Roughly 70 per cent of each group, thirty-five and seventy-four companies respectively, reported they had a policy of favouring purchase in Canada. In each group over a third of the replies indicating such a policy qualified it by stating that Canadian supplies and services were bought only if the terms were equal, or in some cases at the cost of a (usually) small initial price or other disadvantage. The experience with the interviews suggests that an even larger proportion would have so qualified their replies had the question been pressed further. The remaining 30 per cent in each group had no such policy and bought strictly on the basis of favourable terms only. Any bias in the large non-response groups could upset these conclusions, and further analysis of the present replies is probably not warranted.

TABLE 59
COST OF RESEARCH-DEVELOPMENT
RESIDENT-OWNED AND NON-RESIDENT OWNED COMPANIES
WITH ASSETS OF $1 MILLION OR MORE
(Number of firms except as indicated)

Research-development as % of sales	1 Done within Canadian company		2 Purchased from non-affiliates (affiliates) abroad*		3 Purchased from other sources†		4 Total cost		5 Total cost (% distribution)	
	R	NR	R	NR	R	NR	R	NR	R	NR
0	39	64	68	85	69	108	33	44	39	32
Up to 0.5	21	17	6	18	10	5	21	15	25	11
0.6-1.0	6	13	4	7	1	1	4	15	5	11
1.1-2.0	3	20	2	4	—	—	7	22	8	16
2.1-5.0	8	11	—	3	—	—	8	15	10	11
Over 5.0	3	2	—	—	3	6	3	2	4	1
% unspecified‡	5	12	3	17			8	24	10	18
No reply or not available	11	21	13	26	13	40	12	23	—	—
Total	96	160	96	160	96	160	96	160	100	100

NOTE: R refers to resident-owned firms, NR to non-resident owned firms. There is duplication among the columns numbered 1 to 3 in that any single firm could theoretically answer all three columns. The fourth column reflects the total research effort included in (up to three of) the previous columns.

* Purchases from affiliates abroad for non-resident owned firms and from non-affiliated companies for resident-owned firms. It will be recalled that a substantial number of the former receive access to the affiliates' knowledge without explicit charges.

† In the case of non-resident owned firms this refers to firms and other organizations except for foreign affiliates. For resident-owned firms, this refers to firms and other organizations except for non-affiliated companies abroad.

‡ These indicated they were doing research-development as defined but did not give the percentage to sales. Many indicated the research effort was small, probably under one per cent of sales.

Research and Development

The total research effort of a firm can be defined as what it undertakes within the firm plus what it purchases elsewhere. Measured in these terms slightly more of the non-resident owned firms with assets of $1 million or more fostered some research effort in 1959, namely 68 per cent of them as against 61 per cent of the resident-owned firms. What is probably more significant is the fact that a larger proportion of the non-resident owned firms had a total research effort in excess of 0.5 per cent of sales, 39 per cent of them falling into this category compared to 27 per cent of the resident-owned firms. Apart from research-development performed within the Canadian firm, the non-resident owned firm concentrated most of its effort in purchases from affiliates abroad. The resident-owned firm suffers a disadvantage in this respect, as noted in an earlier chapter. It compensates for this in part by purchases from non-affiliated parties. Thus twenty-nine of the resident-owned firms purchased research from outside the Canadian firm compared to only twelve of the non-resident owned firms, excluding purchases from foreign affiliates by the latter. It should be emphasized that the data presented here greatly understate the availability of research-development to the non-resident owned firm, as against its research effort as defined above. In the chapter on research it was pointed out that many direct investment companies have access to the affiliates' knowledge without any explicit payment.

Similar tendencies are apparent if one looks only at research done within the Canadian company. In each group 46 per cent conducted no research-development within the Canadian company. For those with research-development, a somewhat larger proportion of the non-resident owned firms spend in excess of 0.5 per cent of sales on research-development, namely 32 per cent as opposed to 24 per cent of resident-owned firms. This difference between the two sets of firms is concentrated in the two largest size groups shown in table 60. Thus 20 per cent and 12 per cent of the resident-owned firms in the two largest size groups spend over 0.5 per cent of sales on research-development compared to 40 per cent and 31 per cent of the non-resident owned firms. The medians and quartiles for research done within the firm confirm that roughly the same proportion engage in research-development but the non-resident owned firms do more of it. The first quartiles are zero in each case, the medians are 0.1 per cent for resident-owned firms and zero for non-resident owned firms, and the third quartiles are 0.5 per cent of sales and 1.1 per cent of sales respectively. These differences are almost eliminated if comparisons are made only for firms producing fully processed or manufactured products. The first quartiles remain zero in each case, the medians are 0.2 per cent for resident-owned firms and zero for non-resident owned, and the third quartiles are 1.0 per cent and 1.2 per cent respectively.

It is difficult to say much about the industrial distribution of research for the resident-owned firms since so few firms are involved. In both sets of firms the great majority of those with research and development facilities in the Canadian company reported that the facilities were established within the past two decades. A larger portion of the non-resident owned firms with assets of $1 million or more have established such facilities in recent years than is true of the resident-owned firms, however. Thus 56 per cent of the non-resident owned firms with specific facilities devoted to research-

TABLE 60

COST OF RESEARCH-DEVELOPMENT DONE WITHIN THE CANADIAN COMPANY RESIDENT-OWNED AND NON-RESIDENT OWNED COMPANIES WITH ASSETS OF $1 MILLION OR MORE
(Percentages except last line)

Research-development as percentage of sales	Asset size in $ millions							
	1-4.9		5-24.9		25 and over		Total	
	R	NR	R	NR	R	NR	R	NR
0	54	58	43	36	31	31	46	46
Up to 0.5	10	4	33	8	44	34	25	12
0.6-1.0	8	8	7	17	6	3	7	9
1.1-2.0	3	13	7	17	—	16	4	14
2.1-5.0	15	10	3	3	6	9	9	8
Over 5.0	5	—	3	3	—	3	4	1
% unspecified	5	7	3	17	13	3	6	9
Total	100	100	100	100	100	100	100	100
No reply and not available as % of overall total	5	13	14	16	20	9	11	13
Number of firms above	41	82	35	43	20	35	96	160

TABLE 61

NATURE OF CANADIAN RESEARCH PROGRAMS
RESIDENT-OWNED AND NON-RESIDENT OWNED COMPANIES
WITH ASSETS OF $1 MILLION OR MORE
(Number of companies)

Program	All companies		Assets of $25 million or more	
	R	NR	R	NR
Improvement of present products and processes	11	18	3	4
Conceiving and developing new products and processes	6	5	2	1
Combination of above programs	25	44	8	13
Above programs plus programs not primarily committed to specific product or process applications	5	7	—	4
No reply or not available	11	8	3	3
Total*	58	82	16	25

* Totals include only firms which met our definition of research-development and reported either that they had research-development facilities or that they performed research-development in the Canadian firm. Also included are five resident-owned firms and two non-resident owned firms which fell into neither of these categories but bought research from non-affiliated firms or organizations.

development reported these were established in the fifties, as opposed to 40 per cent for resident-owned firms. The figures in earlier periods were respectively 23 per cent and 26 per cent for 1940-1949, 17 per cent and 26 per cent for 1919-1939, and 4 per cent and 8 per cent for the period before 1919. Finally, it will be noted that the research programs of the two sets of firms are broadly similar in nature.[12] About one quarter of each group with such programs reported that improvement of products and processes was a significant part of their program, and about two-thirds

[12]The percentages given below disregard those respondents who did not answer this question.

reported that conceiving and developing new products and processes was a significant part of their program usually along with improvement of existing products and processes. Only about 10 per cent in either group reported that programs not primarily committed to specific product or process applications were a significant part of the program of the Canadian firm. The numbers of firms involved are so small that detailed size breakdowns are probably not justified. Among the firms with assets of $25 million or more which qualified for inclusion in table 61 on research programs, not one of the resident-owned firms considered that uncommitted programs formed a significant part of its research program. Indeed, of the twelve firms with such programs in both sets of firms, fully eight were firms with assets under $25 million.

Where the firms had specific facilities devoted to research-development they were asked to indicate the major reasons for establishing them. Only about two-thirds of the non-resident owned firms with such facilities and half of the resident-owned firms were able to give the major reasons, so perhaps not too much importance should be attached to the results. There is a major difference in the replies which should be noted. Almost half of the non-resident owned firms with assets of $1 million or more gave the need to meet Canadian conditions as a major reason for establishing Canadian research-development facilities.[13] Such reasons as product or process development and the need to meet competition were mentioned with only half the frequency of that just noted. Among the resident-owned firms the need to meet specifically Canadian conditions was mentioned in only one or two cases. Almost half gave competitive pressures as the reason for establishing such facilities while most of the remainder referred to product or process development. No doubt these are related conditions, in that the greater weight given to competitive pressures by the resident-owned firms reflects in good part the impact of competition from non-resident owned firms, with or without modification of products and processes borrowed from parent companies.

Access to the parent's research-development, whether in terms of borrowing of knowledge or use of the parent's facilities for tests, gives an important competitive advantage to non-resident owned companies in comparison with their resident-owned counterparts. This is the case wherever the resident-owned company cannot have access at a comparable cost to a comparable range of facilities by performing such research in the com-

---

[13]See the second section of Chapter 6 for a discussion of the reasons for establishing facilities in all non-resident owned firms.

pany, by engaging in a licensing agreement with another company, or by access to the research of an industry association or government agency. It would be a great over-simplification, accordingly, to think of the competition between the firms as reflecting that between independent resident-owned firms relying solely on their own resources and direct investment companies which have relatively easy access to a large parent research organization abroad. Not all of the parent firms are research conscious and not all are willing to supply the research without an explicit payment or at less than full cost. Moreover, many of the resident-owned firms have tried to compensate for any lack of access to necessary research-development by contracts with otherwise unrelated firms in Canada and abroad. Much industrial knowledge is pooled nationally and internationally in a great variety of ways. This will be apparent from table 59 which shows the distribution of expenditures on research-development for the firms involved. More specifically, fifteen of the ninety-six resident-owned firms with assets of $1 million or more bought research-development and/or "know-how" from non-affiliated companies located abroad. In four other cases payments were made to an industry institute or association located abroad which supplied technical information for an annual fee. The fifteen cases mainly involved agreements with independent firms to produce some of their products, with access to the foreign firms' knowledge as it related to these products, in return for a payment measured usually as a fixed percentage of sales. The access to knowledge, in effect, was the result of an agreement for the Canadian firm to produce an item and was usually restricted to what was necessary for that purpose. Only four or five of the agreements appeared to involve much fuller access to the knowledge of the foreign firms. It will be clear from this that access to the knowledge of foreign firms usually arose through a licensing agreement to produce some of the products of the foreign firm in return for a royalty, while agreements simply to receive information were a minority of the cases. This becomes clearer if one considers the access which the resident-owned firms had to the patents and trademarks of non-affiliated firms located outside Canada. Twenty-two of the ninety-six firms reported such access including nine which had indicated they also had access to research-development and/or know-how. (Thus thirty-two of the ninety-six firms in all had arrangements with unaffiliated firms or industry associations abroad in terms of access either to knowledge, or to legally defined property rights, or both.) Most of these involved access to patents via a licensing agreement which gave the Canadian firm the right to produce a product or products of the foreign firm in return for a payment estimated usually as a percentage of sales. In a few cases access only to trademarks was involved, i.e. the Canadian firm acted as a distributor only. Finally, about two-fifths of the agreements giving the Canadian firm access to the information and/or property rights of the unaffiliated foreign firm also gave the latter access to the knowledge and/or property rights of the Canadian firm. In about half of these cases the access of the foreign firm was limited to information and improvements involving its own products which had been licensed to the Canadian firm; in the remaining cases the independent information and property rights of the Canadian firm were made available to the foreign firm under various terms.

In evaluating the importance of the access which they had to knowledge of all kinds from abroad only one of the resident-owned firms considered it to be highly important (defined as affecting 25 per cent or more of sales), four indicated the importance was moderately high (10 per cent to 15 per cent of sales), and twelve considered it was of relatively little importance (under 10 per cent of sales, in most cases at 1 per cent or 2 per cent). Another six firms referred to various specific benefits which could not be assessed quantitatively. While significant, this is clearly not of the same order of importance as the access reported earlier for the non-resident owned firms even if one considers, as reported by some of the resident-owned firms, that such access bulked large for specific products or divisions of the Canadian firm or had significant qualitative effects on its operations.

The resident-owned firm, in brief, can secure some of the advantages of access to the knowledge of unaffiliated firms located abroad as well as that of firms located in Canada. This is typically a very partial substitute for the access available to most non-resident owned Canadian firms since it is usually restricted in nature as well as paid for at a market price. In addition, the markets for which such rights apply appear to be highly restricted. Only eleven of the twenty-two responses on patents and trademarks indicated the markets for the rights involved; in nine of the eleven the rights applied only to the Canadian market while in two cases they applied to all markets.

In attempting to gain access to the skills of firms located abroad the resident-owned firm can do more than contract to use directly the latter's knowledge and property rights. The two firms can establish a separate Canadian subsidiary in which both the Canadian and foreign parents have a stake in ownership. Eight of the ninety-six resident-owned firms reported they had, or had recently terminated, eleven such subsidiaries which were jointly owned with firms located abroad.[14] These subsidiaries were about evenly divided between cases where the Canadian parent held 50 per cent of the stock and cases where it held over 50 per cent. The management of these subsidiaries is supplied by the Canadian parent, or largely so, while the boards are selected by the two parents in proportion to their owner- ship of the subsidiary. This is a useful way of enabling the Canadian parent to expand into new fields of production while minimizing the risks by draw- ing on the techniques and experience of firms already established in the field. The capital investment involved by the foreign parent might be expected to assure a more direct interest on its part in the success of the subsidiary, in contrast simply with the sale of knowledge and property rights. It does not work well in all cases, however. While four of the firms believed such arrangements to be mutually beneficial the other four in- dicated there was enough dissatisfaction with them that they had ended the arrangements or planned to do so. Problems which can arise vary from a divergence of interests between the parents with the conflicts thus created for the subsidiary, to the difficulty of allocating charges for technical in- formation in a way which is fair to both parents.[15]

Ownership and Finance

The most obvious distinction between the two sets of firms being studied here is the locus of ownership and control of their voting stock. This is evi- dent if one compares the ownership of voting stock for the resident-owned firms in table 62 with the comparable group, with assets of $1 million or more, in table 43 of the preceding chapter. By definition, each of the 160 firms involved in the latter group has a parent located abroad which holds enough of the voting stock, and in most cases 100 per cent, to constitute effective legal control of the Canadian firm. Residents of Canada have effec- tive control of the voting stock of the ninety-six resident-owned firms.

When discussing the ownership pattern of direct investment companies it was noted that a number of them were joint enterprises whose stock was held by Canadian and foreign firms. It was also noted that the line separat- ing resident-owned and non-resident owned firms becomes a thin one at some point, reflecting various degrees of internationalization of ownership

---

[14]These are in addition to any Canadian subsidiaries jointly owned with Canadian firms which are themselves owned by non-residents. Another seven firms, including two in which the Canadian subsidiary bought out the parent, were formerly owned by non-residents but are now independent. Three of these continue to exchange technical information in particular with their former parents.

[15]For a study of joint enterprises, see footnote 4, Chapter 8.

of stock. Five of the ninety-six resident-owned firms identified themselves as joint enterprises whose stock was held equally (or almost so) by Canadian and foreign firms, but the management was the responsibility of the former; there may well be others in the group.

TABLE 62

OWNERSHIP OF VOTING STOCK
RESIDENT-OWNED COMPANIES WITH ASSETS OF $1 MILLION OR MORE
END OF 1959*
(Number of companies)

% held by residents	Asset size in $ millions				% held by non-residents	Country†		
	1.4.9	5-24.9	25 and over	All		U.S.	U.K.	Other
100	18	8	—	26	25 and over	10	1	—
99	9	5	—	14	10-24	7	2	—
76-98	8	19	16	43	2-9	29	22	3
51-75	4	3	3	10	0-1	49	70	92
50% or less	1	—	1	2				
No reply or not available	1	—	—	1	No reply or not available	1	1	1
Total	41	35	20	96	Total	96	96	96

* Excludes directors' qualifying shares.
† In five firms the distribution between United Kingdom and other overseas owners could not be given, and in one other firm the distribution between non-residents in general could not be given. These six were classified as if all the stock was held by residents of the United Kingdom, and under zero for other non-residents. Five of the percentages were from 2-9 per cent, one was from 10-24 per cent.

Perhaps of greater significance is the fact that in most of the resident-owned firms there is a minority non-resident ownership which is most frequently located in the United States but also to a significant extent in the United Kingdom. Only twenty-six of the ninety-six firms are wholly owned by residents of Canada although in another fourteen firms only 1 per cent of voting stock is held by non-residents.[16] The remaining fifty-five

[16]The firms were asked to exclude directors' qualifying shares in giving the distribution of ownership. We took 99 per cent ownership to be equivalent to 100 per cent ownership for the direct investment companies to ensure these were excluded. Such a step did not appear necessary for resident-owned companies since the directors largely reside in Canada. The 99 per cent level is given separately, however.

firms which answered the question reported that over 1 per cent of their voting stock was held by non-residents. In most cases the foreign holding was under 25 per cent of the stock but in twelve cases more than this proportion was held by non-residents. To the extent indicated, the ownership of these resident-controlled firms has been internationalized. This is particularly true of the resident-owned firms with assets of $25 million or more, every one of which reported that a minority of its stock was held by non-residents. In this respect they resemble those larger non-resident controlled firms, fifteen of the thirty-five noted in table 43 above, which also have a minority share ownership.

In most of the resident-owned firms the ownership of voting stock is concentrated. The respondents were asked whether a significant portion of the voting stock, enough to establish effective control, was held by one or a few individuals or companies. In sixty-six of the ninety-six firms the answer was positive. Twelve of the sixty-six were in turn controlled by other resident-owned firms not otherwise represented in this study. The relevant point is that in over half of the resident-owned firms a significant portion of the voting stock was held closely and not subject to everyday trading on the market. This includes ten firms with assets of $25 million or more and nine with assets of $10-24.9 million. Many more of the foreign-owned firms are in this category, of course. In all but seventy-two of the 280 foreign-owned firms discussed in previous chapters the parent held 99-100 per cent of the stock and in a significant portion of the seventy-two the minority share was closely held. The finding for resident-owned firms, added to that for most direct investment companies, suggests that the availability of such shares for market trading is very limited.

There are some interesting differences between the two sets of firms with regard to their sources of funds from 1950 to 1959. The non-resident owned firms have access to a unique source via funds from affiliates abroad. As noted in the preceding chapter, however, beyond the original investment in their early years and except for extraordinary circumstances, most of them are expected to rely on other sources of financing. During the fifties 41 per cent of those with assets of $1 million or more received funds from affiliates abroad. Some received quite substantial amounts; one in five firms, mainly the newer ones, received at least half of their funds from this source. Access to other sources abroad was limited to only 16 per cent of resident-owned firms and 10 per cent of non-resident owned firms. Both sets of firms relied primarily on net income for their funds, including depreciation here since the distinction between it and net income was not always clear. Thus 51 per cent of the non-resident owned firms received at least half of their funds from this source, as did 39 per cent of the resident-owned firms. Even taking into account the difficulty of determining sources in some cases, it still appears that the former were somewhat more reliant on this source. A major difference between the two sets of firms is their degree of reliance on other Canadian sources of funds including, for example, borrowing from the market, financial intermediaries, Canadian affiliates, and banks. Fully 71 per cent of the non-resident owned firms did no such financing, at least on long-term account, against only 38 per cent of the resident-owned firms. Fully 24 per cent of the latter received half or more of their funds from such sources compared with only 5 per cent of the former. In the overall perspective what stands out is the access of many non-resident owned firms to the parent and the relatively greater use by resident-owned firms of domestic sources external to the firm.[17] Among the firms with assets of $25 million or more, over half of the non-resident owned firms had access to funds from the affiliate in the fifties. A substantial minority of both of the largest sets of firms, 40 per cent of the resident-owned and a third of the non-resident owned, had access to other sources outside Canada. Again one notes the major reliance of both on funds internal to the firm and the considerably greater reliance of the resident-owned firms on domestic sources external to the firm.[18]

The non-resident owned firms in this study tend to retain a higher portion of their income on the average. Thus 39 per cent paid no dividends in the fifties as against only 13 per cent of the resident-owned firms. Similarly, 22 per cent paid half or more of net earnings as dividends as against 37 per cent of the resident-owned firms. These differences stand out for each of the asset size groups of firms used here, ie. from $1-4.9 million, $5-24.9 million and $25 million and over. In the last of these, almost a third of the non-resident owned group paid no dividends in the fifties while all of the resident-owned firms paid dividends. Many of the latter clearly have less control over the timing of payments than do the former.

---

[17]It seemed somewhat doubtful at first that as many as eleven resident-owned firms, 12 per cent of the total, could have received 100 per cent of funds from such Canadian sources in the fifties. It was possible to confirm that this was so in five cases. Even if all of the remaining cases were to be split in part, say with net income and depreciation, the emphasis in the text would remain. It should be noted that in a few cases the resident-owned firm is financed by a domestic parent, so that the term "domestic sources external to the firm" is somewhat misleading.

[18]In reading these percentages it should be kept in mind that only thirty non-resident owned firms and twenty resident-owned firms with assets of $25 million or more are involved.

It is interesting to note that the situation does not change much if one looks only at those resident-owned firms which reported that a significant portion of their voting stock was closely held. The distribution of dividends paid as a percentage of earnings for these firms was very similar to that for all of the resident-owned firms. It was noted earlier that the resident-owned firms are older on average than the non-resident owned firms in this study, and it was indicated in the preceding chapter that age is a significant factor in dividend ratios for the latter group of firms. The difference in dividend payments in the fifties as a percentage of net earnings persists, however, if one looks only at those firms in the two groups which were established before the fifties. These findings appear to conform with those for all firms in Canada. It has been estimated that in the period 1952 to 1960 inclusive all direct investment companies in Canada distributed 44 per cent of their net earnings while the comparable average for all companies in Canada, including direct investment companies, was about half of earnings.[19] The average for all resident-owned companies alone would be well in excess of half. As indicated in the text and table 49 of the preceding chapter, the proportion of net earnings distributed by direct investment companies can vary significantly between periods as well as from year to year.[20]

About half of the resident-owned firms with assets of $1 million or more gave some qualitative information on their preferred policy with regard to financing. About half of the replies said, in effect, that there was no such thing, often pointing out that the exact circumstances and costs of financing would vary. For the remainder, expansion by retention of earnings was by far the most frequently mentioned preferred policy while only a few firms mentioned issues of common stock. One fifth of the firms answering the question explicitly preferred to finance within Canada whenever possible and a slightly larger group, while not committing themselves

---

[19]D.B.S., *The Canadian Balance of International Payments, 1960*, p. 22.
[20]It does not appear possible to supplement these findings in detail by comparing the stated dividend policies of the two sets of firms, as distinct from actual payments. Fully eighty-four of the non-resident owned firms and thirty-nine of the resident-owned firms either replied that the question was inapplicable, largely because there were no earnings, or did not answer it. In just over half of the remainder in each case, moreover, the firm had no policy. It is interesting to note, nevertheless, that one-fifth of the non-resident owned firms answering the question on policy regarding dividends replied that they retained earnings for growth as against only one-tenth of the resident-owned firms answering this question. Correspondingly, only one-fifth of the former stated that their policy was to pay a fixed percentage of earnings or a fixed absolute amount as against one third of the latter.

TABLE 63
SOURCES OF FUNDS 1950-1959
RESIDENT-OWNED AND NON-RESIDENT OWNED FIRMS
WITH ASSETS OF $1 MILLION OR MORE

Sources of funds 1950-1959*
(% distribution of number of firms)

Specific source as percentage of all sources	Affiliates abroad	Other sources abroad		Canadian sources outside firm		Net income		Depreciation		Other	
	NR	R	NR	R	NR	R	NR	R	NR	R	NR
All firms with assets of $1 million or more†											
100%	7	—	—	12	4	3	17	—	—	—	—
75-99	4	—	—	4	—	11	16	1	1	—	—
50-74	9	—	1	8	1	25	18	13	6	—	—
25-49	11	2	3	21	7	33	15	38	31	—	—
1-24	11	14	6	17	17	12	17	29	28	19	7
0	59	84	90	38	71	15	17	19	34	81	93
Total	100	100	100	100	100	100	100	100	100	100	100
Firms with assets of $25 million or more											
100%	3	—	—	—	—	—	3	—	—	—	—
75-99	—	—	—	5	—	5	7	—	3	—	—
50-74	7	—	3	20	—	25	20	15	7	—	—
25-49	20	5	7	35	7	40	30	50	53	—	—
1-24	23	35	23	15	47	15	33	25	27	45	20
0	46	60	67	25	47	15	7	10	10	55	80
Total	100	100	100	100	100	100	100	100	100	100	100

NOTE: R refers to resident-owned firms, NR to non-resident owned firms. The data should be read by columns. There are 137 non-resident owned firms and 91 resident-owned firms in each column of section one; the remaining 23 and 5 respectively could not give data for this question. There are 30 non-resident owned and 20 resident-owned firms in each column of section 2; the other five non-resident owned firms could not give this breakdown.

* Data include eight non-resident owned firms and eight resident-owned firms established before 1950 which gave data for a period shorter than 1950-1959. Firms established since 1950 would also cover a shorter period.

† Ten non-resident owned firms could not give precise breakdowns. We have arbitrarily assigned to financing from the parent two cases where the firm could not split between this source and net income; to financing from Canadian sources two cases where the split could not be made between this source and net income; and to net income six cases where the firm could not split between this source and depreciation. All of these involved 100 per cent of funds except for one case of 13 per cent of funds in the first type and one case of 90 per cent in the third. Two resident-owned firms were unable to split their sources between net income and depreciation. Both cases, involving 100 per cent of funds, were allocated to net income.

as to preference, pointed out that all or almost all financing had been done in Canada. It must be admitted that rather few of these were concerned about the loss of control to non-residents. Where reasons were given for these preferences the firms dealt mainly with such factors as the availability and cost of funds, the foreign exchange risks, and the requirement of registration with the United States Securities and Exchange Commission when financing in that country.

Further Tests of Differences Regarding Performance

One further way to explore the differences between the two sets of firms is to consider the views of the officers of the resident-owned firms regarding the characteristics of the non-resident owned firms with which they compete or trade. This method has the advantage of eliciting the views of persons who may have considerable knowledge of some aspects of direct investment firms without being in them. It has the usual disadvantage of a qualitative and complex question placed among the general questions included on the last page of the questionnaire, so, understandably, the response was low. The officers of resident-owned firms were asked if, in their experience, affiliation in itself conferred specific competitive advantages or disadvantages on the direct investment firm compared with its resident-owned counterpart, and whether such affiliation resulted in specific advantages or disadvantages regarding the direct investment company as a source of supply or as a market. Most firms did not answer this question and a number gave rather non-committal replies. Only thirty-two replied in sufficient detail and with sufficient relevance to warrant a brief summary.

With regard to competitive advantages or disadvantages only five firms believed that the direct investment company had no advantage or suffered a net disadvantage as a competitor. The disadvantage they emphasized was the inability of their foreign-owned counterparts to buy or develop products, designs, or machinery more suitable to Canadian market conditions. The remaining twenty-seven firms believed their foreign-owned counterparts had distinct competitive advantages on the whole. The main reason given for this belief was the access which the foreign-owned firm had to the knowledge of the parent, particularly to its research-development and production "know-how". Closely associated with this was a second major reason, namely the access to a wide range of products and components whose development and other costs could usually be spread over a larger volume in the parent. Over one quarter of the companies noted the advantage from the spillover effects of the parents' advertising campaigns in various media, at least where products were identical or nearly so. No other reason was mentioned by more than one or two firms each. Only one firm referred to the easier availability of capital as an advantage for the direct investment firm. No doubt the smaller resident-owned firms would have given greater emphasis to this point.

Almost half of the firms answering this question believed there was no significant advantage or disadvantage to the direct investment firm either as a source of supply or as a market when compared to their resident-owned counterparts. Most of the remainder considered the direct investment firm had certain advantages as a supplier in their experience, particularly in terms of the range of products offered and the technical information available with them. This was offset in the experience of a minority of the respondents by too slow an adaptation of supplies and associated sales procedures to Canadian conditions. On the other hand, most of the remainder believed that from their point of view the direct investment com-

TABLE 64

PER CENT OF NET SAVINGS PAID AS DIVIDENDS 1950-1959
RESIDENT-OWNED AND NON-RESIDENT OWNED COMPANIES
WITH ASSETS OF $1 MILLION OR MORE

Per cent of net earnings paid	All firms		Assets of $25 million or more		All firms over 10 years old	
	R	NR	R	NR	R	NR
0	13	39	—	31	10	30
1-24	14	15	18	16	14	16
25-49	36	25	35	28	38	28
50-74	32	18	35	25	30	21
75-100	5	4	12	—	7	5
Total per cent	100	100	100	100	100	100
Number of firms above	76	131	17	32	69	86
No reply and not applicable	20	29	3	3	18	20
Total firms	96	160	20	35	87	106

NOTE: R refers to resident-owned firms, NR to non-resident owned firms. Seven of the former and six of the latter, established before 1950, gave data for a shorter period than 1950-1959.

pany suffered certain disadvantages as a market for their products. Two specific problems were mentioned, namely, specifications which were determined abroad and not adapted to Canadian conditions and the practice in some firms of favouring trade with affiliates abroad. This type of private commercial preference has already been considered in the chapters on exports and imports.

Finally, in order to further test the effect of ownership on performance, chi-square tests have been made on the differences between the two sets of firms with regard to the proportion of sales in and purchases from the domestic market, and with regard to research and development done within the Canadian firm as a proportion of sales. The chi-square method tests whether two independent samples differ in terms of some particular characteristic. If so, they will differ with regard to the frequency with which the observations fall into the categories in which they are grouped. Essentially what is involved is the comparison of the actual *observed* frequency with which the data fall into the categories involved as against an *expected* frequency based on a test of the null hypothesis. This test indicates whether the observed and expected frequencies are close enough to be likely to have occurred, given the hypothesis that there is no difference between them. If the computed probability that the null hypothesis is true turns out to be small, the null hypothesis can be rejected. It can be concluded, in other words, that the two samples are likely to differ in terms of the particular characteristic involved. The reverse is the case when the computed probability is large. One does not thereby conclusively prove or disprove the point at issue but an assessment is made based on probability. The conclusion can be arrived at by specifying a given level of significance with regard to the probability of the outcome. A 5 per cent level will be used here. If the computed probability falls at or below 5 per cent it will be concluded that there is likely to be a difference in the two sets of data. If the computed probability is above 5 per cent it will be concluded that there is not likely to be a difference between the two sets of data. In the present case the data for sales, purchases and research for the ninety-six resident-owned and 160 non-resident owned firms were set out by categories reflecting the appropriate statistical constraints for this test. This was also done for the sixty-six resident-owned and 107 non-resident owned firms in these two sets of firms which were involved in manufacturing only. The tests were then conducted using the null hypothesis that there is no difference in the frequencies by categories for the two sets of firms. Where the probability is 5 per cent or less it will be concluded that the probability is small that the null hypothesis is correct; it will be concluded, in other words, that there is likely to be a difference due to ownership. It is clear that the test is a limited one in that the differences could reflect some other reason not measured here. It will be recalled that allowance has been made for some other factors: only firms with assets of $1 million or more are included; the firms are very largely from industries in which both resident-owned and non-resident owned firms exist; and separate test results are given for firms engaged only in manufacturing.

For the ninety-six resident-owned and 160 non-resident owned firms the probability that the null hypothesis is correct turns out to be 2 per cent to 2.5 per cent for proportion of sales in Canada, less than 0.1 per cent for proportion of purchases in Canada, and 1 per cent to 2 per cent for research-development done within the Canadian company. At the 5 per cent level of significance the null hypothesis would be rejected in each case and the conclusion drawn that there is likely to be a difference between the two sets of firms for all three characteristics. It was noted earlier, however, that there is a relatively larger representation of purely extractive firms in particular among the resident-owned firms included here, a difference which might well affect the characteristics examined here. If one concentrates only on the sixty-six resident-owned and 107 non-resident owned firms which reported that their type of business was to produce fully processed and manufactured goods, the test results are considerably altered. The probability that the null hypothesis is correct then turns out to be 5.0 per cent to 10 per cent for the proportion of sales in Canada, 2.5 per cent to 5 per cent for the proportion of purchases in Canada, and 10 per cent to 20 per cent for research-development done within the Canadian company. At the 5 per cent level of significance the null hypothesis would be rejected only in the second case and accepted in the other two cases. In other words, one would conclude that there is likely to be a difference between the resident-owned and non-resident owned firms as regards the proportion of purchases in Canada, but that there is unlikely to be a difference with regard to proportion of sales in Canada or research-development performed in the Canadian company.

It is known from other studies that all direct investment firms in Canada taken together sell a relatively larger proportion of their sales abroad and perform relatively more research-development within the Canadian firm than do resident-owned firms. A similar overall comparison between the two sets of firms is not available with regard to the proportion of their purchases in Canada. If these results for given years are representative, they suggest that the non-resident owned firms *as a whole* are more heavily concentrated in export-oriented and research-oriented industries than are the resident-owned firms *as a whole*. What this suggests is that as a group the foreign-owned firms are relatively more heavily represented in those particular extractive and primary manufacturing industries which account for most of exports and, at the same time, more heavily represented in those particular secondary manufacturing industries which account for most research. These overall results are greatly affected by the performance of the relatively few very large firms of both kinds, as is clear from the comparisons earlier of firms with assets of $25 million or more. When like is compared with like, to the extent possible and within the limitations of the present samples, it appears that there is a significant difference in performance of the typical resident-owned and non-resident owned firms only in the case of the proportion of purchases from the domestic market.

That the non-resident owned firm in some industries has advantages over its resident-owned counterpart cannot be doubted from the evidence presented earlier. Unless these are fully offset by the disadvantages which some of them suffer, they should appear in some aspect of its performance compared with resident-owned firms. These need not be the particular aspects of performance which have been emphasized in this study. They could appear in the variety, quality and price of products made available, topics which have not been directly covered in this study. They could also appear in the profits of the direct investment firm. This did not appear to be a topic which could be covered by a private questionnaire survey. Comparative data on profits on an industry basis are available for one year only.[21] They show that profits before taxes for the commodity-producing industries were not very different in 1962, at 14.6 per cent of equity and 9.0 per cent of sales for all firms at least half of whose stock was held by residents and 13.9 per cent of equity and 9.8 per cent of sales for all firms at least half of whose stock was held by non-residents. These are overall measures which hide quite different results by industries in which there are widely different amounts of both foreign and total equity and sales. If one considers the data by the greatest detail available, namely twenty-two major commodity-producing industries, it turns out that in fourteen industries profits as a percentage of equity were higher for the non-resident owned

---

[21]The ratios in this paragraph were derived from data in *Corporations and Labour Unions Returns Act, Report for 1962*, pp. 49-80. There are substantial intercorporate financial items in the financial series of this Report which would be eliminated in a consolidation of the corporate sector of the economy.

firms and in seventeen industries profits as a percentage of sales were higher for the non-resident owned firms. In the fourteen and seventeen industries where they were higher as a percentage of equity and of sales the median difference for the two groups of firms was 3.4 percentage points and 3.5 percentage points respectively. There does not appear to be any systematic tendency for the difference in profitability between the two sets of firms to rise or fall by industries with the increase in the percentage of total equity which is in firms controlled by non-residents. Conclusions from such series must be guarded, however. The return on direct investment involves more than profits. There are a significant number of cases where resident-owned firms have a better profit performance, including some industries where foreign investment is substantial. There are obvious problems of a statistical nature, including the quite different procedures involved in valuing equity and the different degrees of processing of sales by industry. Detailed data are not available for any other year. Finally, the data compare all foreign-owned and all resident-owned firms apart from the smallest in each major industry group, regardless of how different the product mix of the two sets of firms may be within such groups. A more precise answer to the comparative profitability of the two types of firms in similar circumstances would be possible if broadly similar industry sub-groups could be compared, as is done with a limited number of firms elsewhere in this chapter. If subsequent and more detailed returns under the Corporations and Labour Unions Returns Act repeat the differences in profit rates shown in 1962, it might suggest that some part of the advantages of the foreign-owned firm has gone to comparative differences in profits, and eventually in dividends to the parent, rather than in other possible ways noted above.[22]

Data prepared by the Dominion Bureau of Statistics, which are not comparable to the series just noted, can be used to show that profits earned by direct investment firms in Canada have declined as a percentage of total direct investment liabilities over the period 1946-1961.[23] Profits after income and withholding taxes varied between 11 and 13 per cent in the years 1947-1952 inclusive, fell to between 9 and 10 per cent in the years

---

[22]The higher profitability also reflects in part the fact that less than full charges are paid to the parent for some services supplied by it.

[23]This series was derived by dividing the total earnings column of table 49 above, excluding withholding taxes, by the total for direct investment liabilities at the end of each preceding year as shown on p. 126 of D.B.S., *The Canadian Balance of International Payments, 1961 and 1962*. This is a crude estimate in view of valuation and other problems mentioned earlier in this section. It does avoid the problem of inter-corporate transfers mentioned in the previous footnote.

1953-1957 inclusive, and fell sharply to 5 to 8 per cent in 1958-1961. It may be suggested that the latter decline reflects rapid expansion of direct investment in the fifties, an expansion on which returns would come only later, combined with the effects of generally slower economic growth for several years after 1957. Barring cyclical variation such as that in the late fifties and early sixties, the Canadian interest presumably is to have as low a return on direct investment as is consistent with maintaining efficient firms in operation. The benefits of direct investment would be reflected then to a greater extent in the quality and price of the products to the public rather than in the profits accruing to the parent. It is not possible to assess the welfare implications of data on the comparative profits of firms until longer and better series are available.

10
Concluding Comments

The conventional theory of foreign investment states that a country benefits from such investment if the growth of domestic real income associated with it exceeds the return to the foreign owners. This is the case where foreign investment is the lowest-cost way of securing the given increase in real income. The benefits from direct investment extend well beyond the supply of capital. The most important benefit is the transfer of knowledge in all of its forms, including new products, production skills, marketing methods, management ability, and access to extensive research-development facilities. Market contacts and guarantees may also be important, particularly in the case of the sale abroad of primary products and their manufactures in volume. Although it has not been possible to quantify the gains from direct investment in any precise way the nature and extent of these have been spelled out in some detail earlier.

Direct investment also imposes certain constraints and costs on the economy. In the most general sense these constraints involve the usual difficulty confronting a nation which exists in a more rather than a less international context, namely the obligation to so order its affairs as to maintain equilibrium in its balance of payments. Adjustment to changes in the flow of capital is one aspect of this problem. The most obvious cost, a variable, uncertain one, is the return on direct investment which grows as long as the firms are successful and the economy expands. The economy must be sufficiently export oriented or import replacing over time to be able to make these growing payments abroad, if we assume that it is neither desirable nor possible to meet these growing payments indefinitely by further foreign borrowing.

This particular cost has been recognized for some time in the economic literature.[1] It has been dealt with in this study as part of a more general

_____
[1] See Arndt, *op. cit.*, and Penrose, *op. cit.*

criticism of the foreign-owned firm. That criticism is that the international firm may make key decisions which, while maximizing its global profit over time, do not necessarily maximize the interests of the subsidiary or of the country in which the subsidiary is located. As noted in various contexts earlier this results in at least two conflicts. In the first place, it poses a conflict between short-run and long-run situations. Thus it was demonstrated in Chapters 4 and 5 that the view that the parent would not permit competition with its facilities abroad, and would require purchases from such facilities by Canadian subsidiaries, was inconsistent with profit maximization in the long run. It can be argued, however, that apparently short-run circumstances have a way of persisting, that change is not easy or peaceful in a complex organization and hence may be avoided so far as possible, and that in any case the large firm in particular has more objectives than simple profit maximization.[2] Second, it poses a conflict between objectives involving on the one hand international specialization and maximum efficiency and on the other maximum national development of domestic resources and full employment. Many of the criticisms levied against foreign investment by Canadians revolve around the fuller use and development of Canadian facilities and personnel. These criticisms have been quite prevalent in the period of excess capacity in the late fifties and early sixties. They are likely to remain as attention shifts from problems of cyclical full employment to those of maximum national development over time.

This general criticism of the international firm suffers from two defects. In the first place, it has not been verified empirically in any general way. The present study lends only limited support to it. The criticism has been too sweeping and indiscriminate and has not taken sufficient account of the considerable differences which do exist in the performance of the firms involved. Nor has it recognized frequently that these differences are unavoidable given the widely different circumstances facing individual firms. In the second place, the conflict between efficiency and development, insofar as it exists, appears in significant part to be the result not of direct investment as such but of the public policies to which it has responded and within which it operates. Each of these points will be considered in turn.

It is not difficult to find examples of performance by the direct investment company which do not appear to be in the national interest. In every chapter of this volume one can find a group of firms whose operations do not conform in some respect to those announced by succeeding governments to be in the public interest. Some of these standards of performance

---

[2]On this last point see the articles mentioned in footnote 46, Chapter 4.

present a decidedly dual aspect from the point of view of the public benefit. While that interest requires that competent Canadians not be barred from senior positions in the firms involved, for example, it does not follow that Canada is so rich in managerial resources that she can afford to bar the import of such persons. Some of the requested standards of performance are quite unrealistic considering the circumstances facing many firms. Not all firms can be expected to export, for example, when some have comparatively high costs of production or distribution or face tariff barriers abroad. Not all can achieve a high domestic content in purchases if only because some firms enticed to Canada by a high tariff remain unsuited to the Canadian resource and cost structure. In any case, most *generalized* criticisms of such companies are at odds with the available facts on performance. It is the variation in performance which stands out from the data on many aspects of performance, reflecting the differences in the circumstances facing these firms. It is true that these variations can be associated broadly with certain of the characteristics of the firms. The present study cannot claim any scientific precision in analyzing these variables but their treatment here may be a suggestive first step in examining the circumstances under which business performance is determined. It will be of interest to summarize some of these classifications.

Size of firm has been treated throughout as a key variable. It would appear that many of the practices which Canadians have criticized with respect to the direct investment company are more prevalent in the smaller firms. Thus the president was found to be a national of the affiliate in 65 per cent of the firms with assets under $1 million and only 30 per cent of firms with assets of $25 million or more; and only 25 per cent of the former had a resident outside director as against 55 per cent of the latter. There was much more decentralization of decision-making between parent and subsidiary in the larger firms. The median value for the percentage of sales in Canada was 100 per cent for the two smallest size categories (under $1 million and $1-4.9 million) and 95 per cent and 92 per cent for the two largest. The median value for the percentage of purchases in Canada rises from seventy and eighty in the two smallest size categories to 80 and 85 in the two largest. While 58 per cent and 50 per cent of the two smallest size groups did no research-development in Canada only 30 per cent in each of the two largest size groups did no research. About 60 per cent of the first three size groups had unit costs in excess of those of the affiliate on major comparable products compared with 18 per cent for the largest size group. The largest size group had a smaller proportion of firms without a minority stock issue. The smaller firms, however, were more likely to secure funds from the parent and less likely to be paying dividends. No absolute standards have been set for performance in view of the diversity of circumstances facing the firms in this study. In a comparative sense the performance of the largest firms, which comprise the major part of total foreign investment, is better in almost all important respects considered in this study.

The other general variable used, namely control in the United States compared with control overseas, gave much less systematic results. There is a tendency for firms controlled overseas to have a larger proportion of residents among their senior personnel and their board but this does not extend to the president. There is no significant difference in the degree of decentralization of decision-making. Firms owned overseas are better represented among those exporting up to 5 per cent of their output but this is because their industrial mix differs from those owned in the United States. The former are also better represented in the group buying less than 40 per cent of their purchases in Canada, presumably because more of them were established in the fifties. Systematic differences for research, relative unit costs, and numbers issuing shares could not be found. The firms owned overseas were more likely to get funds from the parent and less likely to pay dividends, again presumably because they were younger.

It will be recalled that various aspects of performance were classified by certain other variables and these classifications were examined within three size categories, under $1 million, $1-4.9 million, and $5 million and over. To anticipate the general conclusions, improved performance in terms of more nationals as presidents and more directors as residents tends to be associated with the firms which have a minority share issue and which are less supervised by the affiliate. Improved economic performance in terms of more exports and research, less imports, and smaller cost differences, tends to be associated with certain industries, particularly with primary producers and primary manufactures except as regards research performance; with firms whose products are modified or different compared with the affiliate; and with those whose range of products is narrow relative to the affiliate.

The age of the firm is not associated with improved performance in any systematic way except for one or two limited areas. There was only moderate association between age of firm and Canadianization of senior personnel except for the oldest group of firms. The group with the most extensive supervision declines with age. There is a decline in the proportion of purchases abroad with age only for those making 60 per cent or less of their purchases in Canada, a group which is related in turn to the smallest and newest firms. The more recent firms tend to be more dependent on the parent for funds. In other key respects performance does not improve with age alone.

There was relatively little variation in the nature of senior personnel and degree of supervision when considered by type of business and type of product. The economic aspects of performance were closely associated with these variables. Thus the extractive and integrated producers export more; the percentage of purchases in Canada rises, as one would expect, as one proceeds from assembly to the more rounded forms of operation; and the firms producing fully processed and manufactured products or with integrated operations do more research. By type of product or industry primary producers and primary manufacturing tend to export more and import less, and have a better unit cost position relative to the parent. This difference does not extend to research, which is concentrated in parts of the secondary manufacturing industries.

Compared with firms whose products are identical with those of the affiliate, or almost so, those subsidiaries whose products are substantially modified or not comparable to those of the affiliate have more exports and research and less imports and supervision. The firms whose range of products was narrow relative to the affiliate tended to sell more abroad and to import less than the firms with a product range closer to that of the affiliate. The firms with a very limited product range relative to the affiliate also received more supervision from the affiliate than those with a wide range. Size of firm measured relative to that of the affiliate did not show association with many variables, although research rose markedly with relative size and supervision fell. The degrees of supervision and ownership were associated with senior personnel, in that there were relatively more nationals as presidents and more residents as directors where the super- vision was less and where a minority share issue existed. The degrees of supervision and of ownership were not systematically associated with improved performance in the economic variables, however.

These findings suggest that the effects of ownership on performance are primarily on the nature of senior personnel while economic performance is related largely to other variables. The comparisons with larger resident- owned firms in comparable industries confirm this. There is a difference in the composition of boards and in nationality of senior personnel between larger resident-owned and non-resident owned firms, although residents and nationals are well represented in the latter also. The only systematic difference between them in terms of economic performance, for the variables of exports, imports, and research, is with respect to imports. The non-resident owned firm makes relatively more of its purchases abroad. In addition, of course, such firms have a unique source of financing from the parent abroad, particularly in the early years and under extraordinary circumstances. Their dividend payments, which form a growing but unknown liability to non-residents, tend to be paid less evenly than those by resident-owned firms. It will be recalled that these comparisons were made between a limited number of firms in similar circumstances; specifically, with assets of $1 million or more and, to the extent possible, in comparable industry sub-groups. If one looks simply at *all* resident-owned and non-resident owned firms, reflecting very different industries, sizes and so on, the available data suggest that the foreign-owned firms tend to be more heavily represented in export-oriented and research-oriented industries. While equally comprehensive overall data are not available for imports, it appears that they may be more heavily represented in import-oriented industries as well. All of these conclusions must be tentative, since both the data collected for this study and many of the overall series refer to one or a few years only and suffer from other defects.

The advantages of the foreign-owned firm need not show up in the particular aspects of performance examined in this study, but may show in the quality and price of products made available or in profits to the parent. In any case the resident-owned firm can offset these advantages in part by licensing and other arrangements with otherwise unrelated foreign firms, pooling of research and the like. In part also, the similar performance will reflect adjustments made to meet competition from the foreign-owned firm. This is a point of some importance, since the benefits of foreign techniques accrue to the domestic economy if they are passed on in the form of lower prices and improved products and services rather than accruing simply as profits to the foreign owners. Maximum competition both internally and internationally is necessary to assure that the gains from foreign investment are in fact passed on to the domestic economy. There are not enough good comparative data on profits, much less on other aspects of performance, to permit a judgement on this point; but for the one year for which data are available, the rate of return to the non-resident owned firms exceeded that to resident-owned firms in the majority of industries.

In some cases the performance of the direct investment firm is limited, actually or potentially, by disadvantages peculiar to it. Thus the restricted export franchise of some firms, reflecting market-sharing within the international firm and extra-territorial extension of United States law or regulations, impedes some exports and will impede more to the extent that the firms become more competitive. Much more important, in our view, is the evidence that an inefficient structure of industry inhibits the ability to compete internationally more generally. Some key points in this study suggest that the similarity of performance in economic terms of resident-owned and non-resident owned firms may reflect an equally unsatisfactory level of performance. The great majority of the companies are a small fraction of the parent in size yet they are producing almost the full range of the identical or slightly modified products of the parent. Not surprisingly, their unit costs are in most cases higher than those of the parent on major comparable products. It is difficult to resist the conclusion that many of the potential gains from direct investment may not have accrued to Canada because the inefficient structure of her industry does not permit her to take advantage of them. Much of the poor performance with regard to development of Canadian facilities which is ascribed to foreign-owned firms, and is shared in some respects by their resident-owned counterparts, turns out on closer examination to reflect the economic environment in which the firms operate. Particular emphasis was placed in this connection on tariffs. Historically, the Canadian tariff has played a key role in attracting such firms to Canada (though a lesser role in recent years) leading to an uneconomic proliferation of products and firms. Foreign tariffs and exchange restrictions have helped to limit the market horizons of these firms. Many of the key aspects of the performance of the direct investment company are inexplicable except in terms of tariffs. To the extent that direct investment is a tariff-enforced partial substitute for imports, the continued heavy access to the parent and its foreign sources for components and parts is explained. Similarly, that part which becomes domiciled in Canada because of the tariff and cannot exist without the tariff can hardly be expected to compete internationally through exports on any scale.

The limitations of this position should be clear. Given her tariff, Canada was better off economically having access to direct investment rather than doing without it. Blocking the import of products at world prices and also preventing their production in Canada by international firms would have given Canada the worst of both worlds. The argument here is rather that the tariffs and other restrictions on trade have given Canada both a good deal of foreign ownership and an industrial structure incapable of fully using the advantages of international business connections and of realizing

306   Foreign Ownership of Canadian Industry

the kind of performance demanded by Canadians. It was noted in Chapter 7 that the Canadian tariff has been less important in attracting such firms to Canada since World War II. Tariffs continue, nevertheless, to play an important role in raising costs, in preserving an inefficient number of firms and products, and in limiting market horizons.

If Canadians desire improved performance from the direct investment firm and its resident-owned counterpart, far more attention will have to be given to the structure of industry. Some of the variables considered above are revealing in this respect. It was noted that economic performance improves with absolute size of firm, with greater concentration in certain industries, and with a decreased range of products and greater differentiation relative to the parent. In other words, more scale, more specialization, and more differentiation from the parent, however achieved, are the keys to improved economic performance. They should also permit the nation to take fuller advantage of the special benefits to be derived from direct investment, such as access to research-development facilities and market contacts, which cannot now be exploited with full effectiveness wherever the basic structure of industry is weak. The more competitive environment of industry on an international scale when so re-structured will ensure that the benefits of foreign investment are transmitted to Canadians to a greater extent, rather than going to non-residents by way of unnecessary profits, or into an inefficient proliferation of firms and product lines. Not all foreign investment or associated resident-owned investment must be involved in such re-structuring since much of it is efficient by world standards or enjoys the protection of transfer costs or must be decentralized for other reasons. In addition, the full exploitation of economies of scale does not always require vast markets. In many cases the Canadian market is large enough, or almost so, to support fully efficient operations if sufficient specialization occurs in the industry. What is involved is a matter of degree. More industry needs to be put into such a position if the overall performance of industry is to be improved. The range of production costs relative to the parent suggests that a significant number of firms are capable of reaching an internationally competitive position where transfer costs, including tariffs, are not prohibitive.

To the extent that all of this is achieved the conflicts posed earlier begin to disappear. The interests of the international firm and those of the country within which the subsidiary resides are less likely to diverge when the latter is an efficiently specialized and/or differentiated part of the entire operation. Similarly, the conflict of full employment and efficient operation tends to be minimized in that the efficient operations are more likely to remain in use in times of slack demand. The end result should be an industry more suited to Canada's actual and potential capacities, and capable of yielding both higher living standards and maximum development of Canadian facilities.

What this amounts to is setting a direction of economic policy in which the national economic interest and the interests of the international firm can have more opportunity to coincide and to reinforce one another. Thus it is quite clear that government cannot but be closely concerned with the affairs of direct investment firms, among others. The re-structuring of industry obviously requires a close governmental interest to ensure that the costs do not fall solely on the groups directly involved, that cooperative efforts at change do not become permanent monopoly positions, to negotiate the necessary inter-governmental agreements, and to ensure that the broad direction of change is correct. The need to minimize the special costs or constraints of the international firm, such as the size and variability of income paid abroad and the resistance to some kinds of change over the short run in some firms whose operations are spread internationally, will continue. The strategy of national development should take account of ways of exploiting as greatly as possible the special advantages inherent in contacts with international firms. At the present time, for example, many firms are not able to exploit in a meaningful way the access which they have to the parent's research-development because they are not an efficient source for the product within the international firm. There is often not much point in innovation for a small market, and access to larger markets is conditional on a more efficient cost and product base. Furthermore, in an economy in which the pursuit of profit continues to play a key role there will continue to be divergences of private and public interest which will require public intervention. These divergences may take on added public significance in the context of larger and more specialized firms working in the international markets, since they will pose divergences between national and international welfare from time to time. Finally, the temptation by agencies of the United States government to use subsidiary companies in Canada to implement their own policies can be dealt with only by prompt and vigorous action at the highest governmental level.

The Canadian government's major policy to date with regard to direct investment has been partly hortatory in the sense of urging firms to conduct their operations in order to make maximum use of Canadian personnel and facilities. By differential taxation the government has encouraged direct investment companies to issue 25 per cent or more of their equity shares and to appoint resident directors in proportion. These tax changes were designed to encourage a switch away from foreign equity financing and thus impede the growth of foreign ownership of Canadian industries. It was also believed that minority Canadian participation in stock ownership and directorships was necessary to ensure that the practices of subsidiary companies in Canada would conform to Canadian interests, specifically in the further use or development of domestic production, service, research and management facilities.

The findings of this study raise some serious doubts about the assumptions underlying this approach. In the first place, the implied criticism of the operations of direct investment companies would appear to be too sweeping. The suggestion that many or most of them are acting in a way detrimental to Canadian interests because they are foreign owned is sometimes at variance with the facts, neglects the considerable variation in experience involved, and often fails to trace the inferior performance to its root cause in the environment in which the firms operate. The contrast of the performance of large and small firms and the comparisons of resident-owned and non-resident-owned firms are cases in point. The indiscriminate approach which has tended to be used may reflect a lack of information of the kind necessary for more informed policies, though this does raise the question why the authorities have waited so long to inform themselves. Second, there is little evidence that minority Canadian ownership of 25 per cent and resident directors in proportion will lead to a set of corporate policies more in keeping with Canada's interests.[3] The present data show a difference between partly-owned and wholly-owned companies with respect to senior personnel but not in any systematic way with respect to the economic aspects of performance. One must ask also whether minority shareholders and resident directors would in fact represent "the Canadian interest." Even assuming their views would be the determining ones on any particular issue, a large assumption in many cases, this need not be in the Canadian interest.[4] What is good for the minority shareholders may or

---

[3]The legislation on this is redundant in one respect since most firms already have the required proportion of resident directors.
[4]It has been suggested that if the objective is to have effective Canadian participation in direct investment companies this can sometimes best be done by acquiring a significant interest in the parent company itself. There are cases where the cost of acquiring a 25 per cent interest in the subsidiary would be no more than that of acquiring a smaller but significant interest in the parent and thus becoming the largest single shareholder in the latter. The concentration of ownership may be the key factor in such cases. See the summary of the talk by Maurice F. Strong, *Financial Post*, March 27, 1965.

may not be good for Canada. Where there are generally adverse effects in a particular form of corporate behaviour the corrective steps should be taken by the governments of Canada, the usual representatives of the overall public interest. Third, there is much doubt that this and similar measures will in fact lead to share issues by many subsidiary companies. The structure and operating characteristics of subsidiary companies vary a good deal, hence the logic of public share issues varies a good deal in terms of the interests both of the firm and of the investor. The foreign-owned corporations which do not issue shares cover a great variety of situations, from the small new firm with a few products or processes not far removed from a purely assembly operation to the large well-established firm producing a full range of products largely based on domestic suppliers. The legislation encompasses all of these in an attempt to create the stereotype of a public company with a significant minority share issue and an operating board of directors. It is not even clear that the differential rate of withholding tax which is a key element of the legislation will necessarily serve as an inducement to issue shares in many cases since the tax paid to the Canadian government can be deducted from the tax liabilities of the parent firm to its government.

Quite apart from these questions at the level of the firm, the approach raises some larger economic issues. To the extent that the measures are successful and some firms issue shares in Canada there is a tendency to forego future economic growth simply to buy existing assets. New assets are not necessarily created by this process; there is a tendency, rather, to use scarce Canadian equity capital to replace present foreign equity ownership in existing assets. The actual outcome depends on several variables including what is done by the firm with the funds so acquired. Since there is nothing in this process to make Canada a more attractive place for foreign investment, much of the capital freed by minority Canadian ownership may be exported to affiliates abroad; in this case the outcome is that noted here, assuming Canadian saving habits and foreign borrowing are unchanged. If not paid to the parent or invested in the subsidiary, it could be invested in other Canadian firms. In that case the measures could lead to more firms with minority shareholders but also more firms in which foreign capital is invested. The measure, if it is effective, could reduce the potential for economic growth, but it might have the unexpected effect of spreading direct investment more widely in Canadian industry.

One other conflict which has been posed in parts of this study is that between local autonomy for the subsidiaries and the requirement of centralized approval of some of the key decisions in the international firm.

As much of this book makes clear, direct investment is an extension of management and technical skills and products as well as of capital. Neither the owners nor their trustees are likely to surrender the right of review of major decisions in the great majority of cases. In the last analysis the conflict posed here is not capable of resolution in the sense that the case for full autonomy is really a case against direct investment. Short of this many variations are possible as explained in Chapter 3. Many of the firms studied here enjoy a considerable degree of autonomy, with the qualifications of review of their major decisions on expansion and the related overall financial decisions and an important overall influence through the appointment of key officers. That this does not always yield operational results consistent with maximum use of Canadian facilities has been related in part to some specific disadvantages of the foreign-owned firm. Much more important determinants are the wide differences in the economic situations of different firms and the fact that they frequently operate in an environment which limits improvement of their economic performance. A restructuring of industry along the lines indicated would have conflicting effects in the area of decision-making. Greater specialization, if this involved more integration with the international firm, could well centralize certain areas of decision-making which are now decentralized. It was noted above that firms with only a few products comparable to the parent's were more subject to supervision than those with many products. Offsetting this is the decrease in degree of supervision with the growing absolute and relative size of the firm, particularly if specialization involves differentiation of product, and the fact that the economic and other performance of a kind often identified with autonomy is generally better for the larger firms.

This raises a larger issue, an issue which some consider to be at the heart of the questions surrounding foreign direct investment, which is the assumed threat to the political independence of Canada. It is feared by some that the widespread prevalence of American capital in particular in Canadian industry will involve not only economic but political integration with the United States. The Royal Commission which raised this issue offered no specific evidence on this score apart from listing in a few pages some possibly adverse economic results of direct investment, and the documentation on it in the meantime has been less than satisfactory.[5] The issue clearly involves more than economics and more than direct investment; ultimately it covers all major aspects of the relations between the two countries. It is a theme which runs through Canadian history in one form

---

[5]See the Royal Commission on Canada's Economic Prospects, *Final Report*, p. 390.

or another. No attempt has been made within the confines of this study to evaluate this question in relation to direct investment, but a comment may be made on one or two aspects of the topics studied in this volume which are related to the larger issue.

The evidence from this study suggests that in significant part the direct investment firm has contributed to the development objectives favoured by governmental authorities in recent years. Where it has not done so there are often good economic reasons why it cannot perform as expected, reasons often related to the framework of public policy within which it operates. The fact that Canadian policy has not always been designed to secure the best terms of trade from foreign investment and to take maximum advantage of its special capacities does not negate this point. Much of the evidence presented here suggests that firms, regardless of the nationality of ownership, in most cases operate in response to a given institutional and economic setting in order to improve their economic position. Insofar as private business activity is concerned, the Canadian national interest would appear to require the preservation or attainment of a setting, consistent with other policy objectives, in which the firms' pursuit of gain coincides with increased welfare for the community. Where general industrial practices arise which are clearly against the national interest, whatever the nationality of ownership of the firms, the governments of Canada should be prepared to take corrective action.

The second point is equally important, for at bottom the controversy over direct investment has to do with the extent of internationalization of the economy. Such internationalization carries certain costs because all international trade, capital, corporate and other ties involve interdependence with other countries and impose certain constraints on national policy-making. The direct investment firm imposes some special costs and problems. Notable among costs are the constantly growing and variable payments it requires which necessitate adjustments in the balance of payments and the economy sufficient to finance them. One of the most difficult problems is the temptation by agencies of the United States government to ensure the effectiveness of their policies by extending them to subsidiary companies abroad. This is an area in which a serious threat to Canadian autonomy can occur if Canadian authorities fail to forestall such attempts. Despite these difficulties it does not follow that Canadian independence would be greater by opting out of contact with the international firm. Direct investment has in the past contributed to the strength and diversity of the Canadian economy and to its high living standards. By so doing, for governments which are willing to act, it has enlarged the scope for national policies in both the domestic and international spheres. The direct investment firm may have an even greater role to play in serving Canada's interests in an increasingly shrinking and competitive world where larger economic units are becoming more common. The access to management and technical skills, to research-development, and to market contacts abroad are valuable assets to a country which attempts to put more of its industry on an efficient, expanding, and internationally-competitive basis. The international firm can be an invaluable ally in the process of restructuring Canadian industry to this end, assuming Canadians are willing to make the changes in industrial policy which will take greater advantage of its particular capabilities. More than the direct investment firm will be involved in this process, of course. There is much to be said for an eclectic approach in terms of methods of organizing economic activity so long as these methods are consistent with defined objectives. The resident-owned firm has demonstrated its capacity to dominate certain industries over long periods, for example, as well as to compete in some branches of what are largely foreign-owned industry. Provision of larger pools of equity capital to resident-owned firms may not be sufficient to permit them to rationalize production and to continue to compete with non-resident owned firms. Pooling of research and access to specialized management services may be necessary in some cases to help them overcome their disabilities relative to the direct investment firm, particularly as the latter becomes more efficient. Joint enterprises, licensing of foreign research and development (especially where it is not accompanied by market restriction), government enterprise and the encouragement of direct investment from overseas are all worth considering in specific contexts. The objective is partly to ensure that the direct investment firm meets sufficient competition to guarantee that the benefits are in fact passed on to the public and not simply to their owners in higher profits. The point in part is also to ensure that Canadian capital and skills are mobilized for and equal to the task of exploiting the new opportunities for investment to a greater extent than has been the case with respect to previous opportunities. To the extent that this is accomplished, the proportion of industry which is controlled by non-residents will decline in any case over time.

Appendix A
Additional Tables
by Country of Control

TABLE 65

COMPOSITION OF BOARDS OF DIRECTORS, AMERICAN-OWNED AND LARGER COMPANIES
(Number of companies)

Categories	0	1	2	3	4	5	6	7	8	9	10	11	12	13	14	15	16	17	No reply to question	Not applicable	Total companies	Total number of persons
1. U.S. owned companies only*																						
Management of company	6	36	37	32	17	18	8	4			1								7	61	227	450
Associated with affiliates abroad	8	11	26	48	25	21	12	4	2										9	61	227	528
Resident "outside" directors	104	15	9	9	8	5	1	1	3										11	61	227	154
Other significant owners	143	3	3	4	1														12	61	227	25
Other	126	21	5	1															13	61	227	34
Total number on board†				13	8	36	20	20	15	19	10	6	5	1	4	2		2	5	61	227	1,161
Residents of Canada only	9	26	40	21	15	10	19	9	2	2	4	2	2						5	61	227	576
2. All companies with assets of $25 million or more																						
Management of company	1	2	5	9	6	4	4	1			1								0	3	35	124
Associated with affiliates abroad	2	2	1	9	8	2	5	3	1										0	3	35	132
Resident "outside" directors	15	1	5	3	1	1	1												0	3	35	68
Other significant owners	28	1		1															0	3	35	13
Other	20	7	4	1															0	3	35	18
Total number on board†								2	3	5	6	4	4		3	3		2	2	3	35	356
Residents of Canada only					9	2	3	5	6	4	3								0	3	35	214

* In response to an introductory question "Is the Canadian Board an active one?", 165 replied yes, fifty-four no, seven that there was no board, and one did not answer this question. The composition for the first group only was reported, with allowances for non-responses as indicated.

† The total for number of persons, shown in the last column, will not add vertically because of double counting of persons among the categories shown for some companies. This double counting does not exist in the figure for the total number of persons on the board.

TABLE 66
PROPORTION OF SALES IN CANADA BY AMERICAN-OWNED COMPANIES AND COMPANIES OWNED OVERSEAS
(Number of companies)

Percentage of sales in Canada	American-owned companies by size of assets in $ millions					Companies owned overseas
	Under 1	1-4.9	5-24.9	25 and over	All companies*	All companies
100	63	39	4	0	110	19
95-99	10	21	15	11	62	20
70-94	3	9	8	8	31	6
Below 70	4	2	1	7	15	5
Not available or no response to question	0	1	3	4	9	3
Total	80	72	31	30	227	53

* Includes fourteen companies not classified by size of assets.

TABLE 67
DESTINATION OF EXPORTS, AMERICAN-OWNED COMPANIES WITH EXPORTS
(Percentages by each destination)

Percentage of exports to destination indicated	Distribution of responses by each destination							
	Area				Affiliation			
	U.S.	U.K.	Other sterling area	Other	Parent	Other foreign affiliates of parent	Own subsidiary abroad	Other
100%	24	2	13	7	13	4	0	33
70-99	20	2	3	10	11	1	3	21
30-69	11	5	3	12	10	6	0	10
1-29	14	25	24	18	18	10	0	11
0	31	66	56	54	48	61	9	26
Not relevant	—	—	—	—	—	18	88	—
Total	100	100	100	100	100	100	100	100

NOTE: The data should be read by columns, which total 100 per cent except for rounding. The cases shown as not relevant refer to companies with exports but where the parent companies had no other foreign affiliate or the Canadian company did not have a subsidiary outside Canada. About ninety companies are involved in each column of this table (after excluding those with exports in table 66 which could not give destinations) of which seventeen indicated their type of business was extractive or semi-fabricated products. Six of the seventeen were largely extractive in their operations.

TABLE 68
DESTINATION OF EXPORTS, COMPANIES OWNED OVERSEAS WITH EXPORTS
(Percentages by each destination)

Percentage of exports to destination indicated	Distribution of responses by each destination							
	Area				Affiliation			
	U.S.	U.K.	Other sterling area	Other	Parent	Other foreign affiliates of parent	Own subsidiary abroad	Other
100%	38	4	4	11	4	8	—	54
70-99	10	—	—	11	—	—	—	35
30-69	17	4	4	14	—	—	—	—
1-29	10	25	18	11	30	8	7	—
0	24	68	75	54	67	69	11	12
No relevant	—	—	—	—	—	15	81	—
Total	100	100	100	100	100	100	100	100

NOTE: See note to previous table. About twenty-eight firms are involved in each column of this table, after excluding nineteen without exports and about six with exports which could not give destinations.

TABLE 69
PROPORTION OF PURCHASES IN CANADA
AMERICAN-OWNED COMPANIES AND COMPANIES OWNED OVERSEAS
(Number of companies)

Percentage of purchases in Canada	American-owned companies by size of assets in $ millions					Companies owned overseas
	Under 1	1.4-9	5-24.9	25 and over	All Companies	All Companies
95 and over	11	10	2	3	27	5
90-94	7	10	7	6	32	8
80-89	14	13	5	4	36	11
70-79	10	11	5	5	31	3
60-69	9	9	2	5	28	1
50-59	6	3	1	1	11	2
40-49	2	3	1	1	7	2
30-39	7	5	0	0	12	5
Below 30	9	4	1	0	15	9
Not available or no response	5	4	7	5	28	7
Total	80	72	31	30	227	53

TABLE 70
SOURCES OF IMPORTS, AMERICAN-OWNED COMPANIES WITH IMPORTS
(Percentages by each source)

Percentage of imports from source indicated	Distribution of responses from each source							
	Area				Affiliation			
	U.S.	U.K.	Other sterling area	Other	Parent	Other foreign affiliates of parent	Own subsidiary abroad	Other
100%	49	1	1	2	20	1	0	11
70-99	35	0	0	2	27	1	1	15
30-69	10	3	1	3	25	2	0	22
1-29	2	29	5	19	15	7	0	27
0	3	67	94	75	12	48	9	24
Not relevant	—	—	—	—	—	42	90	—
Total	100	100	100	100	100	100	100	100

NOTE: The data should be read by columns, which total 100 except for rounding. The cases shown as not relevant refer to companies with imports but where the parent companies had no other foreign affiliate or the Canadian company did not have a subsidiary outside Canada. About 175 companies are involved in each column of this table, after excluding those with imports which could not give sources.

TABLE 71
SOURCES OF IMPORTS, COMPANIES OWNED OVERSEAS WITH IMPORTS
(Percentages by each source)

Percentage of imports from source indicated	Distribution of responses from each source							
	Area				Affiliation			
	U.S.	U.K.	Other sterling area	Other	Parent	Other foreign affiliates of parent	Own subsidiary abroad	Other
100%	9	20	—	—	21	—	—	17
70-99	20	27	—	12	30	—	—	20
30-69	14	9	—	2	14	5	—	15
1-29	34	23	—	14	19	5	—	24
0	23	20	100	72	16	73	8	24
Not relevant	—	—	—	—	—	18	92	—
Total	100	100	100	100	100	100	100	100

NOTE: See note to previous table. About forty-three companies are involved in each column of this table after excluding those with imports which could not give sources.

TABLE 72

RESEARCH AND DEVELOPMENT WITHIN THE CANADIAN COMPANY
RESPONDENT AMERICAN-OWNED COMPANIES
(Number of companies)

Research-development as % of sales	Size of assets in $ millions				
	Under 1	1.4-9	5-24.9	25 and over	All Companies
0	49	33	11	6	103
Up to 0.5	4	2	2	10	19
0.6 to 1.0	5	6	4	1	17
1.1 to 2.0	4	9	3	5	21
2.1 to 5.0	4	6	1	3	14
Over 5.0	—	—	—	1	1
% unspecified	2	5	5	1	17
No reply to question	12	11	5	3	35
Total	80	72	31	30	227

TABLE 73

ALL RESEARCH AND DEVELOPMENT BY AMERICAN-OWNED COMPANIES*
(Number of companies)

Research-development as % of sales	Done within the Canadian company	Purchased from affiliates outside Canada	Purchased from other firms or organizations	Total cost of research-development
0	103	121	154	74
Up to 0.5	19	17	4	15
0.6-1.0	17	7	—	16
1.1-2.0	21	8	—	28
2.1-5.0	14	8	—	21
Over 5.0	1	—	1	3
% unspecified†	17	21	5	32
No reply to question	35	45	63	38
Total	227	227	227	227

* There is duplication among the first three columns in the sense that any single firm could theoretically answer all three columns. The fourth column reflects the total research effort included in (up to three of) the previous columns.
† These firms indicated they were doing research-development as defined but did not give the percentage to sales. Many of them indicated the research effort was small, probably under 1 per cent of sales.

Appendix B
Questionnaires and
Covering Letters

September 9, 1960

Dear Sir:

There has been a good deal of discussion in recent years about Canadian companies which are partly or wholly owned by non-residents. I think you will agree that discussion on a matter of such importance should be well informed. Unfortunately, there are large gaps in the information on the characteristics of such companies.

I have undertaken a study to fill in some of these gaps. One part of this study involves the enclosed questionnaire, which is based on interviews with the executives of some eighty companies. The questionnaire is being sent to all companies in Canada in which it is believed that a significant investment by non-residents exists.

I would appreciate your co-operation in filling out the questionnaire as fully as you find possible. May I emphasize, first, that this is an independent academic study and, second, that the material received will be treated as strictly confidential. The participating companies will not be identified, and none of the questionnaire material will be released in a form which might reveal the identity of individual companies. Your specific restrictions, if any, will be respected. If you prefer, please answer anonymously.

No questionnaire can convey adequately the many variations involved in Canadian industry. For this reason, and because of the complexity of one or two items, may I urge you to interpret my questions freely as they apply to your firm. If you find you cannot answer all of the questions asked, even approximately or generally, please answer all you can. I would welcome any further observations, and any documents, on the enclosed or related matters.

Yours very truly,

A. E. Safarian

Associate Professor of Economics

AES/as

QUESTIONNAIRE TO CANADIAN COMPANIES WITH A SUBSTANTIAL NON-RESIDENT OWNERSHIP

Please return to: A. E. SAFARIAN,
Department of Economics and Political Science,
UNIVERSITY OF SASKATCHEWAN,
SASKATOON, CANADA

INSTRUCTIONS

If you cannot give precise figures, your considered estimates will be entirely satisfactory. Where the wording of some questions or choices does not fit your company, please use your own wording. Do not hesitate to combine answers to questions where this seems desirable. The broader questions at the end of the questionnaire should be answered on a separate sheet, by number of question.

The terms parent company or affiliate are used interchangeably to refer to the major or sole shareholder outside Canada. If the Canadian operation is not incorporated in Canada, or your company has no parent or affiliate outside Canada (but has a substantial and widely distributed ownership by non-residents), please answer all questions appropriate to your circumstances and add qualifying comments in other cases. The term Canadian company refers to the operations of facilities located in Canada.

If this questionnaire should have been sent to a more central administrative unit, it would be appreciated if you would forward it. Space is provided at the end of the questionnaire for the names and addresses of any Canadian companies which are associated with your affiliate (but are not covered on this return) to which a separate questionnaire should be sent.

It would be appreciated if nil, not applicable, or other terms were used where necessary, rather than dashes.

A separate copy is provided for your files.

I. NATURE OF THE CANADIAN COMPANY

1. (a) When did the present major or sole shareholder acquire ownership? ....
How was this accomplished?
Establishment of an entirely new company ....
Purchase of or association with an existing company owned by residents .... or by non-residents .... which had been in operation since the year ....
Other, as follows

(b) Country in which your affiliate is located ....
(c) Is the Canadian organization incorporated in Canada? Yes .... No. ....

2. (a) Please underline one of the following to indicate in which type of business the Canadian company is *mainly* engaged: selling agency, assembly, extractive, semi-fabricated products, fully processed or manufactured products, fully or largely integrated production, or other as follows ....
In which type of business is your affiliate mainly engaged? ....

(b) What are the major types of products which are produced in the Canadian company? (Alternatively, indicate broadly the industry which accounts for most of your production.)

(c) Indicate by underlining, or state briefly in your own words, how the Canadian company compares *in general* with its affiliate in the following respects:
Nature of the products of the Canadian company: identical with comparable products of its affiliate, marginally different, substantially modified, not comparable, or ....
If products are comparable:
Range of products in Canada: wider, about the same, majority of affiliate's products, minority, only a few, or ....

1

(d) Please indicate the approximate *percentage* size of the Canadian company relative to its affiliate, by any relevant specified indicator (such as annual sales) ....

3. Please tick the relevant interval for the most recent figures of the Canadian company:

In millions of dollars	Under .5	.5-.9	1-4.9	5-9.9	10-24.9	25-49.9	50-99.9	100 or more
Sales in 1959*								
Book value of assets‡								

*Selling value of factory, mine and mill shipments of the Canadian operations, excluding materials or products purchased and re-sold without further processing.

‡Your most recent figure for gross assets *in Canada* less depreciation and current liabilities.

II. PERSONNEL AND ORGANIZATION

1. For the five senior officers of the Canadian company, please note the following:

	Chairman of the Board	President	Of the next three
(a) Which are resident in Canada?			
Which of the residents were formerly employed with the parent or its affiliates outside Canada?			
(b) Which are nationals of the country in which your affiliate is located?			

2. Is the Canadian Board an active one? Yes .... No ....

If answer is Yes:

(a) Please indicate the composition as follows:

	Number
Senior management of the Canadian company..	
Persons associated with the parent or with its affiliates outside Canada	
Resident "outside" directors, not otherwise associated with parent, with its other affiliates or with Canadian company as employees, legal counsel, or significant owners	
Representatives of other significant owners	
Other	
Total number of directors	
Of which residents of Canada number	

(b) How many times does the Canadian Board usually meet each year?...

How many of these meetings do the representatives of your affiliate usually attend? ....

3. Is there an active management or executive committee with major responsibilities? Yes .... No ....
If Yes, please indicate the composition of the committee by the groups noted in question 2 (a) above.

III. CONTACT WITH PARENT COMPANY OR MAJOR SHAREHOLDER

1. (a) Please specify the officer or division in your affiliate abroad
     (i) to which the Canadian firm is responsible ....
     (ii) to which other foreign affiliates of the parent or major shareholder are responsible ....
   (b) In how many foreign countries, other than Canada, does your affiliate have subsidiaries or branches? ....

2. (a) In general, do you consider that the operations and/or overall policies of the Canadian firm are supervised extensively ...., partly ...., or negligibly .... by your affiliate?

2

(b) Are there special circumstances surrounding your firm which affect the degree of supervision? If so, please explain.

(c) Has there been a significant change over time in the degree to which those associated with your affiliate have been involved in the operations and policies of the Canadian company? If so, can you indicate the nature of the change and any important reasons for it?

(d) Can you indicate whether the degree of involvement by your affiliate differs markedly from that in the case of
    (i) other comparable foreign subsidiaries of your affiliate, if any?

    (ii) comparable domestic subsidiaries of your affiliate, if any?

IV. MARKETING AND PURCHASING

1. For 1959, or for an average of recent years if 1959 is not typical:
    (a) What percentage of the total sales of the Canadian company went to the Canadian market? ....%
    (b) What percentage of the total purchases of the Canadian company (materials and parts, equipment, services) was from suppliers in Canada? ....%
    (c) How were your exports and imports distributed geographically?

	Exports	Imports
United States		
United Kingdom		
Other sterling area countries		
All other countries	100%	100%

    (d) Please indicate approximately the percentage of your total exports going to, and of your total imports coming from:

	Percentage of	
	Exports	Imports
Parent company or major shareholder (including its domestic subsidiaries)..............		
Parent or major shareholder's affiliates in third countries		
Canadian company's subsidiaries or branches located outside Canada		

2. (a) Please indicate the number of subsidiaries and branches of the Canadian company outside Canada, and the number of licenses of all kinds granted by the Canadian firm to affiliated and non-affiliated companies outside Canada.

	Subsidiaries and branches	Licenses to Affiliates	Non-Affiliates
United States			
United Kingdom			
Other sterling area countries			
All other countries			

    (b) What is the ratio of the investment in the Canadian company's subsidiaries and branches outside Canada to that in the Canadian company? ....%

3. (a) Please describe briefly the nature of the export sales organization (including agencies abroad) through which you export, indicating whether your own and/or your affiliates, and whether it differs by countries.

(b) If you export through the parent's export sales organization, please describe how such sales are allocated by it among the various affiliates.

4. Please describe briefly, for your purchases of materials and components, capital equipment, and services (such as insurance, advertising, accounting):

(a) Where the responsibility for policies lies, and what policy you have (if any) regarding country of purchase.

(b) The nature of the organization which does your purchasing, indicating whether your own or/and that of your affiliate.

V. RESEARCH AND DEVELOPMENT

Note: For present purposes, the term "research and development" comprises activities directed to pure or basic research (i.e. to programs not primarily committed to specific product or process applications) and also to conceiving and developing new products, new processes and major changes in products and processes, and bringing them up to the stage of production. Such activities as market and sales research, process and quality control, and geological and geophysical exploration, should be excluded. If in doubt, please use your normal definition and briefly specify its nature.

1. Please estimate the cost of research and development in 1959, as a percentage of your total annual sales:

	% of sales*
(a) Done within the Canadian company (include all direct and indirect operating costs, but exclude capital expenditures)	
(b) Purchased from affiliates outside Canada	
(c) Purchased from all other firms or organizations	
Total as percentage of sales	

*Given the relatively large size of sales, it would be appreciated if ratios were estimated to two decimal places.

2. If you have research and development facilities in the Canadian company:

(a) In what year were these established? .... Can you indicate the major factors which led to their establishment and to any major expansion?

(b) Which of the following are a significant part of the Canadian program: improvement of present products and processes ....; conceiving and developing new products and processes ....; programs not primarily committed to specific product or process applications .... How does this compare with the program of your affiliate?

Are the programs of the two companies largely co-ordinated or significantly different?

(c) On a *relative* basis, are your present expenditures on research and development in Canada roughly the same ...., considerably less ...., or considerably more ...., compared with the program of your affiliate?

4

VI. FINANCIAL

1. (a) Please indicate the percentage distribution of your stock (excluding directors' qualifying shares) and of your debt at the end of 1959 or other recent date.

	Voting Stock	Other Stock	Debt
Parent company or major shareholder			
Non-residents other than affiliates			
Residents	100%	100%	100%

(b) What percentage of the voting stock was held by your affiliate when its relationship with the Canadian company was first established? ....

If your affiliate has increased or decreased its ownership substantially since then, can you outline the change and the date, and why the change was made?

2. (a) *Approximately* what proportion of your funds was obtained from each of the following sources in 1950-59 inclusive (*or* for specified recent years only)

	%
Net financing from—parent or affiliates abroad	
—other sources abroad	
Net financing from Canadian sources	
Net income	
Depreciation and depletion	
Other	100%

(b) What percentage of your net earnings has been paid as dividends since 1950? .... Do you and/or your affiliate have a preferred policy or practice on this?

(c) If there has been a significant *net* withdrawal of capital from Canada in the past decade, please explain the circumstances.

(If you prefer to reply anonymously, please return this questionnaire in a plain envelope.)

Name of company:

Name and position of reporting officer:

If a separate questionnaire should be sent to other Canadian companies which are associated with your affiliate (but are not covered on this return) please list their names and addresses here.

Please Turn Over

Please comment on the following, where relevant, on a separate sheet by number of question.

1. For companies which began operations in Canada, under the present ownership, after 1945.

   Can you indicate the specific reasons, in approximate order of importance, which led to your affiliate's decision to establish operations in Canada?

2. (a) Is there a defined policy or objective on the movement of senior personnel from the parent or its other affiliates to the Canadian company, or on the reverse movement?

   (b) Can you identify any significant historical changes in the characteristics of officers and Board of the Canadian company as defined on page two of the questionnaire?

3. (a) Please describe the more important methods which are used to maintain contact with your affiliate with respect to the operations and policies of the Canadian firm, apart from any representation your affiliate may have on the Canadian Board or executive committee; for example, informal contacts between senior executives, written reports (please specify general nature and frequency), expenditure limits for the executives and Board of the Canadian company, written delineation of responsibilities.

   (b) With respect to the operations and policies of the Canadian company, please describe the degree of decentralization of responsibility and decision making as between persons associated with the Canadian company and those (primarily) associated with your affiliate; for example, with respect to such matters as production planning, financial policies, introducing new products or techniques or markets, capital expansion, marketing, labour relations.

4. (a) In what ways, if any, has the fact of affiliation with companies outside Canada discernibly affected

   (i) the volume, nature, and direction of your exports: for example, guaranteed purchases by affiliates, assignment of markets to be served, contacts with potential customers?

   (ii) the nature, sources, and costs of your purchases: for example, joint purchases with affiliates, contacts with potential suppliers, commitments to particular sources of supply?

   (b) Are your unit costs of production (at the current rate of exchange and at normal volume of operations) typically higher, about the same, or lower than those of your affiliate, on your major comparable products? If unit costs are significantly different, can you indicate the approximate average difference in percentage terms, and the major reasons for the difference?

5. (a) What access do you have to (i) the research and development and (ii) the industrial and other know-how of your affiliate? Please describe the nature of the agreement (formal or informal), broadly what you receive under it, and the terms of payment. (If payment is nil or nominal, is there a specific reason for this?)

   (b) Please describe briefly the access you have to (i) the patents and (ii) the trademarks of your affiliate in terms of the nature of the agreement (license or informal), terms of payment, whether a large portion of your output is involved, and the markets for which the rights apply.

   (c) If not already covered, can you give some quantitative and/or qualitative indication of the importance to your company of the access described in (a) and (b)?

   (d) Please describe briefly the reverse process to (a) and (b), i.e., the access which your affiliate has to the research-development, know-how, patents and trademarks of the Canadian company.

6. (a) For companies whose voting stock is *not* owned wholly by the affiliate.

   Is the remaining voting stock held widely? Why was it established (if not already covered)? Has your experience with an "outside" shareholding been satisfactory or otherwise, from the point of view of the development of the Canadian company and its relations with its affiliate?

   (b) Do you and/or your affiliate have any preferred policies or practices with respect to: the form of capital and extent of financing by your affiliate beyond the original investment in Canada; the form of capital and the extent of financing within Canada? Please explain, including any reasons for the financial procedures and any significant historical changes of which you are aware.

October 7, 1960.

Dear Sir:

There has been a good deal of discussion in recent years about Canadian companies which are largely or wholly owned by non-residents. I have undertaken a study to fill in some of the large gaps in the information on such companies, partly by means of a questionnaire which has been sent to a large number of such companies in Canada.

At the same time, it is important to have some basis for comparisons with these companies. The enclosed questionnaire, which is being sent to many companies which are primarily or wholly owned by residents of Canada, attempts to establish the basis for such comparisons in several key respects.

I would appreciate your co-operation in filling out the questionnaire as fully as you find possible. May I emphasize, first, that this is an independent academic study and, second, that the material received will be treated as strictly confidential. The participating companies will not be identified, and none of the questionnaire material will be released in a form which might reveal the identity of individual companies. Your specific restrictions, if any, will be respected. If you prefer, please answer anonymously.

No questionnaire can convey adequately the many variations involved in Canadian industry. For this reason, and because of the complexity of one or two items, may I urge you to interpret my questions freely as they apply to your firm. If you find you cannot answer all of the questions asked, even approximately or generally, please answer all you can. I would welcome any further observations on the enclosed or related matters.

Yours very truly,

A. E. Safarian,

Associate Professor of Economics.

AES/as

QUESTIONNAIRE TO COMPANIES WHICH ARE OWNED MAINLY OR WHOLLY BY RESIDENTS
OF CANADA

Please return to: A. E. SAFARIAN,
Department of Economics and Political Science,
UNIVERSITY OF SASKATCHEWAN,
SASKATOON, CANADA

INSTRUCTIONS

Where the wording of some questions or choices does not fit your company, please use your own wording. Do not hesitate to combine answers to questions where this seems desirable. The broader questions at the end of the questionnaire should be answered on a separate sheet, by number of question.

The terms company or Canadian company refer to the operations of facilities located in Canada, while affiliates outside Canada refers to your subsidiaries or branches located outside Canada.

If this questionnaire should have been sent to a more central administrative unit, it would be appreciated if you would forward it. Space is provided at the end of the questionnaire for the names and addresses of any Canadian companies which are closely associated with you (but are not covered on this return) to which a separate questionnaire should be sent.

It would be appreciated if nil, not applicable, or other terms were used where necessary, rather than dashes.

A separate copy is provided for your files.

1. NATURE AND ORGANIZATION OF THE CANADIAN COMPANY

1. (a) When was the company established?............................

    (b) Is the Canadian organization incorporated? Yes................No................

    (c) Please underline one of the following to indicate in which type of business the Canadian company is *mainly* engaged: selling agency, assembly, extractive, semi-fabricated products, fully processed or manufactured products, fully or largely integrated production, or other as follows...

    (d) What are the major types of products which are produced in the Canadian company? (Alternatively, indicate broadly the industry which accounts for most of your production)...

2. Please tick the relevant interval for the most recent figures of the Canadian company:

In millions of dollars	Under .5	.5-.9	1-4.9	5-9.9	10-24.9	25-49.9	50-99.9	100 and more
Sales in 1959*								
Book value of assets‡								

*Selling value of factory, mine and mill shipments, excluding materials or products purchased and re-sold without further processing.

‡Your most recent figure for gross assets *in Canada* less depreciation and current liabilities.

3. Is the Board of Directors an active Board? Yes............ No................

If answer is Yes:

    (a) Please indicate the composition as follows: *Number*

    Senior management of the company...

    Representatives of significant owners...

    Resident "outside" directors, not otherwise associated with the company or affiliated companies as employees, legal counsel, or significant owners...

    Other...

                      Total number of directors...

                      Of which residents of Canada number.............................

1

(b) How many times does the Board usually meet each year?................................

4. Is there an active management or executive committee with major responsibilities? Yes................No................
If Yes, please indicate the composition of the committee by the groups noted in question 3 (a) (above).

II. MARKETING AND PURCHASING

1. For 1959, or for an average of recent years if 1959 is not typical:
   (a) What percentage of the company's total sales went to the Canadian market? ....%.
   (b) What percentage of the company's total purchases (materials and parts, equipment, services) was from suppliers in Canada? ....%.
   (c) How were your exports and imports distributed geographically?

	Exports	Imports
United States		
United Kingdom		
Other sterling area countries		
All other countries	100%	100%

2. (a) Please indicate the number of subsidiaries and branches of your company outside Canada, and the number of licenses of all kinds granted by the Canadian firm to affiliated and non-affiliated companies outside Canada.

	Subsidiaries and branches	Licenses to Affiliates	Non-Affiliates
United States			
United Kingdom			
Other sterling area countries			
All other countries			

   (b) If you have subsidiaries and/or branches located outside Canada:

   What percentage of your total exports and total imports is accounted for by your exports to and imports from these affiliates?
   % of exports going to affiliates....................
   % of imports coming from affiliates....................

   What is the ratio of the investment in your subsidiaries and branches outside Canada to that in the Canadian company..............%.

III RESEARCH AND DEVELOPMENT

NOTE: For present purposes, the term "research and development" comprises activities directed to pure or basic research (i.e. to programs not primarily committed to specific product or process applications) and also to conceiving and developing new products, new processes and major changes in products and processes, and bringing them up to the stage of production. Such activities as market and sales research, process and quality control, and geological and geophysical exploration, should be excluded. If in doubt, please use your normal definition and briefly specify its nature.

1. Please estimate the cost of research and development in 1959, as a percentage of your total annual sales:

	% of sales*
(a) Done within the Canadian company (include all direct and indirect operating costs, but exclude capital expenditures)	
(b) Purchased from non-affiliated firms outside Canada	
(c) Purchased from all other firms or organizations	
Total as percentage of sales	

*Given the relatively large size of sales, it would be appreciated if ratios were estimated to two decimal places.

2

2. If you have research and development facilities in the Canadian company:

   (a) In what year were these established? .... Can you indicate the major factors which led to their establishment and to any major expansion?

   (b) Which of the following are a significant part of the Canadian program: improvement of present products and processes................; conceiving and developing new products and processes................; programs not primarily committed to specific product or process applications................

IV. FINANCIAL

1. (a) Please indicate the percentage distribution of your stock (excluding directors' qualifying shares) and of your debt at the end of 1959 or other recent date.

	Voting Stock	Other Stock	Debt
Residents of Canada..			
United States..			
United Kingdom...			
Other non-residents..			
	100%	100%	100%

   (b) Is a significant portion of your voting stock, enough to establish effective "control", held by one or a few individuals or companies? Yes............No................

2. (a) *Approximately* what proportion of your funds was obtained from each of the following sources in 1950-59 inclusive (*or for specified recent years only*):

	%
Net financing from Canadian sources..	
Net financing from sources outside Canada..	
Net income..	
Depreciation and depletion..	
Other...	
	100%

   (b) What percentage of your net earnings has been paid as dividends since 1950? .... Do you have a preferred policy or practice on this?

(If you prefer to reply anonymously, please return this questionnaire in a plain envelope.)

Name of company:

Name and position of reporting officer:

If a separate questionnaire should be sent to affiliated companies in Canada which are not covered on this return, please list their names and addresses here.

Please Turn Over

PLEASE COMMENT ON THE FOLLOWING, WHERE RELEVANT, ON A SEPARATE SHEET
BY NUMBER OF QUESTION

1. Please describe briefly

   (a) The nature of the export sales organization (including agencies abroad) through which you export, indicating whether your own and/or that of other companies, and whether it differs by countries.

   (b) For your purchases of materials and components, capital equipment, and services (such as insurance, advertising, accounting), where the responsibility for policies lies, and what policy you have (if any) regarding country of purchase.

2. (a) If you have access on a continuing or frequent basis to (i) the research and development and/or (ii) the industrial and other know-how of a non-affiliated company located outside Canada, please describe briefly the nature of the agreement, broadly what you receive under it, and the terms of payment.

   (b) If you have access to (i) the patents and/or (ii) the trade-marks of a non-affiliated company located outside Canada, please describe briefly the nature of the agreement, terms of payment, whether a large portion of your output is involved, and the markets for which the rights apply.

   (c) If not already covered, can you give some quantitative and/or qualitative indication of the importance to your company of the access described in (a) and (b)?

   (d) Please indicate whether the agreements noted in (a) and (b) involve access by the non-affiliated firm to your research-development, know-how, patents and trade-marks, and describe the terms of access briefly.

3. Do you have any preferred policies or practices with respect to: the form of capital and the extent of financing inside Canada; the form of capital and the extent of financing outside Canada? Please explain, including any reasons for the financial procedures and any significant historical changes of which you are aware.

4. (a) If your company has been at any time a subsidiary or branch of a company which was located outside Canada, please indicate when and why this relationship was terminated, and what ties are maintained with that company today (apart from any noted earlier).

   (b) If you now have joint ownership of a Canadian company with a company located outside Canada, please outline why joint ownership was preferred; how the ownership, management, and Board of the Canadian company are divided between the owners; and how successful or otherwise the arrangement is proving to be from the points of view of the companies involved. NOTE: If you have recently terminated such an arrangement, your comments on these questions would also be valuable.

5. *In terms of the experience of your firm,* please compare those Canadian firms which are mainly or wholly owned by non-residents with those mainly or wholly owned by residents, as follows:

   (a) Has affiliation with firms outside Canada *in itself* conferred specific competitive advantages or disadvantages on such firms, compared with their Canadian-owned counterparts?

   (b) Has affiliation with firms outside Canada *in itself* resulted in specific advantages or disadvantages from your point of view in dealing with such firms as sources of supply or as markets for your products, as compared with dealing with their Canadian-owned counterparts?

Bibliography

BOOKS AND MONOGRAPHS

Aitken, H. G. *American Capital and Canadian Resources*. Harvard University Press. Cambridge. 1961.

Aitken, H. G. (ed.). *The American Economic Impact on Canada*. Duke University Press. Durham, N.C. 1959.

Allen, F. L. *The Great Pierpont Morgan*. Harper and Brothers. 1949.

Barg, Benjamin. *A Study of United States Control in Canadian Secondary Industry*. Unpublished Ph. D. thesis. Columbia University. 1960.

Barlow, E. R. *Management of Foreign Manufacturing Subsidiaries*. Harvard University Graduate School of Business Administration. Cambridge, Mass. 1953.

Brecher, Irving. *Capital Flows Between Canada and the United States*. Canadian-American Committee. Montreal. 1965.

Brewster, Kingman. *Antitrust and American Business Abroad*. McGraw-Hill. New York. 1958.

Brewster, Kingman. *Law and United States Business in Canada*. Canadian-American Committee. Montreal. 1960.

Cairncross, A. K. *Home and Foreign Investment 1870-1913*. Cambridge University Press. 1953.

Dunning, John H. *American Investment in British Manufacturing Industry*. Allen and Unwin. London. 1958.

English, H. Edward. *Industrial Structure in Canada's International Competitive Position*. The Canadian Trade Committee. Montreal. 1964.

Fayerweather, John. *Management of International Operations*. McGraw-Hill. New York. 1960.

Fenn, Dan H. (ed). *Management Guide to Overseas Operations*. McGraw-Hill. New York. 1957.

Friedmann, Wolfgang and Kalmanoff, George (eds.). *Joint International Business Ventures*. Columbia University Press. 1961.

Gates, Theodore R. and Linden, Fabian. *Costs and Competition: American Experience Abroad*. The National Industrial Conference Board. 1961.

Gordon, Robert Aaron. *Business Leadership in the Large Corporation*. University of California Press. 1961.

Higgins, Benjamin. *Economic Development*. Norton. New York. 1959.

Johnson, Harry G. *The Canadian Quandary: Economic Problems and Policies*. McGraw-Hill. Toronto. 1963.

Lindeman, John and Armstrong, Donald. *Policies and Practices of United States Subsidiaries in Canada*. Canadian-American Committee. Montreal. 1961.

Marshall, Herbert, Southard, Frank A., Jr., and Taylor, Kenneth W. *Canadian-American Industry: A Study in International Investment*. Yale University Press. New Haven. 1936.

Masson, Frances and Whitely, J. B. *Barriers to Trade Between Canada and the United States*. Canadian-American Committee. Montreal. 1960.

Mikesell, Raymond F. (ed.). *U.S. Private and Government Investment Abroad*. University of Oregon Books. Eugene. 1962.

Neufeld, E. P. *The Canadian Development Corporation — An Assessment of the Proposal*. Canadian Trade Committee. Montreal. 1966.

Reuber, G. L. *Britain's Export Trade with Canada*. University of Toronto Press. 1960.

Slater, David W. *Canada's Balance of International Payments — When is a Deficit a Problem?* Canadian Trade Committee. Montreal. 1964.

Smith, Geo. Albert. *Managing Geographically Decentralized Companies*. Harvard University Graduate School of Business Administration. Cambridge. 1958.

Viner, Jacob. *Canada's Balance of International Indebtedness. 1900-1913*. Harvard University Press. Cambridge. 1924.

Articles

Arndt, H. W. "Overseas Borrowing — The New Model." *The Economic Record*. Vol. XXXIII (August 1957). Pp. 247-264.

Arndt, H. W. and Sherk, D. R. "Export Franchises of Australian Companies with Overseas Affiliations." *The Economic Record*. Vol. XXXV (August 1959). Pp. 239-242.

Behrman, J. N. "Promoting Free World Economic Development Through Direct Investment." *Papers and Proceedings of the American Economic Association*. Vol. L. No. 2 (May 1960). Pp. 271-281.

Behrman, J. N. "Licensing Abroad Under Patents, Trademarks, and Know-How by U.S. Companies." *The Patent, Trademark and Copyright Journal of Research and Education.* Vol. 2. No. 2 (June 1958). Pp. 181-277.

Brent, John E. "International Business Machines, World Trade Corporations." International Management Association, Inc. *Case Studies in Foreign Operations.* Special Report No. 1 (New York, 1957). Pp. 11-17.

Breton, Albert. "The Economics of Nationalism." *The Journal of Political Economy.* Vol. LXXII. No. 4 (August 1964). Pp. 376-386.

Currie, A. W. "Canadian Attitudes Toward Outside Investors." *The Canadian Banker.* Vol. 68. No. 1 (Spring 1961). Pp. 22-35.

Dehem, Roger. "The Economics of Stunted Growth." *Canadian Journal of Economics and Political Science.* Vol. 28. No. 4 (November 1962). Pp. 502-510.

Eastman, H. C. "The Canadian Tariff and the Efficiency of the Canadian Economy." *Papers and Proceedings of the American Economic Association.* Vol. LIV. No. 3 (May 1964). Pp. 437-448.

English, H. E. "Automobility — Predicament or Precedent." *The Canadian Banker.* Vol. 72. No. 2 (Summer 1965). Pp. 23-35.

English, H. Edward. "Growth — The Implications of Institutional Factors," in *Growth and the Canadian Economy.* Carleton University. Ottawa. 1965 (Mimeographed).

Frankel, Marvin. "Home Versus Foreign Investment: A Case Against Capital Export." *Kyklos.* Vol. XVIII. Fasc. 3 (1965). Pp. 411-433.

Hartland, Penelope. "Private Enterprise and International Capital." *The Canadian Journal of Economics and Political Science.* Vol. XIX (1953). P. 70.

Higgins, Carter C. "Make-or-Buy Re-Examined." *Harvard Business Review.* Vol. XXXIII. No. 2 (March/April 1955). Pp. 109-119.

Ingram, J. C. "Growth in Capacity and Canada's Balance of Payments." *American Economic Review.* Vol. 47 (March 1957). Pp. 93-104.

Jasay, A. E. "The Social Choice Between Home and Overseas Investment," *The Economic Journal.* Vol. LXX. No. 277 (March 1960). Pp. 105-113.

Jewkes, J. "How Much Science?" *Economic Journal.* Vol. 70 (March 1960). Pp. 1-16.

Johnson, Harry G. "A New Tariff Policy for the Automotive Industries." *Business Quarterly.* Vol. 29. No. 5 (Spring 1964).

Johnson, Harry G. "Canada's Economic Prospects." *The Canadian Journal of Economics and Political Science.* Vol. 24. No. 1 (February 1958). Pp. 104-110.

Johnson, Harry G. "The Bladen Plan for Increased Protection of the Canadian Automotive Industry." *The Canadian Journal of Economics and Political Science.* Vol. 29. No. 2 (May 1963). Pp. 212-238.

Johnson, Harry G. "The Bladen Plan: A Reply." *The Canadian Journal of Economics and Political Science.* Vol. 29. No. 4 (November 1963). Pp. 515-518.

Kemp, Murray C. "Foreign Investment and the National Advantage." *The Economic Record.* Vol. XXXVIII (March 1962). Pp. 56-62.

Kindleberger, C. P. "Obsolescence and Technical Change." *Bulletin of the Oxford Institute of Statistics* (August 1961). Pp. 281-297.

Knapp, J. "Capital Exports and Growth." *Economic Journal.* Vol. LXVII. No. 267 (September 1957). Pp. 432-444. "Comments" by A. G. Ford and Knapp in the September issues for 1958, 1959, and 1960.

Knox, Frank A. "United States Capital Investments in Canada." *The American Economic Review.* Vol. XLVII. No. 2 (May 1957). Pp. 596-609.

Kreinin, Mordechai E. "Comparative Labor Effectiveness and the Leontieff Scarce-Factor Paradox." *The American Economic Review.* Vol. LV. No. 1 (March 1965). Pp. 131-139.

Kuznets, Simon. "Canada's Economic Prospects." *The American Economic Review.* Vol. XLIX. No. 3 (June 1959). Pp. 358-385.

Lewis, W. Arthur. "Economic Development with Unlimited Supplies of Labour." *The Manchester Review* (May 1954).

MacDonald, Neil B. "A Comment: The Bladen Plan for Increased Protection for the Automotive Industry." *The Canadian Journal of Economics and Political Science.* Vol. 29. No. 4 (November 1963). Pp. 505-515.

Maffry, August. "Direct Versus Portfolio Investment in the Balance of Payments." *Papers and Proceedings of the American Economic Association.* "Comment" by Vincent W. Bladen and H. J. Dernburg. Vol. XLIV. No. 2 (May 1954). Pp. 615-633.

McDougall, G. D. A. "The Benefits and Costs of Private Investment from Abroad: A Theoretical Approach." *Bulletin of the Oxford University Institute of Statistics.* Vol. 22. No. 3 (August 1960). Pp. 189-210 (reprinted from *The Economic Record,* March 1960).

Meier, C. G. "Economic Development and the Transfer Mechanism: Canada 1895-1913." *The Canadian Journal of Economics and Political Science.* Vol. XXIX (February 1963). Pp. 1-19.

Monsen, R. Joseph, Jr., and Downs, Anthony. "A Theory of Large Managerial Firms." *The Journal of Political Economy.* Vol. LXXIII. No. 3 (June 1965). Pp. 221-236.

Morse, Chandler. "Potentials and Hazards of Direct International Investment in Raw Materials," in Marion Clawson (ed.). *Natural Resources and International Development.* Johns Hopkins Press. 1964.

Murphy, J. Carter. "International Investment and the National Interest." *The Southern Economic Journal.* Vol. XXVII. No. 1 (July 1960). Pp. 11-17.

National Industrial Conference Board Inc. "Canada: An Expanding Market." *The Conference Board Business Record.* Vol. XV. No. 1 (January 1958).

Penner, Rudolph G. "The Benefits of Foreign Investment in Canada, 1950 to 1956." *Paper* delivered to the Statistics Conference of the Canadian Political Science Association. Vancouver. June 1965.

Penrose, E. T. "Foreign Investment and the Growth of the Firm." *Economic Journal.* Vol. LXVI. No. 262 (June 1956). Pp. 227.

Rosenberg, W. "Capital Imports and Growth — The Case of New Zealand — Foreign Investment in New Zealand, 1840-1958." *Economic Journal.* Vol. LXXI. No. 281 (March 1961). Pp. 93-113. "Comments" by D. J. Delivanis, R. J. Ball and Rosenberg in December 1961 issue.

Safarian, A. E. "The Exports of American-Owned Enterprises in Canada." *Papers and Proceedings of the American Economic Association.* Vol. LIX. No. 3 (May 1964). Pp. 449-458. Comment by C. P. Kindleberger. Pp. 474-477.

Safarian, A. E. "Foreign Ownership and Control of Canadian Industry." In Abraham Rotstein (ed.). *The Prospect of Change.* McGraw-Hill. Toronto. 1965.

Scitovsky, Tibor. "Two Concepts of External Economies." *The Journal of Political Economy* (April 1954). Pp. 143-151.

Singer, H. W. "The Distribution of Gains Between Investing and Borrowing Countries." *Papers and Proceedings of the American Economic Association.* Vol. 40 (1950). Pp. 473-485.

Smyth, J. E. "Financial Disclosures by Subsidiaries." *Queen's Quarterly.* Vol. LXV. No. 3 (Autumn 1958).

Stykolt, S. and Eastman, H. C. "A Model for the Study of Protected Oligopolies." *Economic Journal.* Vol. LXX (June 1960). Pp. 336-347.

Thorp, Willard L. "Canada-United States Economic Relations." *The Canadian Journal of Economics and Political Science.* Vol. 26. No. 2 (May 1960). Pp. 326-334.

Viner, Jacob. "The Gordon Commission Report." *Queen's Quarterly.* Vol. LXIV (Autumn 1957). Pp. 305-325.

Williamson, Oliver E. "Managerial Discretion and Business Behavior." *The American Economic Review.* Vol. LIII. No. 5 (December 1963). Pp. 1032-1057.

Government Of Canada, Government Agencies, Other Governments

Bank of Canada. *Annual Report* of the Governor to the Minister of Finance. Ottawa. 1965.

Canada. *House of Commons. Debates.* Various issues 1963-1966.

Corporations and Labour Unions Returns Act, Report for 1962. 1965.

Department of Scientific and Industrial Research of the United Kingdom. *Estimates of Resources Devoted to Scientific and Engineering Research and Development in British Manufacturing Industry, 1955.* London. 1958.

Department of the Secretary of State for Canada. Annual Summaries and Financial Statements.

Dominion Bureau of Statistics
Canada's International Investment Position, 1926-1954. 1956.
The Canadian Balance of International Payments and International Investment Position. Various years 1955 to 1962-63.
Industrial Research-Development Expenditures in Canada, 1959.
Quarterly Estimates of the Canadian Balance of International Payments. Fourth Quarter. 1965.

Economic Council of Canada. *Second Annual Review.* December 1965.

Hearings and *Reports* of the Royal Commission on Energy. Ottawa.

The Honourable Eric W. Kierans. Minister of Health for Quebec. "The Economic Effects of the Guidelines." Speech delivered to the Toronto Society of Financial Analysts. February 1, 1966.

McColm, George T. "Canadian Surveys of Research and Development." In National Science Foundation. *Methodology of Statistics on Research and Development.* Washington 25, D.C. 1959.

National Research Council. *Annual Reports.*

Notes for an Address by the Minister of Justice (The Honourable Davie Fulton) to the Antitrust Section of the New York State Bar Association. New York. January 28, 1959.

Notes for the speeches by the Honourable Walter L. Gordon, Minister of Finance, to the Sixth Annual Industrial and Municipal Relations Conference, Peterborough, Ontario, October 28, 1964, and to the Albion College Regional Meeting of the American Assembly, Albion, Michigan, May 14, 1965. Department of Finance Press Release.

Parliament of Canada. *Proceedings* of the Special Committee Appointed to Consider the Matter of the Development in Canada of Scientific Research. 10 George V (King's Printer, 1919). Appendix No. 5.

Reports under the Combines Investigations Act.
 Canada and International Cartels. 1945.
 Rubber Products. 1952.

Royal Commission on Canada's Economic Prospects.
 Preliminary Report. 1956.
 E. W. R. Steacie. *Canadian Research Expenditures*. Exhibit 262. March 8, 1956.
 Brief. Security Analysts' Association of Toronto. Exhibit 172. February 1956.
 D. H. Fullerton and H. A. Hampson. *Canadian Secondary Manufacturing Industry*. 1957.
 Irving Brecher and S. S. Reisman. *Canada-United States Economic Relations*. 1957.
 William C. Hood and Anthony Scott. *Output, Labour and Capital in the Canadian Economy*. 1957.
 Final Report. 1958.

U.S. Department of Commerce.
 U.S. Business Investments in Foreign Countries. A Supplement to the Survey of Current Business. Washington, 1960.
 Samuel Pizer and Frederick Cutler. Articles in *Survey of Current Business*. "U.S. Firms Accelerate Capital Expenditures Abroad." October 1964. "U.S. Trade with Foreign Affiliates of U.S. Firms." December 1964. "Financing and Sales of Foreign Affiliates of U.S. Firms." November 1965.
 "Factors Limiting U.S. Investment Abroad." Parts I, 1953 and II, 1954.

U.S. Department of Labor. *Science and Engineering in American Industry*. Washington. Prepared for the National Science Foundation. 1959.

Other Sources

Canadian-American Committee. *Recent Canadian and U.S. Government Actions Affecting U.S. Investment in Canada*. Montreal. 1964.

Canadian Mines Handbook. Northern Miner Press Limited. Toronto.

Empire Trust Letter. Empire Trust Company. No. 60 (October 1958).

Moody's Industrial Manual. Moody's Investors Service Inc. New York.

National Industrial Conference Board. *Corporate Directorship Practices*. Studies in Business Policy. No. 90. New York. 1964.

National Industrial Conference Board. *Scientific Research in Canadian Industry*. Montreal. 1963.

National Science Foundation. *Review of Data on Research and Development*. Washington.

Report of the President's Materials Policy Commission, chaired by William S. Paley. Washington, D.C. 1952.

The Financial Post Corporation Service.

The Financial Post Directory of Directors.

The Financial Post Surveys of Industrials, Mines and Oils.

Unilever Limited. *Anatomy of a Business*. London. 1962.

Articles in the *Economist, Financial Post, Globe and Mail, Investor's Chronicle and Money Market Review, Star Weekly,* and *Toronto Daily Star*.

Index

Index of Subjects

Age of firms:
  by degree of supervision, 91-93, Table 17
  by importance of access to knowledge, 197
  by nationality of president, 55-57
  by ownership of voting stock, 225, Table 44
  by percentage of earnings paid as dividends, 249, Table 51
  by proportion of purchases in Canada, 154, Table 25
  by proportion of resident directors, 70
  by proportion of sales in Canada, 124
  by sources of funds, 240-241, Table 48
  comparison of resident and non-resident owned firms, Table 54, 267
  distribution, Table 4, 40-42
  effect on unit cost difference, 209
Agriculture, ownership of net stock of capital, 12
Automobiles: 105 *n.4*, 115-116, 144, 145 *n.51*

Bank of Canada, comment on guidelines, 256
Boards of directors (*see* Directors, Boards of)
Business, Type of:
  by degree of supervision, 93, Table 17
  by ownership of voting stock, 225, Table 44
  by proportion of purchases in Canada, 154-155, Table 25
  by proportion of resident directors, 70
  by proportion of sales in Canada, 122, 124-125, Table 20
  by research as % of sales, 179, Table 31
  comparison of resident and non-resident owned firms, Table 54, 269

Canada Development Corporation, 26, 26 *n.37*, 218
Canada-United States Joint Committee on Trade and Economic Affairs, 255
Canadian-American Committee, report on United States subsidiaries, 24-25
Capital, fixed, estimates of social and industrial stock, 11-12
Capital flows (*see* Investment and Direct investment)
China, Peoples' Republic of: 106, 144-145, 167
Combines Investigations Act:
  comment on export policy, 113 *n.16*, 118
  effects of affiliation on exports, 137 *n.42*
Comparison of resident-owned and non-resident owned firms:
  boards of directors, 270-273, Table 55
  by age, Table 54, 267
  by export percentage and pattern, 273-274, Tables 56 and 57
  by import percentage and pattern, 274-276, Tables 57 and 58
  by industry classification, 266-267
  by research and development, 280-286, Tables 59, 60 and 61
  by sales organization, 277-278
  by size, Table 54, 267-269
  by type of business, Table 54, 269
  Chi square difference tests on sales, purchases and research, 294-296
  locus of ownership, 286-288, Table 62
  sources of funds, 288-292, Tables 63 and 64
Control, foreign:
  definition, 9 *n.17*, 8-10
  difference between ownership ratio and control ratio, 13

Index of Names